KT-482-591

Sermons for
All Seasons

Sermons for All Seasons

*A Year's Ministry
by Alexander Maclaren, D.D.*

AMG
PUBLISHERS
Chattanooga, TN 37422

Sermons for All Seasons

Originally published
in London by Hodder & Stoughton, 1884,
and in New York by Funk & Wagnalls Company, 1902.

ISBN 0-89957-207-3

Printed in the United States of America

Contents

Foreword

Alexander Maclaren's *Sermons for All Seasons* is a compilation of fifty-two scholarly, insightful sermons. Previously contained in two volumes entitled *A Year's Ministry*, these sermons demonstrate Maclaren's years of experience in ministry; his precise, scholarly approach to the study of Scripture; and the eloquence of this famed expositor and orator.

In creating this new edition, we at AMG Publishers have made a few minor changes to the original works to help make their content more clear to modern readers: We have updated spelling in accordance with how our language has changed over the years; and in some cases, unusual forms of punctuation have been simplified. Readers should also note that the points of current history cited by Maclaren are from Britain in the late 1800s.

Our desire is for these fifty-two sermons to touch their readers in the same way they touched lives when Maclaren spoke them a century ago.

1

The Purifying Influence of Hope

And every man that hath this hope in Him purifieth himself, even as He is pure—1 John 3:3.

That is a very remarkable "and" with which this verse begins. The Apostle has just been touching the very heights of devout contemplation, soaring away up into dim regions where it is very hard to follow—"We shall be like Him, for we shall see Him as He is."

And now, without a pause, and linking his thoughts together by a simple "and" he passes from the unimaginable splendors of the Beatific Vision to the plainest practical talk. Mysticism has often soared so high above the earth that it has forgotten to preach righteousness, and therein has been its weak point. But here is the most mystical teacher of the New Testament insisting on plain morality as vehemently as his friend James could have done.

The combination is very remarkable. Like the eagle he rises, and like the eagle, with the impetus gained from his height, he drops right down on the earth beneath!

And that is not only a characteristic of St. John's teaching, but it is a characteristic of all the New Testament morality—its highest revelations are intensely practical. Its light is at once set to work, like the sunshine that comes ninety millions of miles in order to make the little daisies open their crimson-tipped petals; so the profoundest things that the Bible has to say are said to you and me, not that we may know only, but that knowing me may *do*, and *do* because we *are*.

So John, here: "We shall be like Him, for we shall see Him as He is." "And"—a simple coupling iron for two such thoughts—"every man that hath this hope in Him,"—that is, in Christ, not in himself, as we sometimes read it—"every man that hath this hope," founded on Christ, "purifies himself even as He is pure."

The thought is a very simple one, though sometimes it is somewhat mistakenly apprehended. Put into it general form it is just this: If you expect, and expecting, hope to be like Jesus Christ yonder, you will be trying your best to be like Him here. It is not the mere purifying influence of hope that is talked about, but it is ultimate assimilation to Christ leading to strenuous efforts, each a partial resemblance of Him, here and now. And that is the subject I want to say a word or two about this morning.

I. First, then, notice the principle that is here, which is the main thing to be insisted upon, namely, If we are to be pure, we must purify *ourselves*.

There are two ways of getting like Christ, spoken about in the context. One is the blessed way, that is more appropriate for the higher Heaven, the way of assimilation and transformation by beholding—"If we see Him" we shall be "like Him." That is the blessed method of the Heavens. Yes! But even here on earth it may to some extent be realized. Love always breeds likeness. And there is such a thing, here on earth and now, as gazing upon Christ with an intensity of affection, and simplicity of trust, and rapture of aspiration, and ardor of desire which shall transform us in some measure into His own likeness. John is an example of that for us. It was a true instinct that made the old painters always represent him as like the Master that he sat beside, even in face. Where did John get his style from? He got it by much meditating upon Christ's words. The disciple caught the method of the Master's speech, and to some extent the manner of the Master's vision.

And so he himself stands before us as an instance of the possibility, even on earth, of this calm, almost passive process, and most blessed and holiest method of getting like the Master, by simple gazing, which is the gaze of love and longing.

But, dear brethren, the law of our lives forbids that that should be the only way in which we grow like Christ. "First the blade, then the ear, then the full corn in the ear" was never meant to be the exhaustive, all-comprehensive statement of the method of Christian progress. You and I are not vegetables, and the Parable of the Seed is only one side of the truth about the method of Christian growth. The very word "purify" speaks to us of another condition; it implies impurity, it implies a process which is more than contemplation, it implies the reversal of existing conditions, and not merely the growth upwards to unattained conditions.

And so growth is not all that Christian men need: they need excision, they need casting out of what is in them; they need change as well as growth. "Purifying" they need because they are impure, and growth is only half the secret of Christian progress.

Then there is the other consideration, viz., if there is to be this purifying it must be done by myself. "Ah!" you say, "done by yourself? That is not Evangelical teaching." Well, let us see. Take two or three verses out of this Epistle which at first sight seem to be contradictory of this. Take the very first that bears on the subject: "The blood of Jesus Christ His Son cleanseth us from all sin" (1:7). "If we confess our sins He is faithful and just to forgive us our sins and to cleanse us from all unrighteousness" (4:9). "He that abideth in Him sinneth not" (3:6). "This is the victory that overcometh the world, even our faith" (5:4).

Now, if you put all these passages together, and think about the general effect of them, it comes to this: that our best way of cleansing ourselves is by keeping firm hold of Jesus Christ and of the cleansing powers that lie in Him. To take a very homely illustration—soap and water wash your hands clean, and what you have to do is simply to rub the soap and water onto the hand, and bring them into contact with the foulness. You cleanse yourselves. Yes! Because without the friction there would not be the cleansing. But is it you, or is it the soap, that does the work? Is it you or the water that makes your hands clean? And so when God comes and says, "Wash you, make you clean, put away the evil of your doings, your hands are full of blood," He says in effect, "Take the cleansing that I give you and rub it in, and apply it: and your flesh will become as the flesh of a little child, and you shall be clean."

That is to say, the very deepest word about Christian effort of self-purifying is this—keep close to Jesus Christ. You cannot sin as long as you hold His hand. To have Him with you—I mean by that to have the thoughts directed to Him, the love turning to Him, the will submitted to Him, Him consciously with us in the day's work—to have communion with Jesus Christ is like brining an atmosphere round about us in which all evil will die. If you take a fish out of water and bring it up into the upper air, it writhes and gasps, and is dead presently; and our evil tendencies and sins, drawn up out of the muddy depths in which they live, and brought up into that pure atmosphere of communion with Jesus Christ, are sure to shrivel and to die, and to disappear. We kill all evil by fellowship with the Master. His presence in our lives, by our communion with Him, is like the watchfire that the traveler lights at night—it keeps all the wild beasts of prey away from the fold.

Christ's fellowship is our cleansing, and the first and main thing that we have to do in order to make ourselves pure is to keep ourselves in union with Him, in whom inhere and abide all the energies that cleanse men's souls. Take the unbleached calico and spread it out on the green grass, and let the blessed sunshine come down upon it, and sprinkle it with fair water; and the grass and the moisture and the sunshine will do all the cleansing, and it will glitter in the light "so as no fuller on earth can white it."

So cleansing is keeping near Jesus Christ. But it is no use getting the millrace from the stream into your works unless you put wheels in its way to drive. And our holding ourselves in fellowship with the Master in that fashion is not all that we have to do. There have to be distinct and specific efforts, constantly repeated, to subdue and suppress individual acts of transgression. We have to fight against evil, sin by sin. We have not the thing to do all at once; we have to do it in detail. It is a war of outposts, like the last agonies of that Franco-Prussian war, when the Emperor had abdicated, and the country was really conquered, and Paris had yielded, but yet all over the face of the land combats had to be carried on.

So it is with us. Holiness is not feeling; it is character. You do not get rid of your sins by the act of Divine amnesty only. You are not perfect because you say you are, and feel as if you were, and think you are. God does not make any man pure in his sleep. His cleansing does not dispense with fighting, but makes victory possible.

Then, dear brethren, lay to heart this, as the upshot of the whole matter. First of all, let us turn to Him from whom all the cleansing comes; and then, moment by moment, remember that it is our work to purify ourselves by the strength and the power that is given to us by the Master.

II. The second thought here is this: *This purifying of ourselves is the link or bridge between the present and the future.* "Now are we the sons of God," says John, in the context. That is the pier upon the one side of the gulf. "It doth not yet appear what we shall be, but when He is made manifest we shall be like Him." That is the pier on the other. How are the two to be connected? There is only one way by which the present sonship will blossom and fruit into the future perfect likeness, and that is if we throw across the gulf, by God's help day by day, that bridge of our effort to become like Him.

That is plain enough, I suppose. To speak in somewhat technical terms, the "law of continuity" that we hear so much about, runs on between earth and Heaven. Which, being translated into plain English, is but this—that the act of passing from the limitations and conditions of this transitory life into the solemnities and grandeurs of that future does not alter a man's character, though it may intensify it. It does not make him different from what he was, though it may make him more of what he was, whether its direction be good or bad.

You take a stick and thrust it into water; and because the rays of light pass from one medium to another of a different density, they are refracted and the stick seems bent; but take the human life out of the thick coarse medium of earth and lift it up into the pure rarefied air of Heaven, and there is no refraction; it runs straight on. Straight on! The given direction continues; and in whatever direction my face is turned when I die, thither my face will be turned when I live again.

Do not you fancy that there is any magic in coffins and graves, and shrouds to make men different from their former selves. The continuity runs clean on, the rail goes without a break, though it goes through the Mont Cenis tunnel; and on the one side is the cold of the North, and on the other the sunny South. The man is the same man through death and beyond.

So the one link between sonship here and likeness to Christ hereafter is this link of present, strenuous effort to become like Him day by day in personal purity. For there is another reason, on which I need not dwell, viz., unless there be this daily effort on our part to become like Jesus Christ by personal purity, we shall not be able to "see Him as He is." Death will take a great many veils off men's hearts. It will reveal to them a great deal that they do not know, but it will not give the faculty of beholding the glorified Christ in such fashion as that the beholding will mean transformation. "Every eye shall see Him," but it is conceivable that a spirit shall be so immersed in self-love and in godlessness that the vision of Christ shall be repellent and not attractive; shall have no transforming and no gladdening power. And I beseech you to remember that about that vision, as about the vision of God Himself, the principle stands true; it is "the pure in heart that shall see God" in Christ. And the change from life to the life beyond will not necessarily transform into the image of His dear Son. You make a link between the present and the future by cleansing your hands and your hearts, through faith in the cleansing power of Christ, and direct effort at holiness.

III. Now, I must briefly add finally: that *this self-cleansing* of which I have been speaking is the *offspring and outcome of that "hope"* in my text. It is the child of hope. Hope is by no means an active faculty generally. As the poets have it, she may "smile and wave her golden hair"; but she is not in the way of doing much work in the world. And it is not the mere fact of hope that generates this effort; it is, as I have been trying to show you, a certain kind of hope—the hope of being like Jesus Christ when "we see Him as He is."

I have only two things to say about this matter, and one of them is this: of course, such strenuous effort of purity will only be the result of such a hope as that, because such a hope will fight against one of the greatest of all the enemies of our efforts after purity. There is nothing that makes a man so downhearted in his work of self-improvement as to the constant and bitter experience that it seems to be all of no use; that he is making so little progress; that with immense pains, like a snail creeping up a wall, he gets up, perhaps, an inch or two, and then all at once he drops down, and further down than he was before he started.

Slowly we manage some little patient self-improvement; gradually, inch by inch and bit by bit, we may be growing better, and then there comes some gust and outburst of temptation; and the whole painfully reclaimed soil gets covered up by an avalanche of mud and stones, that we have to remove slowly, barrow load by barrow load. And then we feel that it is all of no use to strive, and we let circumstances shape us, and give up all thoughts of reformation.

To such moods then there comes, like an angel from Heaven, that holy, blessed message, "Cheer up, man! We shall be like Him, for we shall see Him as He is; Every inch that you make now will tell then, and it is not all of no use. Set your heart to the work, it is a work that will be blessed and will prosper."

Again, here is a test for all you Christian people, who say that you look to Heaven with hope as to your home and rest.

A great deal of the religious contemplation of a future state is pure sentimentality, and like all pure sentimentality is either immoral or non-moral. But here the two things are brought into clear juxtaposition, the bright hope of Heaven and the hard work done here below. Now is that what the gleam and expectation of a future life does for you?

This is the only time in John's Epistle that he speaks about hope. The good man, living so near Christ, finds that the present, with its "abiding in Him," is enough for his heart. And though he was the Seer of the Apocalypse, he has scarcely a word to say about the future in this letter of his and when he does it is for a simple and intensely practical purpose, in order that he may enforce on us the teaching of laboring earnestly in purifying ourselves.

My brother, is that your type of Christianity? Is that the kind of inspiration that comes to you from the hope that steals in upon you in your weary hours, when sorrows, and care, and changes, and loss, and disappointments, and hard work weigh you down, and you say, "It would be blessed to pass hence?" Does it set you harder at work than anything else can do? Is it all utilized? Or, if I might use such an illustration, is it like the electricity of the Aurora Borealis, that paints your winter sky with vanishing, useless splendors of crimson and blue? Or, have you got it harnessed to your tram-cars, lighting your houses, driving sewing machines, doing practical work in your daily life? Is the hope of Heaven, and of being like Christ, a thing that stimulates and stirs us every moment to heroisms of self-surrender and to strenuous martyrdom of self-cleansing?

All is gathered up into the one lesson. First, let us go to that dear Lord whose blood cleanseth from all sin, and let us say to Him, "Purge me, and I shall be clean; wash me, and I shall be whiter than snow." And then, receiving into our hearts the powers that purify, in His love and His sacrifice and His life, "having these promises" and these possessions, "Dearly beloved, let us cleanse ourselves from all filthiness of flesh and spirit, perfecting holiness in the fear of the Lord."

2

"The Bridal of the Earth and Sky"

Mercy and truth are met together; righteousness and peace have kissed each other. Truth shall spring out of the earth; and righteousness shall look down from heaven. Yea, the Lord shall give that which is good; and our land shall yield her increase. Righteousness shall go before him; and shall set us in the way of his steps
—Psalm 85:10–13.

This is a lovely and highly imaginative picture of the reconciliation and reunion of God and man, "the bridal of the earth and sky." The Poet-Psalmist, who seems to have belonged to the times immediately after the Return from the exile, in strong faith sees before him a vision of a perfectly harmonious cooperation and relation between God and man. He is not prophesying directly of Messianic times. The vision hangs before him, with no definite note of time upon it. He hopes it may be fulfilled in his own day; he is sure it will, if only, as he says, his countrymen "turn not again to folly." At all events, it will be fulfilled in that far-off time to which the heart of every prophet turned with longing. But, more than that, there is no reason why it should not be fulfilled with every man, at the moment.

It is the ideal, to use modern language, of the relations between Heaven and earth. Only that the Psalmist believed that as sure as that there was a God in Heaven, Who is likewise a God working in the midst of the earth, the ideal might become, and would become, a reality.

So, then, I take it, these four verses all set forth substantially the same thought, but with slightly different modifications and applications. They are a four-fold picture of how Heaven and earth

9

ought to blend and harmonize. This four-fold representation of the one thought is what I purpose to consider now.

I. To begin with, then, take the first verse: "Mercy and truth are met together, righteousness and peace have kissed each other." We have here *the heavenly twin sisters, and the earthly pair that corresponds.* "Mercy and Truth are met together"—that is one personification; "Righteousness and Peace have kissed each other" is another. It is difficult to say whether these four great qualities are to be regarded as all belonging to God, or as all belonging to man, or as all common both to God and man. The first explanation is the most familiar one, but I confess that, looking at the context, where we find throughout an interpenetration and play of reciprocal action as between earth and Heaven, I am disposed to think of the first pair as sisters from the Heavens, and the second pair as the earthly sisters that correspond to them. Mercy and Truth—two radiant angels, like virgins in some solemn choric dance, linked hand in hand, issue from the sanctuary and move amongst the dim haunts of men, making "a sunshine in a shady place," and to them there come forth, linked in a sweet embrace, another pair whose lives depend on the lives of their elder and heavenly sisters, Righteousness and Peace. And so these four, the pair of heavenly origin, and the answering pair that have sprung into being at their coming upon earth; these four, banded in perfect accord, move together, blessing and light-giving amongst the sons of men. Mercy and Truth are the Divine—Righteousness and Peace the earthly.

Let me dwell upon these two couples briefly. "Mercy and Truth are met together" means this: That these two qualities are found braided and linked inseparably in all that God does with mankind; that these two springs are the double fountains from which the great stream of the river of the Water of Life, the forthcoming and the manifestation of God, takes its rise.

"Mercy and Truth." What are the meanings of the two words? Mercy is love that stoops, love that departs from the strict lines of desert and retribution. Mercy is love that is kind when justice might make it otherwise. Mercy is love that condescends to that which is far beneath. Thus the "Mercy" of the Old Testament covers almost the same ground as the "Grace" of the New Testament.

And Truth blends with the mercy. That is to say—truth in a somewhat narrower than its widest sense, meaning mainly God's fidelity to every obligation under which He has come. God's faithfulness to promise, God's fidelity to His past, God's fidelity, in His actions, to His own character, which is meant by that great word, "He sware by *Himself!*"

Thus the sentiment of mercy, the tender grace and gentleness of that condescending love, has impressed upon it the seal of permanence when we say: Grace and truth, mercy and faithfulness, are met together. No longer is love mere sentiment, which may be capricious and may be transient. We can reckon on it, we know the law of its being. The love is lifted up above the suspicion of being arbitrary, or of ever changing or fluctuating. We do not know all the limits of the orbit, but we know enough to calculate it for all practical purposes. God has committed Himself to us, He has limited Himself by His obligations, by His own past. We have a right to turn to Him, and say: "Be what Thou art, and continue to us what Thou hast been unto past ages." And He responds to the appeal. For Mercy and Truth, tender, gracious, stooping forgiving love, and inviolable faithfulness that can never be otherwise, these blend in all His works; "that by two immutable things, wherein it was impossible for God to lie, we might have a strong consolation."

Again, dear brethren, let me remind you, these two are the ideal two, which, as far as God's will and wish are concerned, are the only two that would mark any of His dealings with men. When He is, if I may so say, left free to do as He would, and is not forced to His "strange act" of punishment by my sin and yours, these, and these only, are the characteristics of His dealings.

Nor let us forget—"We beheld His glory, the glory as of the Only Begotten of the Father, *full of grace and truth.*" The Psalmist's vision was fulfilled in Jesus Christ, in whom these sweet twin characteristics, that are linked inseparably in all the works of God, are welded together into one in the living personality of Him who is all the Father's grace embodied; and is the Way and the Truth and the Life.

Turn now to the other side of this first aspect of the union of God and man. "Mercy and truth are met together," these are the Heavenly twins. "Righteousness and peace have kissed each other" —these are the earthly sisters who sprang into being to meet them.

Of course I know that these words are very often applied, by way of illustration, to the great work of Jesus Christ upon the Cross, which is supposed to have reconciled, if not contradictory, at least divergently working sides of the Divine character and government. And we all know how beautifully the phrase has often been employed by eloquent preachers, and how beautifully it has been often illustrated by devout paints.

But beautiful as the adaptation is, I think it is an adaptation, and not the real meaning of the words, for this reason, if for no other, that righteousness and peace are not in the Old Testament regarded as opposites, but as harmonious and inseparable. And so I take it that here we have distinctly the picture of what happens upon earth when Mercy and Truth that come down from Heaven are accepted and recognized—then Righteousness and Peace kiss each other.

Or, to put away the metaphor, here are two thoughts, first that in men's experience and life *righteousness and peace cannot be rent apart.* The only secret of tranquility is to be good. "First of all, King of Righteousness, and after that King of Salem, which is the King of Peace." "The effect of Righteousness shall be peace," as Isaiah, the brother in spirit of this Psalmist, says; and on the other hand, as the same prophet says, "The wicked is like a troubled sea that cannot rest, whose waters cast up mire and dirt; there is no peace, saith my God, to the wicked." But where affections are pure, and the life is worthy, where goodness is loved in the heart, and followed even imperfectly in the daily life, there the ocean is quiet, and "birds of peace sit brooding on the charmed wave." The one secret of tranquility is first to trust in the Lord and then to do good. Righteousness and peace kiss each other.

The other thought here is that Righteousness and her twin sister, Peace, only come in the measure in which the mercy and the truth of God are received into thankful hearts. My brother, have you taken that mercy and that truth into your soul, and are you trying to reach peace in the only way by which any human being can ever reach it—through the path of righteousness, self-suppression, and consecration to Him?

II. Now, take the next phase of this union and cooperation of earth and Heaven, which is given here in the eleventh verse: Truth shall spring out of the earth, and Righteousness shall look down from Heaven." That is, to put it into other words—*God responding to man's truth*. Notice that in this verse one member from each of the two pairs that have been spoken about in the previous verse is detached from its companion, and they are joined so as to form for a moment a new pair. Truth is taken from the first couple; Righteousness from the second, and a third couple is thus formed.

And notice, further, that each takes the place that had belonged to the other. The Heavenly Truth becomes a child of earth; and the earthly Righteousness ascends "to look down from Heaven." The process of the previous verse in effect is reversed. "Truth shall spring out of the earth, Righteousness shall look down from Heaven." That is to say: Man's truth shall begin to grow and blossom in answer, as it were, to God's Truth that came down upon it. Which being translated into other words is this: where a man's heart has welcomed the mercy and the truth of God there shall spring up in that heart, not only the righteousness and peace, of which the previous verse is speaking, but specifically a faithfulness not all unlike the faithfulness which it grasps. If we have a God immutable and unchangeable to build upon, let us build upon Him immutability and unchangeableness. If we have a Rock on which to build our confidence, let us see that our confidence that we build upon it is rocklike too. If we have a God that cannot lie, let us grasp His faithful Word with an affiance that cannot falter. If we have a truth in the Heavens, absolute and immutable, on which to anchor our hopes, let us see to it that our hopes, anchored thereon, are sure and steadfast. What a shame it would be that we should bring the vacillations and fluctuations of our own insincerities and changeableness to the solemn, fixed unutterableness of that Divine Word! We ought to be faithful, for we build upon a faithful God.

And then the other side of this second picture. Righteousness shall "look down from Heaven." Not in its judicial aspect merely, but as the perfect moral purity that belongs to the Divine Nature, which shall bend down a loving eye upon the men beneath, and mark the springings of any imperfect good and thankfulness in our hearts; joyous as the husbandman beholds the springing of his crops in the fields that he has sown.

God delights when He sees the first faint flush of green which marks the springing of the good seed in the else barren hearts of men. No good, no beauty of character, no meek rapture of faith, no aspiration Godwards is ever wasted and lost, for His eye rests upon it. As Heaven, with its myriad stars, bends over the lowly earth, and in the midnight when no human eye beholds, sees all, so God sees the hidden confidence, the unseen "truth" that springs to meet His faithful Word. The flowers that grow in the pastures of the wilderness, or away upon the wild prairies, or that hide in the clefts of the inaccessible mountains, do not "waste their sweetness on the desert air" for God sees them.

It may be an encouragement and quickening to us to remember that wherever the tiniest little bit of truth springs upon the earth, the loving eye—not the eye of a great taskmaster—but the eye of the Brother, Christ, which is the eye of God, looks down. "Wherefore we labor, that whether present or absent, we may be well-pleasing unto Him."

III. And then there is the third aspect of this ideal relation between earth and Heaven, the converse of the one we have just now been speaking of, set forth in the next verse: "Yea, the Lord shall give that which is good and our land shall yield her increase." That is to say: *man responding to God's gift.* You see that the order of things is reversed in this verse from the former one. It recurs to the order with which we originally started. "The Lord shall give that which is good." In figure, that refers to all the skyey influence of dew, rain, sunshine, passing breezes, and still, ripening autumn days; in the reality it refers to all the motives, powers, impulses, helps, furtherances by which He makes it possible for us to serve Him and love Him, and bring forth fruits of righteousness.

And so the thought which has already been hinted at is here more fully developed and dwelt upon, this great truth, that earthly fruitfulness is possible only by the reception of Heavenly gifts. As sure as every leaf that grows is mainly water that the plant has got from the clouds, and carbon that it has got out of the atmosphere, so surely will all our good be mainly drawn from Heaven and Heaven's gifts. As certainly as every lump of coal that you put upon your fire contains in itself sunbeams that have been locked up for all these millenniums that have passed since it waved green in the forest, so certainly does every good deed embody in itself gifts from above. And no man is pure except by impartation; and every good thing and every perfect thing cometh from the Father of Lights.

So let us learn the lesson of absolute dependence for all purity, virtue, and righteousness on His bestowment, and come to Him and ask Him evermore to fill our emptiness with His own gracious fullness, and to lead us to be what He commands and would have us to be.

And then there is the other lesson out of this phase of the ideal relation between earth and Heaven, the lesson of what we ought to do with the gift. "The earth yields her increase," by laying hold of the good which the Lord gives, and by reason of that received good quickening all the germs. Ah! Dear brethren, wasted opportunities, neglected moments, uncultivated talents, gifts that are not stirred up; rain and dew and sunshine, all poured upon us and no increase—is not that the story of much of all our lives, and of the whole of some lives?

Are we like Eastern lands where the trees have been felled, and the great irrigation works and tanks have been allowed to fall into disrepair, and so when the bountiful treasure of the rains comes, all that it does is to swell for half a day the discolored stream that carries away some more of the arable land; and when the sunshine comes, with its swift, warm powers, all that it does is to bleach the stones and scorch the barren sand? "The earth which *drinketh in the rain* that cometh oft upon it, and yieldeth herbs meet for them by whom it is dressed, receiveth the blessing of God." Is it true about you that the earth yieldeth her increase, as it is certainly true that "the Lord giveth that which is good"?

IV. And now the last thing which is here, the last phrase of the fourfold representation of the ideal relation between earth and Heaven, is "Righteousness shall go before Him and shall set us in the way of His steps." That is to say, *God teaching man to walk in*

His footsteps. There is some difficulty about the meaning of the last clause of this verse, but I think that having regard to the whole context and to that idea of the interpenetration of the Heavenly with the human which we have seen running through it, the reading in our English Bible gives substantially, though somewhat freely, the meaning. The clause might literally be rendered "make His footsteps for a way." It comes to substantially the same thing as is expressed in our English Bible. Righteousness, God's moral perfectness, is set forth here in a twofold phase. First as a herald going before Him and preparing His path.

The Psalmist in these words draws tighter than ever the bond between God and man. It is not only that God sends His messengers to the world, nor only that His loving eye looks down upon it, nor only "that he gives that which is good"; but it is that the whole Heaven, as it were, lowers itself to touch earth, that God comes down to dwell and walk among men. The Psalmist's mind is filled with the thought of a present God who moves amongst mankind, and has His "footsteps" on earth. This herald Righteousness prepares God's path, which is just to say that all His dealing with mankind—which, as we have seen, have mercy and faithfulness for their signature and stamp—are rooted and based in perfect rectitude.

The second phase of the operation of righteousness is, that that majestic herald, the Divine purity which moves before Him, and "prepares in the desert a highway for the Lord,"—that that very same righteousness comes and takes my feeble hand, and will lead my tottering footsteps into God's path, and teach me to walk, planting my little foot where He planted His. The highest of all thoughts of the ideal relation between earth and Heaven, that of likeness between God and man, is trembling on the Psalmist's lips. Men may walk in God's ways—not only in the ways that please Him, but in the ways that are like Him. "Be ye therefore perfect, even as your Father which is in Heaven is perfect."

And the likeness can only be a likeness in moral qualities—a likeness in goodness, a likeness in purity, a likeness in aversion from evil, for the other attributes and characteristics are His peculiar property; and no human brow can wear the crown that He wears. But though His mercy can but, from afar off, be copied by us, the righteousness that moves before Him, and engineers God's path through the wilderness of the world, will come behind Him and nurse-like lay hold of our feeble arms and teach us to go in the way God would have us to walk.

Ah, brethren! That is the crown and climax of the harmony between God and man, that His mercy and His truth, His gifts and His grace have all led us up to this: that we take His righteousness as our pattern, and try in our poor lives to reproduce its wondrous beauty. Do not forget that a great deal more than the Psalmist dreamed of, you Christian men and women possess, in the Christ Who of God is made unto us righteousness, in Whom Heaven and earth are joined forever, in Whom man and God are knit in strictest bonds of indissoluble friendship; and Who, having prepared a path for God in His mighty mission and by His sacrifice on the Cross, comes to us; and, a the Incarnate Righteousness, will lead us in the paths of God, leaving us an example, that "we should follow in His steps."

3

The Work and Armor of the Children of the Day

Let us, who are of the day, be sober, putting on the breastplate of faith and love; and for a helmet, the hope of salvation—1 Thessalonians 5:8.

THIS letter to the Thessalonians is the oldest book of the New Testament. It was probably written within something like twenty years of the Crucifixion; long, therefore, before any of the Gospels were in existence. It is, therefore, exceedingly interesting and instructive to notice how this whole context is saturated with allusions to our Lord's teaching, as it is preserved in these Gospels; and how it takes for granted that the Thessalonian Christians were familiar with the very words.

For instance: "Yourselves know perfectly that the day of the Lord so cometh as a thief in the night" (5:2). How did these people in Thessalonica know that? They had been Christians for a year or so only; they had been taught by Paul for a few weeks only, or a month or two at the most. How did they know it? Because they had been told what the Master had said: "If the good man of the house had known at what hour the thief would come, he would have watched, and would not have suffered his house to be broken up."

And there are other allusions in the context almost as obvious—"The children of the light." Who said that? Christ, in His words: "The children of this world are wiser than the children of light." "They that sleep, sleep in the night, and if they be drunken, are drunken in the night." Where does that metaphor come from? "Take heed lest at any time ye be over-charged with surfeiting and drunkenness, and the cares of this life, and so that day come upon you unawares." "Watch, lest coming suddenly he find you sleeping!"

So you see all the context reposes upon, and presupposes the very words, which you find in our present existing Gospels, as the words of the Lord Jesus. And this is all but contemporaneous, and quite independent evidence of the existence in the Church, from the beginning, of a traditional teaching respecting Christ in verbal correspondence with the teaching which is now preserved for us in that four-fold record of His life.

Take that remark for what it is worth; and now turn to the text itself with which I have to deal this morning. The whole of the context may be said to be a little dissertation upon the moral and religious uses of the doctrine of our Lord's second coming. In my text these are summed up in one central injunction which has preceding it a motive that enforces it, and following it a method that ensures it. "Let us be sober." That is the center thought; and it is buttressed upon either side by a motive and a means. "Let us who are of the day," or "since we are of the day, be sober." And let us *be* it by "putting on the breastplate, and helmet of faith, love, and hope." These, then, are the three points which we have to consider.

I. First, this central injunction, into which all the moral teaching drawn from the second coming of Christ is gathered—"Let us be sober." Now, I do not suppose we are altogether to omit any reference to the literal meaning of this word. The context seems to show that, by its reference to night as the season for drunken orgies. Temperance is moderation in regard not only of the evil and swinish sin of drunkenness, which is so manifestly contrary to all Christian integrity and nobility of character, but in regard of the far more subtle temptation of another form of sensual indulgence—gluttony. The Christian Church needed to be warned of that, and if these people in Thessalonica needed the warning I am quite sure that we need it. There is not a nation on earth which needs it more than Englishmen. I am no ascetic, I do not want to glorify any outward observance, but any doctor in England will tell you that the average Englishman eats and drinks a great deal more than is good for him. It is melancholy to think how many professing Christians have the edge and keenness of their intellectual and spiritual life blunted by the luxurious and senseless table-abundance in which they habitually indulge. I am quite sure that water from the spring and barley-bread would be a great deal better for their souls and for their bodies too, in the case of many people that call themselves Christians. Suffer a word of exhortation! And do not let it be neglected because it is brief and general. Sparta, after all, is the best place for a man to live in, next to Jerusalem.

But, passing from that, let us turn to the higher subject with which the Apostle is here evidently mainly concerned. What is the meaning of the exhortation "Be sober?" Well, first let me tell you what I think is not the meaning of it. It does not mean an unemotional absence of fervor in your Christian character.

There is a kind of religious teachers who are always preaching down enthusiasm, and preaching up what they call a "sober standard of feeling" in matters of religion. By which, in nine cases out of ten, they mean precisely such a tepid condition as is described in much less polite language; when the Voice from Heaven says, "Because thou art neither cold nor hot I will spew thee out of My mouth." That is the real meaning of the "sobriety" that some people are always desiring you to cultivate. I should have thought that the last piece of furniture which any Christian Church in the nineteenth century needed was a refrigerator! A poker and a pair of bellows would be very much more needful for them. For, dear brethren, the truths that you and I profess to believe are of such a nature, so tremendous either in their joyfulness and beauty, or in their solemnity and awfulness, that one would think that if they once got into a man's head and heart, nothing but the most fervid and continuous glow of a radiant enthusiasm would correspond to their majesty and overwhelming importance. I venture to say that the only consistent Christian is the enthusiastic Christian; and that the only man that will ever do anything in this world for God or man worth doing, is the man who is not *sober*, according to that cold-blooded definition which I have been speaking about, but who is all ablaze with an enkindled earnestness that knows no diminution and no cessation.

Paul, the very man that is exhorting here to sobriety, was the very type of an enthusiast all his life. So Festus thought him mad, and even in the Church at Corinth there were some to whom in his fervor, he seemed to be "beside himself." (2 Cor. 5:13).

Oh! For more of that insanity! You may make up your minds to this; that any men or women that are in thorough earnest, either about Christianity or about any other great, noble, lofty, self-forgetting purpose, will have to be content to have the old Pentecostal charge flung at them: "These men are full of new wine!" Well for the Church, and well for the men who deserve the taunt; for it means that they have learned something of the emotion that corresponds to such magnificent and awful verities as Christian faith converses with.

I did not intend to say so much about that; I turn now for a moment to the consideration of what this exhortation really means. It means, as I take it, mainly this: the prime Christian duty of self-restraint in the use and the love of all earthly treasures and pleasures.

I need not do more than remind you how, in the very make of a man's soul, it is clear that unless there be exercised rigid self-control he will go all to pieces. The make of human nature, if I may so say, shows that it is not meant for a democracy but a monarchy.

Here are within us many passions, tastes, desires, most of them rooted in the flesh, which are as blind as hunger and thirst are. If a man is hungry, the bread will satisfy him all the same whether he steals it or not; and it will not necessarily be distasteful even if it be poisoned. And there are other blind impulses and appetites in our nature which ask nothing except this: "Give me my appropriate gratification, though all the laws of God and man be broken in order to get it!"

And so there has to be something like an eye given to these blind beasts, and something like a directing hand laid upon these instinctive impulses. The true temple of the human spirit must be built in stages, the broad base laid in these animal instincts; above them and controlling them the directing and restraining will; above it the understanding which enlightens it and them; and supreme over all the conscience with nothing between it and Heaven. Where that is not the order of the inner man, you get wild work. You have set "beggars on horseback," and we all know where they go! The man who lets passion and inclination guide is like a steamboat with all the furnaces banked up, with the engines going full speed, and nobody at the wheel. It will drive on to the rocks, or wherever the bow happens to point, no matter though death and destruction lie beyond the next turn of the screw. That is what you will come to unless you live in the habitual exercise of rigid self-control.

And that self-control is to be exercised mainly, or at least as one very important form of it, in regard of our use and estimate of the pleasures of this present life. Yes! It is not only from the study of a man's make that the necessity for a very rigid self-government appears, but the observation of the conditions and circumstances in which he is placed points the same lesson. All round about him are hands reaching out to him drugged cups. The world with all its fading sweets comes tempting him, and the old fable fulfills itself—Whoever takes that Circe's cup and puts it to his lips and quaffs deep, turns into a swine, and sits there imprisoned at the feet of the sorceress forevermore!

There is only one thing that will deliver you from that fate, my brother. "Be sober" and in regard of the world and all that it offers to us—all joy, possession, gratification—"set a knife to thy throat if thou be a man given to appetite." There is no noble life possible on any other terms—not to say there is no Christian life possible on any other terms—but suppression and mortification of the desires of the flesh and of the spirit. You cannot look upwards and dowards at the same moment. Your heart is only a tiny room after all, and if you cram it full of the world, you relegate your Master to the stable outside. "Ye cannot serve God and Mammon." "Be sober," says Paul, then, and cultivate the habit of rigid self-control in regard of this present. Oh! What a melancholy, solemn thought it is that hundreds of professing Christians in England, like vultures after a full meal, have so gorged themselves with the garbage of this present life that they cannot fly, and have to be content with moving along the ground, heavy and languid. Christian men and women, are you keeping yourselves in spiritual health by a very sparing use of the dainties and delights of earth? Answer the question to your own souls and to your Judge.

II. And now let me turn to the other thoughts that lie here. There is, secondly, a motive which backs up and buttresses this exhortation. "Let us who are of the day," or as the Revised Version has it a little more emphatically and correctly, "Let us, since we are of the day, be sober." "The day"; what day? The temptation is to answer the question by saying, of course the specific day which was spoken about in the beginning of the section, "the day of the Lord," that coming judgment by the coming Christ. But I think that although, perhaps, there may be some allusion here to that specific day, still, if you will look at the verses which immediately precede my text, you will see that in them the Apostle has passed from the thought of "the day of the Lord" to that of day in general. That is obvious, I think, from the contrast he draws between the "day" and the "night"—the darkness and the light. If so, then, when he says "the children of the day" he does not so much mean—though that is quite true—that we are, as it were, akin to that Day of Judgment, and may therefore look forward to it without fear, and in quiet confidence, lifting up our heads because our redemption draws nigh; but rather he means that Christians are the children of that which expresses knowledge, and joy, and activity. Of these things the day is the emblem, in every language and in every poetry. The day is the time when men see and hear, the symbol of gladness and cheer all the world over.

And so, says Paul, you Christian men and women belong to a joyous realm, a realm of light and knowledge, a realm of purity and righteousness. You are children of the light; a glad condition which involves many glad and noble issues. Children of the light should be brave, children of the light should not be afraid of the light, children of the light should be cheerful, children of the light should be buoyant, children of the light should be transparent, children of the light should be hopeful, children of the light should be pure, and children of the light should walk in this darkened world, bearing their radiance with them; and making things, else unseen, visible to many a dim eye.

But while these emblems of cheerfulness, hope, purity, and illumination are gathered together in that grand name, "Ye are children of the day," there is one direction especially in which the Apostle thinks that that consideration ought to tell, and that is the direction of its self-restraint. "*Noblesse oblige!*"; the aristocracy are bound to do nothing low or dishonorable. The children of the light are not to stain their hands with anything foul. Chambering and wantonness, slumber and drunkenness, the indulgence in the appetites of the flesh—all that may be fitting for the night, it is clean incongruous with the day.

Well, if you want that turned into pedestrian prose—which is not more clear but a little less emotional—it is just this: You Christian men and women belong—if you are Christians—to another state of things from that which is lying round about you; and therefore you ought to live in rigid abstinence from these things that are round about you.

That is plain enough surely, nor do I suppose that I need to dwell on that thought at any length. We belong to another order of things, says Paul; we carry a day with us in the midst of the night. What follows from that? Do not let us pursue the wandering lights and treacherous will-o'-the-wisps that lure men into bottomless bogs where they are lost. If we have light in our dwellings while Egypt lies in darkness, let it teach us to eat our meat with our loins girded, and our staves in our hands, not without bitter herbs, and ready to go forth into the wilderness. You do not belong to the world in which you live, if you are Christian men and women; you are only camped here. Your purposes, thoughts, hopes, aspirations, treasures, desires, delights, go up higher. And so, if you are children of the day, be self-restrained in your dealings with the darkness.

III. And, last of all, my text points out for us a method by which this great precept may be fulfilled: "Putting on the breastplate of faith and love, and for a helmet the hope of salvation."

That, of course, is the first rough draft, occurring in Paul's earliest epistle, of an image which recurs at intervals and in more or less expanded form in other of his letters, and is so splendidly worked out in detail in the grand picture of the Christian armor in the Epistle to the Ephesians.

I need not do more than just remind you of the difference between that finished picture and this outline sketch. Here we have only defensive and not offensive armor, here the Christian graces are somewhat differently allocated to the different parts of the armor.

Here we have only the great triad of Christian graces, so familiar on our lips: faith, hope, charity. Here we have faith and love in the closest possible juxtaposition, and hope somewhat more apart; the breastplate, like some of the ancient hauberks, made of steel and gold, is framed and forged out of faith and love blended together. And faith and love are more closely identified in fact than faith and hope, or than love and hope. For faith and love have the same object, and are all but contemporaneous. Wherever a man lays hold of Jesus Christ by faith, there cannot but spring up in his heart love to Christ; and there is no love without faith. So that we may almost say that faith and love are but the two throws of the shuttle, the one in the one direction and the other in the other; whereas hope comes somewhat later in a somewhat remoter connection with faith, and has a somewhat different object from these other two. Therefore it is here slightly separated from its sister graces. Faith, love, hope—these three form the defensive armor that guard the soul; and these three make self-control possible. Like a diver in his dress, who is let down to the bottom of the wild, far-weltering ocean, a man whose heart is girded by faith and charity, and whose head is covered with the helmet of hope, may be dropped down into the wildest sea of temptation and of worldliness, and yet will walk dry and unharmed through the midst of its depths, and breathe air that comes from a world above the restless surges.

And in like manner the cultivation of faith, charity, and hope is the best means for securing the exercise of sober self-control.

It is an easy thing to say to a man, "Govern yourself!" It is a very hard thing with the powers that any man has at his disposal to do it. As somebody said about an army joining the rebels, "It's a bad job when the extinguisher catches fire!" And that is exactly the condition of things in regard to our power of self-government. The powers that should control are largely gone over to the enemy, and become traitors.

"Who shall keep the very keepers?" is the old question, and here is the answer: You cannot execute the gymnastic feat of "erecting yourself above yourself" any more than a man can take himself by his own coat collar and lift himself up from the ground with his own arms. But you can cultivate faith, hope, and charity, and these three, well cultivated and brought to bear upon your daily life, will do the governing for you. Faith will bring you into communication with all the power of God. Love will lead you into a region where all the temptations round you will be touched as by an Ithuriel spear, and will show their own foulness. And Hope will turn away your eyes from looking at the tempting splendor around, and fix them upon the glories that are above.

And so the reins will come into your hands in an altogether new manner, and you will be able to be king over your own nature in a fashion that you did not dream of before, if only you will trust in Christ, and love Him, and fix your desires on the things above.

Then you will be able to govern yourself when you let Christ govern you. The glories that are to be done away that gleam round you like foul, flaring tallow-candles, will lose all their fascination and brightness, by reason of the glory that excels, the pure starlike splendor of the white inextinguishable lights of Heaven.

And when by Faith, Charity and Hope you have drunk of the new wine of the Kingdom, the drugged and opiate cup which a sorceress world presents, jewelled though it be, will lose its charms, and it will not be hard to turn from it and dash it to the ground.

God help you, brother, to be "sober," for unless you are, you cannot see the Kingdom of God!

4

The Last Beatitude of the Ascended Christ

Blessed are they that do His commandments, that they may have right to the Tree of Life, and may enter in through the gates into the city—Revelation 22:14.

The Revised Version reads, "Blessed are they that wash their robes, that they may have the right to come to the Tree of Life."

That may seem a very large change to make, from "keep his commandments" to "wash their robes," but in the Greek it is only a change of three letters in one word, one in the next, and two in the third. And the two phrases, written, look so like each other that a scribe hasty, or, for the moment, careless, might very easily mistake the one for the other. There can be no doubt whatever that the reading in the Revised Version is the correct one. Not only is it sustained by a great weight of authority, but also it is far more in accordance with the whole teaching of the New Testament than that which stands in our Authorized Version.

"Blessed are they that do His commandments, that they might have right to the Tree of Life," carries us back to the old law, and has no more hopeful a sound in it than the thunders of Sinai. If it were, indeed, among Christ's last words to us, it would be a most sad instance of His "building again the things He had destroyed." It is relegating us to the dreary old round of trying to earn Heaven by doing good deeds; and I might almost say it is "making the Cross of Christ of none effect." The fact that that corrupt reading came so soon into the Church and has held its ground so long, is to me a very singular proof of the difficulty which men have always had in keeping themselves up to the level of the grand central Gospel-truth: "Not by works of righteousness which we have done, but by His mercy, He saved us."

"Blessed are they that wash their robes, that they may have right to the Tree of Life," has the clear ring of the New Testament music about it, and is in full accord with the whole type of doctrine that runs through this book; and is not unworthy to be almost the last word that the lips of the Incarnate Wisdom spoke to men from Heaven. So then, taking that point of view, I wish to look with you at the three things that come plainly out of these words: First, that principle that if men are clean it is because they are cleansed; "Blessed are they that wash their robes." Second, it is the cleansed who have unrestrained access to the source of life. And last, it is the cleansed that pass into the society of the city. Now, let me deal with these three things:

First, if we are clean it is because we have been made so. The first beatitude that Jesus Christ spoke from the mountain was, "Blessed are the poor in spirit." The last beatitude that He speaks from Heaven is, "Blessed are they that wash their robes." And the act commended in the last is but the outcome of the spirit extolled in the first. For they who are poor in spirit are such as know themselves to be sinful men; and those who know themselves to the sinful men are they who will cleanse their robes in the blood of Jesus Christ.

I need not remind you, I suppose, how continually this symbol of the robe is used in Scripture as an expression for moral character. This Book of the Apocalypse is saturated through and through with Jewish implications and allusions, and there can be no doubt whatever that in this metaphor of the cleansing of the robes there is an allusion to that vision that the Apocalyptic seer of the Old Covenant, the prophet Zecharias, had when he saw the High Priest standing before the altar clad in foul raiment, and the word came forth, "Take away the filthy garments from him." Nor need I do more than remind you how the same metaphor is often on the lips of our Lord Himself, notably in the story of the man that had not on the wedding garment, and in the touching and beautiful incident in the parable of the Prodigal Son, where the exuberance of the father's love bids them cast the best robe round the rags and the leanness of his long lost boy. Nor need I remind you how Paul catches up the metaphor, and is continually referring to an investing and a divesting, the putting on and the putting off of the new and the old man. In this same Book of the Apocalypse, we see, gleaming all through it, the white robes of the purified soul: "They shall walk with Me in white, for they are worthy." "I beheld a great multitude, whom no man could number, who had washed their robes and made them white in the blood of the Lamb."

And so there are gathered up into these last words, all these allusions and memories, thick and clustering, when Christ speaks from Heaven and says, "Blessed are they that wash their robes."

Well then, I suppose we may say roughly, in our more modern phraseology, that the robe thus so frequently spoken of in Scripture answers substantially to what we call character. It is not exactly the man, and yet it is the man. It is the self, and yet it is a kind of projection and making visible of the self, the vesture which is cast round "the hidden man of the heart."

This mysterious robe, which answers nearly to what we mean by character, is made by the wearer.

That is a solemn thought. Every one of us carries about with him a mystical loom, and we are always weaving—weave, weave, weaving—this robe which we wear, every thought a thread of the warp, every action a thread of the weft. We weave it, as the spider does its web, out of its own entrails, if I might so say. We weave it, and we dye it, and we cut it, and we stitch it, and then we put it on and wear it, and it sticks to us. Like a snail that crawls about your garden patches, and makes its shell by a process of secretion from out of its own substance, so you and I are making that mysterious, solemn thing that we call character, moment by moment. It is our own self, modified by our actions. Character is the precipitate from the stream of conduct which, like the Nile Delta, gradually rises solid and firm above the parent river and confines its flow.

The next step that I ask you to take is one that I know some of you do not like to take, and it is this: All the robes are foul. I do not say all are equally splashed, I do not say all equally thickly spotted with the flesh. I do not wish to talk dogmas, I wish to talk experience;

and I appeal to your own consciences, with this plain question, that every man and woman among us can answer if they like: Is it true or is it not, that the robe is all dashed with mud caught on the foul ways, with stains in some of us of rioting and banqueting and revelry and drunkenness; sins of the flesh that have left their marks upon the flesh; but with all of us grey and foul as compared with the whiteness of His robe who sits above us there?

Ah! Would that I could bring to all hearts that are listening to me now, whether the hearts of professing Christians or no, that consciousness more deeply than we have ever had it, of how full of impurity and corruption our characters are. I do not charge you with crimes; I do not charge you with guilt in the world's eyes, but, if we seriously ponder over our past, have we not lived, some of us habitually, all of us far too often, as if there were no God at all, or as if we had nothing to do with Him? And is not that godlessness, practical Atheism, the fountain of all foulness from which black brooks flow into our lives and stain our robes?

The next step is, the foul robe can be cleansed. My text does not go any further in a statement of the method, but it rests upon the great words of this Book of the Revelation, which I have already quoted for another purpose, in which we read, "they washed their robes, and made them white in the blood of the Lamb." And the same writer, in his Epistle, has the same paradox, which seems to have been, to him, a favorite way of putting the central Gospel truth: "The blood of Jesus Christ cleanses from all sin." John saw the paradox, and saw that the paradox helped to illustrate the great truth that He was trying to proclaim, that the red blood whitened the black robe, and that in its full tide there was a limpid river of water of life, clear as crystal, proceeding out of the Cross of Christ.

Guilt can be pardoned, character can be sanctified. Guilt can be pardoned! Men say: "No! We live in a universe of inexorable laws: 'What a man soweth that he must also reap.' If he has done wrong he must inherit the consequences."

But the question whether guilt can be pardoned or not has only to do very remotely with consequences. The question is not whether we live in a universe of inexorable laws, but whether there is anything in the universe but the laws; for forgiveness is a personal act and has only to do secondarily and remotely with the consequences of a man's doings. So that, if we believe in a personal God, and believe that He has got any kind of living relation to men at all, we can believe—blessed be His name!—in the doctrine of forgiveness; and leave the inexorable laws full scope to work, according as His wisdom and His mercy may provide. For the heart of the Christian doctrine of pardon does not touch those laws, but the heart of it is this: "O Lord! Thou wast angry with me, but Thine anger is turned away, Thou hast comforted me!" So guilt may be pardoned.

Character may be sanctified and elevated. Why not, if you can bring a sufficiently strong new force to bear upon it? And you can bring such a force, in the blessed thought of Christ's death for me, and in the gift of His love. There is such a force in the thought that He has given Himself for our sin. There is such a force in the Spirit of Christ given to us through His death to cleanse us by His presence in our hearts. And so I say, the blood of Jesus Christ, the power of His sacrifice and Cross, cleanses from all sin, both in the sense of taking away all my guilt, and in the sense of changing my character into something loftier and nobler and purer.

Men and women! Do you believe that? If you do not, why do you not? If you do, are you trusting to what you believe, and living the life that befits the confidence?

One word more. The washing of your robes has to be done by you. "Blessed are they that wash their robes." On one hand is all the fullness of cleansing, on the other is the heap of dirty rags that will not be cleansed by you sitting there and looking at them. You must bring the two into contact. How? By the magic band that unites strength and weakness, purity and foulness, the Savior and the penitent; the magic band of simple affiance, and trust and submission of myself to the cleansing power of His death and of His life.

Only remember, "Blessed are they that *are washing*," as the Greek might read. Not once and for all, but a continuous process, a blessed process running on all through a man's life.

These are the conditions as they come from Christ's own lips, in almost the last words that human ears, either in fact or in vision, heard Him utter. These are the conditions under which noble life, and at least Heaven, are possible for men; namely, that their foul characters shall be cleansed, and that continuously, by daily recurrence and recourse to the Fountain opened in His sacrifice and death.

Friends, you may know much of the beauty and nobleness of Christianity, you may know much of the tenderness and purity of Christ, but if you have not apprehended Him in this character, there is an inner sanctuary yet to be trod, of which your feet know nothing, and the sweetest sweetness of all you have not yet tasted, for it is His forgiving love and cleansing power that most deeply manifest His Divine affection and bind us to Himself.

II. The second thought that I would suggest is that these cleansed ones, and by implication these only, have unrestrained access to the source of life: "Blessed are they that wash their robes, that they may have right 'to the Tree of Life'." That, of course, carries us back to the old mysterious narrative at the beginning of the Book of Genesis.

Although it does not bear very closely upon my present subject, I cannot help pausing to point out one thing, how remarkable and how beautiful it is that the last page of the Revelation should come bending round to touch the first page of Genesis. The history of man began with angels with frowning faces and flaming swords barring the way to the Tree of Life. It ends here with the guard of Cherubim withdrawn; or rather, perhaps, sheathing their swords and becomg guides to the no longer forbidden fruit, instead of being its guards. That is the Bible's grand symbolical way of saying that all between—the sin, the misery, the death—is a parenthesis. God's purpose is not going to be thwarted, and the end of His majestic march through human history is to be men's access to the Tree of Life from which, for the dreary ages that are but as a moment in the great eternities, they were barred out by their sin.

However, that is not the point that I meant to say a word about. The Tree of Life stands as the symbol here of an external source of life. I take "life" to be used here in what I believe to be its predominant New Testament meaning, not bare continuance in existence, but a full blessed perfection and activity of all the faculties and possibilities of the man, which this very Apostle himself identifies with the knowledge of God and of Jesus Christ. And that life, says John, has an external source in Heaven as on earth.

There is an old Christian legend, absurd as a legend, beautiful as a parable, that the cross on which Christ was crucified was made out of the wood of the Tree of Life. It is true in idea, for He and His work will be the source of all life, for earth and for Heaven, whether of body, soul, or spirit. They that wash their robes have the right of unrestrained access to Him in Whose presence, in that loftier state, no impurity can live.

I need not dwell upon the thought that is involved here, of how, while on earth and in the beginnings of the Christian career, life is the basis of righteousness; in that higher world, in a very profound sense, righteousness is the condition of fuller life.

The Tree of Life, according to some of the old Rabbinical legends, lifted its branches, by an indwelling motion, high above impure hands that were stretched to touch them, and until our hands are cleansed through faith in Jesus Christ, its richest fruit hangs unreachable, golden, above our heads. Oh! Brother, the fullness of the life of Heaven is granted only to them who, drawing near Jesus Christ by faith on earth, have thereby cleansed themselves from all filthiness of the flesh and spirit?

III. Finally, those who are cleansed, and they only, have entrance into the society of the city.

There again we have a whole series of Old and New Testament metaphors gathered together. In the old world the whole power and splendor of great kingdoms was gathered in their capitals, Babylon and Nineveh in the past, Rome in the present. To John, the forces of evil were all concentrated in that city on the Seven Hills. To him, the antagonistic forces which were the hope of the world were all concentrated in the real ideal city which he expected to come down from Heaven: the New Jerusalem. And he and his brother who wrote the Epistle to the Hebrews, whoever *he* was—trained substantially in the same school—have taught us the same lesson that our picture of the future is not to be of a solitary or self-regarding Heaven, but of "a city which hath foundations."

Genesis began with a garden, man's sin sent him out of the garden. God, out of evil evolves good, and for the lost garden comes the better thing, the found city. "Then comes the statelier Eden back to man." For surely it is better that men should live in the activities of the city than in the sweetness and indolence of the garden; and manifold and miserable as are the sins and the sorrows of great cities, the opprobria of our modern so-called civilization, yet still the aggregation of great masses of men for worthy objects generates a form of character, and sets loose energies and activities which no other kind of life could have produced.

And so I believe a great step in progress is set forth when we read of the final condition of mankind as being their assembling in the city of God. And surely there, amidst the solemn troops and sweet societies, the long-loved, long-lost, will be found again. I cannot believe that like the Virgin and Joseph, we shall have to go wandering up and down the streets of Jerusalem when we get there, looking for our dear ones. "Knew ye not that I should be in the Father's house?" We shall know where to find them.

> We shall clasp them again
> And with God be the rest.

The city is the emblem of security and of permanence. No more shall life be as a desert march, with changes which only bring sorrow, and yet a dreary monotony amidst them all. We shall dwell amid abiding realities, ourselves fixed in unchanging, but ever growing completeness and peace. The tents shall be done with, we shall inhabit the solid mansions of the city which hath foundations, and shall wonderingly exclaim, as our unaccustomed eyes gaze on their indestructible strength, "What manner of stones, and what buildings are here!"; and not one stone of these shall ever be thrown down.

Dear friends, the sum of all my poor words now is the earnest beseeching of every one of you to bring all your foulness to Christ, who alone can make you clean. "Though thou wash thee with nitre, and take thee much soap, yet thine iniquity is marked before Me, saith the Lord." "The blood of Jesus Christ cleanseth from all sin." Submit yourselves, I pray you, to its purifying power, by humble faith. Then you will have the true possession of the true life today, and will be citizens of the city of God, even while in this far-off dependency of that great metropolis. And when the moment comes for you to leave this prison-house, an angel "mighty and beauteous, though his face be hid," shall come to you, as once of old to the sleeping Apostle. His touch shall wake you, and lead you, scarce knowing where you are or what is happening, from the sleep of life, past the first and second ward, and through the iron gate that leads unto the city. Smoothly it will turn on its hinges, opening to you of its own accord, and then you will come to yourself and know of a surety that the Lord hath sent His angel, and that he has led you into the home of your heart, the city of God, which they enter as its fitting inhabitants who wash their robes in the blood of the Lamb.

5

Luther: A Stone
on the Cairn

*For David, after he had served his own generation by
the will of God, fell on sleep, and was laid unto his fathers and saw corruption. But He, Whom God raised
again, saw no corruption—Acts 13:36, 37.*

I take these words as a motto rather than as a text. You will have
anticipated the use which I purpose to make of them in connection with the Luther Commemoration. They set before us, in
clear sharp contrast, the distinction between the limited transient
work of the servants and the unbounded, eternal influence of the
Master. The former are servants, and that but for a time; they do
their work, they are laid in the grave, and as their bodies resolve into
their elements, so their influence, their teaching, the institutions
which they may have founded, disintegrate and decay. He lives. His
relation to the world is not as theirs; He is "not for an age, but for
all time." Death is not the end of His work. His Cross is the eternal foundation of the world's hope. His life is the ultimate, perfect
revelation of the Divine Nature which can never be surpassed, or
fathomed, or antiquated. Therefore, the last thought, in all com-
memorations of departed teachers and guides, should be of Him
Who gave them all the force that they had; and the final word
should be, "they were not suffered to continue by reason of death,
this Man continueth ever."

In the same spirit, then, as the words of my text, and taking them
as giving me little more than a starting point and a framework, I
draw from them some thoughts appropriate to the occasion.

I. First, we have to think about the limited and transient work
of this great servant of God.

The miner's son who was born in that little Saxon village four hundred years ago presents at first sight a character singularly unlike the traditional type of medieval Church fathers and saints. Their ascetic habits and the repressive system under which they were trained withdraw them from our sympathy; but this sturdy peasant, with his full-blooded humanity, unmistakably a man, and a man all round, is a new type, and looks strangely out of place among doctors and medieval saints.

His character, though not complex, is many-sided and in some respects contradictory. The face and figure that look out upon us from the best portraits of Luther tell us a great deal about the man. Strong, massive, not at all elegant; he stands there firm and resolute, on his own legs, grasping a *Bible* in a muscular hand. There is plenty of animalism—a source of power as well as of weakness—in the thick neck; an iron will in the square chin; eloquence on the full, loose lips; a mystic, dreamy tenderness and sadness in the steadfast eyes—altogether a true king and a leader of men!

The first things that strike one in the character are the iron will that would not waver, the indomitable courage that knew no fear, the splendid audacity that, single-handed, sprang into the arena for a contest to the death with Pope, Emperors, superstitions and devils; the insight that saw the things that were "hid from the wise and prudent," and the answering sincerity that would not hide what he saw, nor say that he saw what he did not.

But there was a great deal more than that in the man. He was no mere brave revolutionary; he was a cultured scholar, abreast of all the learning of his age, capable of logic-chopping and scholastic disputation on occasion, and but too often the victim of his own over-subtle refinements. He was a poet, with a poet's dreaminess and waywardness, fierce alterations of light and shade, sorrow and joy. All living things whispered and spoke to him, and he walked in communion with them all. Little children gathered round his feet, and he had a big heart of love for all the weary and the sorrowful.

Everybody knows how he could write and speak. He made the German language, as we may say, lifting it up from a dialect of boors to become the rich, flexible, cultured speech that it is. And his Bible, his single-handed work, is one of the colossal achievements of man; like Stonehenge or the Pyramids. "His words were half-battles," "they were living creatures that had hands and feet"; his speech, direct, strong, homely, ready to borrow words from the kitchen or the gutter, is unmatched for popular eloquence and impression. There was music in the man. His flute solaced his lonely hours in his home at Wittemberg; and the Marseillaise of the Reformation, as that grand hymn of his has been called, came, words and music, from his heart. There was humor in him, coarse horseplay often; an honest, hearty, broad laugh frequently, like that of a Norse god! There were coarse tastes in him, tastes of the peasant folk from whom he came, which clung to him through life and kept him in sympathy with the common people, and intelligible to them. And with all, there was a constitutional melancholy, aggravated by his weary toils, perilous fightings, and fierce throes, which led him down often into the deep mire where there was no standing and which sighs through all his life. The penitential psalms and Paul's wail, "O! Wretched man that I am," perhaps never woke more plaintive echo in any human heart than they did in Martin Luther's.

Faults he had, gross and plain as the heroic mold in which he was cast. He was vehement and fierce often; he was coarse and violent often. He saw what he did see so clearly that he was slow to believe that there was anything that he did not see. He was oblivious of counter-balancing considerations, and given to exaggerated, incautious, unguarded statements of precious truths. He too often aspired to be a driver rather than a leader of men, and his strength of will became obstinacy and tyranny. It was too often true that he had dethroned the Pope of Rome to set up a pope at Wittemberg. And foul personalities came from his lips, according to the bad controversial fashion of his day, which permitted a license to scholars that we now forbid to fishwives.

All that has to be admitted; and when it is all admitted, what then? This is a fastidious generation; Erasmus is its heroic type a great deal more than Luther—I mean among the cultivated classes of our day—and that very largely because in Erasmus there is no quick sensibility to religious emotion as there is in Luther, and no inconvenient fervor. The faults are there—coarse, plain, palpable—

and perhaps more than enough has been made of them. Let us remember, as to violence, that he was following the fashion of the day; that he was fighting for his life; that when a man is at death-grips with a tiger he may be pardoned if he strikes without considering whether he is going to spoil the skin or not; and that, on the whole, you cannot throttle snakes in a graceful attitude. Men fought then with bludgeons; they fight now with dainty polished daggers, dipped in cold colorless poison of sarcasm. Perhaps there was less malice in the rougher old way than in the new.

The faults are there, and nobody who was not a fool would think of painting that homely Saxon peasant-monk's face without the warts and the wrinkles. But it is quite as unhistorical, and a great deal more wicked, to paint nothing but the warts and wrinkles; to rake all the faults together and make the most of them and present them in answer to the question: "What sort of a man was Martin Luther?"

As to the work that he did, like the work of all of us, it had its limitations and it will have its end. The impulse that he communicated, like all impulses that are given from men, will wear out its force. New questions will arise, of which the dead leaders never dreamed, and in which they can give no counsel. The perspective of theological thought will alter, the center of interest will change, a new dialect will begin to be spoken. So it comes to pass that all religious teachers and thinkers are left behind, and that their words are preserved and read rather for their antiquarian and historical interest than because of any impulse or direction for the present which may linger in them, and if they founded institutions, these, too, in their time will crumble and disappear.

But I do not mean to say that the truths which Luther rescued from the dust of centuries, and impressed upon the conscience of Teutonic Europe, are getting antiquated. I only mean that his connection with them and his way of putting them, had its limitations and will have its end; "This man, having served his own generation by the will of God, was gathered to his fathers, and saw corruption."

What *were* the truths, what was his contribution to the illumination of Europe, and to the Church? Three great principles, which perhaps closer analysis might reduce to one; but which for popular use, on such an occasion as the present, had better be kept apart, will state his service to the world.

There were three men in the past who, as it seems to me, reach out their hands to one another across the centuries: Paul, St. Augustine, and Martin Luther. Three men very like each other, all three of them joining the same subtle speculative power with the same capacity of religious fervor, and of flaming up at the contemplation of Divine truth. All of them gifted with the same exuberant, and to fastidious eyes, incorrect eloquence. All three trained in a school of religious thought of which each respectively was destined to be the antagonist and all but the destroyer.

The young Pharisee, on the road to Damascus, blinded, bewildered, with all that vision flaming upon him, sees in its light his past, that he thought had been so pure, and holy, and God-serving, and amazedly discovers that it had been all a sin and a crime, and a persecution of the Divine One. Beaten from every refuge, and lying there, he cries: "What wouldst Thou have me to do, Lord?"

The young Manichean and profligate in the fourth century, and the young monk in his convent in the 15th, passed through a similar experience, different in form, identical in substance, with that of Paul, the persecutor. And so Paul's gospel, which was the description and explanation, the rationale of his own experience, became their gospel; and when Paul said, "Not by works of righteousness which our own hands have done, but by His mercy He saved us" (Titus 3:5), the great voice from the North African shore, in the midst of the agonies of barbarian invasions and a falling Rome, said "Amen." "Man lives by faith," the voice from the Wittemberg convent, a thousand years after, amidst the unspeakable corruption of that phosphorescent and decaying renaissance, answered across the centuries, "It is true!" "Herein is the righteousness of God revealed from faith to faith." Luther's word to the world was Augustine's word to the world; and Luther and Augustine were the echoes of Saul of Tarsus; and Paul learned his theology on the Damascus road, when the voice bade him go and proclaim "forgiveness of sins, and inheritance among them which are sanctified by faith that is in Me" (Acts 26:18). That is Luther's first claim on our gratitude, that he took this truth from the shelves where it had reposed, dust-covered, through centuries, that he lifted this truth from the bier where it had lain, smothered with sacerdotal garlands, and called with a loud voice, "I say unto thee, arise!" and that now the commonplace of Christianity is this: All men are sinful men, justice condemns us all. Our only hope is God's infinite mercy. That mercy comes to us all in Jesus Christ who died for us, and he that gets that into his heart by simple faith, he is forgiven, pure, and he is an heir of Heaven.

There are other aspects of Christian truth which Luther failed to apprehend. The Gospel is, of course, not only a way of reconciliation and forgiveness. He pushed his teaching of the uselessness of good works as a means of salvation too far. He said rash and exaggerated things in his vehement way about the "justifying power" of faith alone. Doubtless his language was often exaggerated, and his thoughts one-sided, in regard to subjects that need very delicate handling and careful definition. But after all that is admitted, it remains true that his strong arm tossed aside the barriers and rubbish that had been piled across the way by which prodigals could go home to their Father, and made plain once more the endless mercy of God, and the power of humble faith. He was right when he declared that whatever heights and depths there may be in God's great revelation, and however needful it is for a complete apprehension of the truth as it is in Jesus that these should find their place in the creed of Christendom, still the firmness with which that initial truth of man's sinfulness and his forgiveness and acceptance through simple faith in Christ is held, and the clear earnestness with which it is proclaimed, are the test of a standing or a falling Church.

And then, closely connected with this central principle, and yet susceptible of being stated separately, are the other two; of neither of which do I think it necessary to say more than a word. Side by side with that great discovery—for it was a discovery—by the monk in his convent, of Justification by faith, there follows the other principle of the entire sweeping away of all priesthood, and the direct access to God of every individual Christian soul. There are no more external rites to be done by a designated and separate class. There is One sacrificing Priest, and one only, and that is

Jesus Christ, Who has sacrificed Himself for us all, and there are no other priests, except in the sense in which every Christian man is a priest and minister of the most high God. And no man comes between me and my Father; and no man has a right to do anything for me which brings me any grace, except insofar as my own heart opens for the reception, and my own faith lays hold of the grace given.

Luther did not carry that principle so far as some of us modern non-conformists carry it. He left illogical fragments of sacramentarian and sacerdotal theories in his creed and in his Church. But, for all that, we owe mainly to him the clear utterance of that thought, the warm breath of which has thawed the ice chains which held Europe in barren bondage. Notwithstanding the present portentous revival of sacerdotalism, and the strange turning again of portions of society to these beggarly elements of the past, I believe that the figments of a sacrificing priesthood and sacramental efficacy will never again permanently darken the sky in this land, the home of the men who speak the tongue of Milton, and owe much of their religious and political freedom to the Reformation of Luther.

And the third point, which is closely connected with these other two, is this, the declaration that every illuminated Christian soul has a right and is bound to study God's Word without the Church at its elbow to teach what to think about it. It was Luther's great achievement that, whatever else he did, he put the Bible into the hands of the common people. In that department and region, his work, perhaps, bears more distinctly the traces of limitation and imperfection than anywhere else, for he knew nothing—how could he?—of the difficult questions of this day in regard to the composition and authority of Scripture, nor had he thought out his own system or done full justice to his own principle.

He could be as inquisitorial and as dogmatic as any Dominican of them all. He believed in force; he was as ready as all his fellows were to invoke the aid of the temporal power. The idea of the Church, as helped and sustained, which means fettered, and weakened, and paralyzed, by the civic government, bewitched him as it did his fellows. We needed to wait for George Fox, and Roger Williams, and more modern names still before we understood fully what was involved in the rejection of priesthood, and the claim that God's Word should speak directly to each Christian soul. But for all that, we largely owe to Luther the creed that looks in simple faith to Christ: a Church without a priest, in which every man is a priest of the Most High, the only true democracy that the world will ever see; and a Church in which the open Bible and the indwelling spirit are the guides of every humble soul within its pale. These are his claims on our gratitude.

Luther's work had its limitations and its imperfections, as I have been saying to you. It will become less and less conspicuous as the ages go on. It cannot be otherwise. That is the law of the world. As a whole green forest of the carboniferous era is represented now in the rocks by a thin seam of coal, no thicker than a sheet of paper, so the stormy lives and the large works of the men that have gone before, are compressed into a mere film and line in the great cliff that slowly rises above the sea of time and is called the history of the world.

II. Be it so! Be it so! Let us turn to the other thought of our text, the perpetual work of the abiding Lord. "He Whom God raised up saw no corruption." It is a fact that there are thousands of men and women in the world today who have a feeling about that eighteen-centuries-dead Galilean carpenter's son that they have about nobody else. All the great names of antiquity are but ghosts and shadows, and all the names in the Church and in the world, of men whom we have not seen, are dim and ineffectual to us. They may evoke our admiration, our reverence, and our wonder, but none of them can touch the heart. And here is this unique, anomalous fact that men and women by the thousand love Jesus Christ, the dead One, the unseen One, far away back there in the ages, and feel that there is no mist of oblivion between them and Him.

This is because He does for you and me what none of these other men can do. Luther talked about a cross, Christ *died* on it. "Was Paul crucified for you?" There is the secret of His undying hold upon the world. The further secret lies in this, that He is not a past force but a present one. He is no exhausted power but a power mighty today; working in us, around us, on us, and for us—a living Christ: "This Man Whom God raised up from the

dead saw no corruption." The others move away from us like figures in a fog, dim as they pass into the mists, having a blurred half-
spectral outline for a moment, and then gone.

That death has a present and a perpetual power. He has offered one sacrifice for sins forever; and no time can diminish the efficacy of His cross, nor our need of it, nor the full tide of blessings
which flow from it to the believing soul. Therefore do men cling to
Him today as if it was but yesterday that He had died for them.
When all other names carved on the world's records have become
unreadable, like forgotten inscriptions on decaying gravestones,
His shall endure forever, deep graven on fleshly tables of the heart.
His Revelation of God is the highest truth. Till the end of time
men will turn to His life for their clearest knowledge and happiest
certainty of their Father in heaven. There is nothing limited or
local in His character or works. In His meek beauty and gentle perfectness, He stands so high above us all that, today, the inspiration
of His example and the lessons of His conduct touch us as much as
if He had lived in this generation, and will always shine before
men as their best and most blessed law of conduct. Christ will not
be antiquated till He is outgrown, and it will be some time before
that happens.

But Christ's work is not the only abiding influence of His earthly
life and death. He is not a past force, but a present one. He is putting
forth fresh powers today, working in and for and by all who love
Him. We believe in a living Christ.

Therefore, the final thought in all our grateful commemoration
of dead helpers and guides should be, of the undying Lord. He
sent whatsoever power was in them. He is with His Church today,
still giving to men the gifts needful for their times. Aaron may die
on Hor, and Moses be laid in his unknown grave on Pisgah, but the
Angel of the Covenant, who is the true leader, abides in the pillar of
cloud and fire, Israel's guide in the march, and covering shelter in repose. That is our consolation in our personal losses when our dear
ones are "not suffered to continue by reason of death." He who gave
them all their sweetness is with us still, and has all the sweetness
which He lent them for a time. So, if we have Christ with us, we
cannot be desolate.

Looking on all these men, who in their turn have helped forward His cause a little way, we should let their departure teach us His presence, their limitations His all-sufficiency, their death His life.

Luther was once found, at a moment of peril and fear, when he had need to grasp unseen strength, sitting in an abstracted mood, tracing on the table with his finger the words, *"Vivit! vivit!"*— "He lives! He lives!" It is our hope for ourselves, and for His truth, and for mankind. Men come and go; leaders, teachers, thinkers, speak and work for a season and then fall silent and impotent. He abides. They die, but He lives. They are lights kindled, and therefore sooner or later quenched, but He is the true light from which they draw all their brightness, and He shines forevermore. Other men are left behind and as the world glides forward, are wrapped in ever-thickening folds of oblivion, through which they shine feebly for a little while, like lamps in a fog, and then are muffled in invisibility. We honor other names, and the coming generations will forget them, but "His name shall endure forever, His name shall continue as long as the Sun, and men shall be blessed in Him; all nations shall call Him blessed."

6

What the World Called the Church, and What the Church Calls Itself

The disciples were called Christians first in Antioch.
—Acts 11:26.

Nations and parties, both political and religious, very often call themselves by one name, and are known to the outside world by another. These outside names are generally given in contempt; and yet they sometimes manage to hit the very center of the characteristics of the people on whom they are bestowed; and so by degrees get to be adopted by them, and worn as an honor.

So it has been with the name "Christian." It was given at the first, by the inhabitants of the Syrian city of Antioch, to a new sort of people who had sprung up among them, and whom they could not quite make out. They would not fit into any of their categories, and so they had to invent a new name for them. It is never used in the New Testament by Christians about themselves. It occurs here in this text; it occurs in Agrippa's half-contemptuous exclamation: "You seem to think it is a very small matter to make me—me, a king! A Christian; one of those despised people!" And it occurs once more, where the Apostle Peter is specifying the charges brought against them. "If any man suffer as a Christian, let him not be ashamed; but let him glorify God on this behalf" (1 Pet. 4:16). That sounds like the beginning of the process which has gone on ever since, by which the nickname, flung by the sarcastic men of Antioch, has been turned into the designation by which, all over the world, the followers of Jesus Christ have been proud to call themselves.

Now in this verse there are the outside names by which the world calls the followers of Jesus Christ, and one of the many interior names by which the Church called itself. I have thought it might be profitable this morning for us to put all the New Testament names for Christ's followers together, and think about them.

I. So, to begin with, we deal with this name given by the world to the Church, which the Church has adopted. Observe the circumstances under which it was given. A handful of large-hearted, brave men, anonymous fugitivies belonging to the little Church in Jerusalem, had come down to Antioch; and there, without premeditation, without authority, almost without consciousness—certainly without knowing what a big thing they were doing—they took, all at once, as if it were the most natural thing in the world, a great step by preaching the Gospel to pure heathen Greeks. And so began the process by which a small Jewish sect was transformed into a worldwide church. The success of their work in Antioch, among the pure heathen population, has for its crowning attestation this, that it compelled the curiosity-hunting, pleasure-loving, sarcastic Antiocheans to find out a new name for this new thing; to write out a new label for the new bottles into which the new wine was being put. Clearly the name shows that the Church was beginning to attract the attention of outsiders.

Clearly, it shows, too, that there was a novel element in the Church. The earlier disciples had been all Jews, and could be lumped together along with their countrymen, and come under the same category. But here is something that could not be called either Jew or Greek, because it embraces both. The new name is the first witness to the cosmopolitan character of the primitive Church. Then clearly, too, the name indicates that in a certain dim, confused way, even these superficial observers had got hold of the right notion of what it was that *did* bind these people together. They called them "Christians"—Christ's men, Christ's followers. But it was only a very dim refraction of the truth that had got to them; they had no notion that "Christ" was not a proper name, but the designation of an office; and they had no notion that there was anything peculiar or strange in the bond which united its adherents to Christ. Hence they called His followers "Christians" just as they would have called Herod's followers "Herodians," in the political world, or Aristotle's followers "Aristotelians" in the philosophical world. Still, in their groping way, they had put their finger on the fact that the one thing that held this heterogeneous mass together, the one bond that bound up Jew and Gentile, barbarian, Scythian, bond and free into one vital unity, was a personal relation to a living person. And so they said—not understanding the whole significance of it, but having got hold of the right end of the clue—they said, "They are Christians!" "Christ's people," "the followers of this Christ."

And their very blunder was a felicity. If they had called them "Jesuits" that would have meant the followers of the mere man. They did not know how much deeper they had gone when they said, not followers of Jesus, but "followers of Christ," for it is not Jesus the Man, but Jesus Christ, the Man with His office, that makes the center and the bond of the Christian Church.

These, then, are the facts, and the fair inferences from them. A plain lesson here lies on the surface. The Church—that is to say the men and women who make its members—should draw to itself the notice of the outside world. I do not mean by advertising, and ostentation, and sounding trumpets, and singularities, and affectations. None of all these are needed. If you are live Christians it will be plain enough to outsiders. It is a poor comment on your consistency if, being Christ's followers, you can go through life unrecognized even by "them that are without." What shall we say of leaven which does *not* leaven, or of light which does *not* shine, or of salt which does *not* repel corruption? It is a poor affair if, being professed followers of Jesus Christ, you do not impress the world with the thought that "here is a man who does not come under any of our categories, and who needs a new entry to describe *him.*" The world ought to have the same impression about you which Haman had about the Jews: "Their laws are diverse from all people."

Christian professors! Are the world's names for themselves enough to describe you by, or do you need another name to be coined for you in order to express the manifest characteristics that you display? The Church that does not *provoke* the attention (I use the word in its etymological, not its offensive sense), the Church that does not call upon itself the attention and interest of outsiders is not the Church as Jesus Christ meant it to be, and it is not a Church that is worth keeping alive; and the sooner it has decent burial the better for itself and the world too!

There is another thing here; viz: This name suggests that the clear impression made by our conduct and character, as well as by our words, should be that we belong to Jesus Christ. The eye of an outside observer may be unable to penetrate the secret of the deep sweet tie uniting us to Jesus, but there should be no possibility of the most superficial and hasty glance overlooking the fact that we *are* His. He should manifestly be the center and the guide, the impulse and the pattern, the strength and the reward of our whole lives. We are Christians. That should be plain for all folks to see, whether we speak or be silent. Brethren, is it so with you? Does your life need no commentary of your words in order that men should know what is the hidden spring that moves all its wheels; what is the inward spirit that coordinates all its motions into harmony and beauty? It is true that like "the ointment of the right hand which betrayeth itself," your allegiance to Jesus Christ, and the overmastering and supreme authority which He exercises upon you, and upon your life, "cannot be hid"? Do you think that, without your words, if you, living the way you do, were put down into the middle of Pekin, as these handful of people were put down into the middle of the heathen city of Antioch, the wits of the Chinese metropolis would have to invent a name for you, as the clever men of Antioch did for these people; and do you think that if they had to invent a name, the name that would naturally come to their lips, looking at you, would be "Christians," "Christ's men"? If you do not, there is something wrong.

The last thing that I say about this first part of my text is this. It is a very sad thing, but it is a thing that is always occurring, that the world's inadequate notions of what makes a follower of Jesus Christ, get accepted by the Church. Why was it that the name "Christian" ran all over Christendom in the course of a century and a half? I believe very largely because it was a conveniently vague name; because it did not describe the deepest and sacredest of the bonds that unite us to Jesus Christ. Many a man is quite willing to say, "I am a Christian," who would hesitate a long time before he said, "I am a believer," "I am a disciple." The vagueness of the name, the fact that it erred by defect in not touching the central, deepest relation between man and Jesus Christ, made it very appropriate to the declining spirituality and increasing formalism of the Christian Church in the post-Apostolic age. It is a sad thing when the Church drops its standard down to the world's standard of what it ought to be, and swallows the world's name for itself, and its converts.

II. I turn now to set side by side with this vague, general, outside name the more specific and *interior* names, if I may so call them, by which Christ's followers at first knew themselves. The world said, "You are Christ's men," and the names that I am going to gather for you, and say a word about now, might be taken as being the Church's explanation of what the world was fumbling at when it so called them. There are four of them; of course, I can only just touch on them.

The first is in this verse: *"disciples."* The others are *believers, saints, brethren.* These four are the Church's own christening of itself; its explanation and expansion, its deepening and heightening of the vague name given by the world.

As to the first, *disciples,* any concordance will show that the name was employed almost exclusively during the time of Christ's life upon earth. It is the only name for Christ's followers in the Gospels; it occurs also, mingled with others, in the Acts of the Apostles; and it never occurs any more.

The name "disciple," then, carries us back to the historical beginning of the whole matter, when Jesus was looked upon as a Rabbi having followers called disciples; just as were John the Baptist and his followers, Gamaliel and his school, and many a one besides. It sets forth Christ as being the Teacher, and His followers as being His adherents, His scholars, who learned at His feet.

Now that is always true. *We* are Christ's scholars quite as much as the men who heard and saw with their eyes and handled with their hands of the Word of Life. Not by words only, but by gracious deeds and fair spotless life, He taught them and us and all men to the end of time, our highest knowledge of God of Whom He is the final revelation, our best knowledge of what men should and shall be by His perfect life in which is contained all morality, our only knowledge of that future in that He has died, and is risen and lives to help and still to teach. He teaches us still by the record of His life, and by the living influence of that Spirit whom He sends forth to guide us into all truth. He is the Teacher, the only Teacher, the Teacher for all men, the Teacher of all truth, the Teacher forevermore. He speaks from Heaven. Let us give heed to His voice. But that Name is not enough to tell all which He is to us, or we to Him, and so after He had passed from earth, it unconsciously and gradually dropped out of the lips of the disciples, as they felt a deepened bond uniting them to Him who was not only the Teacher of the Truth, which was Himself, but was their sacrifice and Advocate with the Father. And for all who hold the, as I believe, essentially imperfect conception of Jesus Christ as being mainly a Teacher, either by word or by pattern; whether it be put into the old form or into the modern form of regarding Him as the Ideal and Perfect Man, it seems to me a fact well worthy of consideration that the name of Disciple and the thing expressed by it, were speedily felt by the Christian Church to be inadequate as a representation of the bond that knit them to Him. He is our Teacher, we His scholars. He is more than that, and a more sacred bond unites us to Him. As our Master we owe Him absolute submission. When He speaks, we have to accept His dictum. What He says is truth, pure and entire. His utterance is the last word upon any subject that He touches, it is the ultimate appeal, and the Judge that ends the strife. We owe Him submission, an open eye for all new truth, constant docility, as conscious of our own imperfections, and a confident expectation that He will bless us continuously with high and as yet unknown truths that come from His inexhaustible stores of wisdom and knowledge.

2. Teacher and scholars move in a region which, though it be important, is not the central one. And the word that was needed next to express what the early Church felt Christ was to them, and they to Him, lifts us into a higher atmosphere altogether—*Believers*, they who are exercising not merely intellectual submission to the dicta of the Teacher, but who are exercising living trust in the person of the Redeemer. The belief which is faith is altogether

a higher thing than its first stage, which is the belief of the understanding. There is in it the moral element of trust. We believe a truth, we trust a Person; and the trust which we are to exercise in Jesus Christ, and which knits us to him, is the trust in Him, not in any character that we may choose to ascribe to Him, but in the character in which He is revealed in the New Testament—Redeemer, Savior, Manifest God—and therefore, the Infinite Friend and Helper of our souls.

That trust, my brethren, is the one thing that binds men to God, and the one thing that makes us Christ's men. Apart from it, we may be very near Him, but we are not joined to Him. By it, and by it alone, the union is completed, and His power and His grace flow into our spirits. Are you, not merely a "Christian," in the world's notion, being bound in some vague way to Jesus Christ, but are you a Christian in the sense of trusting your soul's salvation to Him?

3. Then, still further, there is another name, *saints*. It has suffered perhaps more at the hands both of the world and of the Church than any other. It has been taken by the latter and restricted to the dead, and further restricted to those who excel, according to the fantastic, ascetic standard of medieval Christianity. It has suffered from the world in that it has been used with a certain bitter emphasis of resentment at the claim of superior purity supposed to be implied in it, and so has come to mean on the world's lips a pretender to be better than other people, whose actions contradict his claim. But the name belongs to all Christ's followers. It makes no claim to special purity, for the central idea of the word "saint" is not purity. Holiness, which is the English for the Latinized "sanctity," holiness which is attributed in the Old Testament to God first, to men only secondarily, does not primarily mean *purity,* but *separation.* God is holy, inasmuch as by that whole majestic character of His, He is lifted above all bounds of creatural limitations, as well as above man's sin. A sacrifice, the Sabbath, a city, a priest's garment, a miter, all these things are "holy," not when they are *pure,* but when they are devoted to Him. And men are holy, not because they are clean, but because by free self-surrender they have consecrated themselves to Him.

Holiness is consecration; that is to say, holiness is giving myself up to Him to do what He will with. "I am holy" is not the declaration of the fact "I am pure," but the declaration of the fact, "I am thine, O Lord." So the New Testament idea of saint has in it these elements: consecration, consecration resting on faith in Christ, and consecration leading to separation from the world and its sin. And that glad yielding of oneself to God, as wooed by His mercies, and thereby drawn away from communion with our evil surroundings and from submission to our evil selves, must be a part of the experience of every true Christian. All His people are saints, not as being pure, but as being given up to Him, in union with Whom alone will the cleansing powers flow into their lives and clothe them with "the righteousness of saints." Have you thus consecrated yourself to God?

4. The last name is *brethren*, a name which has been much maltreated both by the insincerity of the Church, and by the sarcasm of the world. "Brethren!" an unreal appellation which has meant nothing and been meant to mean nothing, so that the world has said that our "brethren" signified a good deal less than their "brothers." " 'Tis true, 'tis pity; pity 'tis, 'tis true."

But what I want you to notice is that the main thing about that name "brethren" is not the relation of the brethren to one another, but their common relation to their Father.

When we call ourselves as Christian people, "brethren," we mean first, this: that we are the possessors of a supernatural life, which has come from one Father, and which has set us in altogether new relations to one another, and to the world round about us. Do you believe that? If you have got any of that new life which comes through faith in Jesus Christ, then you are the brethren of all those that possess the same.

As society gets more complicated, as Christian people get unlike each other in education, in social position, in occupation, in their general outlook into the world, it gets more and more difficult to feel what is nevertheless true: that any two Christian people, however unlike each other, are nearer each other in the very roots of their nature, than a Christian and a non-Christian, however like each other. It is difficult to feel that, and it is getting more and more difficult, but for all that it is a fact.

And now I wish to ask you, Christian men and women who are listening to me now, whether you feel more at home with people who love Jesus Christ, as you say *you* do, or whether you like better to be with people who do not.

There are some of you that choose your intimate associates, whom you ask to your homes and introduce to your children as desirable companions, with no reference at all to their religious character. The duties of your position, of course, oblige each of you to be much among people who do not share your faith, and it is cowardly and wrong to shrink from the necessity. But for Christian people to make choice of heart friends, or close intimates among those who have no sympathy with their professed belief about, and love to Jesus Christ, does not say much for the company he keeps, and if your friends are picked out for other reasons, and their religion is no part of their attraction, it is not an unfair conclusion that there are other things for which you care more than you do for faith in Jesus Christ and love to Him. If you deeply feel the bond that knits you to Christ, and really live near to Him, you will be near your brethren. You will feel that "blood is thicker than water," and however like you may be to irreligious people in many things, you will feel that the deepest bond of all knits you to the poorest, the most ignorant, the most unlike you in social position; ay! and the most unlike you in theological opinion, that love the Lord Jesus Christ in sincerity.

Now that is the sum of the whole matter. And my last word to you is this: Do not you be contented with the world's vague notions of what makes Christ's man. I do not ask you if you are Christians; plenty of you would say: "Oh, yes! of course I am!"

I do not ask you that; *I* do not ask you anything; but I pray you to ask yourselves these four questions: "Am I Christ's scholar?" "Am I believing on Him?" "Am I consecrated to Him?" "Am I the possessor of a new life?" And never give yourselves rest until you can say, humbly and yet confidently, "Yes! Thank God, I am!"

7

Faith Conquering the World

This is the victory that overcometh the world, even our faith—1 John 5:4.

No New Testament writer makes such frequent use of the metaphors of combat and victory as this gentle Apostle John. None of them seem to have conceived so habitually of the Christian life as being a conflict, and in none of their writings does the clear note of victory in the use of that word "overcometh" ring out so constantly as it does in those of the very Apostle of Love. Equally characteristic of John's writings is the prominence which he gives to the still contemplation of, and abiding in, Christ. These two conceptions of the Christian life appear to be discordant, but are really harmonious.

There is no doubt where John learned the phrase. Once he had heard it at a time and in a place which stamped it on his memory forever. "Be of good cheer, I have overcome the world." said Christ, an hour before Gethsemane. Long years since then had taught John something of its meaning, and had made him to understand how the Master's victory might belong to the servants. Hence in this letter he has much to say about "overcoming the wicked one," and the like; and in the Apocalypse we never get far away from hearing the shout of victory, whether we consider the sevenfold promises of the letters that stand at the beginning of the visions, or whether we listen to such sayings as this: "They overcame by the blood of the Lamb," or the last promise of all: "He that overcometh shall inherit all things."

Thus bound together by that link, as well as by a great many more, are all the writings which the tradition of the Church has attributed to this great Apostle.

But to come to the words of my text. They appear in a very remarkable context here. If you read a verse or two before, you will get the full singularity of their introduction. "This is the love of God," says he, "that we keep His commandments: and His commandments are not grievous." They *are* very heavy and hard in themselves; it is very difficult to do right, and to walk in the ways of God, and to please Him. His commandments *are* grievous, *per se;* a heavy burden, a difficult thing to do—but let us read on: "They are not grievous, *for* whatsoever is born of God"—keepeth the commandments? No! "Whatsoever is born of God *overcometh the world*." That, thinks John, is the same thing as keeping God's commandments. "This is the victory that overcometh the world, even our faith." Notice, then, first, What is the true notion of conquering the world? Secondly, How may that victory be ours?

I. What is the true notion of conquering the world? Let us go back to what I have already said. Where did John learn the expression? Who was it that first used it? It comes from that never-to-be-forgotten night in that upper room; where, with His life's purpose apparently crushed into nothing, and the world just ready to exercise its last power over Him by killing Him, Jesus Christ breaks out into such a strange strain of triumph, and in the midst of apparent defeat lifts up that clarion note of victory: "I have overcome the world!"

He had not made much of it, according to usual standards, had He? His life had been the life of a poor man. Neither fame nor influence, nor what people call success, had He won, judged from the ordinary points of view, and at three-and-thirty is about to be murdered; and yet He says, "I have beaten it all, and here I stand a conqueror!" That threw a flood of light for John, and for all who had listened to Christ, on the whole conditions of human life, and on what victory and defeat, success and failure in this world mean. Not so do men usually estimate what conquering the world is. Not so do you and I estimate it when we are left to our own folly and our own weakness. Our notion of being victorious in life is when each man, according to his own ideal of what is best, manages to wring that ideal out of a reluctant world. Or, to put it into plainer words, a man desires, say, conspicuous notoriety and fame. He accounts that he has conquered when he scrambles over all his fellows, and writes his name, as boys do, upon a wall, higher than anybody else's name, with a bit of chalk, in writing that the next winter's storm will obliterate! That is victory! The Manchester ideal says, "Found a big business and make it pay." That is to conquer! Other notions, higher and nobler than that, all partake of the same fallacy that if a man can get the world, the sum of external things, into his grip, and squeeze it as one does a grape, and get the last drop of sweetness out of it into his thirsty lips, he is a conqueror.

Well, you may get all that, whatever it is, that seems to you best, sweetest, most needful, most toothsome and delightsome—you may get it all; and in a sense you may have conquered the world, and yet you may be utterly beaten and enslaved by it. Do you remember the old story (I make no apology for the plainness of it) of the man who said to his commanding officer, "I have taken a prisoner." "Bring him along with you." "He won't let me." "Come yourself, then." "I can't." So you think you have conquered the world when it yields you the things you want, and all the while it has conquered and captivated *you*.

You say "Mine!" It would be a great deal nearer the truth if the possessions, or the love, or the wealth, or the culture, or whatever else it may be that you have set your desire upon, were to rise up and say you are theirs! Utterly beaten and enslaved many a man is by the things that he vainly fancies *he* has mastered and conquered. If you think of how in the process of getting, you narrow yourselves; of how much you throw away; of how eyes become blind to beauty or goodness or graciousness; of how you become the slaves of the thing that you have won; of how the gold gets into a man's blood and makes his complexion as yellow as jaundice—if you think of all that, and how desperate and wretched you would be if in a minute it was all swept away, and how it absorbs your thoughts in keeping it and looking after it, say, is it you who are its master, or it that is yours?

Now let us turn for a moment to the teaching of this Epistle. Following in the footsteps of Jesus Christ Himself, the poor man, the beaten man, the unsuccessful man, may yet say, "I have overcome the world." What does that mean? Well, it is built upon this—the world, meaning thereby the sum total of outward things considered as apart from God—the world and God we make to be antagonists to one another. And the world woos me to trust to it, to love it; crowds in upon my eye and shuts out the greater things beyond; absorbs my attention, so that if I let it have its own way I have no leisure to think about anything but itself. And the world conquers me when it succeeeds in hindering me from seeing, loving, holding communion with and serving my Father, God.

On the other hand, I conquer it when I lay my hand upon it and force it to help me to get nearer Him, to get liker Him, to think more often of Him, to do His will more gladly and more constantly. The one victory over the world is to bend it to serve me in the highest things: the attainment of a clearer vision of the Divine nature, the attainment of a deeper love to God Himself, and of a more glad consecration and service to Him. That is the victory, when you can make the world a ladder to lift you to God. That is its right use, that is victory, when all its tempting voices do not draw you away from listening to the Supreme Voice that bids you keep His commandments. When the world comes between you and God as an obscuring screen, it has conquered you. When the world comes between you and God as a transparent medium, you have conquered it. To win victory is to get it beneath your feet and stand upon it, and reach up thereby to God.

Now, dear brethren, that is the plain teaching of all this context, and I would lay it upon your hearts and upon my own. Do not let us be deceived by the false estimates of the men around us. Do not let us forget that the one thing we have to live for is to know God, and to love and to please Him, and that every life is a disastrous failure, whatsoever outward artificial apparent success it may be enriched and beautified with, that has not accomplished that.

You rule Nature, you coerce winds and lightnings and flames to your purposes. Rule the world! Rule the world by making it help you to be wiser, gentler, nobler, more gracious, more Christ-like, more Christ-conscious, more full of God, and more like to Him, and then you will get the deepest delight out of it. If a man wanted to find a winepress that should squeeze out of the vintage of this world its last drop of sweetest sweetness, he would find it in constant recognition of the love of God, and in the coercing of all the outward and the visible to be his help thereto.

There are the two theories: the one that we are all apt to fall into, of what success and victory is; the other the Christian theory. Ah! Many a poor, battered Lazarus, full of sores, a pauper and a mendicant at Dives' gate; many a poor old cottager; many a lonely woman in her garret; many a man that has gone away from Manchester, for instance, unable to get on in business, and obliged to creep into some corner and hide himself, not having succeeded in making a fortune, is the victor! And many a Dives, fettered by his own possessions, and the bond-slave of his own successes, is beaten by the world shamefully and disastrously! Pray and strive for the purged eyesight which shall teach you what it is to conquer the world, and what it is to be conquered by it.

II. And now let me turn for a moment to the second of the points that I have desired to put before you; viz., the method by which this victory over the world, of making it help us to keep the commandments of God, is to be accomplished. We find, according to John's fashion, a three-fold statement in this context upon this matter, each member of which corresponds to and heightens the preceding. We read thus: "Whatsoever is born of God overcometh the world." "This is the victory that overcometh the world," or, more accurately, "*hath overcome* the world, even our faith." Who is He that overcometh the world? He that believeth that Jesus Christ is "the Son of God." Wherein there are, speaking roughly, these three statements, that the true victory over the world is won by a new life, born of and kindred with God; that that life is kindled in men's souls through their faith; that the faith which kindles that supernatural life, the victorious antagonist of the world, is the definite, specific faith in Jesus as the Son of God. These are the three points which the Apostle puts as the means of conquest of the world.

The first consideration, then, suggested by these statements is that the one victorious antagonist of all the powers of the world which seek to draw us away from God, is a life in our hearts kindred with God, and derived from God.

Now I know that a great many people turn away from this central representation of Christianity as if it were mystical and intangible. I desire to lay it upon your hearts, dear brethren, that every Christian man has received and possesses through the open door of his faith, a life supernatural, born of God, kindred with God, therefore having nothing kindred with evil, and therefore capable of meeting and mastering all the temptations of the world.

It is a plain piece of common sense, that God is stronger than this material universe, and that what is born of God partakes of the Divine strength. But there would be no comfort in that, nor would it be anything germane and relevant to the Apostle's purpose, unless there was implied in the statement what in fact is distinctly asserted more than once in this Epistle, that every Christian man and woman may claim to be thus born of God. Hearken to the words that almost immediately precede our text, "Whosoever believeth that Jesus is the Christ, is born of God." Hearken to other words which proclaim the same truth. "To as many as received Him, to them gave He power to become the sons of God, which were born, not of the will of the flesh, nor of the will of man, but of God." He does come with all the might of His regenerating power into our poor natures, if and when we turn ourselves with humble faith to that dear Lord; and He breathes into our deadness a new life, with new tastes, new desires, new motives, new powers, making us able to wrestle with and to overcome the temptations that were too strong for us.

Mystical and deep as this thought may be, God's nature is breathed into the spirits of men that will trust Him! And if you will put your confidence in that dear Lord, and live near Him, into your weakness will come an energy born of the Divine, and you will be able to do all things in the might of the Christ who strengthens you from within, and is the life of your life, and the soul of your soul. To the little beleaguered garrison surrounded by strong enemies through whom they cannot cut their way, the king sends reliefs who force their passage into the fortress, and hold it against all the power of the foe. You are not left to fight by yourselves, you can conquer the world if you will trust to that Christ, trusting in Whom God's own power will come to your aid, and God's own Spirit will be the strength of your spirit.

And then there is the other way of looking at this same thing; viz., you can conquer the world if you will trust in Jesus Christ, because such trust will bring you into constant, living, loving contact with the Great Conqueror. There is a beautiful accuracy and refinement in the language of these three clauses which is not represented in our Authorized Version. The central one which I have read as my text this morning might be translated as it is translated in the Revised Version: "This is the victory that hath overcome the world, even our faith." By which I suppose the Apostle means very much what I am saying now; viz., that my faith brings me into contact with that one great victory over the world which for all time was won by Jesus Christ. I can appropriate Christ's conquest to myself if I trust Him. The might of it and some portion of the reality of it passes into my nature in the measure in which I rely upon Him. He conquered once for all, and the very remembrance of His conquest, by faith will make me strong, will "teach my hands to war and my fingers to fight." He conquered once for all, and His victory will pass, with electric power, into my life if I trust Him. I am brought into living fellowship with Him. All the stimulation of example, and all that lives lofty and pure can do for us, is done for us in transcendant fashion by the life of Jesus Christ. And all that lives lofty and pure can never do for us is done in unique fashion by the life and death of Him Whose life and death are alike the victory over the world and the pattern for us.

So if we join ourselves to Him by faith, and bring into our daily life, in all its ignoble effort, in all its little duties, in all its wearisome monotonies, in all its triviality, the thought, the illuminating thought, the ennobling thought, of the victorious Christ our companion and our Friend—*in hoc signo vinces*—in this sign thou shalt conquer! They who keep hold of His hand see over the world and all its falsenesses and fleetingnesses. They who trust in Jesus are more than conquerors by the might of His victory.

And then there is the last thought, which, though it be not directly expressed in the words before us, is yet closely connected with

them. You can conquer the world if you will trust Jesus Christ, because your faith will bring into the midst of your lives the grandest and most solemn and blessed realities. Faith is the true anesthesia
of the soul; the thing that deadens it to the pains and the pleasures
that come from this fleeting life. As for the pleasures, I remember
reading lately of some thinker of our own land who was gazing
through a telescope at the stars, and turned away from the solemn
vision with one remark: "I don't think much of our county families!" And if you will look up at Christ through the telescope of
your faith, it is wonderful what Lilliputians the Brobdignagians
round about you will dwindle into, and how small the world will
look, and how coarse the pleasures.

If a man goes to Italy, and lives in the presence of the pictures
there, it is marvellous what daubs the works of art, that he used to
admire, look when he comes back to England again. And if he has
been in communion with Jesus Christ, and has found out what
real sweetness is, he will not be over-tempted by the coarse dainties
that people eat here. Children spoil their appetites for wholesome
food by sweetmeats; we very often do the same in regard to the
bread of God, but if we have once really tasted it, we shall not
care very much for the vulgar dainties on the world's stall.

Dear brethren, set your faith upon that great Lord, and the
world's pleasures will have less power over you, and as for its
pains—

> There's nothing either good or bad,
> But thinking makes it so.

If a man does not think that the world's pains are of much account, they are not of much account. He who sees athwart the
smoke of the fire of Smithfield, the face of the Captain of his warfare, Who has conquered, will dare to burn and will not dare to deny
his Master or his Master's truth. The world may threaten in hope of
winning you to its service, but if its threats, turned into realities, fail
to move you, it is the world which inflicts, and not you who suffer,
that is beaten. In the extremest case they "kill the body and after that
have no more that they can do," and if they have done all they
can, and have not succeeded in wringing the recantation from the
locked lips, they are beaten, and the poor dead martyr that they

could only kill has conquered them and their torments. So fear not all that the world can do against you. If you have got a little spark of the light of Christ's presence in your heart, the darkness will not be very terrible, and you will not be alone.

So, brethren, two questions: Does your faith do anything like that for you? If it does not, what do you think is the worth of it? Does it deaden the world's delights? Does it lift you above them? Does it make you conqueror? If it does not, do you think it is worth calling faith?

And the other question is: Do you want to beat, or to be beaten? When you consult your true self, does your conscience not tell you that it were better for you to keep God's commandments than to obey the world? Surely there are many young men and women in this place today who have some desires high, and true, and pure, though often stifled, and overcome, and crushed down; and many older folk who have glimpses, in the midst of predominant regard for the things that are seen and temporal, of a great calm, pure region away up there that they know very little about.

Dear friends, my one word to you all is: Get near Jesus Christ by thought, and love, and trust. Trust to Him and to the great love that gave itself for you. And then bring Him into your life, by daily reference to Him of it all: and by cultivating the habit of thinking about Him as being present with you in the midst of it all, and so holding His hand, you will share in His victory; and at the last, according to the climax of His sevenfold promises, "To Him that overcometh will I give to sit down with Me on My throne, even as I also overcame, and am sat down with My Father on His Throne."

8

"In Remembrance of Me"

This do in remembrance of Me—1 Corinthians 11:24.

This Epistle to the Corinthians is prior in date to any of the Gospels, consequently we have, in the section from which my text is taken, the earliest account of the institution of the Lord's Supper. More than that, the account is entirely independent of the oral tradition which may be supposed to have preceded the written Gospels among the Christian communities. For the Apostle distinctly affirms, in the immediate context, that he received this narrative of the institution of the Lord's Supper from none of the guests in that upper chamber, but from the host Himself.

By what means the communication was made it boots not to inquire; vision, or ecstasy, or special revelation, we know not how. But if language have any meaning, we have here an account which the repeater of it to the Corinthian Church declares he got straight from the lips of the risen Lord Himself.

Consequently the words before us, and the whole section, of which they are a part, afford us a means of tracing up the celebration of the Lord's Supper to a period very near in time to the death of Christ, and thus yield to us a very strong presumption, in addition to that of the Gospel narrative, of the historical accuracy of the story, and a valuable indication of the aspect in which it was regarded by the primitive belief of Christendom.

The occasion for the utterance of the words of my text is also very characteristic of the Apostle Paul, and instructive to us: If it had not been for some abuses in the Corinthian Church, we should never have had here from his lips one word about this ordinance; and in that event there would have been scarcely any reference in the whole New Testament to the Lord's supper beyond the short narratives in three out of the four Gospels.

These entirely incidental, fragmentary, sparse references in the New Testament to all matters of Church organization, polity, and ritual, ought to be very instructive to us as to where the true center of gravity lies, and ought to rebuke the attempts that are made to lift any of these outward things, the form of the sheepfold or any of the modes of worship, into a position of more than secondary importance. I heard someone say, a day or two ago, that the Emperor of Russia, with Nihilists round about him ready to blow him up, spends most of his time in designing buttons for the uniforms of his soldiers; and I think Christian men who waste time and strength over such questions at this day are not much wiser than that. However, that is not what I wanted to talk about this morning. I desire to take these words as foundation of a few remarks in reference to the purpose and meaning of the great rite of Christendom—the Lord's Supper.

I. And first, let us regard it as a memorial. Now, observe that the words which I have read are even stronger in the original than they are in our translation. "This do in remembrance of Me" might mean "This do because you remember." But the real rendering is: "This do for a remembrance of Me"; "in order that you may remember," or "lest you forget." And the words are all but a verbatim quotation of those used in the institution of that Passover which our Lord, with sovereign authority, brushed aside in order to make room for His own memorial rite. "This day shall be unto you for a memorial," says the law of the Passover. The Lord's Supper was grafted upon and meant to supersede the older feast. And the words forming our text must obviously be supposed to have distinct reference to those of Exodus, and to be meant to substitute for the memories so stirring to Jewish national pride and devout feeling, the remembrance of Him as the one thing needful.

Notice also that this is Christ's own distinct statement of the purpose of the Lord's Supper, "for a 'remembrance,' in order to bring Me again to your recollection." I suppose He is likely to have put foremost the main purpose of the ceremonial, and I suppose that if there be any *alleged* purposes of it, of which there is no hint to be gathered from His own distinct statement of what the meaning of the rite is, that is a strong argument against these. So I want you to mark that Christ Himself has told us that this rite is meant to bring Him to our remembrance, and that He has given us no other statement of its purpose but that. Nor will you find anywhere in the New Testament any statement of the purpose of the Lord's Supper additional to this. And so I say that all our theories about the meaning and value and virtue of this Communion Service must be found within the four corners of that word: "This do for a remembrance of Me!"—a memorial rite, and as far as I know, nothing more whatsoever. Nothing more, certainly, insofar as Christ's own solemn declaration of its purpose, and of His intention in establishing it, can be supposed to go.

Notice further about this first part of my subject: of what the Lord's Supper is a memorial; viz., "A memorial of Me," of Me! I do not need to dwell upon what I have hinted already, the remarkable way in which Christ deals, as One Who has authority, with the sacredest rite of the nation to which He and His Apostles belonged; brushing aside the thing that for centuries had been the very Palladium of their national life, and the vital center of their national worship; and saying in effect: "Moses and that old redemption that you have heard about all these centuries, are antiquated; and a mere flickering taper light as compared with the redemption that I bring. You have remembered him and his deliverance; forget him! Lo, the shadow passes, and here I stand, the substance! Do this; never mind about your old Passover; that is done with, wheeled away into a corner and forgotten. Do this in remembrance no longer of dead Pharaohs and exhausted deliverances, but do this in remembrance of an everloving friend and helper; and of a redemption that shall never pass away. 'In remembrance of Me!' "

What a marvelous, unique, majestic prevision that was, that from that little room in some upper chamber in that obscure corner of the world, looked all down the ages and expected that to the end of time men would turn to Him with passionate thankfulness, and with a flame of love ever leaping in their hearts! And more wonderful still, the forecast has been true, and the memory of millions turns to one thing in the past as the center of life, the Cross of Christ, and to one thing in the future as the fountain of Hope—the Throne of the crucified Christ. "Do this in remembrance of Me."

And as majestic as is the authority so tender and gracious is the condescension: "Do *this* for a remembrance." He does not rely upon His mighty love and sacrifice for the remembrance, the grateful remembrance of the world, but He consents and condescends to trust some portion of our remembrance of Him to mere outward things. The world, time, sense, the material and the visible come rushing in upon us and make us forget. Like a snowstorm in an American winter, our atmosphere is all filled with the flying motes, almost impalpable, of the thick driving trifles that hide the sky from us. The fluttering flakes of ever-recurring cares and duties, joys, and sorrows, obscure the blue and the Christ Who is there.

And so He takes and uses for once the things of time and sense to fight the things of time and sense with, and says: "The visible shall serve Me in this one instance; and the material elements shall conspire to help you to remember My great love."

Surely we need all the help we can get to keep His memory vivid and fresh in spite of the pressure of the visible and temporal. If it be possible to bring Him and His great world of love before our minds through the help of sight as well as by the hearing of the ear, we shall be armed with double armor.

The purpose of Christ in instituting this rite is simply that men should have presented to them in visible form, as well as in audible form by the spoken voice, the facts on which their salvation depends. Although the differences are infinite in regard of the sacredness of the person and thing to be remembered, shall I shock any of you if I say that I know no difference in kind between the bread and the wine that is for a memorial of Christ's dying love, and the handkerchief dipped in blood, sent from the scaffold by a dying King with the one message: "Remember!" "Do this for a memorial of me!"

II. I come to the next point that I wish to touch on; viz., the Lord's Supper as being what is called a means of grace; or, less technically, a source of religious profit and growth. Now, if what I have been saying about the one purpose of this Communion rite be true, there follows from it, as a matter of course, this: that the only way by which this or any other outward ceremony can do a man any good is by its fulfilling the purpose for which it was appointed, and setting him to think of and feel the truth that is in Jesus Christ. I know only one way by which what theologians call grace can get into men's souls, and that is through the occupation of a man's understanding, heart, and will, with Jesus Christ and the Gospel that tells of Him. To think of Him, to contemplate Him, to love Him, and to yield the submission of the will and the life to Him: that is, at bottom, the one channel through which all God's grace comes to a man's heart; and the good that any outward thing does us, the good that any act of worship does us, that any rite or ceremony whatsoever does us, is only this: that it brings before us the truth on which our hopes depend, and knits to our contemplation and our heart the Christ and His love; and the measure in which it does that is the exact measure of the blessing that it works upon us.

I can find nothing more than this in this Communion, except only that it is obedience to a definite command of Jesus Christ, and so has the blessing which always follows upon obedience to Him. These two, the blessing that comes from obedience to His commandment and the blessing that comes from having our thoughts turned to Him, and faith and hope excited and kindled towards Him, these exhaust, as far as I know, the whole of the good that that Communion Service does to any man.

And I think all that is confirmed very strongly by the remarks in the context about the mischief that it sometimes does to people. We read there words which superstition has laid hold of in order to darken the whole horizon, and turn the whole purpose of the Lord's Supper to another thing altogether from what it was in its original institution. We read in the context about an unworthy partaking, and that unworthy partaking is defined. "Whoso eateth and drinketh" (*not* "unworthily," for that word in that verse is an unauthorized supplement) "eateth and drinketh judgment to Himself, not discerning the Lord's Body."

That is to say, unworthy participation is a participation which does not use the external symbols as a means of turning thought and feeling to Christ and His death; and unworthy participation does a man harm, as unworthy handling of any outward rite does.

I preach a sermon. I try with words here to lead men to look to Jesus Christ. If my poor attempt fail and my words come between you and Him rather as an obscuring medium than as a transparent medium, then my sermon does you harm. You read a hymn. The hymn is meant to lead you up to Christ your Savior in aspiration and devotion. If it does not do that, then it does you harm.

If through the outward ritual we see Christ, we get all the good that the outward ritual can do us. If through the outward rite we do not see Him, if the colored glass stay the eye instead of leading it on, then the rite does us harm. To my judgment the difference between the Lord's Supper, and its operation upon the Christian life, and a sermon or a prayer or the reading of a chapter or any other piece of Christian worship and service and their operation lies here; that, first, one is more definitely a commandment than the other; second, that the one presents the truth more directly to the understanding through the ear, and that the other presents it in symbolical and pictorial form through the eye, and third, that in the participation of the Lord's Supper there is an increased sacredness by reason of the sacredness of the thing of which it is a memorial, and by reason that it is a more personal profession of faith therein. These points, I think, exhaust all that the New Testament tells in reference to its sanctity.

And sure I am that neither it nor anything else can do a man spiritual good, except by one way, and on one condition. All outward rites and forms are "schoolmasters to bring us to Christ." If they do that they help us, if they do not, they hurt us. The one condition of spiritual blessing is union with Him, the one means of union with Him is the exercise of faith and love towards Him. If the rite strengthen this, it has blessed you; if it does not, it is a curse to you.

How the whole fabric of superstitious sacerdotalism and externalism that has cursed God's Church for centuries disappears when once men find out that there is nothing to help them but only their grasp of Jesus Christ, and that the only way of grasping Him is by faith and love, and that the only good of anything ritual is as subserving that, and perchance stimulating and increasing these!

III. And so, lastly, and briefly, there is another aspect of this rite, which is set forth in these words; namely, the Lord's Supper as a witness for Christian truth.

"This do for a remembrance of Me!" I do not dwell further upon what I have already said about the significance of that extraordinary self-consciousness which here claims to the end of time the reverence, the regard, the remembrance of humanity. Nor do I merely mean that the Lord's Supper, by reason of its very early origin and the history of Christianity, is a witness as to the belief predominant at the point of origin. But what I mean is this: Christ Himself, if we accept the story of the Gospels and of this chapter, has appointed this institution and selected for us, by the pointing of His finger, the part of His mission which He considers the vital and all-important center: "Do this in remembrance of Me!" "This is My body, broken for you. This is the new covenant in My blood, shed for many," according to the other version in one of the Gospels, "for the remission of sins."

There is the heart of Christ's work, my brother. That death is the kernel of objective Christianity. Not His words, not His loving deeds of mercy, not His tenderness, to nothing of all these does He point us. They are all included and subordinated, but He points us to His violent death; for from the fact that "body" and "blood" are contemplated apart, it is clear that not merely death, but a violent death was in His mind. He points us to His violent death, as if He said, "There is the thing that is to touch hearts and change lives, and bind men to Me with endless bonds of deep and life-transforming gratitude."

Christ Himself has taught us that what He will have to be remembered through all generations is the fact that He died, the fact that He died for us, the fact that in His blood is the covenant of our pardon, and of our peace with God. Forms of Christianity which have let go the Incarnation and the Atonement do not know what to make of the Lord's Supper. There is no room for it among them, and practically you will find that such forms of Christianity have relegated it to a corner, and have almost disused it. They who do not feel that Christ's death is their peace, do not feel that the rite that commemorates the broken Body and the shed Blood is the center of Christian worship.

I dare say I am speaking to people this morning who regard it as a very unnecessary part of Christian service. My brother, Jesus Christ knew what He meant by His work quite as well as you do, and he thought that the part of it which most concerns us to remember was this: "that He died for our sins, according to the Scriptures." I commend that thought to you, and point to that table as a witness to every man and woman who believes that this Communion was established by Jesus Christ Himself, that the center of Christian truth and of the Gospel of Christ is the good news of His death on the Cross for the sins of the whole world.

And now I ask you, dear brethren, to remember this, that as plain and distinct as the teaching is of this ordinance in reference to what is the living heart of Christ's work for us, so plain and distinct is its teaching in reference to what is our way of making that work ours.

We eat that we may live, we take the bread that perisheth into our lips, masticate and swallow and the food is assimilated to our body, and so we are nourished.

We take Christ. "Believe and thou hast eaten," says Augustine. We take Christ, the fact of His death, of His love, of His personal life for us today, and by faith we partake of Him, and the body is assimilated to the food, and so in that higher region we live. If we are to have life in us, it must be by no outward connection through ritual and ceremony, but by an inward possession of that which ritual and ceremony proclaim; namely, the life of Him Who lived that we may be partakers of His Resurrection, the death of Him Who died that in Him we too might die to self and sin.

This table preaches to us all, "My flesh is meat indeed, and My blood is drink indeed." And it preaches no less emphatically the other great word, "Whoso eateth My flesh and drinketh My blood hath eternal life; and I will raise him up at the last day."

9

How to Sweeten the Life of Great Cities

The priests repaired every one over against his house
—Nehemiah 3:28.

The condition of our great cities has lately been forced upon public attention, and all kinds of men have been offering their panaceas. I am not about to enter upon that discussion, but as we are making a collection this morning for our Manchester City Mission I am glad to seize the opportunity of saying one or two things which I think very much need to be said to individual Christian people about their duty in the matter. "Every man over against his house," is the principle I want to commend to you this morning as going a long way to solve the problem of how to sweeten the foul life of our modern cities.

The story from which my text is taken does not need to detain us long. Nehemiah and his little band of exiles have come back to a ruined Jerusalem. Their first care is to provide for their safety, and the first step is to know the exact extent of their defenselessness. So we have the account of Nehemiah's midnight ride among the ruins of the broken walls. And then we read of the cooperation of all classes in the work of reconstruction. "Many hands made light work." Men and women, priests and nobles, goldsmiths, apothecaries, merchants, all seized trowel or spade, and wheeled and piled. One man puts up a long length of wall, another can only venture a little bit; another undertakes the locks, bolts, and bars for the gates. Roughly and hastily the work is done. The result, of course, is very unlike the stately structures of Solomon's or of Herod's time, but it is enough for shelter. We can imagine the sigh of relief with which they looked upon the completed circle of their rude fortifications.

The principle of division of labor in our text is repeated several times in this list of the builders. It was a natural one; a man would work all the better when he saw his own roof mutely appealing to be defended, and thought of the dear ones that were there. But I take these words mainly as suggesting some thoughts applicable to the duties of Christian people in view of the spiritual wants of our great cities.

I. I need not do more than say a word or two about the *ruins which need repair*. If I dwell rather upon the dark side than on the bright side of city life I shall not be understood as forgetting that the very causes which intensify the evil of a great city quicken the good—the friction of multitudes and the impetus thereby given to all kinds of mental activity. Here among us there is much that is admirable and noble: much public spirit, much wise and benevolent expenditure of thought and toil for the general good, much conjoint action by men of different parties, earnest antagonism and earnest cooperation, and a free, bracing intellectual atmosphere, which stimulates activity. All that is true, though, on the other hand, it is not good to live always within hearing of the clatter of machinery and the strife of tongues; and the wisdom that is born of solitary meditation and quiet thought is less frequently met with in cities than the cleverness that is born of intercourse with men, and newspaper reading.

But there is a tragic other side to all that, which mostly we make up our minds to say little about and to forget. I confess that I have been rather surprised that the "Bitter Cry of Outcast London," and of "Squalid Liverpool" should have been so much of a discovery. The indifference which has made that ignorance possible, and has in its turn been fed by the ignorance, is in some respects a more shocking phenomenon than the vicious life which it has allowed to rot and to reek unheeded.

Most of us have got so familiarized with the evils that stare us in the face every time we go out upon the pavements, that we have come to think of them as being inseparable from our modern life, like the noise of a carriage wheel from its rotation. And is it so then? It is indeed inevitable that within a stone's throw of our churches and chapels there should be thousands of men, and women who have never been inside a place of worship since they were christened; and have no more religion than a horse? Must it be that the shining structure of our modern society, like an old Mexican temple, must be built upon a layer of living men, flung in for a foundation! Can it not be helped that there should be streets in Manchester into which it is unfit for a decent woman to go by day alone, and unsafe for a brave man to venture after nightfall? Must men and women huddle together in dens where decency is as impossible as it is for swine in a sty? Is it an indispensable part of our material progress and wonderful civilization that vice and crime and utter irreligion and hopeless squalor should go with it? Can all that bilge water really not be pumped out of the ship? If it be so, then I venture to say that, to a very large extent, progress is a delusion, and that the simple life of agricultural communities is better than this unwholesome aggregation of men.

The beginning of Nehemiah's work of repair was that sad midnight ride round the ruined walls. So there is a solemn obligation laid on Christian people to acquaint themselves with the awful facts, and then to meditate on them, till sacred, Christ-like compassion, pressing against the floodgates of the heart, flings them open, and lets out a stream of helpful pity and saving deeds.

"If thou forbear to deliver them that are drawn unto death, those that ready to be slain; if thou sayest: Behold! We knew it not! Doth not He that pondereth the heart consider it; and shall He not render to every man according to his works?"

II. So much for my first point. My second is: the ruin is to be repaired mainly by the old Gospel of Jesus Christ. Far be it from me to pit remedies against each other. The causes are complicated, and the cure must be as manifold as the causes. For my own part I believe that, in regard of the condition of the lowest of our outcast population, drink and lust have done it almost all, and that for all but an infinitesimal portion of it, intemperance is directly or indirectly the cause. That has to be fought by the distinct preaching of abstinence, and by the invoking of legislative restrictions upon the traffic. Wretched homes have to be dealt with by sanitary reform, which may require municipal and parliamentary action. Domestic discomfort has to be dealt with by teaching wives the principles of domestic economy. The gracious influence of art and music, pictures and window gardening, and the like, will lend their aid to soften and refine. Coffee taverns, baths and wash-houses, workmen's clubs, and many other agencies are doing real and good work. I, for one, say, God speed to them all, and willingly help them so far as I can.

But, as a Christian man, I believe that I know a thing that if lodged in a man's heart, will do pretty nearly all which they aspire to do; and while I rejoice in the multiplied agencies for social elevation, I believe that I shall best serve my generation, and I believe that ninety-nine out of a hundred of you will do so too by trying to get men to love and fear Jesus Christ the Savior. If you can get His love into a man's heart, that will produce new tastes and new inclinations, which will reform, and sweeten, and purify faster than anything else does.

They tell us that Nonconformist ministers are never seen in the slums; well, that is a libel! But I should like to ask why it is the Roman Catholic priest is seen there more than the Nonconformist minister. Because the one man's congregation is there, and other man's is not, which being translated into other words is this: the religion of Jesus Christ mostly keeps people out of the slums, and certainly it will take a man out of them if once it gets into his heart, more certainly and quickly than anything else will.

So, dear friends, if we have in our hearts and in our hands this great message of God's love, we have in our possession the germ out of which all things that are lovely and of good report will grow. It will purify, elevate, and sweeten society, because it will make individuals pure and strong, and homes holy and happy. We do not need to draw comparisons between this and other means of reparation, and still less to feel any antagonism to them or the benevolent men who work them; but we should fix it in our minds that the principles of Christ's Gospel adhered to by individuals and therefore by communities, would have rendered such a condition of things impossible, and that the true repair of the ruin wrought by evil and ignorance, in the single soul, in the family, the city, the nation, the world, is to be found in building anew on the One Foundation which God has laid, even Jesus Christ, the Living Stone, Whose pure life passes into all who are grounded and founded on Him.

III. Lastly, this remedy is to be applied by the individual action of Christian men and women on the people nearest them.

"The priests repaired every one over against his own house." We are always tempted in the face of large disasters, to look for heroic and large remedies, and to invoke corporate action of some sort, which is a great deal easier for most of us than the personal effort that is required. When a great scandal and danger like this of the condition of the lower layers of our civic population is presented before men, for one man that says, "What can *I* do?" there are twenty who say, "Somebody should do something. Government should do something. The Corporation should do something. This, that, or the other aggregate of men should do something." And the individual calmly and comfortably slips his neck out of the collar and leaves it on the shoulders of these abstractions.

As I have said, there are plenty of things that need to be done by these somebodies. But what they do (they will be a long time in doing it) when they do get to work will only touch the fringe of the question, and the substance and the center of it *you* can set to work upon this afternoon if you like, and not wait for anybody either to set you the example or to show you the way.

If you want to do people good you can; but you have got to pay the price for it. That price is personal sacrifice and effort. The example of Jesus Christ is the all-instructive one in the case. People talk about Him being their pattern, but they often forget that whatever more there was in Christ's Cross and Passion there was this in it: the exemplification for all time of the one law by which any reformation can be wrought on men—that a sympathizing man shall give himself to do it, and that by personal influence alone men shall be drawn and won from out of the darkness and filth. A loving heart and a sympathetic word, the exhibition of a Christian life and conduct, the fact of going down into the midst of evil and trying to lift men out of it, are the old-fashioned and only magnets by which men are drawn to purer and higher life. That is God's way of saving the world—by the action of single souls on single souls. Masses of men can neither save nor be saved. Not in groups, but one by one, particle by particle, soul by soul, Christ draws men to Himself, and He does His work in the world through single souls on fire with His love, and tender with pity learned of Him.

So, dear friends, do not think that any organization, any corporate activity, any substitution of vicarious service, will solve the problem. It will not. There is only one way of doing it, the old way that we must tread if we are going to do anything for God and our fellows: "The priests repaired everyone over against his own house."

Let me briefly point out some very plain and obvious things which bear upon this matter of individual action. Let me remind you that if you are a Christian man you have in your possession the thing which will cure the world's woe, and possession involves responsibility. What would you think of a man who had a specific for some pestilence that was raging in a city, and was contented to keep it for his own use, or at most for his family's use, when his brethren were dying by the thousand, and their corpses polluting the air? And what shall we say of men and women who call themselves Christians, who have some faith in that great Lord and His mighty sacrifice; who know that the men they meet with every day of their lives are dying for want of it, and who yet themselves do absolutely nothing to spread His name, and to heal men's hurts? What shall we say? God forbid that we should say they are not Christians; but God forbid that anybody should flatter them with the notion that they are anything but most inconsistent Christians.

Still further, need I remind you that if we have found anything in Jesus Christ which has been peace and rest for ourselves, Christ has thereby called us to this work? He has found and saved us, not only for our own personal good. That, of course, is the prime purpose of our salvation, but not its exclusive purpose. He has saved us too, in order that the Word may be spread through us to those beyond. "The Kingdom of Heaven is like leaven, which a woman took and hid in three measures of meal until the whole was leavened," and every little bit of the dough, as it received into itself the leaven, and was transformed, became a medium for transmitting the transformation to the next particle beyond it and so the whole was at last permeated by the power. We get the grace for ourselves that we may pass it on; and as the Apostle says: "God hath shined into our hearts that we might give the light of the knowledge of the glory of God in the face of Jesus Christ."

And you *can* do it, you Christian men and women, every one of you, and preach Him to somebody. The possession of His love gives the commission; ay! and it gives the power. There is nothing so mighty as the confession of personal experience. Do not you think that when that first of Christian converts, and first of Christian preachers went to his brother, all full of what he had discovered, his simple saying, "We have found the Messiah," was a better sermon than a far more elaborate proclamation would have been? My brother! If you have found Him, you can say so; and if you can say so, and your character and your life confirm the words of your lips, you will have done more to spread His name than much eloquence and many an orator. All can preach, who can say, "We have found the Christ."

The last word I have to say is this: there is no other body that can do it but you. They say: "What an awful thing it is that there are no churches or chapels in these outcast districts!" If there were they would be what the churches and chapels are now—half empty. Bricks and mortar built up into ecclesiastical forms are not the way to evangelize this or any other country. It is a very easy thing to build churches and chapels. It is not such an easy thing—I believe it is an impossible thing (and that the sooner the Christian Church gives up the attempt the better)—to get the Godless classes into any church or chapel. Conducted on the principles upon which churches and chapels must needs at present be conducted, they are for another class altogether; and we had better recognize it, because then we shall feel that no multiplication of buildings like this in which we now are, for instance, is any direct contribution to the evangelization of the waste spots of the country, except insofar as from a center like this there ought to go out much influence which will originate direct missionary action in places and fashions adapted to the outlying community.

Professional work is not what we want. Any man, be he minister, clergyman, Bible-reader, city missionary, who goes among our godless population with the suspicion of pay about him is the weaker for that. What is needed besides is that ladies and gentlemen that are a bit higher up in the social scale than these poor creatures, should go to them themselves; and excavate and work. Preach, if you like, in the technical sense; have meetings, I suppose, necessarily; but the personal contact is the thing, the familiar talk, the simple exhibition of a loving Christian heart, and the unconventional proclamation in free conversation of the broad message of the love of God in Jesus Christ. Why, if all the people in this chapel who can do that would do it, and keep on doing it, who can tell what an influence would come from some hundreds of new workers for Christ? And why should the existence of a church in which the workers are as numerous as the Christians be a Utopian dream? It is simply the dream that perhaps a church might be conceived to exist all the members of which had found out their plainest, most imperative duty, and were really trying to do it.

No carelessness, no indolence, no plea of timidity or business shift the obligation from your shoulders if you are a Christian. It is your business, and no paid agents can represent you. You cannot buy yourselves substitutes in Christ's army as they used to do in the militia by a guinea subscription. We are thankful for the money, because there are kinds of work to be done that unpaid effort will not do. But they ask for your money; Jesus Christ asks for yourself, for your work and will not let you off as having done your duty because you have paid your subscription. No doubt there are some of you who, from various circumstances, cannot yourselves do work among the masses of the outcast population. Well, but you have got people by your side whom you can help. The question which I wish to ask of my Christian brethren and sisters this morning is this: Is there a man, woman, or child living to whom you ever spoke a word about Jesus Christ? Is there? If not, do not you think it is time that you began?

There are people in your houses, people that sit by you in your counting-house, on your college benches, who work by your side in mill or factory or warehouse, who cross your path in a hundred ways, and God has given them to you that you may bring them to Him. Do you set yourself, dear brother, to work and try to bring them. Oh! If you lived nearer Jesus Christ you would catch the sacred fire from Him; and like a bit of cold iron lying beside a magnet, touching Him, you would yourselves become magnetic and draw men out of their evil and up to God.

Let me commend to you the old pattern: "The priests repaired every one over against his house"; and beseech you to take the trowel and spade, or anything that comes handiest, and build in the bit nearest you some living stones on the true Foundation.

10

The Triple Rays Which Make the White Light of Heaven

> *His servants shall serve Him; and they shall see His face; and His name shall be in their forehead*
> —Revelation 22:3, 4.

One may well shrink from taking words like these for a text. Their lofty music will necessarily make all words of ours seem thin and poor. The great things about which they are concerned are so high above us, and known to us by so few channels that usually he who says least speaks most wisely about them. And yet it cannot be but wholesome if in a reverent spirit of no vain curiosity, we do try to lay upon our hearts the impressions of the great, though they be dim, truths which gleam from these words. I know that to talk about a future life is often a most sentimental, vague, unpractical form of religious contemplation, but there is no reason at all why it should be so. I wish to try now very simply to bring out the large force and wonderful meaning of the words which I have ventured to read. They give us three elements of the perfect state of man: Service, Contemplation, Likeness. These three are perfect and unbroken.

I. The first element, then, in the perfect state of man is perfect activity in the service of God. Now the words of our text are remarkable in that the two expressions for "servant" and "serve" are not related to one another in the Greek, as they are in the English, but are two quite independent words; the former meaning literally "a slave," and the latter being exclusively confined in Scripture to one kind of service. It would never be employed for any service that a man did for a man; it is exclusively a religious word, and means only the service that men do for God, whether in specific acts of so-called worship or in the wider worship of daily life. So that if we have not here the notion of priesthood, we have one very closely approximating towards it; and the representation is that the activity of the redeemed and perfected man, in the highest ideal condition of humanity, is an activity which is all worship, and is directed to the revealed God in Christ.

That, then, is the first thought that we have to look at. Now, it seems to me to be a very touching confession of the weariness and unsatisfactoriness of life in general that the dream of the future which has unquestionably the most fascination for most men, is that which speaks of it as Rest. The religion which has the largest number of adherents in the world—the religion of the Buddhists—formally declares existence to be evil, and preaches as the highest attainable good, something which is scarcely distinguishable from annihilation. And, even though we do not go so far as that, what a testimony it is of burdened hearts and mournful lives, and work too great for the feeble limits of our powers, that the most natural thought of a blessed future is as rest! It is easy to laugh at people for singing hymns about sitting upon green and flowery mounts, and counting up the labors of their feet. But oh, it is a tragical thought that whatsoever shape a life has taken, howsoever full of joy and sunshine and brightness it may be, deep down in the man there is such an experience as that the one thing he wants is repose and to get rid of all the trouble and toil.

Now, this representation of my text is by no means contradictory, but it is complementary, of that other one. The deepest rest and the highest activity coincide. They do so in God Who "worketh hitherto" in undisturbed tranquility; they may do so in us. The wheel that goes round in swiftest rotation seems to be standing still. Work at its intensest, which is pleasurable work, and level to the capacity of the doer, is the truest form of rest. In vacuity there are stings and torment; it is only in joyous activity which is not pushed to the extent of strain and unwelcome effort that the true rest of man is to be found. And the two verses in this Book of Revelation about this matter, which look at first sight to be opposed to each other, are like the two sides of a sphere, which unite and make the perfect whole. "They rest from their labors." "They rest *not*, day nor night."

From their labors, yes; from toil disproportioned to faculty, yes! From unwelcome work, yes! From distraction and sorrow, yes! But from glad praise and vigorous service, never! Day nor night. And so with the full apprehension of the sweetness and blessedness of the tranquil Heaven, we say: It is found only there, where His servants serve Him. Thus the first thought that is presented here is that of an activity delivered from all that makes toil on earth burdensome and unwelcome; and which, therefore, is coincident with the deepest and most perfect repose.

It may seem strange to think of a blessed life which has no effort in it, for effort is the very salt and spice of life here below, and one can scarcely fancy the perfect happiness of a spirit which never has the glow of warmth that comes from exercise in overcoming difficulties. But perhaps effort, and antagonism, and strain, and trial have done their work on us when they have molded our characters, and when "school is over we burn the rod"; and the discipline of joy may evolve nobler graces of character than ever the discipline of sorrow did. At all events, we have to think of work which also is repose, and of service in which is unbroken tranquility.

Then there is further involved in this first idea, the notion of an outer world, on which and in which to work; and also the notion of the resurrection of the body, in which the active spirit may abide, and through which it may work.

Perhaps it may be that they who sleep in Jesus, in the period between the shuffling off of this mortal coil and the breaking of that day when they are raised again from the dead, are incapable of exertion in an outer sphere. Perhaps, it may be, that by reason of the absence of that glorified body of the Resurrection, they sleep in Jesus in the sense that they couch at the Shpeherd's feet within the fold until the morning comes, when He leads them out to new pastures. It may be. At all events, this we may be sure of, that if it be so they have no desires in advance of their capacities; and of this also I think we may be sure, that whether they themselves can come into contact with an external Universe or not, Christ is for them in some measure what the body is to us here now, and the glo-rified body will be hereafter; that being absent from the body they are present with the Lord, and that He is as it were the Sensorium by which they are brought into contact with and have a knowledge of external things, so that they may rest and wait and have no work to do, and have no effort to put forth, and yet be conscious of all that befalls the loved ones here below, may know them in their affliction, and not be untouched by their tears.

But all that is a dim region into which we have not any need to look. What I emphasize is, the service of Heaven means rest, and the service of Heaven means an outer universe on which, and a true bodily frame with which, to do the work which is delight.

The next point is this: such service must be in a far higher sphere and a far nobler fashion that the service of earth. That is in accordance with the analogy of the Divine dealings. God rewards work with more work. The powers that are trained and exercised and proved in a narrower region are lifted to the higher. As some poor peasant girl, for instance, whose rich voice has risen up in the harvest field only for her own delight and that of a handful of listeners, heard by someone who detects its sweetness, may be car-ried away to some great city, and charm kings with her tones, so the service done in some little corner of this remote rural province of God's universe, apprehended by Him, shall be rewarded with a wider platform, and a nobler area for work. "Thou hast been faith-ful in a few things, I will make thee ruler over many things." God sends forth His children to work as apprentices here, and when they are "out of their time," and have "got a trade," He calls them home, not to let their faculties rest unused, but to practice on a larger theater what they have learned on earth.

One more point must be noticed; viz., that the highest type of Heaven's service must be service for other people. The law for Heaven can surely not be more selfish than the law for earth, and that is, "He that is chiefest amongst you let him be your servant." The law for the perfect man can surely not be different from the law for the Master, and the law for Him is, "Even Christ pleased not Himself." The perfection of the child can surely not be different from the perfection of the Father, and the perfection of the Father is: "He maketh His sun to 'shine,' and His blessings to come on the unthankful and on the good."

So then the highest service for man is the service of others; how, where, or whom, we cannot tell. We, too, may be "ministering spirits, sent forth to minister" (Heb. 1:14), but at all events not on ourselves can our activities center; and not in self-culture can be the highest form of our service to God.

The last point about this first matter is simply this: that this highest form of human activity is all to be worship; all to be done in reference to Him; all to be done in submission to Him. The will of the man in his work is to be so conformed to the will of God as that, whatsoever the hand on the great dial points to, that the hand on the little dial shall point to also. Obedience is joy and rest. To know and to do His will is Heaven. It is Heaven on earth insofar as we partially attain to it, and when with enlarged powers and all imperfections removed, and in a high sphere, and without interruptions we do His commandments, hearkening to the voice of His word, then the perfect state will have come. Then shall we enter into the liberty of the glory of the children of God when, as His slaves, we serve Him in the unwearied activities done for Him, which make the worship of Heaven.

II. Next, look at the second of the elements here: "They shall see His face." Now that expression "seeing the face of God" in Scripture seems to me to be employed in two somewhat different ways, according to one of which the possibility of seeing the face is affirmed, and according to the other of which it is denied.

The one may be illustrated by the Divine word to Moses: "Thou canst not see My face. There shall no man see Me and live." The other may be illustrated by the aspiration and the confidence of one of the psalms: "As for me, I shall behold Thy face in righteousness."

A similar antithesis, which is apparently a contradiction, may be found in setting side by side the words of our Savior: "Blessed are the pure in heart, for they shall see God," with the words of the Evangelist: "No man hath seen God at any time." I do not think that the explanation is to be found altogether in pointing to the difference between present and possible future vision, but rather I think the Bible teaches what reason would also teach: that no corporeal vision of God is ever possible; still further, that no complete comprehension and knowledge of Him is ever possible, and, as I think further, that no direct knowledge of, or contact with, God in Himself is possible for finite man, either here or yonder. And the other side lies in such words as these, which I have already quoted: "Blessed are the pure in heart for they shall see God." "As through a glass darkly, but then face to face." Where is the key to the apparent contradiction? Here, I think: Jesus Christ is the manifest God, in Him only do men draw near to the hidden Deity, the King Invisible, Who dwelleth in the light that is inaccessible.

Here on earth we see by faith, and yonder there will be a vision, different in kind, most real, most immediate and direct, not of the hidden Godhood in itself, but of the revealed Godhood manifest in Jesus Christ, Whom in His glorified corporeal Manhood we shall perceive, with the organs of our glorified body, Whom, in His Divine beauty we shall know and love with heart and mind, in knowledge direct, immediate, far surpassing in degree, and different in kind from, the knowledge of faith which we have of Him here below. But the infinite Godhood that lies behind all revelations of Deity shall remain as it has been through them all, the King invisible, Whom no man hath seen or can see. They shall see His face insofar as they shall hold communion with and through their glorified body and have the direct knowledge of Christ the revealed Deity.

Whether there be anything more, I know not; I think there is not, but this I am sure of, that the law for Heaven and the law for earth alike are, "He that hath seen Me hath seen the Father."

But there is another point I would touch upon in reference to this second thought of our text; viz., its connection with the previous representation, "They shall serve Him"; that is work in an outer sphere; "they shall see His face"; that is contemplation. These two, the life of work and the life of devout communion—the Martha and the Mary of the Christian experience—are antagonistic here below, and it is hard to reconcile their conflicting, fluctuating claims and to know how much to give to the inward life of gazing upon Christ, and how much to the outward life of serving Him. But says my text, the two shall be blended together. "His servants shall serve Him," nor in all their activity shall they lose the vision of His face. His servants "shall see His face," nor in all the still blessedness of their gaze upon Him shall they slack the diligence of the unwearied hands, or the speed of the willing feet. The Rabbis taught that there were angels who serve, and angels who praise, but the two classes meet in the perfected man, whose services shall be praise, whose praise shall be service. They go forth to do His will, yet are ever in the House of the Lord. They work and gaze; they gaze and work. Resting they serve, and serving they rest; perpetual activity and perpetual vision are theirs. "They serve Him, and see His face."

III. The last element is, "His name shall be in their forehead." That is, as I take it, a manifest likeness to the Lord Whom they serve is the highest element in the perfect state of redeemed men. We hear a good deal in this Book of the Revelation about writing the names and numbers of persons and of powers upon men's faces and foreheads; as for instance, you remember we read about the "number of the beast" written upon his worshipers, and about "the name of the New Jerusalem, and the name of my God" being written as a special reward, "upon him that overcomes." The metaphor, as I suppose, is taken from the old cruel practice of branding a slave with the name of his master. And so the primary idea of this expression, "His slaves shall bear His name upon their foreheads," is that their ownership shall be conspicuously visible to all who look.

But there is more than that in it. How is the ownership to be made visible? By His name being on their foreheads. What is "His name"? Universally in Scripture "His name" is His revealed character, and so we come to this: the perfect men shall be known to belong to God in Christ, because they are like Him. The ownership shall be proved by the likeness, and that likeness shall no longer be hidden in their *hearts*, no longer be difficult to make out, so blurred and obliterated the letters of the name, by the imperfections of their lives and their selfishness and sin; but it shall flame in their foreheads, plain as the inscription on the high priest's miter that declared him to be consecrated to the Lord.

And so that lovely and blessed thought is here of a perfect likeness in moral character, at all events, and a wonderful approximation and resemblance in other elements of human nature to the glorified humanity of Jesus Christ our Lord, which shall be the token that we are His.

Oh! What a contrast to the partial ownership, proved to be partial by our partial resemblance here on earth! We say, as Christian men and women, that we bear His name. Is it written so that men can read it, or is it like the name of some person traced in letters of gas jets over a shopfront, half blown out by every gust of wind that comes? Is that the way in which His name is written on your heart and character? My brother! A possibility great and blessed opens before us of a nobler union with Him, a closer approximation, a clearer vision, a more perfect resemblance. "We shall be like Him, for we shall see Him as He is!"

One last word. These three elements—service, contemplation, likeness—these three are not different in kind from the elements of a Christian man's life here. You can enjoy them all sitting in these pews; in the bustle and the hurry of your daily life, you can have every one of them. If you do not enjoy them here you will never have them yonder. If you have never served anybody but yourself, how shall death make you His servant? If all the days of your life you have turned away your ear when He has been saying to you, "Seek ye my face," what reason is there to expect that when death's hammer smashes the glass through which you have seen darkly, "the steady whole of that awful face" will be a pleasant sight to you? If all your life you have been trying, as some of you men and women, old and young, have been trying, and are trying now, to engrave the name of the beast upon your foreheads, what reason have you to expect that when you pass out of this life the foul signs shall disappear in a moment, and you will bear in your brow "the marks of the Lord Jesus" in their stead? No! No! These things do not happen; you have got to begin here as you mean to end yonder. Trust Him here, and you will see Him there. Serve Him here, and you will serve Him yonder. Write His new Name upon your heart, and when you pass from the imperfections of life you will bear His Name on your foreheads.

And if you do not—I lay this upon the consciences of you all—if you do not you will see Christ, and you will not like it! And you will bear, not the Image of the Heavenly, which is life, but the image of the earthy, which is death and hell!

11

The Secret of Gladness

And Jesus said unto them, Can the children of the bridechamber mourn as long as the bridegroom is with them?—Mark 2:19

This is part of our Lord's answer to the question put by John's disciples as to the reason for the omission of the practice of fasting by his followers. The answer is very simple. It is, "My disciples do not fast because they are not sad." And the principle which underlies the answer is a very important one. It is this: that all outward forms of religion, appointed by man, ought only to be observed when they correspond to the feeling and disposition of the worshiper. That principle cuts up all religious formalism by the very roots. The Pharisee said, "Fasting is a good thing in itself, and meritorious in the sight of God." The modern Pharisee says the same about many externals of ritual and worship, Jesus Christ says "No! The thing has no value except as an expression of the feeling of the doer." Our Lord did not object to fasting; He expressly approved of it as a means of spiritual power. But he did object to the formal use of it or of any outward form. The formalist's form, whether it be the elaborate ritual of the Catholic Church, or the barest Nonconformist service, or the silence of a Friends' meetinghouse, is rigid, unbending and cold, like an iron rod. The true Christian form is elastic, like the stem of a palm tree, which curves and sways and yields to the wind, and has the sap of life in it. If any man is sad, let him fast; "if any man is merry, let him sing psalms." Let his ritual correspond to his spiritual emotion and conviction.

But the point which I wish to consider now is not so much this, as the representation that is given here of the reason why fasting was incongruous with the condition and disposition of the disciples. Jesus says, "We are more like a wedding party than anything else. Can the children of the bridechamber mourn as long as the bridegroom is with them?"

The "children of the bridechamber" is but another name for those who were called the "friends" or companions "of the bridegroom." According to the Jewish wedding ceremonial it was their business to conduct the bride to the home of her husband, and there to spend seven days in festivity and rejoicing, which were to be so entirely devoted to mirth and feasting that the companions of the bridegroom were by the Talmudic ritual absolved even from prayer and from worship, and had for their one duty to rejoice.

And that is the picture that Christ holds up before the disciples of the ascetic John as the representation of what He and His friends were most truly like. Very unlike our ordinary notion of Christ and His disciples as they walked the earth! The presence of the Bridegroom made them glad with a strange gladness, which shook off sorrow as the down on a seabird's breast shakes off moisture, and leaves it warm and dry, though it floats amidst boundless seas. I wish today to meditate with you on this secret of imperviousness to sorrow arising from the felt presence of the Christ.

There are three subjects for consideration arising from the words of my text: The Bridegroom, the presence of the Bridegroom, the joy of the Bridegroom's presence.

I. Now with regard to the first, a very few words will suffice. The first thing that strikes me is the singular appropriateness, and the delicate pathetic beauty in the employment of this name by Christ in the existing circumstances. Who was it that had first said, "He that hath the bride is the bridegroom, but the friend of the bridegroom that standeth by and heareth him, rejoiceth greatly because of the bridegroom's voice. This my joy therefore is fulfilled"? Why, it was the master of these very men who were asking the question. John's disciples came and said, "Why do not your disciples fast?" And our Lord reminded them of their own teacher's words when he said, "The friend of the bridegroom can only be glad." And so He would say to them, "In your master's own conception of what I am, and of the joy that comes from my presence, you have an answer to your question. He might have taught you who I am, and why it is that the men that stand around Me are glad."

But this is not all. We cannot but connect this name with a whole circle of ideas found in the Old Testament, especially with that most familiar and almost stereotyped figure which represents the union between Israel and Jehovah, under the emblem of the marriage bond. The Lord is the husband, and the nation that He has loved and redeemed and chosen for Himself is the wife; unfaithful and forgetful, often requiting love with indifference, and protection with unthankfulness, and needing to be put away, and debarred of the society of the husband who still yearns for her; but a wife still, and in the new time to be joined to Him by a bond that shall never be broken and a better covenant.

And so Christ lays His hand upon all that old history and says, "It is fulfilled here in Me." A familiar note in Old Testament Messianic prophecy too is caught and echoed here, especially that grand marriage ode of the forty-fifth Psalm, in which he must be a very prosaic or very deeply prejudiced reader who hears nothing more than the shrill wedding greetings at the marriage of some Jewish king with a foreign princess. Its bounding hopes and its magnificent sweep of vision are a world too wide for such interpretation. The Bridegroom of that psalm is the Messiah, and the Bride is the Church.

I need only refer in a sentence to what this indicates of Christ's self-consciousness. What must He, who takes this name as His own, have thought Himself to be to the world, and the world to Him? He steps into the place of the Jehovah of the Old Testament, and claims as His own all these great and wonderful prophecies. He promises love, protection, communion, the deepest, most mystical union of spirit and heart with Himself; and He claims quiet, restful confidence in His love, absolute, loving obedience to His authority, reliance upon His strong hand and loving heart, and faithful cleaving to Him. The Bridegroom of humanity, the Husband of the world, if it will only turn to Him, is Christ Himself.

II. But a word as to the presence of the Bridegroom. It might seem as if this text condemned us who love an unseen and absent Lord to exclusion from the joy which is made to depend on His presence. Are we in the dreary period when "the bridegroom is taken away" and fasting appropriate?

Surely not. The time of mourning for an absent Christ was only three days; the law for the years of the Church's history between the moment when the uplifted eyes of the gazers lost Him in the symbolic cloud and the moment when He shall come again is, "Lo, I am with you always." The absent Christ is the present Christ. He is really with us, not as the memory or the influence of the example of the dead may be said to remain, not as the spirit of a teacher may be said to abide with his school of followers. We say that Christ has gone up on high and sits on the right hand of God. The right hand of God is His active power. Where is "the right hand of God?" It is wherever His divine energy works. He who sits at the right hand of God is thereby declared to be wherever the Divine energy is in operation, and to be Himself the wielder of that Divine Power. I believe in a local abode of the glorified human body of Jesus Christ now, but I believe likewise that all through God's Universe, and eminently in this world, which He has redeemed, Christ is present in His consciousness of its circumstances, and in the activity of His influence, and in whatsoever other incomprehensible and unspeakable mode Omnipresence belongs to a Divine Person. So that He is with us most really, though the visible, bodily Form is no longer by our sides.

That Presence which survives, which is true for us here today, may be a far better and more blessed and real thing than the presence of the mere bodily Form in which He once dwelt. We may have lost something by His going away in visible form; I doubt whether we have. We have lost the manifestation of Him to the sense, but we have gained the manifestation of Him to the spirit. And just as the great men, who are only men, need to die and go away in order to be measured in their true magnitude and understood in their true glory; and just as when a man is in among the mountains he cannot tell which peak is the dominant one, but when he gets away a little bit across the sea and looks back, distance helps to measure magnitude and reveal the sovereign summit which towers above all the rest, so looking back across the ages with the foreground between us and Him of the history of the Christian Church ever since, and noticing how other heights have sunk beneath the waves and have been wrapped in clouds, and have disappeared behind the great round of the earth, we can tell how high this One is; and know better than they knew Who it is who moves among men in the form of a servant, even the Bridegroom of the Church and of the world. "It is expedient for you that I go away." And Christ is, or ought to be, nearer to us today in all that constitutes real nearness, in our apprehension of His essential character, in our reception of His holiest influences, than He ever was to them who walked beside Him on the earth.

But, brethren, that presence is of no use at all to us unless we daily try to realize it. He was with these men whether they would or no. Whether they thought about Him or no, there He was; and just because His presence did not at all depend upon their spiritual condition, it was a lower kind of presence than that which you and I have now, and which depends for us altogether on our realizing it by the turning of our hearts to Him, and by the daily contemplation of Him amidst all the bustle and the struggle.

Do you, as you go about your work feel His nearness and try to keep the feeling fresh and vivid, by occupying heart and mind with Him, by referring everything to His supreme control? By trusting yourselves utterly and absolutely in His hand, and gathering round you, as it were, the sweetness of His love by meditation and reflection, do you try to make conscious to yourselves your Lord's presence with you? If you do, that presence is to you a blessed reality; if you do not, it is a word that means nothing and is of no help, no stimulus, no protection, no satisfaction, no sweetness to you whatever. The children of the Bridegroom are glad only when, and as, they know that the Bridegroom is with them.

III. And now a word, last of all, about the joy of the Bridegroom's presence. What was it that made these rude lives so glad when Christ was with them; filling them with strange new sweetness and power? The charm of personal character, the charm of contact with one whose lips were bringing to them fresh revelations of truth, fresh visions of God, whose whole life was the exhibition of a nature, beautiful, and noble, and pure, and tender and sweet, and loving, beyond anything they had ever seen before.

Ah, brethren, there is no joy in the world like that of companionship, in the freedom of perfect love, with one who ever keeps us at our best, and brings the treasures of ever fresh truth to the mind, as well as beauty of character to admire and imitate. That is one of the greatest gifts that God gives, and is a source of the purest joy that we can have.

Now you may have all that and much more in Jesus Christ. He will be with us if we do not drive Him away from us, as the source of our purest joy, because He is the all-sufficient object for our love.

Oh! You men and women who have been wearily seeking in the world for love that cannot change, for love that cannot die and leave you; you who have been made sad for life by irrevocable losses, or sorrowful in the midst of your joy by the anticipated certain separation which is to come, listen to this One who says to you: "I will never leave thee, and My love shall be round thee forever"; and recognize this, that there is a love which cannot change, which cannot die, which has no limits, which never can be cold, which never can disappoint, and therefore, in it, and in His presence there is unending gladness.

He is with us as the source of our joy, because He is the Lord of our lives, and the absolute Commander of our Wills. To have One present with us Whose loving word it is delight to obey, and Who takes upon Himself all responsibility for the conduct of our lives, and leaves us only the task of doing what we are bid—that is peace, that is gladness, of such a kind as none else in the world gives.

He is with us as the ground of perfect joy because He is the adequate object of all our desires, and the whole of the faculties and powers of a man will find a field of glad activity in leaning upon Him, and realizing His presence. Like the Apostle whom the old painters loved to represent lying with his happy head on Christ's heart, and his eyes closed in a tranquil rapture of restful satisfaction, so if we have Him with us and feel that He is with us, our spirits may be still, and in the great stillness of fruition of all our wishes and the fulfillment of all our needs, may know a joy that the world can neither give nor take away.

He is with us as the source of endless gladness in that He is the defense and protection for our souls. And as men live in a victualed fortress, and care not though the whole surrounding country may be swept bare of all provision, so when we have Christ with us we may feel safe, whatever befalls, and "in the days of famine we shall be satisfied."

He is with us as the source of our perfect joy because His presence is the kindling of every hope that fills the future with light and glory. Dark or dim at the best, trodden by uncertain shapes, casting many a deep shadow over the present, that future lies, except we see it illumined by Christ, and have Him by our sides. But if we possess His companionship, the present is but the parent of a more blessed time to come; and we can look forward and feel that nothing can touch our gladness, because nothing can touch our union with our Lord.

So, dear brethren, from all these thoughts and a thousand more which I have no time to dwell upon, comes this one great consideration, that the joy of the presence of the Bridegroom is the victorious antagonist of all sorrow and mourning. "Can the children of the bridechamber mourn whilst the bridegroom is with them?" The answer sometimes seems to be, "Yes, they can!" Our own hearts, with their experience of tears, and losses, and disappointments, seem to say: "Mourning is possible, even while He is here. We have our own share, and we sometimes think, more than our share of the ills that flesh is heir to."

And we have, over and above them, in the measure in which we are Christians, certain special sources of sorrow and trial, peculiar to ourselves alone; and the deeper and truer our Christianity the more of these shall we have. But notwithstanding all that, what will the felt presence of the Bridegroom do for these griefs that will come? Well, it will limit them for one thing; it will prevent them from absorbing the whole of our nature. There will always be a Goshen in which there is light in the dwelling, however murky may be the darkness that wraps the land. There will always be a little bit of soil above the surface, however weltering and wide may be the inundation that drowns our world. There will always be a dry and warm place in the midst of the winter, a kind of greenhouse into which we may get from out of the tempest and the fog. The joy of the Bridegroom's presence will last through the sorrow, like a spring of fresh water welling up in the midst of the sea. We may have the salt and the sweet waters mingling in our lives, not sent forth by one fountain, but flowing in one channel.

Our joy will sometimes be made sweeter and more wonderful by the very presence of the mourning and the grief. Just as the pillar of cloud, that glided before the Israelites through the wilderness, glowed into a pillar of fire as the darkness deepened, so, as the outlook around becomes less and less cheery and bright, and the night falls thicker and thicker, what seemed to be but a thin grey wavering column in the blaze of the sunlight will gather warmth and brightness at the heart of it when the midnight comes.

You cannot see the stars at twelve o'clock in the day; you have to watch for the dark hours ere heaven is filled with glory. And so sorrow is often the occasion for the full revelation of the joy of Christ's presence.

Why have so many Christian men so little joy in their lives? Because they look for it in all sorts of wrong places, and seek to wring it out of all sorts of sapless and dry things. "Do men gather grapes of thorns?" If you put the berries of the thorn into the winepress, will you get sweet sap out of them? That is what you are doing when you take gratified earthly affections, worldly competence, fulfilled ambitions, and put them into the press, and think that out of these you can squeeze the wine of gladness. No, no, brethren, dry and sapless and juiceless they all are. There is one thing that gives a man worthy, noble, eternal gladness, and that is the felt presence of the Bridegroom.

Why have so many Christians so little joy in their lives?

A religion like that of John's disciples and that of the Pharisees is a poor affair. A religion of which the main features are law and restriction and prohibition, cannot be joyful. And there are a great many people who call themselves Christians, and have just got religion enough to take the edge off worldly pleasures, and yet they have not got enough to make fellowship with Christ a gladness for them.

There is a cry among us for a more cheerful type of religion. I re-echo the cry, but am afraid that I do not mean by it quite the same thing that some of my friends do. A more cheerful type of Christianity means to many of us a type of Christianity that will interfere less with my amusements; a more indulgent doctor that will prescribe a less rigid diet than the old Puritan type used to do. Well, perhaps they went too far; I do not care to deny that. But the only cheerful Christianity is a Christianity that draws its gladness from deep personal experience of communion with Jesus Christ. There is no way of men being religious and happy except being profoundly religious, and living very near their Master, and always trying to cultivate that spirit of communion with Him which shall surround them with the sweetness and the power of His felt presence. We do not want Pharisaic fasting, but we do want that the reason for not fasting shall not be that Christians like eating better, but that their religion must be joyful because they have Christ with them, and therefore cannot choose but sing, as a lark cannot choose but carol. "Religion has no power over us, but as it is our happiness," and we shall never make it our happiness, and therefore never know its beneficent control, until we lift it clean out of the low region of outward forms and joyless service, into the blessed heights of communion with Jesus Christ, "whom having not seen we love."

I would that Christian people saw more plainly that joy is a duty, and that they are bound to make efforts to obey the command, "Rejoice in the Lord always," no less than other precepts. If we abide in Christ, His joy will abide in us, and our joy will be full. We shall have in our hearts a fountain of true joy which will never be turbid with earthly stains, nor dried up by heat, nor frozen by cold. If we set the Lord always before us our days may be at once like the happy hours of the children of the bridechamber, bright with gladness and musical with song; and also, saved from the enervation that sometimes comes from joy, because they are like the patient vigils of the servants who wait for the Lord, when He shall return from the wedding. So strangely blended of fruition and hope, of companionship and solitude, of feasting and watching, is the Christian life here, until the time comes when His friends go in with the Bridegroom to the banquet, and drink forever of the new joy of the kingdom.

12

The Lesson of Memory

*Thou shalt remember all the way which the Lord
thy God led thee these forty years in the wilderness, to
humble thee, and to prove thee, to know what was in
thine heart whether thou wouldst keep His commandments or no*—Deuteronomy 8:2.

The strand of our lives usually slips away smoothly enough,
but days such as this, the last Sunday in a year, are like the
knots on a sailor's log, which, as they pass through his fingers, tell
him how fast it is being paid out off the reel, and how far it has run.

They suggest a momentary consciousness of the swift passage
of life, and naturally lead us to a glance backward and forward, both
of which occupations ought to be very good for us. The dead flat
upon which we live here may be taken as an emblem of the low present in which most of us are content to pass our lives, affording
nowhere a distant view, and never enabling us to see more than a
street's length ahead of us. It is a good thing to get up upon some little elevation sometimes, and take a wider view, backward and forward.

And so this morning I venture to let the season preach to us, and
to confine myself simply to suggesting for you one or two very plain
and obvious thoughts which may help to make our retrospect wise
and useful. And there are two main considerations which I wish to
submit. The first is, what we ought to be chiefly occupied with as
we look back; and secondly, what the issue of such a retrospect
ought to be.

I. What we should be mainly occupied with as we look back.
Memory, like all other faculties, may either help us or hinder us. As
the man, so will be his remembrance. The tastes which rule his

present will determine the things that he likes best to think about in the past. There are many ways of going wrong in our retrospect. Some of us, for instance, prefer to think with pleasure about things that ought never to have been done, and to give a wicked immortality to thoughts that ought never to have had a being. Some men's tastes and inclinations are so vitiated and corrupted that they find a joy in living their badnesses over again. Some of us, looking back on the days that are gone, select by instinctive preference for remembrance, the vanities and frivolities and trifles which were the main things in them while they lasted. Such a use of the great faculty of memory is like the folly of the Egyptians who embalmed cats and vermin. Do not let us be of those, who have in their memories nothing but rubbish, or something worse, who let down the dragnet into the depths of the past and bring it up full only of mud and foulnesses, and of ugly monsters that never ought to have been dragged into the daylight.

Then there are some of us who abuse memory just as much by picking out, with perverse ingenuity, every black bit that lies in the distance behind us, all the disappointments, all the losses, all the pains, all the sorrows. Some men look back and say, with Jacob in one of his moods, "Few and evil have been the days of the years of my life!" Yes! And the same man, when he was in a better spirit said, and a great deal more truly, "The God that fed me all my life long, the angel which redeemed me from all evil." Do not paint like Rembrandt, even if you do not paint like Turner. Do not dip your brush only in the blackness, even if you cannot always dip it in molten sunshine!

And there are some of us who, in like manner, spoil all the good that we could get out of a wise retrospect by only looking back in such a fashion as to feed a sentimental melancholy, which is, perhaps, the most profitless of all the ways of looking backward.

Now here are the two points, in this verse of my text, which would put all these blunders and all others right, telling us what we should chiefly think about when we look back, and from what point of view the retrospect of the past must be taken in order that it should be salutary. "Thou shalt remember all the way by which the Lord thy God hath led thee." Let memory work under the distinct recognition of Divine guidance in every part of the past. That is the *first* condition of making the retrospect blessed. "To humble thee and to prove thee, and to know what was in thine heart, whether thou wouldst keep His commandments or no." Let us look back with a clear recognition of the fact that the use of life is to test, and reveal, and to make character. This world, and all its outward engagements, duties and occupations, is but a scaffolding, on which the builders may stand to rear the true temple, and when the building is reared you may do what you like with the scaffolding. So we have to look back on life from this point of view, that its joys and sorrows, its ups and downs, its work and repose, all the vicissitudes and sometimes contrariness of its circumstances and conditions, are all for the purpose of making *us*, and of making plain to ourselves, what we are. "To humble thee"; that is, to knock the self-confidence out of us, and to bring us to say: "I am nothing and Thou art everything; I myself am a poor weak rag of a thing that needs Thy hand to stiffen me, or I shall not be able to resist or to do." That is one main lesson that life is meant to teach us. Whoever has learnt to say by reason of the battering and shocks of time, by reason of sorrows and failures, by reason of joys, too, and fruition, "Lord, I come to Thee as depending upon Thee for everything," has got the supreme good out of life, and has fulfilled the purpose of the Father, who has led us all these years, to humble us into the wholesome diffidence that says, "Not in myself, but in Thee is all my strength and my hope."

I need not do more than remind you of the other cognate purposes which are suggested here. Life is meant, not only to bring us to humble self-distrust, as a step towards devout dependence on God, but also to reveal us to ourselves, for we only know what we are by reflecting on what we have done; and the only path by which self-knowledge can be attained is the path of observant recollection of our conduct in daily life.

Another purpose for which the whole panorama of life is made to pass before us, and for which all the gymnastics of life exercise us, is that we may be made submissive to the great Will, and may keep His commandments.

These thoughts then should be with us in our retrospect, and our retrospect will be blessed: First, we are to look back and see God's guidance everywhere, and second, we are to judge of the things that we remember by their tendency to make character, to make us humble, to reveal us to ourselves, and to knit us in glad obedience to our Father God.

II. And now turn to the other consideration which may help to make remembrance a good; viz., the issues to which our retrospect must tend, if it is to be anything more than sentimental recollection.

First let me say: Remember and be thankful. If what I have been saying be true, as to the standard by which events are to be tried; if it be the case that the main fact about things is their power to mold persons and to make character, then there follows, very plainly and clearly, that all things that come within the sweep of our memory may equally contribute to our highest good.

Good does not mean pleasure. Bright being may not always be well being, and the highest good has a very much nobler meaning than comfort and satisfaction. And so, realizing the fact that the best of things is that they shall make us like God, then we can turn to the past and judge it wisely, because then we shall see that all the diversity, and even the opposition of circumstances and events, may cooperate towards the same end. Suppose two wheels in a great machine, one turns from right to left and the other from left to right, but they fit into one another, and they both produce one final result of motion. So the movements in my life which I call blessings and gladness, and the movements in my life which I call sorrows and tortures; these may work into each other, and they will do so if I take hold of them rightly, and use them as they ought to be used. They will tend to the highest good whether they be light or dark; even as night with its darkness and its dews has its ministration and mission of mercy for the wearied eye no less than day with its brilliancy and sunshine; even as the summer and the winter are equally needful, and equally good for the crop. So in our lives it is good for us, sometimes, that we be brought into the dark places; it is good for us sometimes that the leaves be stripped from the trees, and the ground be bound with frost.

And so for both kinds of weather, dear brethren, we have to remember and be thankful. It is a hard lesson, I know for some of us. There may be some listening to me whose memory goes back to this dying year as the year that has held the sorest sorrow of their lives; to whom it has brought some loss that has made earth dark. And it seems hard to tell quivering lips to be thankful, and to bid a man, whose eyes fill with tears, to be grateful, as he looks back on such a past. But yet it is true that it is good for us to be drawn or to be driven to Him; it is good for us to have to tread even a lonely path if it makes us lean more on the arm of our Beloved. It is good for us to have places made empty if, as in the year when Israel's King died, we shall thereby have our eyes purged to behold the Lord sitting on the Royal Seat.

> Take it on trust a little while
> Thou soon shalt read the mystery right,
> In the full sunshine of His smile.

And for the present let us try to remember that He dwelleth in the darkness as in the light, and that we are to be thankful for the things that help us to be near Him, and not only for the things that make us outwardly glad. So I venture to say even to those of you who may be struggling with sad remembrances, remember and be thankful.

I have no doubt there are many in this congregation who look back, if not upon a year desolated by some blow that never can be repaired, yet upon a year in which failing resources and declining business, or diminished health, or broken spirits, or a multitude of minute but most disturbing cares and sorrows do make it hard to recognize the loving Hand in all that comes. Yet to such, too, I would say, "All things work together for good," therefore all things are to be embraced in the thankfulness of our retrospect.

The second, and simple practical suggestion that I make is this: Remember, and let the memory lead to contrition. Perhaps I am speaking to some men or women for whom this dying year holds the memory of some great lapse from goodness; some young man who for the first time has been tempted to sensuous sin; some man who may have been led into slippery places in regard to business integrity. I draw a "bow at a venture" when I speak of such things;

perhaps somebody is listening to me who would give a great deal if he or she could forget a certain past moment of this dying year which makes their cheeks hot yet while they think of it. To such I say: Remember! Go close into the presence of the black thing, and get the consciousness of it driven into your heart; for the remembrance is the first step to deliverance from the load, and to your passing, emancipated from the bitterness, into the year that lies before you.

But even if I have not people here to whom such remarks would apply, let us all summon up to ourselves the memories of these bygone days. In all the three hundred and sixty-five of them, my friend, how many moments stand out distinct before you as moments of high communion with God? How many times can you remember of devout consecration to Him? How many, when, as the people on the Riviera reckon the number of days on the season in which, far across the water, they have seen Corsica, you can remember this year to have beheld, faint and far away, "the mountains that are round about" the Jerusalem that is above? How many moments do you remember of consecration and service, of devotion to your God and your fellows? Oh! What a miserable, low-lying stretch of God-forgetting monotony our life looks when we are looking back at it in the mass. One film of mist is scarcely visible, but when you get a mile of it you can tell what it is—oppressive darkness. One drop of muddy water does not show its pollution, but when you get a pitcherful of it you can see how thick it is. And so a day or an hour looked back upon may not reveal the true godlessness of the average life, but if you will take the twelve-month and think about it, and ask yourselves a question or two about it, I think you will feel that the only attitude for any of us in looking back across a stretch of such brown barren moorland is that of penitent prayer for forgiveness and for cleansing.

But I daresay that some of you say: "Oh! I look back and I do not feel anything of that kind of thing that you describe; I have done my duty and nobody can blame me. I am quite comfortable in my retrospect. Of course there have been imperfections; we are all human, and these need not trouble a man." Let me ask you, dear brother, one question: Do you believe that the law of a man's life is,

"Thou shalt love the Lord thy God with all thy heart, and with all thy soul, and with all thy strength, and with all thy mind, and thy neighbor as thyself?" Do you believe that that is what you ought to do? Have you done it? If you have not, let me beseech you not to go out of this year, across the artificial and imaginary boundary that separates you from the next, with the old guilt upon your back, but go to Jesus Christ, and ask Him to forgive you, and then you may pass into the coming twelvemonth without the intolerable burden of unremembered, unconfessed, and therefore unforgiven sin.

The next point that I would suggest is this: Let us remember in order that from the retrospect we may get practical wisdom. It is astonishing what unteachable, untamable creatures men are. They gain wisdom by experience about all the little matters of daily life, but they do not seem to do so about the higher. Even a sparrow gets to understand a scarecrow after a time or two, and any rat in a hole will learn the trick of a trap. But you can trick men over and over again with the same inducement, and, even while the hook is sticking in their jaws, the same bait will tempt them once more. That is very largely the case because they do not observe and remember what has happened to them in bygone days.

There are two things that any man, who will bring his reason and common sense to bear upon the honest estimate and retrospect of the facts of his life, may be fully convinced of. These are, first, his own weakness. One main use of a wise retrospect is to teach us where we are weakest. What an absurd thing it would be if the inhabitants of a Dutch village were to let the sea come in at the same gap in the same dyke a dozen times! What an absurd thing it would be if a city were captured over and over again by assault from the same point, and did not strengthen its defenses there! But that is exactly what you do; and all the while, if you would only think about your own past lives wisely and reasonably, and like men with brains in your heads, you might find out where it was that you were most open to assault; what it was in your character that needed most strengthening, what it was wherein the devil caught you most quickly, and so build yourselves up in the most defenseless points.

Do not look back for sentimental melancholy; do not look back with unavailing regrets; do not look back to torment yourselves with useless self-accusation; but look back to see how good God has been, and look back to see where you are weak and pile the wall higher there, and so learn practical wisdom from retrospect.

Another phase of practical wisdom which memory should give is deliverance from the illusions of sense and time. Remember how much the world has ever done for you in bygone days. Why should you let it befool you once again? If it has proved itself a liar when it has tempted you with gilded offers that came to nothing, and with beauty that was no more solid than the "Easter eggs" that you buy in the shops, painted sugar with nothing inside, why should you believe it when it comes to you once more? Why not say, "Ah! Once burnt twice shy! You have tried that trick on me before, and I have found it out!" Let the retrospect teach us how hollow life is without God, and let it so draw us nearer to Him.

The last thing that I would say is: Let us remember that we may hope. It is the prerogative of Christian remembrance, that it merges into Christian hope. The forward look and the backward look are really but the exercise of the same faculty in two different directions. Memory does not always imply hope, we remember sometimes because we do not hope, and try to gather round ourselves the vanished past because we know it never can be a present or a future. But when we are occupied with an unchanging Friend, whose love is inexhaustible, and whose arm is unwearied, it is good logic to say, "It has been, therefore it shall be."

With regard to this fleeting life, it is a delusion to say, "tomorrow shall be as this day, and much more abundant," but with regard to the life of the soul that lives in God, that is true, and true forever. The past is a specimen of the future. The future for the man who lives in Christ is but the prolongation, and the heightening into superlative excellence and beauty of all that is good in the past and in the present. As the radiance of some rising sun may cast its bright beams into the opposite sky, even so the glowing past behind us flings its purples and its golds and its scarlets onto the else-dim curtain of the future.

Remember that you may hope. A paradox, but a paradox that is a truth in the case of Christians whose memory is of a God that has loved and blessed them; whose hope is in a God that changes never; whose memory is charged with every good and perfect gift that came down from the Father of Lights, whose hope is in that same Father, "with whom is no variableness, neither shadow of turning." So on every stone of remembrance, every Ebenezer on which is graved, "Hitherto hath the Lord helped us," we can mount a telescope, if I may so say, that will look into the furthest glories of the heavens, and be sure that the past will be magnified and perpetuated in the future. Our prayer may legitimately be, "Thou hast been my help, leave me not, neither forsake me!" And His answer will be, "I will leave thee not until I have done that which I have spoken to thee of." Remember that you may hope, and hope because you remember.

13

Now! Now!—Not By-and-By

A Sermon to the Young

And as Paul reasoned of righteousness, temperance, and judgment to come, Felix trembled, and answered, Go thy way for this time; when I have a convenient season, I will call for thee—Acts 24:25.

Felix and his brother had been favorite slaves of the Emperor, and had won great power at court. At the date of this incident he had been for some five or six years the procurator of the Roman province of Judea; and how he used his power the historian Tacitus tells us in one of his bitter sentences, in which he says, "He wielded his kingly authority with the spirit of a slave, in all cruelty and lust."

He had tempted from her husband Drusilla, a daughter of that Herod whose dreadful death is familiar to us all; and his court reeked with blood and debauchery. He is here face to face with Paul for the second time. On a former interview he had seen good reason to conclude that the Roman Empire was not in much danger from this one Jew whom his countrymen, with suspicious loyalty, were charging with sedition; and so he had allowed him a very large margin of liberty.

On this second occasion he had sent for him evidently not as a judge, but partly with a view to try to get a bribe out of him, and partly because he had some kind of languid interest, as most Romans then had, in Oriental thought, some languid interest perhaps too in this strange man. Or he and Drusilla were possibly longing for a new sensation, and not indisposed to give a moment's glance at Paul, with his singular ideas.

So they called for the Apostle, and the guilty couple got a good deal more than they bargained for. Paul does not speak to them as a Greek philosopher, anxious to please high personages, might have done, but he goes straight at their sins; "He reasons of righteousness" with the unjust judge, "of temperance" with the self-indulgent, sinful pair, "of the judgment to come" with these two, who thought that they could do anything they liked with impunity. Christianity has sometimes to be exceedingly rude in reference to the sins of the upper classes.

As Paul goes on, a strange fear began to creep about the heart of Felix. It is the watershed of his life that he has come to, the crisis of his fate. Everything depends on the next five minutes. Will he yield? Will he resist? The tongue of the balance trembles and hesitates for a moment and then, but slowly, the wrong scale goes down. "Go thy way for this time."

Ah! If he had said, "Come and help me to get rid of this strange fear," how different all might have been! The metal was at the very point of melting. What shape would it take? It ran into the wrong mold, and, as far as we know, it was hardened there. "It might have been once, and he missed it, lost it forever." No sign marked out that moment from the common uneventful moments, though it saw the death of a soul.

Now, my dear young friends, I am not going to say anything more to you of this man and his character, but I wish to take this incident and its lessons and urge them on your hearts and consciences.

I. Let me say a word or two about the fact, of which this incident is an example, and of which I am afraid many of your lives would furnish other examples, that men lull awakened consciences to sleep and excuse delay in deciding for Christ by half-honest promises to attend to religion at some future time.

"Go thy way for this time" is what Felix is really anxious about. His one thought is to get rid of Paul and his disturbing message for the present. But he does not wish to shut the door altogether. He gives a sop to his conscience to stop its barking, and he probably deceives himself as to the gravity of his present decision by the lightly-given, and well-guarded promise with its indefiniteness, "When I have a convenient season I will send for thee." The thing he really means is, Not now, at all events: the thing he hoodwinks himself with is, By-and-by. Now that is what I know some of you are doing; and my purpose and earnest prayer is to bring you tonight to the decision which by one vigorous act of your wills will settle the question for the future as to which God you are going to follow.

So, then, I have just one or two things to say about this first part of my subject. Let me remind you that however beautiful, however gracious, however tender, and full of love and mercy, and good tidings the message of God's love in Jesus Christ is, there is another side to it, a side which is meant to rouse men's consciences and to awaken men's fears.

You bring a man like the man in this story, Felix, or a very much better man than he—any of us who are here tonight—into contact with these three thoughts: "Righteousness, temperance, judgment to come," and the effect of a direct appeal to moral convictions will always be more or less to awaken a sense of failure, insufficiency, defect, sin; and to create a certain creeping dread that if I set myself against the great law of God, that law of God will have a way of crushing me. The fear is well founded, and not only does the contemplation of God's *law* excite it. God's Gospel comes to us, and just because it is a gospel, and is intended to lead you and me to love and trust Jesus Christ, and give our whole hearts and souls to Him—just because it is the best "good news" that ever came into the world—it begins often (not always, perhaps) by making a man feel what a sinful man he is, and how he has gone against God's law, and how there hang over him, by the very necessities of the case and the constitution of the universe, consequences bitter and painful. Now, I believe that there are very few people who, like you, come occasionally into contact with the preaching of the truth, who have not had their moments when they felt "Yes! It is all true, it is all true. I *am* bad, and I *have* broken God's law, and there is a dark lookout before me!" I believe that most of us know what that feeling is.

And now my next step is that the awakened conscience is just like the sense of pain in the physical world, it has got a work to do, and a mission to perform. It is meant to warn you off dangerous ground. Thank God for pain! It keeps off death many a time. And in like manner thank God for a swift conscience that speaks. It is meant to ring an alarm-bell to us, to make us, as the Bible has it, "flee for refuge to the hope that is set before us." My imploring question to my young friends now is, "Have you used that sense of evil and wrongdoing, when it has been aroused in your consciences, to lead you to Jesus Christ, or what have you done with it?"

There are two men in this book of the Acts of the Apostles who pass through the same stages of feeling up to a certain point, and then they diverge. And the two men's outline history is the best sermon that I can preach upon this point. Felix becoming afraid, re-coils, shuts himself up, puts away the thing that disturbs him and settles himself back into his evil. The Philippian jailer becoming afraid (the phrases in the original being almost identical), like a sensible man tries to find out the reason of his fear, and how to get rid of it; and falls down at the Apostles' feet and says, "Sirs, what must I do to be saved?"

The fear is not meant to last; it is of no use in itself. It is only an impelling motive that leads us to look to the Savior, and the man who uses it so has used it rightly. Yet there comes in many a heart that transparent self-deception of delay. "They all with one accord began to make excuse." It is the history today as it was the history then. It is the history in such a congregation as this. There will be dozens, I was going to say hundreds, who will leave this chapel tonight feeling that my poor word has gone a little way into their hardened hide; but settling themselves back into their carelessness, and forgetting all impressions that have been made. O dear young friend, do not do that, I beseech you. Do not stifle the wholesome alarm, and cheat yourself with the notion of a little delay!

II. And now, I wish next to pass very swiftly in review before you, some of the reasons why we fall into this habit of self-de-ceiving, indecision, and delay. "Go thy way," would be too sharp and unmistakable if it were left alone, so it is fined off: "I will not commit myself beyond today." "For this time go thy way, and when I have a convenient season I will call for thee."

What are the reasons for such an attitude as that? Let me enu-merate one or two of them as they strike me: First there is the in-stinctive, natural wish to get rid of a disagreeable subject, much as a man without knowing what he is doing twitches his hand away from the surgeon's lancet. So a great many of us do not like, and no wonder we do not like, these thoughts of the old Book about "righteousness, and temperance and judgment to come," and make a natural effort to get our minds away from the contemplation of the subject because it is painful and unpleasant. Do you think it would be a wise thing for a man, if he began to suspect that he was insolvent, to refuse to look into his books or to take stock, and let things drift, till there was not a halfpenny in the pound for anybody? What do you suppose his creditors would call him? They would not compliment him on either his honesty or his prudence, would they? And is it not the part of a wise man, if he begins to see that something is wrong, to get to the bottom of it, and as quickly as possible, to set it right? And what do you call people who, suspecting that there may be a great hole in the bottom of the ship, never man the pumps or do any caulking, but say, "Oh! She will very likely keep afloat until we get into harbor"?

Do not you think it would be a wiser thing for you if, *because* the subject is disagreeable, you would force yourself to think about it until it became agreeable to you? You can change it if you will, and make it not at all a shadow or a cloud, or a darkness over you. And you can scarcely expect to claim the designation of wise and prudent orderers of your lives until you do. Certainly it is not wise to shuffle a thing out of sight because it is not pleasing to think about.

Then there is another reason. A number of you young people say, "Go thy way for this time," because you have got a notion that it is time enough for you to begin to think about serious things and be religious when you get a bit older. And some of you even, I daresay, have an idea that religion is all very well for people who are turned sixty and are going down the hill, but that it is quite unnecessary for you. Shakespeare puts a grim word into the mouth of one of his characters, which sets the theory of many of us in its true light, when, describing a dying man calling on God, he makes the narrator say: "I, to comfort him, bid him he should not think of God. I hoped there was no need to trouble himself with any such thoughts yet."

Some of my hearers practically live on that principle, and are tempted to regard thoughts of God as in place only among medicine bottles, or when the shadows of the grave begin to fall cold and damp on our path. "Young men will be young men," "We must sow our wild oats," "You can't put old heads on young shoulders," and such like sayings, often practically mean that vice and godlessness belong to youth, and virtue and religion to old age, just as flowers to spring and fruit to autumn. Let me beseech you not to be deceived by such a notion; and to search your own thoughts and see whether it be one of the reasons which leads you to say, "Go thy way for this time."

Then again, some of us fall into this habit of putting off the decision for Christ, not consciously, not by any distinct act of saying "No! I will not," but simply by letting the impressions made on our hearts and consciences be crowded out of them by cares and enjoyments and pleasures and duties of this world. If you had not so much to do at Owen's College, you would have time to think about religion. If you had not so many parties and balls to go to, you would have time to nourish and foster these impressions. If you had not your place to make in the warehouse, if you had not this, that, and the other thing to do; if you had not love, and pleasure, and ambition, and advancement, and mental culture to attend to, you would have time for religion; but as soon as the seed is sown and sower's back turned, hovering flocks of light-winged thoughts and vanities pounce down upon it and carry it away seed by seed. And if some stray seed here and there remains and begins to sprout, the ill weeds which grow apace, spring up with ranker stems and choke it. "The cares of this world, and the deceitfulness of riches, and the lusts of other things entering in, choke the word," and efface the impression made upon your hearts.

Here tonight some serious thought is roused; by tomorrow at midday it has all gone. You did not intend it to go, you did not set yourself to banish it, you simply opened the door to the flocking in of the whole crowd of the world's cares and occupations, and away went the shy solitary thought that, if it had been cared for and tended, might have led you at last to the cross of Jesus Christ. Do not allow yourselves to be drifted by the swaying current of earthly cares from the impressions that are made upon your consciences, and from the duty that you know you ought to do!

And then some of you fall into this attitude of delay, and say to the messenger of God's love: "Go thy way for this time," because you do not like to give up something that you know is inconsistent with His love and service. Felix would not part with Drusilla, nor disgorge the ill-gotten gain of his province. Felix therefore was obliged to put away from him the thoughts that looked in that direction. I wonder if there is any young man listening to me now who feels that if he lets my words carry him where they seek to carry him, he will have to give up "fleshly lusts which war against the soul." I wonder if there is any young woman listening to me now, who feels that if she lets my words carry her where they would carry her, she will have to live a different life from what she has been doing, to have more of a high and a noble aim in it, to live for something else than pleasure. I wonder if there are any of you who are saying, "I cannot give up that." My dear young friend! "If thine eye offend thee, pluck it out and cast it from thee! It is better for thee to enter into life blind than with both eyes to be cast into hell fire."

Reasons for delay, then, are these: first, getting rid of an unpleasant subject; second, thinking that there is time enough; third, letting the world obliterate the impressions that have been made; and fourth, shrinking from the surrender of something that you know you will have to give up.

III. And now let me very briefly, as my last point, put before you one or two of the reasons which I would fain might be conclusive with you for present decision to take Christ for your Savior and your Master.

And I say, do not delay, but *now* choose Him for your Redeemer, your Friend, your Helper, your Commander, your All; because delay is really decision the wrong way. Do not delay, but take Jesus Christ as the Savior of your sinful souls, and rest your hearts upon Him tonight before you sleep; because there is no real reason for delay. No season will be more convenient than the present season. Every time is the right time to do the right thing, every time is the right time to begin following Him. There is nothing to wait for. There is no reason at all except their own disinclination, why every man and woman in this place now should not now grasp the cross of Christ as their only hope for forgiveness and acceptance, and yield themselves to that Lord, to live in His service forever. Let not this day pass without your giving yourselves to Jesus Christ, because every time that you have this message brought to you, and you refuse to accept it, or delay to accept it, you make yourselves less capable of receiving it another time.

If you take a bit of phosphorus and put it upon a slip of wood, and ignite the phosphorus, bright as the blaze is, there drops from it a white ash that coats the wood and makes it almost incombustible. And so when the flaming conviction, laid upon your hearts, has burnt itself out, it has coated the heart, and it will be very difficult to kindle the light there again. Felix said, "Go thy way, when I have a more convenient season I will send for thee." Yes! And he did send for him, and he talked with him often. He repeated the conversation, but we do not know that he repeated the trembling. He often communed with Paul, but it was only once that he was alarmed. You are less likely to be touched by the Gospel message, for every time that you have heard it and put it away. That is what makes my place here so terribly responsible, and makes me feel that my words are so very feeble in comparison with what they ought to be. I know that I may be doing harm to men just because they listen and are not persuaded, and so go away less and less likely to be touched.

Ah! Dear friends, you will, perhaps, never again have as deep impressions as you have now or at least, they are not to be reckoned upon as probable, for the tendency of all truth is to lose its power by repetition, and the tendency of all emotion which is not acted upon is to become fainter and fainter. And so I beseech you that now you would cherish any faint impression that is being made upon your hearts and consciences. Let it lead you to Christ; and take Him for your Lord and Savior now.

I say to you: Do that now, because delay robs you of large blessing. You will never want Jesus Christ more than you do today. You need Him in your early hours. Why should it be that a portion of your lives should be left unfilled by that rich mercy? Why should you postpone possessing the purest joy, the highest blessing, the Divinest strength? Why should you put off welcoming your best Friend into your heart. Why should you?

I say to you again, take Christ for your Lord, because delay inevitably lays up for you bitter memories and involves dreadful losses. There are good Christian men and women, I have no doubt, in this world now, who would give all they have if they could blot out of the tablets of their memories some past hours of their lives, before they gave their hearts to Jesus Christ. I would have you ignorant of such transgression. Oh! Young men and women! If you grow up into middle life not Christians, then should you ever become so, you will have habits to fight with, and remembrances that will smart and sting; and some of you, perhaps, remembrances that will pollute even though you are conscious that you are forgiven. It is a better thing not to know the depths of evil than to know them and to have been raised from them. You will escape infinite sorrows by an early cleaving to Christ your Lord.

And last of all, I say to you, give yourselves tonight to Jesus Christ, because no tomorrow may be yours. Delay is gambling, very irrationally, with a very uncertain thing—your life and your future opportunities. "You know not what shall be on the morrow."

Six and twenty years I have preached in Manchester these annual sermons to the young. Ah! How many of those who heard the early ones are laid in their graves; and how many of them were laid in *early* graves; and how many of them said, as some of you are saying, When I get older I will turn religious. And they never got older. It is a commonplace word that, but I leave it on your hearts. You have no time to lose.

Do not delay, because delay is decision in the wrong way; do not delay because there is no reason for delay; do not delay because delay robs you of a large blessing; do not delay because delay lays up for you, if ever you come back, bitter memories; do not delay because delay may end in death. And for all these reasons come as a sinful soul to Christ the Savior; and ask Him to forgive you, and follow in His footsteps. And do it now! "Today, if ye will hear His voice, harden not your hearts."

14

Salt without Savor

Ye are the salt of the earth; but if the salt have lost its savor, wherewith shall it be salted? It is henceforth good for nothing, but to be cast out, and to be trodden under foot of men—Matthew 5:13.

These words must have seemed ridiculously presumptuous, when they were first spoken, and they have too often seemed mere mockery and irony in the ages since. A Galilean peasant, with a few of his rude countrymen who had gathered round him, stands up there on the mountain, and says to them, "You, a handful, are the people who are to keep the world from rotting, and to bring it all its best light." Strange when we think that Christ believed that these men were able to do these grand functions because they got their power from Himself! Stranger still to think that notwithstanding all the miserable inconsistencies of the professing Church ever since, yet, on the whole, the experience of history has verified these words! And some wise men may curl their lips with a sneer as they say about us Christians, "*Ye* are the salt of the earth!" Yet the most progressive, and the most enlightened, and the most moral portion of humanity has derived its impulse to progress, its enlightenment about the loftiest things, and the purest portion of its morality from the men who received their power to impart these from Jesus Christ.

And so, dear brethren, I have to say two or three things now, which I hope will be plain, and earnest and searching, about the function of the Christian Church, and of each individual member of it, as set forth in these words; about the solemn possibility that the qualification for that function may go away from a man; about the grave question as to whether such a loss can ever be repaired; and about the certain end of the saltless salt.

I. First, then, as to the high task of Christ's disciples as here set forth. "Ye are the salt of the earth!" The metaphor wants very little explanation, however much enforcement it may require. It involves two things: a grave judgment as to the actual state of society, and a lofty claim as to what Christ's followers are able to do to it.

A grave judgment as to the actual state of society. It is corrupt and tending to corruption. You do not salt a living thing. You salt a dead one that it may not be a rotting one. And, says Christ, by implication, what He says plainly more than once in other places: "Human society, without My influence, is a carcass that is rotting away and disintegrating. And you, faithful handful, who have partially apprehended the meaning of My mission, and have caught something of the spirit of My life, you are to be rubbed into that rotting mass to sweeten it, to arrest decomposition, to stay corruption, to give flavor to its insipidity, and to save it from falling to pieces of its own wickedness. Ye are the *salt* of the earth."

Now, it is not merely because we are the bearers of a truth that will do all this that we are thus spoken of, but we Christian men are to do it by the influence of conduct and character.

There are two or three thoughts suggested by this metaphor. The chief one is that of our power and therefore our obligation to arrest the corruption round us, by our own purity. The presence of a good man, according to the old superstition, prevented the possessed from playing their tricks. The presence of a good man hinders the devil from having elbow room to do his work. Do you and I exercise a repressive influence (if we do not do anything better), so that evil and low-toned life is ashamed to show itself in our presence and skulks back as do wrong-doers from the bull's-eye of a policeman's lantern. It is not a high function, but it is a very necessary one, and it is one that all Christian men and women ought to discharge: rebuking and hindering the operation of corruption, even if they have not the power to breathe a better spirit into the dead mass.

But the example of Christian men is not only repressive. It ought to tempt forth all that is best and purest and highest in the people with whom they come in contact. Every man who does right helps to make public opinion in favor of doing right; and every man who lowers the standard of morality in his own life helps to lower it in the community of which he is a part. And so in a thousand ways that I have no time to dwell upon here, the men that have Christ in their hearts and something of Christ's conduct and character repeated in theirs are to be the preserving and purifying influence in the midst of this corrupt world.

There are two other points that I name, and do not enlarge upon. The first of them is: salt does its work by being brought into close contact with the thing which it is to work upon. And so we, brought into contact as we are with plenty of evil and wickedness by many common relations of friendship, of kindred, of business, of proximity, of citizenship, and the like—we are not to seek to withdraw ourselves from contact with the evil. The only way by which the salt can purify is by being rubbed into the corrupted thing.

And once more, salt does its work silently, inconspicuously, gradually. "Ye are the light of the world," says Christ in the next verse. Light is far-reaching and brilliant, flashing that it may be seen. That is one side of Christian work, the side that most of us like best, the conspicuous kind of work. Ay! But there is a very much humbler, and, as I fancy, a very much more useful kind of work that we have all to do. We shall never be the "light of the world," except on condition of being "the salt of the earth." You have to do the humble, inconspicuous, silent work of checking corruption by a pure example before you can aspire to do the other work of raying out light into the darkness, and so drawing men to Christ Himself.

Now, brethren, why do I say all these common threadbare platitudes, as I know they are? Simply in order to plant upon them this one question to the heart and conscience of you Christian men and women: Is there anything in your life that makes this text, in its application to you, anything else than the bitterest mockery?

II. The grave possibility of the salt losing its savor.

There is no need for asking the question whether that is a physical fact or not, whether in the natural realm it is possible for any forms of matter that have saline taste to lose it by any cause. That does not at all concern us. The point is that it is possible for us, who call ourselves, and are, Christians to lose our penetrating pungency, which stays corruption; to lose all that distinguishes us from the men that we are to better.

Now I think that nobody can look upon the present condition of professing Christendom; or, in a narrower aspect, upon the present condition of English Christianity; or in a still narrower, nobody can look round upon this congregation; or in the narrowest view, none of us can look into our own hearts, without feeling that this saying comes perilously near being true of us. And I beg you, dear Christian friends, while I try to dwell on this point to ask yourselves this question: Lord, is it I? and not to be thinking of other people whom you may suppose the cap will fit.

There is, then, manifest on every side, first of all the obliteration of the distinction between the salt and the mass into which is inserted, or to put it into other words, Christian men and women swallow down bodily, and practice thoroughly, the maxims of the world, as to life, and what is pleasant, and what is desirable, and as to the application of morality to business. There is not a hair of difference in that respect between hundreds and thousands of professing Christian men, and the irreligious man who has his office up the same staircase. I know, of course, that there are in every communion saintly men and women who are laboring to keep themselves unspotted from the world, but I know, too, that in every communion there are those whose religion has next to no influence on their general conduct, and does not even keep them from corruption, to say nothing of making them sources of purifying influence. You cannot lay the flattering unction to your souls that the reason why there is so little difference between the Church and the world today is because the world has got so much better. I know that to a large extent the principles of Christian ethics have permeated the consciousness of a country like this, and have found their way even among people who make no profession of being Christians at all. Thank God for it; but that does not explain it all.

If you take a red-hot ball out of a furnace and lay it down upon a frosty moor, two proccesses will go on—the ball will lose its heat and the surrounding atmosphere will gain. There are two ways by which you equalize the temperature of a hotter and a colder body: the one is by the hot one getting cold, and the other is by the cold one getting hot. If you are not warming the world, the world is freezing you. Every man influences all round about him, and receives influences from them, and if there be not more exports than imports, if there be not more influences and mightier influences raying out from him than coming into him, he is a poor creature, and at the mercy of circumstances. "Men must either be hammers or anvils"; must either give blows or receive them. I am afraid that a great many of us who call ourselves Christians get a great deal more harm from the world than we ever dream of doing good to it. Remember this, "you are the salt of the earth," and if you do not salt the world, the world will rot you.

Is there any difference between your ideal of happiness and the irreligious one? Is there any difference between your notion of what is pleasure, and the irreligious one? Is there any difference in your application of the rules of morality to daily life, any difference in your general way of looking at things from the way of the ungodly world? Yes, or No? Is the salt being infected by the carcass, or is it purifying the corruption? Answer the question, brother, as before God and your own conscience.

Then there is another thing. There can be no doubt but that all round and shared by us, there are instances of the cooling of the fervor of Christian devotion. That is the reason for the small distinction in character and conduct between the world and the Church today. An Arctic climate will not grow tropical fruits, and if the heat has been let down, as it has been let down, you cannot expect the glories of character and the pure unworldliness of conduct that you would have had at a higher temperature. Nor is there any doubt but that the present temperature is, with some of us, a distinct *loss* of heat. It was not always so low. The thermometer has gone down.

There are, no doubt, people listening to me who had once a far more vigorous Christian life than they have today; who were once far more aflame with the love of God than they are now. And although I know, of course, that as years go on emotion will become less vivid, and feeling may give place to principle, yet I know no reason why, as years go on, fervor should become less, or the warmth of our love to our Master should decline. There will be less sputtering and crackling when the fire burns up; there may be fewer flames; but there will be a hotter glow of ruddy unflaming heat. That is what ought to be in our Christian experience.

Nor can there be any doubt, I think, but that the obliteration of the distinction between us and the world, and the decay of the fervor of devotion which leads to it, are both to be traced to a yet deeper cause, and that is the loss or diminution of actual fellowship with Jesus Christ. It was that which made these men "salt." It was that which made them "light." It is that, and that alone, which makes devotion burn fervid, and which makes characters glow with the strange saintliness that rebukes iniquity, and works for the purifying of the world.

And so I would remind you that fellowship with Jesus Christ is no vague exercise of the mind but is to be cultivated by three things, which I fear me are becoming less and less habitual among professing Christians: Meditation, the study of the Bible, private prayer. If you have not these, and you know best whether you have them or not, no power in Heaven or earth can prevent you from losing the savor that makes you salt.

III. Now, I come to the next step, and that is the solemn question, Is there a possibility of re-salting the saltless salt, of restoring the lost savor? "Wherewithal shall it be salted?" says the Master. That is plain enough, but do not let us push it too far. If the Church is meant for the purifying of the world and the Church itself needs purifying, is there anything in the world that will do it? If the army joins the rebels, is there anything that will bring back the army to submission? Our Lord is speaking about ordinary means and agencies. He is saying in effect, if the one thing that is intended to preserve the meat loses its power, is there anything lying about that will salt that? So far, then, the answer seems to be—No!

But Christ has no intention that these words should be pushed to this extreme, that if salt loses its savor, if a man loses the pungency of his Christian life, he cannot get it back, by going again to the source from which he got it at first. There is no such implication in these last words. There is no obstacle in the way of a penitent returning to the fountain of all power and purity, nor of the full restoration of the lost savor, if a man will only bring about a full reunion of himself with the source of the savor.

Dear brethren! The message is to each of us; the same pleading words, which the Apocalyptic seer heard from Heaven, come to you and me: "Remember, therefore, from whence thou art fallen, and repent, and do the first works." And all the savor and the sweetness that flow from fellowship with Jesus Christ will come back to us in larger measure than ever, if we will return unto the Lord. Repentance and returning will bring back the saltness to the salt, and the brilliancy to the light.

IV. But one last word warns us what is the certain end of the saltless salt. As the other Evangelist puts it: "It is neither good for the land nor for the dunghill." You cannot put it upon the soil; there is no fertilizing virtue in it. You cannot even fling it into the rubbish heap; it will do mischief there. Pitch it out into the road; it will stop a cranny somewhere between the stones when once it is well trodden down by men's heels. That is all it is fit for. God has no use for it, man has no use for it. If it has failed in doing the only thing it was created for, it has failed altogether. Like a knife that will not cut, or a lamp that will not burn, it may have a beautiful handle, a beautiful stem, it may be highly artistic and decorated; does it cut, does it burn? If not, it is a failure altogether, and in this world there is no room for failures. The poorest living thing of the lowest type will jostle the dead thing out of the way. And so, for the salt that has lost its savor, there is only one thing to be done with it—cast it out, and tread it under foot.

Yes! Where are the Churches of Asia Minor, the patriarchates of Alexandria, of Antioch, of Constantinople; the whole of that early Syrian, Palestinian Christianity; where are they? Where is the Church of North Africa, the Church of Augustine? "Trodden under foot of men!" Over the archway of a mosque in Damascus you can read the half-obliterated inscription: "Thy Kingdom, O Christ, is an everlasting Kingdom." And above it: "There is no God but God, and Mohammed is His prophet!" The salt has lost his savor, and been cast out.

And does anybody believe that the Churches of Christendom are eternal in their present shape? I see everywhere the signs of disintegration in the existing embodiments and organizations that set forth Christian life. And I am sure of this, that in the days that are coming to us, the storm in which we are already caught, all dead branches will be whirled out of the tree. So much the better for the tree! And a great deal that calls itself organized Christianity will have to go down because there is not vitality enough in it to stand. For you know it is low vitality that catches all the diseases that are going; and it is out of the sick sheep's eyeholes that the ravens peck the eyes. And it will be the feeble types of spiritual life, the inconsistent Christianities of our churches, that will yield the crop of apostates and heretics and renegades, and that will fall before temptation.

Brethren, remember this: Unless you go back close to your Lord, you will go farther away. The deadness will deepen, the coldness will become icier and icier; you will lose more and more of the life, and show less and less of the likeness, and purity, of Jesus Christ until you come to this (I pray God that none of us come to it): "Thou hast a name that thou livest, and art dead." Dead!

My brother, let us return unto the Lord our God, and keep nearer Him than we ever have done, and bring our hearts more under the influence of His grace, and cultivate the habit of communion with Him; and pray and trust, and leave ourselves in His hands, that His power may come into us, and that we in the beauty of our characters, and the purity of our lives, and the elevation of our spirits, may witness to all men that we have been with Christ; and may, in some measure, check the corruption that is in the world through lust.

15

The Lamp and the Bushel

*Ye are the light of the world. A city that is set on a hill
cannot be hid. Neither do men light a candle and put it under
the bushel, but on the candlestick, and it giveth light unto all
that are in the house. Let your light so shine before men,
that they may see your good works and glorify your Father
which is in Heaven—Matthew 5:14, 15, 16.*

The conception of the office of Christ's disciples contained in
these words is a still bolder one than that expressed by the
preceding metaphor, which we considered last Sunday. "Ye are the
salt of the earth" implied superior moral purity and power to arrest
corruption. "Ye are the light of the world" implies superior spiritual illumination, and power to scatter ignorance.

That is not all the meaning of the words, but that is certainly in
them. So then, our Lord here gives His solemn judgment that the
world without Him and those who have learned from Him, is in a
state of darkness; and that His followers have that to impart which
will bring certitude and clearness of knowledge, together with purity and joy and all the other blessed things which are "the fruit of
the light."

That high claim is illustrated by a very homely metaphor. In
every humble house from which His peasant followers came, there
would be a lamp—some earthen saucer with a little oil in it, in
which a wick floated—a rude stand to put it upon; a meal-chest or
a flour bin; and a humble pallet on which to lie. These simple
pieces of furniture are taken to point this solemn lesson. "When you
light your lamp you put it on the stand, do you not? You light it in
order that it may give light; you do not put it under the meal-mea-
sure nor the bed. So I have kindled you that you may shine, and put
you where you are that you may give light."

And the same thought, with a slightly different turn in the application, lies in that other metaphor, which is enclosed in the middle of this parable about the light. "A city that is set on a hill cannot be hid." Where they stood on the mountain, no doubt, they could see some village perched upon a ridge for safety, with its white walls gleaming in the strong Syrian sunlight; a landmark for many a mile round. So says Christ, "The City which I found, the true Jerusalem, like its prototype in the Psalm, is to be conspicuous for situation, that it may be the joy of the whole earth."

I have ventured to take all this somewhat long text this morning because all the parts of it hold so closely together, and converge upon the one solemn exhortation with which it closes, and which I desire to lay upon your hearts and consciences, "Let your light so shine before men." I make no pretensions to anything like an artificial arrangement of my remarks, but simply follow the words in the order in which they lie before us.

I. First, just a word about the great conception of a Christian man's office which is set forth in that metaphor: "Ye are the light of the world." That expression is wide; "generic," as they say. Then in the unfolding of this little parable our Lord goes on to explain what kind of a light it is to which He would compare His people—the light of a lamp kindled. Now that is the first point that I wish to deal with. Christian men individually, and the Christian Church as a whole, shine by derived light. There is but One who is light in Himself. He who said, "I am the light of the world, he that followeth Me shall not walk in darkness," was comparing Himself to the sunshine, whereas when He said to us, "Ye are the light of the world; men do not light a lamp and put it under a bushel," He was comparing us to the kindled light of the lamp, which had a beginning and will have an end.

Before, and independent of, His historical manifestation in the flesh, the Eternal Word of God, who from the beginning was the Life, was also the light of men; and all the light of reason and of conscience, all which guides and illumines, comes from that one source, the Everlasting Word, by whom all things came to be and consist. "He was the true light which lighteth every man that cometh into the world."

And further, the historic Christ, the Incarnate Word, is the source for men of all true revelation of God and themselves, and of the relations between them; the Incarnate Ideal of humanity, the Perfect Pattern of conduct, who alone sheds beams of certainty on the darkness of life, who has left a long trail of light as He has passed into the dim regions beyond the grave. In both these senses He is the light, and we gather our radiance from Him.

We shall be "light" if we are "in the Lord." It is by union with Jesus Christ that we partake of His illumination. A sunbeam has no more power to shine if it be severed from the sun than a man has to give light in this dark world if He be parted from Jesus Christ. Cut the current and the electric light dies, slacken the engine and the electric arc becomes dim, quicken it and it burns bright. So the condition of my being light is my keeping unbroken my communication with Jesus Christ; and every variation in the extent to which I receive into my heart the influx of His power and of His love is correctly measured and represented by the greater or the lesser brilliancy of the light with which I reflect His beauty. "Ye were some time darkness, but now are ye light in the Lord." Keep near to Him, and a firm hold of His hand and then you will be light.

And now I need not dwell for more than a moment or two upon what I have already said is included in this conception of the Christian man as being light. There are two sides to it: one is that all Christian people who have learned to know Jesus Christ and have been truly taught of Him do possess a certitude and clearness of knowledge which make them the lights of the world. We advance no claims to any illumination as to other than moral or religious truth. We leave all the other fields uncontested. We bow humbly with confessed ignorance and with unfeigned gratitude and admiration before those who have labored in them as our teachers, but if we are true to our Master, and true to the position in which He has placed us, we shall not be ashamed to say that we believe ourselves to know the truth, insofar as men can ever know it, about the all-important subject of God and man, and the bond between them.

Today there is need, I think, that Christian men and women should not be reasoned or sophisticated or cowed out of their confidence that they have the light because they do know God. It is proclaimed as the ultimate word of modern thought that we stand in the presence of a power which certainly is, but of which we can know nothing except that it is altogether different from ourselves, and that it ever tempts us to believe that we can know it, and ever repels us into despair. Our answer is, "Yes! We could have told you that long ago, though not altogether in your sense; you have got hold of half a truth, and here is the whole of it: No man hath seen God at any time, nor can see Him! (a Gospel of despair, verified by the last words of modern thinkers). "The only begotten Son, which is in the bosom of the Father, He hath declared Him."

Christian men and women! "Ye are the light of the world." Darkness in yourselves, ignorant about many things, ungifted with lofty talent, you have got hold of the deepest truth; do not be ashamed to stand up and say, even in the presence of Mars' Hill, with all its Stoics and Epicureans: "Whom ye ignorantly"—alas! not worship—"Whom ye ignorantly speak of, Him declare we unto you."

And then there is the other side, which I only name, moral purity. Light is the emblem of purity as well as the emblem of knowledge, and if we are Christians we have within us, by virtue of our possession of an indwelling Christ, a power which teaches and enables us to practice a morality high above the theories and doings of the world. But upon this there is the lesser need to dwell, as it was involved in our consideration of the previous figure of the salt.

II. And now the next point that I would make is this: following the words before us, the certainty that if we are light we shall shine. The nature and property of light is to radiate. It cannot choose but shine; and in like manner the little village perched upon a hill there, glittering and twinkling in the sunlight, cannot choose but be seen. So, says Christ, "If you have Christian character in you, if you have Me in you, such is the nature of the Christian life that it will certainly manifest itself." Let us dwell upon that for a moment or two. Take two thoughts: All earnest Christian conviction will demand expression; and all deep experience of the purifying power of Christ upon character will show itself in conduct.

All earnest conviction will demand expression. Everything that a man believes has a tendency to convert its believer into its apostle. That is not so in regard to common everyday truths, nor in regard even of truths of science, but in regard to all moral truth. For example, if a man gets a vivid and an intense conviction of the evils of intemperance and the blessings of abstinence, look what a fiery vehemence of propagandism is at once set to work! And so all round the horizon of moral truth which is intended to affect conduct. It is of such a sort that a man cannot get it into brain and heart without causing him before long to say, "This thing has mastered me, and turned me into its slave; and I must speak according to my convictions."

That experience works most mightily in regard to Christian truth, as the highest. What shall we say, then, of the condition of Christian men and women if they have not such an instinctive need of utterance? Do you ever feel this in your heart: "Thy word shut up in my bones was like a fire. I was weary of forbearing, and I could not stay"? Professing Christians! Do you know anything of the longing to speak your deepest convictions, the feeling that the fire within you is burning through all envelopings, and will be out?

What shall we say of the men that have it not? God forbid I should say there is no fire, but I do say that if the fountain never rises into the sunlight above the dead level of the pool there can be very little pressure at the main; that if a man has not the longing to speak his religious convictions, those convictions must be very hesitating and very feeble; that if you never felt, "I must say to somebody I have found the Messiah," you have not found Him in any very deep sense, and that if the light that is in you can be buried under a bushel it is not much of a light after all, and needs a great deal of feeding and trimming before it can be what it ought to be.

On the other hand, all deep experience of the purifying power of Christ upon character will show itself in conduct. It is all very well for people to talk about having received the forgiveness of sins and the inner sanctification of God's Spirit. If you have, let us see it, and let us see it in the commonest, pettiest things of daily life. The communication between the inmost experience and the outermost conduct is such as that if there be any real revolution deep down, it will manifest itself in the daily life. I make all allowance for the loss of power in transmission, for the loss of power in friction. I am glad to believe that you and I, and all our imperfect brethren, are a great deal better in heart than we ever manage to show ourselves to be in life. Thank God for the consolation that may come out of that thought, but, notwithstanding, I come back to my point that making all such allowance, and setting up no impossible standard of absolute identity between duty and fact in this present life, yet, on the whole if we are Christian people with any deep central experience of the cleansing power and influence of Christ and His grace, we shall show it in life and in conduct. Or, to put it into the graphic and plain words of my text, if we are light we shall shine.

III. Again, and very briefly, this obligation of giving light is still further enforced by the thought that that was Christ's very purpose in all that He has done with us and for us. The homely figure here implies that *He* has not kindled the lamp to put it under the bushel, but that *His* purpose in lighting it was that it might give light.

God has made us partakers of His grace, and has given it to us to be light in the Lord, for this among other purposes, that we should impart that light to others.

No creature is so small that it has not the right to expect that its happiness and welfare shall be regarded by God as an end in His dealings with it; but no creature is so great that it has the right to expect that its happiness or well being shall be regarded by God and itself as God's only end in His dealings with it. He gives us His grace, His pardon, His love, the quickening of His Spirit by our union with Jesus Christ; He gives us our knowledge of Him, and our likeness to Him—what for? "For my own salvation, for my happiness and well being," you say. Certainly, blessed be His name for His love and goodness! But is that all His purpose? Paul did not think so when he said, "God who commanded the light to shine out of darkness hath shined into our hearts [that we might give to others] the light of the knowledge of the glory of God in the face of Jesus Christ." And Christ did not think so when He said, "Men do not light a candle and put it under a bushel, but that it may give light to all that are in the house." "Heaven doth with us as we with torches do: not light them for themselves." The purpose of God is that we may shine. The lamp is kindled not to illumine itself, but that it may "give light to all that are in the house."

Consider again, that while all these things are true, there is yet a solemn possibility that men, even good men, may stifle and smother and shroud their light. You can, and I am afraid a very large number of you do this, by two ways. You can bury the light of a holy character under a whole mountain of inconsistencies. If one were to be fanciful, one might say that the bushel or meal-chest meant material well-being, and the bed, indolence, and love of ease. I wonder how many Christian men and women in this place this morning have buried their light under the flour bin and the bed, so interpreted. How many of us have drowned our consecration and devotion in foul waters of worldly lusts, and have let the love of earth's goods, of wealth and pleasure, and creature love, come like a poisonous atmosphere round the lamp of our Christian character, making it burn dim and blue.

And we can bury the light of the Word under cowardly and sheepish and indifferent silence. I wonder how many of us have done that. Like blue-ribbon men that button their greatcoats over their blue ribbons when they go into company where they are afraid to show them, there are plenty of Christian people who are devout Christians at the Communion Table who would be ashamed to say they were so in the miscellaneous company of a railway carriage or a *table d'hote*. There are professing Christians who have gone through life in their relationships to their fathers, sisters, wives, children, friends kindred, their servants and dependents, and have never spoken a loving word for their Master. That is a sinful hiding your light under the bushel and the bed.

IV. And so the last word, into which all this converges, is the plain duty: If you are light, shine! "Let your light so shine before men," says the text, "that they may see your good works and glorify your Father which is in Heaven."

In the next chapter our Lord says, "Take heed that ye do not your alms before men to be seen of them. Thou shalt not be as the hypocrites are; for they love to pray standing in the synagogues that they may be seen of men." What is the difference between the two sets of men and the two kinds of conduct? The motive makes the difference for one thing, and for another thing, "Let your light so shine" does not mean "take precautions that your goodness may come out into public," but it means "Shine!" You find the light, and the world will find the eyes, no fear of that! You do not need to seek "to be seen of men," but you do need to shine that men may see.

The lighthouse-keeper takes no pains that the ships tossing away out at sea may behold the beam that shines from his lamp, but all that he does is to feed it and tend it. And that is all that you and I have to do—tend the light, and do not, like cowards, cover it up. Modestly, but yet bravely, carry out your Christianity, and men will see it. Do not be as a dark lantern, burning with the slides down and illuminating nothing and nobody. Live your Christianity, and it will be beheld.

And remember, candles are not lit to be looked at. Candles are lit that something else may be seen by them. Men may see God through your words, through your conduct, that never would have beheld Him otherwise, because His beams are too bright for their dim eyes. And it is an awful thing to think that the world always—*always*—takes its conception of Christianity from the Church, and neither from the Bible nor from Christ; and that it is you and your like, you inconsistent Christians; you people who say your sins are forgiven and are doing the old sins day by day which you say are pardoned; you low-toned, unpraying, worldly Christian men, who have no elevation of character and no self-restraint of life and no purity of conduct above the men in your own profession and in your own circumstances all round you—it is you who are hindering the coming of Christ's Kingdom, it is you who are the standing disgraces of the Church, and the weaknesses and diseases of Christendom. I speak strongly, not half as strongly as the facts of the case would warrant; but I lay it upon all your consciences as professing Christian people to see to it that no longer your frivolities, or doubtful commercial practices, nor low, unspiritual tone of life, your self-indulgence in household arrangements, and a dozen other things that I might name—that no longer do they mar the clearness of your testimony for your Master, and disturb with envious streaks of darkness the light that shines from His followers.

None who have not seen its power can suppose how effectual such a witness may be. Example does tell. A holy life curbs evil, ashamed to show itself in that pure presence. A good man or woman reveals the ugliness of evil by showing the beauty of holiness. More converts would be made by a Christlike Church than by many sermons. Oh! If you professing Christians knew your power and would use it, if you would come closer to Christ, and catch more of the light from His face, you might walk among men like very angels, and at your bright presence darkness would flee away, ignorance would grow wise, impurity be abashed and sorrow comforted.

Be not content, I pray you, till your own hearts are fully illumined by Christ, having no part dark, and then live as remembering that you have been made light that you may shine. "Arise, shine, for thy light is come, and the glory of the Lord is risen upon thee!"

16

Man's True Treasure in God

The Lord is the portion of mine inheritance and of my cup; Thou maintainest my lot. The lines are fallen unto me in pleasant places; yea, I have a goodly heritage
—Psalm 16:5, 6.

We read, in the law which created the priesthood in Israel, that "the Lord spake unto Aaron, Thou shalt have no inheritance in their land, neither shalt thou have any part among them. I am thy part and thine inheritance among the children of Israel" (Num. 17:20). Now there is an evident allusion to that remarkable provision in this text. The Psalmist feels that in the deepest sense he has no possession among the men who have only possessions upon earth, but that God is the treasure which he grasps in a rapture of devotion and self-abandonment. The priest's duty is his choice. He will "walk by faith and not by sight."

Are not all Christians priests? And is not the very essence and innermost secret of the religious life this, that the heart turns away from earthly things and deliberately accepts God as its supreme good, and its only portion? These first words of my text contain the essence of all true religion.

The connection between the first clause and the others is closer than many readers perceive. The "lot" which "Thou maintainest," the "pleasant places," the "goodly heritage," all carry on the metaphor, and all refer to God as Himself the portion of the heart that chooses and trusts Him. "Thou maintainest my lot." He Who is our inheritance also guards our inheritance, and whosoever has taken God for his possession has a possession as sure as God can make it. "The lines are fallen to me in pleasant places; yea, I have a goodly heritage." The heritage that is goodly is God Himself. When a man chooses God for his portion, then, and then only, is he satisfied; "satisfied with favor, and full of the goodness of the Lord." Let me try and expand and enforce those thoughts, with the hope that we may catch something of their fervor and their glow.

I. The first thought, then, that comes out of the words before us is this: all true religion has its very heart in deliberately choosing God as my supreme good.

"The Lord is the portion of my inheritance and of my cup." The two words which are translated in our version "portion" and "inheritance" are substantially synonymous. The latter of them is used continually in reference to the share of each individual, or family, or tribe in the partition of the land of Canaan. There is a distinct allusion, therefore, to that partition in the language of our text; and the two expressions, part or "portion," and "inheritance," are substantially identical, and really mean just the same as if the single expression had stood: "The Lord is my portion."

I may just notice in passing that these words are evidently alluded to in the New Testament, in the Epistle to the Colossians, where Paul speaks of God "having made us meet for the portion of the inheritance of the saints in light."

And then the "portion of my cup" is a somewhat strange expression. It is found in one of the other Psalms, with the meaning "fortune," or "destiny," or "sum of circumstances which make up a man's life." There may be, of course, an allusion to the metaphor of a feast here, and God may be set forth as "the portion of my cup," in the sense of being the refreshment and sustenance of a man's soul. But I should rather be disposed to consider that there is merely a prolongation of the earlier metaphor, and that the same thought as is contained in the figure of the "inheritance" is expressed here (as in common conversation it is often expressed) by the word "cup"; namely, that which makes up a man's portion in this life. It is used with such a meaning in the well-known words: "My cup runneth over," and in another shape in, "The cup which My Father hath given Me, shall I not drink it?" It is the sum of circumstances which make up a man's "fortune." So the double metaphor presents the one thought of God as the true possession of the devout soul.

Now how do we possess God? We possess things in one fashion and persons in another. The lowest and most imperfect form of possession is that by which a man simply keeps other people off material good, and asserts the right of disposal of it as he thinks proper. A blind man may have the finest picture that ever was painted; he may call it his, that is to say, nobody else can sell it, but what good is it to him? A lunatic may own a library as big as the Bodleian, but what use is it to him? Does the man who draws the rents of a mountainside, or the poet or painter, to whom its cliffs and heather speak far-reaching thoughts, most truly possess it? The highest form of possession, even of things, is when they minister to our thought, to our emotion, to our moral and intellectual growth. We possess even them, really, according as we know them and hold communion with them.

But when we get up into the region of persons, we possess them in the measure in which we understand them, and sympathize with them, and love them. Knowledge, intercourse, sympathy, affection; these are the ways by which men can possess men, and spirits, spirits. A man who gets the thoughts of a great teacher into his mind and has his whole being saturated by them may be said to have made the teacher his own. A friend or a lover owns the heart that he or she loves, and which loves back again; and not otherwise do we possess God.

Such ownership must be, from its very nature, reciprocal. There must be the two sides to it. And so we read in the Bible, with equal frequency: the Lord is the "inheritance of His people," and His people are "the inheritance of the Lord." He possesses me, and I possess Him (with reverence be it spoken) by the very same tenure; for whoso loves God has Him, and whom He loves He owns. There is deep and blessed mystery involved in this wonderful prerogative, that the loving believing heart has God for its possession and indwelling Guest; and people are apt to brush such thoughts aside as mystical. But like all true Christian mysticism, it is intensely practical.

We have God for ours first in the measure in which our minds are actively occupied with thoughts of Him. We have no merely mystical or emotional possession of God to preach. There is a real, adequate knowledge of Him in Jesus Christ. We know God, His character, His heart, His relations to us, His thoughts of good concerning us, sufficiently for all intellectual and for all practical purposes. I wish to ask you a plain question. Do you ever think about Him?

There is only one way of getting God for yours, and that is by bringing Him into your life by frequent meditation upon His sweetness, and upon the truths that you know about Him. There is no other way by which a spirit can possess a spirit, that is not cognizable by sense, except only by the way of thinking about Him, to begin with. All else follows that. That is how you hold your dear ones when they go to the other side of the world. That is how you hold God Who dwells on the other side of the stars. There is no way to "have" Him, but through the understanding accepting Him, and keeping firm hold of Him. Men and women that from Monday morning to Saturday night never think of His name, how do they possess God? And professing Christians who never remember Him all the day long—what absurd hypocrisy it is for them to say that God is theirs!

Yours, and never in your mind! When your husband, or your wife, or your child goes away from home for a week, do you forget them as utterly as you forget God? Do you have them in any sense if they never dwell in the "study of your imagination," and never fill your thoughts with sweetness and with light?

And so again, when the heart turns to Him and when all the faculties of our being, will, and hope, and imagination, and all our affections and all our practical powers, when they all touch Him, each in its proper fashion, then and then only can we in any reasonable and true sense be said to possess God.

Thought, communion, sympathy, affection, moral likeness, practical obedience, these are the way—and not by mystical raptures only—by which, in simple prose fact, is it possible for the finite to grasp the infinite; and for a man to be the *owner* of God.

Now there is another consideration very necessary to be remembered, and that is that this possession of God involves, and is possible only by, a deliberate act of renunciation. The Levite's example that is glanced at in my text is always our law. You must have no part or inheritance among the sons of earth if God is to be your inheritance. Or, to put it into plain words, there must be a giving up of the material and the created if there is to be a possession of the Divine and the Heavenly. There cannot be *two* supreme, any more than there can be two pole-stars, one in the north, and the other in the south, to both of which a man can be steering.

You cannot stand with—

> One foot on land, and one on sea,
> To one thing constant never.

If you are going to have God as your supreme good you must empty your heart of earth and worldly things, or your possession of Him will be all words and imagination and hypocrisy. Brethren! I wish to bring that message to your consciences today.

And what is this renunciation? There must be, first of all, a fixed, deliberate, intelligent conviction lying at the foundation of my life that God is best, and that He and He only is my true delight and desire. Then there must be built upon that intelligent conviction that God is best, the deliberate turning away of the heart from these material treasures. Then there must be the willingness to abandon the outward possession of them, if they come in between us and Him. Just as travellers in old days who went out looking for treasures in the western hemisphere were glad to empty out their ships of their less-precious cargo in order to load them with gold, you must get rid of the trifles, and fling these away if ever they so take up your heart that God has no room there. Or, rather, perhaps, if the love of God in any real measure, however imperfectly, once gets into a man's soul, it will work there to expel and edge-out the love and regard for earthly things.

Just as when the chemist collects oxygen in a vessel filled with water, as it passes into the jar it drives out the water before it; the love of God, if it come into a man's heart in any real sense, in the measure in which it comes will deliver him from the love of the world.

But between the two there is warfare so internecine and endless that they cannot co-exist: and here, today, it is as true as ever it was that if you want to have God for your portion and your inheritance you must be content to have no inheritance among your brethren, nor part among the sons of earth.

Men and women! Are you ready for that renunciation! Are you prepared to say, "I know that the sweetness of Thy presence is the truest sweetness that I can taste, and lo! I give up all besides and my own self."

> O God of good, the unfathomed sea,
> Who would not yield himself to Thee?

And remember, that nothing less than these are Christianity— the conviction that the world is second and not first; that God is best, love is best, truth is best; knowledge of Him is best; likeness to Him is best; the willingness to surrender all if it come in contest with His supreme sweetness. He who turns his back upon earth by reason of the drawing power of the glory that excels is a Christian. The Christianity that only trusts to Christ for deliverance from the punishment of sin and so makes religion a kind of fire insurance is a very poor affair. We need the lesson pealed into our ears as much as any generation has ever done, Ye cannot serve God and mammon. A man's real working religion consists in his loving God most and counting His love the sweetest of all things.

II. Now let me turn to the next point that is here; viz., that this possession is as sure as God can make it. "Thou maintainest my lot." Thou art Thyself both my heritage and the guardian of my heritage. He who possesses God, says the text, therefore, by implication, is lifted above all fear and chance of change.

The land, the partition of which among the tribes lies at the bottom of the allusive metaphor of my text, was given to them under the sanction of a supernatural defense; and the law of their continuance in it was that they should trust and serve the unseen King. It was He, according to the theocratic theory of the Old Testament, and not chariots and horses, their own arm and their own sword, that kept them safe, though the enemies on the north and the enemies on the south were big enough to swallow up the little kingdom at a mouthful.

And so, says the Psalmist allusively, in a similar manner the Divine Power surrounds the man who chooses God for his heritage, and nothing shall take that heritage from him.

The lower forms of possession by which men are called the owners of material goods are imperfect, because they are all precarious and temporary. Nothing really belongs to a man if it can be taken from him. What we may lose we can scarcely be said to have. They *are* mine, they *were* yours, they *will be* somebody else's tomorrow. While we have them we do not have them in any deep sense; we cannot retain them, they are not really ours at all. The only thing that is worth calling mine is something that so passes into and saturates the very substance of my soul that, like a piece of cloth dyed in the grain, as long as two threads hold together the tint will be there. That is how God gives us Himself, and nothing can take Him out of a man's soul. He, in the sweetness of His grace, bestows Himself upon man, and guards His own gift, in the heart, which is Himself. He who dwells in God and God in him, lives as in the inmost keep and citadel. The noise of battle may roar around the walls, but deep silence and peace are within. The storm may rage upon the coasts, but he who has God for his portion dwells in a quiet inland valley where the tempests never come. No outer changes can touch our possession of God. They belong to another region altogether. Other goods may go, but this is held by a different tenure. The life of a Christian is lived in two regions: in the one his life has its roots, and its branches extend to the other. In the one there may be whirling storms and branches may toss and snap, while in the other to which the roots go down, may be peace. Root yourselves in God, making Him your truest treasure, and nothing can rob you of your wealth.

We here in this commercial community see plenty of examples of great fortunes and great businesses melting away like yesterday's snow. And surely the difficulties and perplexities in which much of our Lancashire trade is involved today might preach to some of you this lesson: Set not your hearts on that which can pass, but make your treasure that which no man can take from you.

Then, too, there is the other thought. He will help us so that no temptations shall have power to make us rob *ourselves* of our treasure. None can take it from us but ourselves, but we are so weak and surrounded by temptations so strong that we need Him to aid us if we are not to be beguiled by our own treacherous hearts into parting with our highest good. A handful of feeble Jews were nothing against the gigantic might of Assyria, or against the compacted strength of civilized Egypt, but there they stood, on their rocky mountains, defended not by their own strength but by the might of a present God. And so, unfit to cope with the temptations round us as we are, if we cast ourselves upon His power and make Him our supreme delight, nothing shall be able to rob us of that possession and that sweetness.

And there is just one last point that I would refer to here on this matter of our stable possession of God. It is very beautiful to observe that this Psalm, which, in the language of my text, rises to the very height of spiritual and, in a good sense, mystical devotion, recognizing God as the One good for souls, is also one of the Psalms which has the clearest utterance of the faith in immortality. Just after the words of my text we read these others, in which the Old Testament confidence in a life beyond the grave reaches its very climax: "Thou wilt not leave my soul in Sheol, neither wilt Thou suffer Thine holy one to see corruption. Thou wilt show me the path of life; in Thy presence is fullness of joy; at Thy right hand there are pleasures forevermore."

That connection teaches us that the measure in which a man feels his true possession of God here and now, is the measure in which his faith rises triumphant over the darkness of the grave, and grasps with unfaltering confidence the conviction of an immortal life. The more we know that God is our portion and our treasure, the more sure, and calmly sure, we shall be that a thing like death cannot touch a thing like that, that the mere physical fact is far too small and insignificant a fact to have any power in such a region as that; that death can no more affect a man's relation to God, Whom he has learned to love and trust, than you can cut thought or feeling with a knife. The two belong to two different regions. Thus we have here the Old Testament faith in immortality shaping itself out of the Old Testament enjoyment of communion with God, with a present God. And you will find the very same process of thought in that seventy-third Psalm, which stands in some respects side by side with this one as containing the height of mystical devotion, joined with a very clear utterance of the faith in immortality: "Whom have I in Heaven but Thee, and there is none upon earth that I desire beside

Thee! Thou wilt guide me with Thy counsel, and afterwards receive me to glory."

So Death himself cannot touch the heritage of the man whose heritage is the Lord. And his ministry is not to rob us of our treasures as he robs men of all treasures besides (for "their glory shall not descend after them") but to give us, instead of the "earnest of the inheritance," the bit of turf by which we take possession of the estate, the broad land in all the amplitude of its sweep, into our perpetual possession. "Thou maintainest my lot." Neither death nor life shall separate us from the love of God which is in Christ Jesus our Lord!

III. And then the last thought here is that he who thus elects to find his treasure and delight in God is satisfied with his choice. "The lines"—the measuring-cord by which the estate was parted off and determined—"are fallen in pleasant places; yea!"—not as our Bible has it, merely "I have a *goodly* heritage," putting emphasis on the fact of possession—but "the heritage is goodly *to me*," putting emphasis on the fact of subjective satisfaction with it.

I have no time to dwell upon the thoughts that spring from these words. Take them in the barest outline. No man who makes the worse choice of earth instead of God ever, in retrospect, said, "I have a goodly heritage." One of the later Roman emperors, who was one of the best of them, said, when he was dying: "I have been everything, and it profits me nothing." No creature can satisfy your whole nature. Portions of it may be fed with their appropriate satisfaction, but as long as we feed on the things of earth there will always be part of our being like an unfed tiger in a menagerie, growling for its prey while its fellows are satisfied for the moment. You can no more give your heart rest and blessedness by pitching worldly things into it than they could fill up Chat Moss, when they made the first Liverpool and Manchester Railway, by throwing in cartloads of earth. The bog swallowed them and was none the nearer being filled.

No man who takes the world for his portion ever said, "The lines are fallen to me in pleasant places." For the make of your soul as plainly cries out, "God!" as a fish's fins declare that the sea is its element, or a bird's wings mark it out as meant to soar. Man and

God fit each other like the two halves of a tally. You will never get rest or satisfaction, and you will never be able to look at the past with thankfulness nor at the present with repose, nor into the future with hope, unless you can say, "God is the strength of my heart, and my portion forever." But oh! If you do, then you have a goodly heritage, a heritage of still satisfaction, a heritage which suits and gratifies, and expands all the power of a man's nature, and makes him ever capable of larger and larger possession of a God Who ever gives more than we can receive, that the overplus may draw us to further desire, and the further desire may more fully be satisfied.

The one, true, pure, abiding joy is to hold fellowship with God and to live in His love. The secret of all our unrest is the going out of our desires after earthly things. They fly forth from our hearts like Noah's raven, and nowhere amid all the weltering flood can find a resting place. The secret of satisfied repose is to set our affections thoroughly on God. Then our wearied hearts, like Noah's dove returning to its rest, will fold their wings and nestle fast by the throne of God. "All the happiness of this life," said William Law, "is but trying to quench thirst out of golden *empty* cups." But if we will take the Lord for "the portion of our cup," we shall never thirst.

Let me beseech you to choose God in Christ for your supreme good and highest portion; and having chosen, to cleave to your choice. So shall you enter on possession of good that truly shall be yours, even "that good part, which shall not be taken away from you."

And lastly, remember that if you would have God, you must take Christ. He is the true Joshua, who puts us in possession of the inheritance. He brings God to you—to your knowledge, to your love, to your will. He brings you to God, making it possible for your poor sinful souls to enter His presence by His blood, and for your spirits to possess that Divine Guest. "He that hath the Son hath the Father"; and if you trust your souls to Him who died for you and cling to Him as your delight and your joy, you will find that both the Father and the Son come to you and make Their home in you. Through Christ the Son you will receive power to become sons of God, and if children, then heirs, heirs of God, because joint heirs with Christ.

17

God's True Treasure in Man

The Lord's portion is His people; Jacob is the lot of His inheritance—Deuteronomy 32:9.

Jesus Christ (Who) gave Himself for us, that He might redeem us from all iniquity and purify unto Himself a peculiar people—Titus 2:14.

In my last sermon I dealt with the thought that man's true treasure is in God. My text then was, "The Lord is the portion of my inheritance; Thou maintainest my lot," and the following words. You observe the correspondence between these words and those of my first text: "The Lord's portion is His people; Jacob is the lot of His inheritance." The correspondence in the original is not quite so marked as it is in our Authorized Version, but still the idea in the two passages is the same.

You may remember that I said then that persons could possess persons only by love, sympathy, and communion. From that it follows that the possession must be mutual; or, in other words, that only he can say, "Thou art mine," who can say, "I am thine." And so to possess God and to be possessed by God are but two ways of putting the same fact. "The Lord is the portion of His people," and "The Lord's portion is His people," are the same truth in a double form.

Then my second text clearly quotes the well-known utterance that lies at the foundation of the national life of Israel: "Ye shall be unto me a peculiar treasure above all people," and claims that privilege, like all Israel's privileges, for the Christian Church. In like manner, Peter (1 Pet. 2:9) quotes the same words "a peculiar people," as properly applying to Christians. I need scarcely remind you that "peculiar" here is used in its proper original sense of "belonging to," or, as the Revised Version gives it, "a people for God's own possession," and has no trace of the modern significance of "singular." Similarly, we find Paul in his Epistle to the Ephesians giving both sides of the idea of the inheritance, in intentional juxtaposition, when he speaks (1:14) of the "earnest of our inheritance until the redemption of God's own possession." In the words before us we have the same idea, and this text tells us besides how Christ, the revealer of God, wins men for Himself, and what manner of men they must be whom He counts as His.

Therefore, there are, as I take it, three things to be spoken about now. First, God has a special ownership in some people. Second, God owns these people because He has given Himself to them. Third, God possesses, and is possessed by, His inheritance, that He may give and receive services of love. Or, in briefer words, I have to speak about this wonderful thought of a special Divine ownership: what it rests upon and what it involves.

Now first, "The Lord's portion is His people; Jacob is the lot of His inheritance." Put side by side with that other words of the Old Testament: "All souls are Mine," or the utterance of the Hundredth Psalm rightly translated: "It is He that hath made us, and to Him we belong." There is a right of ownership and possession inherent in the very relation of Creator and creature, so that the Being made is wholly and altogether at the disposal and is the property of Him who makes him.

But is that enough for God's heart? Is that worth calling ownership at all? An arbitrary tyrant in an unconstitutional kingdom, or a slave-owner, may have the most absolute right of property over his subject or his slave; may have the right of entire disposal of all his industry, of the profit of all his labor, may be able to do anything he likes with him, may have the power of life and death; but such ownership is only of the husk and case of a man. The man himself may be free, and may smile at the claim of possession. "They may *own* the body, and after that they have no more that they can do." That kind of authority and ownership, absolute and utter, to the point of death, may satisfy a tyrant or a slave-driver; it does not satisfy the loving heart of God. It is not real possession at all. In what sense did Nero own Paul when he shut him up in a prison and cut his head off? Does the slave-owner own the man whom he whips within an inch of his life and who dare not do anything without his permission? Does God in any sense that corresponds with the yearning of infinite love own the men who reluctantly obey Him, and are simply, as it were, tools in His hands? He covets and longs for a deeper relationship and tenderer ties, and though all creatures are His, and all men are His servants and His possession, yet, like certain regiments in our own British army, there are some who have the right to bear in a special manner on their uniform and on their banners the emblazonment, "The King's Own." "The Lord's portion is His people; Jacob is the lot of His inheritance."

Well then, the next thought is that the special relationship of possession is constituted by mutual love. I said at the beginning of these remarks that the only ways by which spiritual beings can possess each other are by love, sympathy, and communion, and that these must necessarily be mutual. We have a perfect right to apply the human analogy here; in fact, we are bound to do it if we would rightly understand such words as those of my text; and it just leads us to this, that the one thing whereby God reckons that He possesses a man at all is by His love falling upon that man's heart and soaking into it, and by the springing up in the heart of a corresponding affection. The men who welcome the Divine love that goes through the whole world, "seeking such to worship it," and to trust it, and to be its treasure, and who, therefore, lovingly yield to the loving Divine will and take it for their law, these are the men whom He regards as His portion and the lot of His inheritance. So "God is mine," "I am God's," are two sides of one truth; "I possess Him" and "I am possessed by Him" are but the statement of one fact expressed from two points of view. In the one case you look upon it from above, in the other case you look upon it from beneath. All the sweet commerce of mutual surrender and possession which makes the joy of our hearts in friendship and in domestic life we have the right to lift up into this loftier region, and find in it the best teaching of what makes the special bond of mutual possession between God and man.

Deep words of Scripture point in that direction. Those parables of our Lord's: the lost sheep, the lost coin, the lost son, in their inifinite beauty, while they contain a great deal besides this, do contain this in their several ways. The money, the animal, the man, belong to the woman of the house, to the shepherd, to the father. Each is lost in a different fashion, but the most clear revelation is given in the last parable of the three, which explains the other two. The son was "lost" when he did not love the father, and he was "found" by the father when he returned the yearning of the father's heart.

And so, dear brethren, it ever is: the one thing that knits men to God is that the silken bond of love let down from the Heaven should by our own hand be wrapped round our own hearts, and then we are united to Him. We are His and He is ours by the same double action; His love manifested by Him and His love received by us.

Now there is nothing in all that of favoritism. The declaration that there are people who have a special relationship to the Divine heart may be so stated as to have a very ugly look, and it often has been so stated as to be nothing more than self-complacent Pharisaism, which values a privilege principally because its possession is an insult to somebody else who has not it.

There has been plenty of Christianity of that sort in the world, but rightly looked at there is nothing of it in the thoughts of these texts. There is only this: it cannot but be that men who yield to God and love Him and try to live near Him and do righteousness, are His, in a manner that those who steel themselves against Him and turn away from Him are not. It should be joy to believe that while all creatures have a place in His heart, and all His creatures are flooded with His benefits and get as much of Him as ever they can hold, the men who recognize the source of their blessing and turn to it with grateful hearts are nearer Him than those who do not do so. Let us take care, lest for the sake of seeming to preserve the impartiality of His love, we have destroyed all in Him that makes His love worth having. If to Him the good and the bad, the men who fear Him and the men who fear Him not, are equally satisfactory, and in the same manner the objects of an equal love, then He is not a God who has pleasure in righteousness; and if He is not a God who has pleasure in righteousness, He is not a God for me to trust to. We are not giving countenance to the notion that God has any stepchildren, any petted members of His family, when we cleave to this truth that they who have welcomed His love into their hearts are dearer to Him than those who have closed the door against it.

And there is one more point here about this matter of ownership on which I dwell for a moment; namely, that this conception of certain men being in a special sense God's possession and inheritance means also that He has a special delight in, and lofty appreciation, of them.

All this material creation exists for the sake of growing good men and women. That is the use of the things that are seen and temporal; they are like greenhouses built for the Great Gardener's use in striking and furthering the growth of His plants; and when He has got the plants He has got what He wanted, and you may pull the greenhouse down if you choose. So God estimates and teaches us to estimate the relative value and greatness of the material and the spiritual in this fashion: that He tells us in effect that all these magnificences and magnitudes round us are small and vulgar as compared with this—a heart in which wisdom and Divine truth and the love and likeness of God have attained to some tolerable measure of maturity and of strength. "These are His jewels," as the Roman matron said about her two boys. The Great Father looks upon the men who love Him as His jewels; and having got the jewels, the rock in which they were embedded and preserved may be crushed when you like. "They shall be Mine," said the Lord, "My treasures, in that day which I make."

And so, my brother, all the insignificance of man, as compared with the magnitude and duration of the universe, need not stagger our faith that the divinest thing in the universe is a heart that has learned to love God and aspire after Him, and should but increase our wonder and our gratitude, for that Christ who has been "mindful of man, and has visited the son of man," in order that He might give Himself for men, and so might win men for Himself.

II. That brings me, and very briefly, to the other points that I desire to deal with this morning. The second one which is suggested to us from my second text in the Epistle to Titus is that God owns men because God has given Himself to man.

The Apostle puts it very strongly in the Epistle to Titus: "The glorious appearing of the great God and our Savior Jesus Christ, Who gave Himself for us," "that He might purify unto Himself a *people for a possession.*"

Israel, according to one metaphor, was God's son, begotten by that great redeeming act of deliverance from the captivity of Egypt. (Deut. 32:6–19). According to another metaphor, Israel was God's bride, wooed and won for His own by that same act. Both of which just point to the thought that in order to get man for His own, He has to give Himelf to man. The very height and sublimity of that truth is found in the Christian fact which the Apostle points to here. We need not depart from human analogies here either. Christ gave Himself to us that He might get us for Himself. Absolute possession of others is only possible at the price of absolute surrender to them. No human heart ever gave itself away unless it was convinced that the heart to which it gave itself had given itself to it.

On the lower levels of human experience, the only thing that binds one man to another in utter submission is the conviction that that other has given himself in absolute sacrifice for him. A doctor goes into the wards of a hospital with his life in his hands, and because he does, he wins the respect, confidence, and affection of all who are there. You cannot buy a heart with anything less than a heart. In the barter of the world it is not skin for skin, but it is self for self. If you want to own me, you must give yourself altogether to me; and the measure in which teachers and guides, and preachers and philanthropists of all sorts make conquests of men is the measure in which they make themselves sacrifices for men.

All that is true, and is lifted to its superlative truth in the great central fact of the Christian faith. But there is more than human analogy here. Christ is not only self-sacrifice in the sense of surrender, but He is sacrifice in the sense of giving Himself for our propitiation and forgiveness. He has not only given Himself to us, He has given Himself for us. And there, and on that, is built, and on that alone, has He a right to build, or have we a right to yield, His claim of absolute authority over each of us.

He has died for us, therefore the springs of our life are at His disposal; and the strongest motives which can sway our wills are set in motion by His touch. His death, says this text, redeems us from iniquity and purifies us. That points to its power in delivering us from the service and practice of sin. He buys us from the despot whose slaves we were, and makes us His own in the hatred of evil and the doing of righteousness. Moved by His death, we become capable of heroisms and martyrdoms of devotion to Him. Brethren! It is only as that self-sacrificing love touches us, which died for our sins upon the Cross, that the diabolical chain of selfishness shall be broken from our affections and our wills, and we shall be led "into a large place" of glad surrender of ourselves to the sweetness and the gentle authority of His omnipotent love.

III. The last thought which I suggest is the issues to which the mutual possession points. God owns men, and is owned by them, in order that there may be a giving and receiving of mutual services of love.

"The Lord's portion is His people." That, in the Old Testament, is always laid as the foundation of certain obligations under which He has come, and which He will abundantly discharge. What is a great landlord expected to do to his estate? "What ought I to have done to my vineyard?" the Divine Proprietor asks through the mouth of His servant the prophet. He ought to till it, He ought not to starve it; He ought to fence it; He ought to cast a wall about it; He ought to reap the fruits. And He does all that for His inheritance. God's honor is concerned in His portion not being waste. It is not to be a garden of the sluggard, by which people who pass can see the thorns growing there. So He will till it, He will plow it, He will pick out the weeds; and all the discipline of life will come to us and the plowshare will be driven deep into the heart that "the peaceable fruit of righteousness" may spring up. He will fence His vineyard. Round about His inheritance His hand will be cast; within His people His spirit will dwell. No harm shall come near thee if thy love is given to Him. Safe and untouched by evil, thou shalt walk if thou walk with God. "He that toucheth you toucheth the apple of Mine eye." The soul that trusts Him He accepts in pledge, and before any evil can befall it He must be overcome by a stronger than He, who can take away from Him His goods, "He is able to keep that which I Have committed unto Him against that day." "The Lord's portion is His people" and "none shall pluck them out of His hand."

And on the other side, what do we owe to God as belonging to Him? What does the vineyard owe the husbandman? Fruit. We are His, therefore we are bound to absolute submission. "Ye are not your own." Life, circumstances, occupations, all; we hold them at His will. We have no more right of property in anything than a slave in the bad old days had in his cabin and patch of ground. They belonged to the master to whom he belonged. Let us recognize our stewardship and be glad to know ourselves His, and all events and things which we sometimes think ours, to be His also.

We are His, therefore we owe absolute trust. The slave has at least this blessing in his lot, that he need have no anxieties. Nor need we. We belong to God, and He will take care of us. A rich man's horses and dogs are well cared for, and our Owner will not leave us unheeded. Our well being involves His good name. Leave anxious thought to masterless hearts which have to front the world with nobody at their backs. If you are God's, you will be looked after.

We are His, therefore we are bound to live to His praise. That is the conclusion which one Old Testament passage draws. "This people have I formed for Myself; they shall show forth My praise" (Is. 43:21). The Apostle Peter quotes these words immediately after those from Exodus, which describe Israel as "a people for God's own possession," "that ye should show forth the praises of Him who hath called you." Let us then live to His glory, and remember that the servants of the king are bound to stand to their colors amid rebels, and that they who know the sweetness of possessing God and the blessedness of yielding to His supreme control should tell what they have found of His goodness, and "show forth the honor of His name, and make His praise glorious." Let not all the magnificent and wonderful expenditure of Divine longing and love be in vain, nor run off your hearts like water poured upon a rock. Surely the sun's flames leaping leagues high, they tell us, in tongues of burning gas, must melt everything that is near them. Shall we keep our hearts sullen and cold before such a fire of love? Surely that superb and wonderful manifestation of the love of God in the Cross of Christ should melt into running rivers of gratitude all the ice of our hearts.

"He gave Himself for me!" Let us turn to Him and say, "Lo! I give myself to Thee. Thou art mine. Make me Thine by the constraint of Thy love, to utterly and so saturate my spirit with Thyself that it shall not only be Thine, but in a very deep sense it shall be Thee, and that it may be no more I that live but Christ that liveth in me."

18

The Present and the Future Inheritance—God's in Us and Ours in God

Which is the earnest of our inheritance until the redemption of the purchased possession—Ephesians 1:14.

I have chosen these words this morning, and ventured to isolate them from their connection because of their bearing upon the subject of our last two sermons. You will observe that the Apostle here is evidently intending to bring together the two aspects of the reciprocal possession of God by believers, and of believers by God, which has occupied us in these discourses.

"The Holy Spirit of promise," given to all who believe, is here declared to dwell in and to seal believers as the "earnest" of their "inheritance"; while, on the other hand, that sealing is declared to last until, or, as seems more probably the rendering of the proposition here, to be done with a view unto, the full redemption of God's purchased "possession." So that the two halves of the thought are intentionally brought together in these words of our text. And about both of them—God's possession of us and our possession of God—it is asserted or implied that they are partially realized here, and are to be realized more fully in the future.

An "earnest" is a portion of the estate which is paid over to the purchaser on the completion of the purchase as the token that all is his and will come into his hands in due time. Like that part of a man's wages given to him in advance when he is engaged; like the shilling put into the hand of a recruit; like the half-crown given to the farm servant at the hiring fair; like the bit of turf that in some old ceremonials used to be solemnly presented to the sovereign on his

163

investiture; it is a portion of the whole possession, the same in kind but a very tiny portion, which yet carries with it the acknowledgment of ownership and the assurance of full possession.

So, says my test, the Spirit of God is the "earnest of the inheritance," a small portion of it granted to us today and the pledge that all shall be granted in the future. And the same idea of present imperfection is suggested in the corresponding clause, which speaks about God's *entire* purchase (for such is the emphasis in the original) of His possession as also a thing of the future.

So, then, here are the three points that I purpose to consider: first, the imperfect present; second, the present, imperfect as it is, still a guarantee and pledge of the future; and lastly, the perfect future which is the outcome of the imperfect present.

I. First a word about this imperfect present, which is put here as being on the one side the earnest of our inheritance and on the other side as being God's partial acquisition of us as His Possession.

Now you may remember, perhaps, that in the former sermons I said that we possess God in the measure in which we know Him, love Him, and have communion and sympathy with Him. These things, knowledge, love, communion, sympathy, make a very real and a very precious possession of God, and he who has God thus has Him as truly, though not as prefectly, as the angels in Heaven that bow before His throne.

But though that is true, there is yet another aspect of this possession of God suggested in the words of my text. The Holy Spirit of promise comes to every man who believes in Jesus Christ and enters into his heart and becomes his. That is the truest way in which man possesses God. The greatest gift that my faith brings down to me from Heaven is the gift of an indwelling Spirit—of an indwelling God. For the Spirit of God *is* God. He who has God in his heart by the dwelling there in mystic reality of the Divine Spirit, possesses Him as truly as he possesses love or memory, imagination or hope.

There can be no possession deeper, none greater, none more real than the possession which every one of us may have of an indwelling God for our life and our peace. It passes all human analogy. Love gives us the ownership, most really and most sweetly, of the hearts that we love; but after all the yearning desires for union and experience of oneness in sympathy, the awful wall of partition between spirits remains. Life may, and death must, separate, but he who has God's Divine Spirit with him has God for the life of his life and the soul of his soul. And we possess Him when, by faith in Jesus Christ, the Spirit of God dwells in our hearts.

But most real and most blessed as that union and possession is, my text tells us it is incomplete.

I need not dwell upon that in order to prove it; I only want to apply and urge the truth for a moment. We have an Infinite Spirit to dwell with us; how finite and little is our possession of it! The Spirit of God is set forth in Scripture under the symbol of "a rushing, mighty wind," and you and I say that we are Christ's and that we have Him. How does it come, then, that our sails flap idly on the mast, and we lie becalmed and making next to no progress? The Spirit of God is set forth in Scripture under the symbol of "flaming tongues of fire," and you and I say that we have it; how is it, then, that this thick-ribbed ice is round our hearts and our love is all so tepid? The Spirit of God is set forth in Scripture under the symbol of "rivers of water," and you and I say that we possess it. How is it, then, that so much of our hearts and of our natures is given up to barrenness, and dryness, and deadness? Oh, brethren, with an Infinite Spirit for our Guest and Indweller, any of us who look at our own hearts must feel that my text is too surely true, and that the present possession of God by the best of us is but a partial and incomplete possession.

And the same facts of wavering faith, cold affection, and imperfect consecration which show how little we have of God show likewise how little God has of us. We say that we are His, and live to please ourselves. We protest to belong to another, and to that other we render fragments of ourselves and scarcely even fragments of our time and of our efforts. His! And yet all day long never thinking of him. His! And yet from morning till night never refraining from a thing because we know it is contrary to His will, or spurred to do a thing that is contrary to ours because we know it is His. His! And yet we wallow in selfishness. His! And yet we live Godless. Christian men and women! It is only a little corner of your souls that really belongs to God. Alas, alas! For the imperfections and incompleteness of our possession of God, of Whom we hold but the merest shred, and of His possession of us, Who has conquered such a little strip of the whole field of our nature.

Now do not forget that this incompleteness of possession, looked at in both aspects, is to a certain extent inevitable and must go with us all through life. And so do not let any of us rush precipitately to the conclusion that we are *not* Christians because we find what poor Christians we are. Do not let us say, "If there were any reality in my faith it would be not a dotted line, but one continuous and unbroken." Do not let us write bitter things against ourselves because we find that we have only got "the earnest of the inheritance" and that the inheritance has not yet come.

And, on the other hand, do not make a pillow for laziness of that most certain truth, nor, because there must always be imperfections in the Christian career here, apply that as an excuse for the individual instances of imperfection as they crop up. You know, when you are honest with yourselves, that each breach of continuity in your faith and obedience might have been prevented. You know that there was no inevitable necessity for your doing that piece of badness that rises in your memory; that there was no reason that could not have been overcome for any failure of consecration or wavering of faith or act of disobedience and rebellion which has ever marked your course. Granted, that imperfection is the law, but also remember that the individual instances of imperfection are to be debited not to law but to us, and are not to be lamented over as inevitable, though painful, issues of our condition, but to be confessed as sins. "My fault, O Lord! My fault and mine only."

Many Christian people forget that if our present condition be, as it certainly is, necessarily imperfect, it ought also to be, and it will be if there be any vital force of Christian principle within us, constantly and indefinitely approximating to the ideal standard of perfection that gleams there ahead of us. Or, to put it into plainer English, if you have life you will grow. If there be any real possession of the inheritance, it will be like the rolling fences that they used to have in certain parts of the country, where a squatter settled himself down upon a bit of a royal forest and had a hedge that could be moved outwards and shifted on by degrees, till, from having begun with a little bit big enough for a cabbage garden, he ended with a piece big enough for a farm.

And that is what we are always to do, to be always acquiring, "adding field to field" in the great inheritance that is ours. But a mournfully large number of professing Christians have lost the very notion of progress and content themselves with saying, "Oh! We shall always be imperfect. As long as we are here in this world we cannot make ourselves different." No! You cannot make yourselves perfect but if you are not growing at all, I would pray you to ask yourselves if you are living at all. Do not be content, as so many of you are, to be like invaders, who, after years of occupation, are unable to advance beyond the strip of shore which they seized at first, while all the interior lies unconquered and in arms against them.

So remember that if we have any real possession of God or God of us, it will not only be an imperfect possession but an imperfect possession daily becoming more complete.

II. Now turn to the second thought here: that this imperfect present in its very imperfection is a prophecy and a pledge of a perfect future. The "earnest of our inheritance" points on to the full "redemption of the purchased possession."

The facts of Christian experience are such as that they inevitably lead up to the conclusion that there is a life beyond. All that is good and blessed about religion, our faith, the joy that comes from our faith, the sweetness of communion, the aspiration after the increase of fellowship with Him; all these, to the man who enjoys them, are the best proof that they are going to last forever and that death can have no power over them. "Like thoughts whose very sweetness yieldeth proof that they are born for immortality."

To love, to know, to reach the hands out through the shows of time and sense, and to grasp an unseen reality that lies away beyond, is, to any man who has ever experienced the emotion and done the thing, one of the strongest of all demonstrations that nothing belonging to this dusty low region of the physical can touch that immortal aspiration that knits him to God; but that whatsoever may befall the husk and shell of him, his faith, his love, his obedience, his consecration, are eternal, and may laugh at death and the grave. And

I believe that even to the men who have not that experience, the fact of religious emotion, the fact of worship, ought to be one of the best demonstrations of a future life.

But I pass that with these simple remarks, and touch another thing: the very incompleteness of our possession of God, and of God's possession of us, points onwards to, and, as it seems to me, demands a future. The imperfection, as well as the present attainments of our Christian experience, proclaim a coming time. That we are no better than we are, being as good as we are, seems to make it inconceivable that this evidently half-done work is going to be broken off short at the side of the grave.

Here is a certain force acting in a man's nature, the power of God's good Spirit, evidently capable of producing effects of entire transformation. Such being the cause, who, looking at the effects, can doubt that sometime and somewhere there will be less disproportion between the two? The engine is evidently not working full power. The characters of Christians at the best are so inconsistent and contradictory that they are evidently only in the making. It is clear that we are looking at unfinished work, and surely the great Master Builder who has laid such a foundation-stone, tried and precious, will not begin to build and be unable to finish. Every Christian life, at its best and noblest, shows, as it were, the ground plan of a great structure partly carried out—a bit of walling here, vacancy there, girders spanning wide spaces, but gaping for a roof, a chaos and a confusion. It may look a thing of shreds and patches, and they that pass by the way begin to mock. But the very fact that it is incomplete prophesies to wise men of the day when the headstone shall be brought with shouting, and the flag hoisted on the roof tree. Fools and children, says the proverb, should not see half-done work; certainly they should not judge it.

Wait a bit. There comes a time when tendencies shall be facts, and when influences shall have produced their appropriate effects; and when all that is partial and broken shall be consummate and entire in the Kingdom beyond the stars. Wait! And be sure that the good and the bad, so strangely blended in Christian experience, are alike charged with the prophecy of a glorious and perfect future.

III. Then, lastly, my text in the one clause asserts and in the other implies that the future is the perfecting of the present.

The "earnest" points onwards to an inheritance the same in kind, but immensely greater in degree. The "redemption of the possession" is a somewhat singular expression, for we are accustomed to regard the great act of redemption as already past in the sacrifice of Christ upon the Cross. But the expression is employed here, as in several other places, to express not so much the act of purchase, the paying of the price of our salvation, which is done once for all and long ago, as the historical working out of the results of that price paid in the *entire* deliverance of the *whole* nature of man from *every* form of captivity to *anything* that would prevent his *full* possession by God.

A very essential part of that entire deliverance is that which the Apostle calls the redemption of the body (Rom. 8:23), and which he there puts in contrast with the present possession of the "*firstfruits* of the Spirit," as here the redemption is contrasted with the *earnest* of the Spirit. That full deliverance takes place, according to this Epistle (4:30) at a definite future period called, therefore, "the day of redemption," which is, I suppose, the time when the whole man, body, soul and spirit, in the Resurrection glory shall be delivered from every form of evil, limitation, and sin; and shall be lifted up into the full light and knowledge of God. Then God will possess men, when the whole man is capable of holding or possessing God. Then redemption will be completed in effect, which was completed in cause and in purchase when He said, "It is finished," and bowed His head and died.

Time will not allow me to dwell upon the many thoughts involved here. One is that the main hope and glory of that future is the perfect possession of and by God.

"We shall know even as we are known." "Through a glass darkly, but then face to face," says Paul, suggesting great changes in the degree of our knowledge of, and friendly communion with, God, but also seeming to imply some unknown changes in the manner of our beholding, which may be connected with the new powers of that "body of glory" like our Lord's which will then be ours. It is quite conceivable that the physical universe may have qualities as real as light and heat, and scent and sound, which we could appreciate if we had other senses appropriate, as we have sight and touch and smell and hearing. And so it is quite conceivable that when clothed upon with our "house which is from Heaven," which will have a great many more windows in it than the earthly house of this tabernacle, which is built for stormy weather, there will be sides and aspects of the Divine nature that we do not know anything about today which shall be communicable and communicated to us.

Be that as it may, a deeper knowledge, a fixed love, an unbroken communion, with all distractions and interruptions swept clean away forever, so that we shall dwell forevermore in the House of the Lord, these are the plain elements which make the very Heaven of heavens, and which ought to make the joy of our hope. In the measure in which we know and love Him, in that measure shall we be known and loved by Him. He and we shall be so interwoven as that we shall be inseparable. We shall cleave to God and God shall cleave to us.

Oh! How small and insignificant all other notions of a future life are as compared with that! The accidents of locality and circumstance should ever be kept subordinate in the pictures which imagination may draw of what is beheld through "the gates ajar" by "little pilgrims in the unseen." The representations which seem to aim at making another world as like this one as may be, dwarf its greatness and tend to obscure the conditions of entering into its rest. "It doth not yet appear what we shall be" is as much a revelation as "When He shall appear we shall be like Him." As a great painter concentrates finish and light on the face of his sitter, and purposely keeps the rest of the picture slight, there is one face that should fill the dim, dark curtain of the future—the face of Christ—and all else may be thrown in in mere sketchy outline. We know that future chiefly by negations and by symbols, and the one positive fact is that we shall have Him and He will possess us. It is enough for the disciple that he be as, and that he be with and have his Master.

It is a solemn thought that this ultimate perfect possession of and by God is evolved from a germ which must be planted now if it is to flourish there. "The child is father of the man." Every present is the result of all the past; every future will be the result of the past and the present. Everybody admits that about this life, but there are some of us who seem to forget it with regard to another world.

We know too little of the effect that is produced upon men by the change of death to dogmatize; but one may be quite sure that the law of continuity will go on into the other world. Or, to put it into plainer English, a man on the other side of the grave will be the same as he was on this side. The line will run straight on; it may be slightly refracted by passing from an atmosphere of one density to another of a different, but it will be very slightly. The main direction will be the same.

What is there in death that can change a man's will? I can fancy death making an idiot wise, because idiocy comes from physical causes. I can fancy death giving people altogether different notions of the folly of sin; but I do not know anything in the physical fact of death or in the accompanying alterations that it produces upon spiritual consciousness, insofar as they are known to us, that can alter the dominant bias and set of a man's nature. It seems to me more likely that it will intensify that dominant bias, whatever it is; that good men will become better, and bad men worse when the limitations of incomplete organs are gone. At all events, do not run risks with such a very shaky hypothesis as that death will change the main direction of your life, but remember that what a man sows he shall reap, that the present is the parent of the future, and that unless we have the earnest of the inheritance here and pass into the other world, bearing that earnest in our hands, there seems little reason why we should expect that, when we stand before Him empty-handed, we can claim a portion therein.

I was passing a little town garden a day or two ago, which the owner had got a young weeping willow that he had put in the plot in front of his door. He had bent down its branches and put them round the hoop of an old wine cask to teach them to droop. And after a bit, when they have been set, he will take away the hoop, but though it be done, the branches will never spring upwards, wherever you transplant the tree.

Are you doing that with your souls? If you give them the downward set they will keep it though the earth to which you have fastened them be burned up with fervent heat, and the soul be transplanted into another region.

Let me beseech you to yield yourself to God in Christ, and by faith, love, and true submission to take Him for your treasure and your King. Then Heaven will perfect the partial knowledge and incomplete service of earth and will be the consummation and not the contradiction of your life here. Let it be true of you that there is none on earth whom you desire besides God, and it will be true that He will be for you the very Heaven of heavens.

19

The Servant of the Lord and His Blessing

Unto you first, God, having raised up His Servant, sent Him to bless you, in turning away every one of you from your iniquities—Acts 3:26 (Revised Version).

Six weeks passed between the crucifixion and Pentecost. The incidents recorded in this chapter must certainly have occurred very soon, if not immediately, after the Day of Pentecost. The entire revolution in the whole tone and bearing of the disciples, in that short space of a couple of months, is a problem that needs accounting for. The greatness of the change is nowhere more conspicuous than in the instance of the Apostle Peter himself: two months before, frightened out of all his faith by a saucy maidservant and a few hangers-on at Pilate's court; two months before, having buried all his hopes in his Master's grave; and now grown all at once into a hero, with altogether a new insight into Christian truth. How had it all come about? Is it to be believed that nothing had happened but Christ's death? How could that have cleared and strengthened these men's conceptions and faith? How could that have bound them far more closely together than ever they had been before? Something is wanted to account for the change.

If you bring in the Resurrection and the Ascension, and the gift of the Holy Spirit, you get an adequate explanation. If you try to get rid of these for the sake of eliminating the supernatural from the history, you get rid of the supernatural and you make it unnatural; a psychological contradiction in blank, staring antagonism to all the possibilities of the action of sane men.

These words come out of one of the three addresses belonging to this period which are preserved for us in the Book of the Acts—addresses which, in certain respects, are unlike both what the Apostles said and thought before, and what they said and thought afterwards. They bear traces of a transition period, and the facts that we meet in them some forms of speech which we do not find at a subsequent period, and that also we do not meet in them some teaching that afterwards appeared in the course of the development of Christian doctrine, are very valuable evidence that these are authentic records of the first days of the Church.

I. In dealing with these words, we may notice first the boldness and loftiness of the claim which is here made for Jesus Christ.

Long ago Peter had said, "Thou art the Christ, the Son of the living God." And as long as Jesus Christ had been with them none of them wavered in that belief; but the Cross shattered all that for a time and the sad-faced two who went down to Emmaus represented accurately the feelings of all their brethren when they said, with such a bitter emphasis upon the past tense, "We *trusted* that it had been He that should have redeemed Israel." In the interval between the death and resurrection, Jesus Christ was in the same category as "Theudas which had boasted himself to be somebody, and was slain, and all, as many as obeyed him, were scattered and brought to nought." (Acts 5:36). There had been plenty of pretenders to the Messiahship, and death had disposed of all their claims. And so it would have been with Christ and you would never have heard anything about Him unless He had risen from the dead. But the faith and hope in His Messiahship which had died with Him on the Cross rose with Him to newness of life—crucified in weakness and raised in strength and glory—as we see from such words as these of Peter here, in which he proclaims with new meaning and emphasis the mission of his Master: "God, having raised up His Son Jesus, sent Him to bless you."

Now the characteristic of these early addresses contained in the second, third and fourth chapters of the Acts, is the clear decisiveness with which they put forward Christ as the fulfillment of Jewish prophecy. It seems as if the Cross and the Resurrection had poured a flood of light on the Old Testament. Psalm and prophecy assume new significance. Lawgiver and monarch have a new purpose. They point onwards to Him, and "all they that go before cry, Hosanna, blessed be He that cometh in the name of the Lord." If we could read these discourses with sympathy for the speaker and think of them as the eager words of a man awed and surprised and gladdened as the new light floods his mind, we should know them better. To us they are rigid and cold, like iron bars; but they were all hot and fluid when they poured from his lips like metal from the furnace.

Almost every word here has reference to some great utterance of the past, which now for the first time Peter is beginning to understand.

For instance, "God, having *raised up* His Son Jesus." Now in these words there is no reference to the Resurrection, but if you look back for a verse or two you will see what there is a reference to. "Moses truly said unto the fathers: A prophet shall the Lord your God *raise up* unto you of your brethren, like unto me; Him shall ye hear in all things whatsoever He shall say unto you." And what can be more clear here than that the Apostle is claiming that the ancient prophecy of a prophet like unto his brethren, raised up by God, is fulfilled in Jesus Christ? Now that prediction from the Pentateuch, no doubt, refers to the prophetic order and the word "a prophet" is not primarily a singular, meaning an individual, but a collective, meaning a class. But still the order does not come up to the ideal of the prophecy, as was seen even before a person appeared who did. For the appendix to the Book of Deuteronomy is plainly referring to the prophecy, and declaring the shortcomings of the whole prophetic order when it sadly says, "And there arose *not* a prophet since in Israel like unto Moses." When these words were added we do not know. Evidently they presuppose the existence of a series of prophets extending through a considerable period, and if we adopted modern theories of the date of the book, these would increase the significance of these last words, considered as the verdict of experience on the inferiority of all the prophets to the great law-giver in certain specified respects. That saying at the close of the book of the law is a confession of unfulfilled hopes which still burn on, though disappointed for weary years, and still spread before God His own promise as in unspoken prayer that He would accomplish His own word on which He had caused men to hope. And it seems a perfectly legitimate position to say that the prophetic order itself was a prophecy by reason of the very incompleteness of the noble men who composed it, and that not only by their words, but by their office and by their limitations, they pointed onwards to Him who is the perfect Revealer of God to man, the perfect Inspirer, to whom God gives not His Spirit by measure, nor at intervals, and who not only, like the great law-giver, beheld God face to face, but from the beginning dwelt in the bosom of the Father and therefore declares Him perfectly to men. The manifold methods and fragmentary portions of the revelations to the prophetic order are surpassed by the one final and complete utterance in the Son, given to the world forevermore as noonday outshines the twilight dawn. He is chief of the prophets as He is Prince of all the kings of the earth and the Priest. And all this is hinted and implied in that one significant and pregnant word, "God, having *raised up* His Son."

Another great claim for Christ is suggested by that other word, "His *Son* Jesus." Now those of you who use the Revised Version will see that for "Son" is substituted "Servant," and rightly. This is not the place to enter into any discussion of the reasons for that change, but I may just perhaps in two or three sentences explain it sufficiently to my hearers who do not follow the original. The Greek word, then, which our Authorized Version translates "Son" and the Revised Version translates "Servant" means, literally, a "boy" or a "child," and like our own English equivalent, is sometimes used with the meaning of "a servant." For instance, we talk about "a boy," or "a maid," or "a man," meaning thereby to express the fact of service in a graceful and gentle way; to cover over the harsher features of authority. So the centurion in Matthew's Gospel, when he comes to Christ and asks Him to heal his little page, calls him "his boy," which our Bible properly translates as "servant"— the same word that is employed here. The reasons for adopting "servant" here rather than "son" are these: that the New Testament has a distinct expression for the "Son of God," which is not the word employed here; and that the Septuagint—the Greek version of the Old Testament—has the same expression which is employed here as the translation of the well-known phrase occurring especially in Isaiah's prophecy, "the Servant of the Lord."

Now it is interesting to notice that this expression, "the Servant of God," as applied to Jesus Christ, only occurs at this period. We never find it earlier, we never find it later. We find it here and here only, in this sermon of Peter's, and in some other words of his in the next chapter. All together, it occurs four times in these two chapters, and never again. Does not that look like the frequent repetition of a new thought which had just come to a man and was taking up his whole mind for the time? The Cross and the Resurrection had opened his eyes to see that the dim majestic figure that looked out on him from the prophecy had had a historical existence in the dear Master whom he had lived beside; and we can almost perceive the gladness and surprise swelling his heart as he thinks, "Ah! Then *He* is 'My servant whom I upheld.' Of whom speaketh the prophet this? Wonder of wonders, it is of Jesus of Nazareth, and we are His witnesses." It is not strange that that name should be ever on his lips in these days.

If you turn to the second half of Isaiah's prophecies, you will find that they might almost be called the biography of the Servant of the Lord. And while I quite admit, in the same way as I admitted about the "Prophet like unto me," that the collective Israel is often intended by the title "the Servant of the Lord," there remain other parts of the prophecy—the shining summits of the table-land, as it were—which cannot apply to any class, but have distinctly a person for their subject, and which cannot apply to any person but One, that is the Person who died and lived again.

For instance, is there any fact in the history of any community or any person which can correspond to the words, "when His soul shall make an offering for sin He shall see His seed"? Who is it whose death is the birth of His children, whom after His death He will see? Who is it whose death is His own voluntary act? Who is it whose death is a sacrifice for others' sin? Who is it whose days are protracted after death, and who carries out more prosperously the pleasure of the Lord after He has died? Surely there is but One of whom these things, and many more that are said of the Servant of the Lord, are true.

But that name on Peter's lips is not only a reference to prophecy, but it is a very beautiful revelation of the impression of absolute perfection which Christ's character made. Here was a man who "had companied with Him all the time that the Lord Jesus went in and out among them," who knew Him through and through; and the impression made upon him, when he came to think of his Master's life, was this: "All the time that I saw Him there was never a trace of anything but obedience. All His life was pure and perfect submission to the Divine will." Jesus asserted the same thing for Himself in many words. No consciousness of sin or incompleteness ever found utterance from His lips, but, on the other hand, words unexampled in the serenity of their claim to absolute purity: "I do always the things that please Him"; "Which of you convinceth Me of sin?" Strange claims from one who is meek and lowly of heart! Stranger still, the world, not usually tolerant of pretensions to sanctity, has allowed and endorsed the claim, and these humble friends of His, who stood by and watched Him, who summered and wintered with Him, bear eager witness to His perfect life.

So the claim rises up into yet loftier regions; for clearly enough, a perfect and stainless man is either an impossible monster or something more. And they who fully believe that God's will was absolutely and exclusively and completely done by Jesus Christ, in all consistency, if they will carry out their principles, must go a step further and say, "He that perfectly did the Father's will was more than one of us stained and sinful men." There is one biography, and there is but one, on the title page of which might be written, "Lo, I come. I delight to do Thy will, O my God," and the last page of which might truly bear, "He did no sin, neither was guile found in His mouth"—and God and man, and Heaven with its attendant angels, and hell with its baffled Prince, would attest the words.

II. Now, turn to the next point that comes out of the words before us, the dawning vision of a kingdom of worldwide blessings.

Peter and all his brethren had had their full share of Jewish prejudices. But I suppose that when they found the tongues of fire sitting on their heads, and when they found themselves speaking in so many different languages, even they began to apprehend that they had been entrusted with a worldwide gospel; and Pentecost taught them, if it taught nobody else, that Christ's Kingdom was to cover all the earth. The words before us mark very clearly the growing of that consciousness of the worldwide destination of the Gospel, while yet the Jewish prerogative of precedence is firmly held. "Unto you *first*," that was the law of the apostolic working. But they were beginning to learn that if there were a "first," there must also be a "second," and that the very words of promise to the father of the nation which he had just quoted pointed to "all the nations of the earth" being blessed in the seed of Abraham.

If Israel was first to receive the blessing, it was only that through Israel it might flow over into the whole Gentile world. That is the true spirit of "Judaism," which is so often spoken of as "narrow" and "exclusive." There is nothing clearer in the Old Testament than that, according to its view, the fire is kindled in Israel that it may give warmth to all who are in the house, and the candle is lighted in Israel in order that it might shed light on all the chambers of the world. Israel was the first recipient, in order that it might be the transmitter of God's light and knowledge to all the world. That was the genius of "Judaism," and that is Peter's faith here.

Then again, what grand confidence is here! What a splendid audacity of faith it is for the Apostle with his handful of friends to stand up in the face of his nation to say, "This Man, whom you hung on a tree, is going to be the blessing of the whole world."

Why! It is like the old Roman story of putting up to auction in the Forum the very piece of land that the enemy's camp was pitched upon, while their tents were visible over the wall. So magnificent was their confidence that victory is certain.

And how did all that come? Was all that heroism and enthusiasm of confident success born out of the grave of a dead man, do you think? I do not believe it, and I do not think anybody that has an eye for the probabilities of human conduct will believe it. But the Resurrection was the foundation of it, and explains it as nothing else can do.

III. The last thing to be observed here is the purely spiritual conception of what Christ's blessing is. "To bless you in turning away every one of you from his iniquities."

What has become of all the Jewish notions of the blessings of Messiah's Kingdom? Most of them, no doubt, had faded away, as the meaning of and need for the Cross began to be more clear, and the high and pure conception of Christ's work which it teaches began to take definiteness in their minds. That had not been the kind of kingdom of which they had dreamed when they had sought to be first in it. But now the Cross had taught Peter that, as he says in one of his other early discourses, Him hath God raised up a Prince and a Savior to give, strange gift for a prince to have in his hand, "to give repentance unto Israel, and remission of sins."

The heart, then, of Christ's work for the world is deliverance from sin. That is what man needs most. There are plenty of other remedies offered for the world's ills: culture, art, new political and social arrangements, progress of science and the like. God forbid that I should say a word that might seem to depreciate these, but I tell you, and your own consciences tell you, that the disease goes deeper than these things can cure. The Bible diagnoses the disease grimly and gravely, because it knows it can cure it. You may as well try to put out Vesuvius with a teaspoonful of cold water as to cure the sickness of humanity with anything that does not grapple with the fundamental mischief, and that is a wicked heart. There is only one Man who ever pretended He could deal with that, and that is Jesus Christ. And it took *Him* all His power to deal with it; but He did it! And there is only one way by which *He* could deal with it, and that was by dying for it, and He did it! So He has conquered.

"Canst thou draw out leviathan with a hook?" When you can lead a crocodile out of the Nile with a bit of silk thread round his neck, you will be able to overcome the plague of the world, and that of your own heart, with anything short of the great sacrifice made by Jesus Christ.

The one thing the world wants is the blessing He alone can give, and that blessing is deliverance from sin. No man will understand Christ's Gospel unless He begins there. I believe that the secret of most of the mistaken and partial views of Christian truth lies here, that people have not got into their hearts and consciences a sense of their own sinfulness. And so you get a tepid, self-sufficient and superficial Christianity; and you get ceremonials, and high and dry morality, masquerading under the guise of religion: and you get Unitarian and semi-Unitarian tendences in churches and preachers and thinkers. But if once there came a wholesome, living consciousness of what is meant when men say, "We are sinners," all such mutilated Christianity would crumble because it would be felt to be all inadequate to the needs of the conscience.

So, brethren, I beseech you to put yourself in the right place to understand the Gospel by the recognition of that fact. But do not stop there. More than the right understanding of Christianity is at stake. It is a matter of life and death for you to put yourselves in the right place to receive Christ's richest blessing. You can only do that by feeling in your own conscience the fact of your own personal sin, and so coming to Him to do for you what you cannot do for yourselves, and no one but He can do for you, deliver you from your sins by His forgiving love, and turn you from the inclination to them by His sanctifying Spirit.

And notice how strongly the text puts the individuality of this process. "Everyone," or rather, "each one" singly to be turned, and so, as it were, universality reached through the multitude of single souls. If all kindreds of earth are to be blessed, they are to be blessed one by one, as every one is turned from his iniquities. The inadequate notions of Christianity that I have been speaking about are all characterized by this among other things: that they regard it as a social system diffusing social blessings and operating on communities by elevating the general tone and quickening the public conscience, and so on. Christianity does do that. But it begins with dealing with men one by one, and men must deal one by one with it, or they will never get its highest blessings.

Christ is like a great King, who, passing through the streets of His capital, scatters His *largesse* over the multitude, but He reserves His richest gifts for the men who enter His presence chamber. Even those of us who have no close personal union with Him receive of His gifts. Every man, woman and child in England is better and purer today because Christ died on the Cross. But for their deepest needs and their highest blessings, they must go to Christ by their own personal faith. As the old mystics defined prayer, so I might define faith: the flight of the solitary soul to the only Christ. You must go to Him by yourself and for yourself, and receive into your own hands the blessing which is for the world. The strait gate, like the wicket at some public hall, takes in one at a time. Blessed be God! There is nothing to pay as you pass through, and when you pass you enter into a large place.

20

The Gradual Healing of the Blind Man

And Jesus cometh to Bethsaida; and they bring a blind man unto Him, and besought Him to touch him. And He took the blind man by the hand, and led him out of the town; and when He had spit on his eyes, and put His hands upon him, He asked him if he saw aught. And he looked up, and said, I see men as trees walking. After that He put His hands upon his eyes and made him look up; and he was restored and saw every man clearly—Mark 8:22–25.

This miracle, which is only recorded by the Evangelist Mark, has about it several very peculiar features. Some of these it shares with one other of our Lord's miracles, which also is found only in this Gospel, and which occurred nearly about the same time; that miracle of healing the deaf and dumb man recorded in the previous chapter. Both of them have these points in common: that our Lord takes the sufferer apart and works His miracle in privacy; that in both there is an abundant use of the same singular means—our Lord's touch, and the saliva upon His finger—and that in both there is the urgent injunction of entire secrecy laid upon the recipient of the benefit.

But this miracle had another peculiarity, in which it stands absolutely alone, and that is that the work is done in stages; that the power which at other times has but to speak and it is done, here seems to labor, and the cure comes slowly; that in the middle, Christ pauses and, like a physician trying the experiment of a drug, asks the patient if any effect is produced, and getting the answer that some mitigation is realized, repeats the application and perfect recovery is the result.

Now, how unlike that is to all the rest of Christ's miraculous working we do not need to point out, but the question may arise, what is the meaning, and what the reason, and what the lessons of this unique and anomalous form of miraculous working? It is to that question that I wish to turn now, for I think that the answer will open up to us some very precious things in regard to that great Lord, the revelation of whose heart and character is the inmost and the loftiest meaning both of His words and of His works.

I take these three points of peculiarity to which I have referred: the privacy, the strange and abundant use of means veiling the miraculous power, and the gradual, slow nature of the cure. I see in them these three things: Christ isolating the man that He would heal; Christ stooping to the sense-bound nature by using outward means; and Christ making His power work slowly, to keep abreast of the man's slow faith.

I. First, then, here we have Christ isolating the man whom He wanted to heal. Now there may have been something about our Lord's circumstances and purposes at the time of this miracle which accounted for the great urgency with which at this period He impresses secrecy upon all around Him. What that was it is not necessary for us to inquire here, but this is worth noticing, that in obedience to this wish, on His own part, for privacy at the time, He covers over with a veil His miraculous working and does it quietly, as one might almost say, in a corner. He never sought to display His miraculous working; here He absolutely tries to hide it. That fact of Christ taking pains to conceal His miracle carries in it two great truths: first, about the purpose and nature of miracles in general, and second, about His character, as to each of which a few words may be said.

This fact of a miracle done in intended secrecy and shrouded in deep darkness suggests to us the true point of view from which to look at the whole subject of miracles.

People say they were meant to be attestations of His Divine mission. Yes, no doubt that is true partially, but that was never the sole or even the main purpose for which they were wrought; and when anybody asked Jesus Christ to work a miracle for that purpose only, He rebuked the desire and refused to gratify it. He wrought the miracle, not coldly, in order to witness to His mission, but every one of them was the token, because it was the outcome, of His own sympathetic heart, brought into contact with human need. And instead of the miracles of Jesus Christ being cold, logical proofs of His mission, they were all glowing with the earnestness of a loving sympathy, and came from Him at sight of sorrow as naturally as rays from the sun.

Then, on the other hand, the same fact carries with it, too, a lesson about His character. Is not He here doing what He tells us to do: "Let not thy left hand know what thy right hand doeth?" He dares not wrap His talent in a napkin; He would be unfaithful to His mission if He hid His light under a bushel. All goodness "does good by stealth," even if it does not "blush to find it fame," and that universal mark of true benevolence marked His. He had to solve in His human life what we have to solve, the problem of keeping the narrow path between ostentation of powers and selfish concealment of faculty; and He solved it thus, leaving us an example that we should follow in His steps.

But that is somewhat aside from the main purpose to which I wanted to turn in these first remarks. Christ did not invest the miracle with any of its peculiarities for His own sake only. All that is singular about it, will, I think, find its best explanation in the condition and character of the subject, the man on whom it was wrought. What sort of a man was he? Well, the narrative does not tell us much, but if we use our historical imagination and our eyes we may learn something about him. First, he was a Gentile; the land in which the miracle was wrought was the half-heathen country on the east side of the Sea of Galilee. In the second place, it was other people who brought him; he does not come of his own accord. Then again, it is their prayer that is mentioned, not his—he asks nothing.

You see him standing there, hopeless, listless, not believing that this Jewish stranger is going to do anything for him, with his impassive blind face glowing with no entreaty to reenforce his companions' prayers. And suppose he is a man of that sort, with no expectation of anything from this Rabbi, how is Christ to get at him? It is no use talking to him. His eyes are shut, so he cannot see the sympathy beaming in His face. There is one thing possible—to lay hold of Him by the hand; and the touch, gentle, loving, firm, says this, at least: "Here is a man who has some interest in me, and whether He can do anything or not for me, He is going to try something." Would not that kindle an expectation in him? And is it not in parable just exactly what Jesus Christ does for the whole world? Is not that act of His by which He put out His hand and seized the unbelieving limp hand of the blind man that hung by his side the very same, in principle, as that by which He "taketh hold of the seed of Abraham," and is made like to His brethren? Is not the mystery of the Incarnation and the meaning of it wrapped up as in a germ in that little simple incident, "He put out His hand and touched him?"

Is there not in it, too, a lesson for all you goodhearted Christian men and women, in all your work? If you want to do anything for your Master and brethren, there is only one way to do it—to come down to their level and get hold of their hands, and then there is some chance of doing them good. We must be content to take the hands of beggars if we are to make the blind to see.

And then, having thus drawn near to the man and established in his heart some dim expectation of something coming, He gently draws him away out of the little village. I wonder no painter has ever painted that, instead of repeating *ad nauseam* two or three scenes out of the Gospels. I wonder none of them has ever seen what a parable it is—the Christ leading the blind man out into solitude before He can say to him, "Behold!" How as they went, step by step, the poor blind eyes not telling the man where they were going, or how far away he was being taken from his friends, his conscious dependence upon this stranger would grow! How he would feel more and more at each step, "I am at His mercy! What *is* He going to do with me?" And how thus there would be kindled in his heart some beginnings of an expectation, as well as some surrendering of himself to Christ's guidance! These two things, the expectation and the surrender, have in them, at all events, some faint beginnings and rude germs of the highest faith, to lead up to which is the purpose of all that Christ here does.

And is not that what He does for us all? Sometimes by sorrows, sometimes by sickbeds, sometimes by shutting us out from chosen spheres of activity, sometimes by striking down the dear ones at our sides and leaving us lonely in the desert. Is He not saying to us in a thousand ways, "Come ye yourselves apart into a desert place"? As Israel was led into the wilderness that God might "speak to her heart," so often Christ draws us aside, if not by outward providences such as these, yet by awaking in us that solemn sense of personal responsibility and making us feel our solitude, that He may lead us to feel His all-sufficient companionship.

Ah! brethren, here is a lesson from all this: if you want Jesus Christ to give you His highest gifts and to reveal to you His fairest beauty, you must be alone with Him. He loves to deal with single souls. Our lives, many of them, can never be outwardly alone. We are jammed up against one another in such a fashion, and the hurry and pressure of city life is so great with us all that it is often impossible for us to find the outward secrecy and solitude. But a man may be alone in a crowd; the heart may be gathered up into itself, and there may be a still atmosphere round about us in the shop and in the market, and among the busy ways of men, in which we and Christ shall be alone together. Unless there be, I do not think any of us will see the King in His beauty or the far-off land. "I was left alone, and I saw this great vision" is the law for all true beholding.

So, dear brethren, try to feel how awful this earthly life of ours is in its necessary solitude; that each of us by himself must shape out his own destiny, and make his own character; that every unit of the swarms upon our streets is a unit that has to face the solemn facts of life for and by itself; that alone you live, that alone you will die; that alone you will have to give account of yourself before God, and in the solitude let the hand of your heart feel for His hand that is stretched out to grasp yours, and listen to Him saying, "Lo! I am with you always, to the end of the world." There was no dreariness in the solitude when it was *Christ* who "took the blind man by the hand and led him out of the city."

II. We have Christ stooping to a sense-bound nature by the use of material helps. No doubt there was something in the man, as I have said, which made it advisable that these methods should be adopted. If he were the sort of person that I have described, slow of faith, not much caring about the possibility of cure, and not having much hope that anything would come of it, then we can see the fitness of the means adopted; the hand laid upon the eyes, the finger possibly moistened with saliva touching the ball, the pausing to question, the repeated application. They make a ladder by which his hope and confidence might climb to the apprehension of the blessing. And that points to a general principle of the Divine dealings. God stoops to a feeble faith and gives to it outward things by which it may rise to an apprehension of spiritual realities.

Is not that the meaning of the whole complicated system of Old Testament revelation? Is not that the meaning of the altars, and priests, and sacrifices, and the old cumbrous apparatus of the Mosaic law? Was it not all a picture book in which the infant eyes of the race might see in a material form deep spiritual realities? Was not that the meaning and explanation of our Lord's parabolic teaching? He veils spiritual truth in common things that He may reveal it by common things: taking fishermen's boats, their nets, a sower's basket, a baker's dough, and many another homely article, and finding in them the emblems of the loftiest truth.

Is not that the meaning of His own Incarnation? It is no use talking to men about God, let them see Him; no use preaching about principles, give them the facts of His life. Revelation does not consist in the setting forth of certain propositions about God, but in the exhibition of the acts of God in a human life.

> And so the Word was flesh and wrought
> With human hands the creed of creeds.

And still further, may we not say that this is the inmost meaning and purpose of the whole frame of the material universe? It exists in order that, as a parable and a symbol, it may proclaim the things that are unseen and eternal. Its depths and heights, its splendors, and its energies are all in order that through them spirits may climb to the apprehension of the "King eternal, immortal, invisible," and the realities of His spiritual kingdom.

So in regard to all the externals of Christianity, forms of worship, ordinances, and so on, all these, in like manner, are provided in condescension to our weakness, in order that by them we may be lifted above themselves; for the purpose of the temple is to prepare for the time and the place where the seer "saw no temple therein." They are but the cups that carry the wine, the flowers whose chalices bear the honey, the ladders by which the soul may climb to God Himself, the rafts upon which the precious treasure may be floated into our hearts.

If Christ's touch and Christ's saliva healed, it was not because of anything in them, but because He willed it so; and He Himself is the source of all the healing energy. Therefore, let us keep these externals in their proper place of subordination, and remember that in Him, not in them, lies the healing power; and that even Christ's touch may become the object of superstitious regard, as it was when that poor woman who came through the crowd to lay her finger on the hem of His garment, thinking that she could bear away a surreptitious blessing without the conscious outgoing of His power. He healed her because there was a spark of faith in her superstition, but she had to learn that it was not the hem of the garment but the loving will of Christ that cured, in order that the dross of superstitious reliance on the outward vehicle might be melted away, and the pure gold of faith in His love and power might remain.

III. Lastly, we have Christ accommodating the pace of His power to the slowness of the man's faith.

The whole story, as I have said, is unique, and especially that part of it, "He put His hands upon him, and asked him if he saw aught." One might have expected an answer with a little more gratitude in it, with a little more wonder in it, with a little more emotion in it. Instead of these it is almost surly, or at any rate strangely reticent— a matter-of-fact answer to the question, and there an end. As our Revised Version reads it better: "I see men, for I behold them as trees walking." Curiously accurate! A dim glimmer had come into the eye, but there is not yet distinctness of outline or sense of magnitude, which must be acquired by practice. The eye has not yet been educated, and it was only because these blurred figures were in motion that he knew they were not trees. "After that He put His hands upon his eyes and made him look up." Or as the Revised Version has it with a better reading, "and he looked steadfastly." An eager straining of the new faculty to make sure that he had got it, and to test its limits and its perfection. "And he was restored and saw all things clearly."

Now I take it that the worthiest view of that strangely protracted process, broken up into two halves by the question that is dropped into the middle, is this: that it was determined by the man's faith and was meant to increase it. He was healed slowly because he believed slowly. His faith was a condition of his cure, and the measure of it determined the measure of the restoration; and the rate of the growth of his faith settled the rate of the perfecting of Christ's work on him. As a rule, faith in His power to heal was a condition of Christ's healing, and that mainly because our Lord would rather have men believing than sound of body. They often wanted only the outward miracle, but He wanted to make it the means of insinuating a better healing into their spirits. And so, not that there was any necessary connection between their faith and the exercise of His miraculous power, but in order that He might bless them with His best gifts, He usually worked on the principle, "According to your faith be it unto you." And here, as a nurse or a mother with her child might do, He keeps step with the little steps, and goes slowly because the man goes slowly.

Now both the gradual process of illumination and the rate of that process as determined by faith are true for us. How dim and partial a glimmer of light comes to many a soul at the outset of the Christian life! How little a new convert knows about God and self and the starry truths of His great revelation! Christian progress does not consist in seeing new things, but in seeing the old thing more clearly: the same Christ, the same Cross, only more distinctly and deeply apprehended, and more closely incorporated into my very being. We do not grow away from Him, but we grow into knowledge of Him. The first lesson that we get is the last lesson that we shall learn, and He is the Alpha at the beginning, and the Omega at the end of the alphabet, the letters of which make up our knowledge for earth and Heaven.

But then let me remind you that just in the measure in which you expect blessing of any kind, illumination and purifying and help of all sorts from Jesus Christ, just in that measure will you get it. You can limit the working of Almighty power and can determine the rate at which it shall work on you. God fills the water pots to the brim, but not beyond the brim; and if, like the woman in the Old Testament story, we stop bringing vessels, the oil will stop flowing. It is an awful thing to think that we have the power, as it were, to turn a stopcock and so increase or diminish or cut off altogether the supply of God's mercy and Christ's healing and cleansing love in our hearts. You will get as much of God as you want and no more. The measure of your desire is the measure of your capacity, and the measure of your capacity is the measure of God's gift. "Open thy mouth wide and I will fill it." And if your faith is heavily shod and steps slowly, His power and His grace will step slowly along with it, keeping rank and step. "According to your faith shall it be unto you."

Ah! Dear friends, "Ye are not straitened in Me, ye are straitened in yourselves." Desire Him to help and bless you, and He will do it. Expect Him to do it, and He will do it. Go to Him like the other blind man, and say to Him, "Jesus, Thou Son of David, have mercy on me, that I may receive my sight," and He will lay His hand upon you, and at any rate a glimmer will come, which will grow in the measure of your humble, confident desire, until at last He takes you by the hand and leads you out of this poor little village of a world, and lays His finger for a brief moment of blindness upon your eyes and asks you if you see aught. Then you look up, and the first face that you behold shall be His, whom you saw "as through a glass darkly" with your dim eyes in this twilight world.

May that be your experience and mine, through His mercy!

21

The Name above Every Name

Therefore let all the house of Israel know assuredly that God hath made that same Jesus, Whom ye have crucified, both Lord and Christ—Acts 2:36.

It is no part of my purpose at this time to consider the special circumstances under which these words were spoken, or even to enter upon an exposition of their whole scope. I select them for one reason: the occurrence in them of the three names by which we designate our Savior—Jesus, Christ, Lord. To us they are very little more than three proper names; they were very different to these men who listened to the characteristically vehement discourse of the Apostle Peter. It wanted some courage to stand up at Pentecost and proclaim on the housetop what he had spoken in the ear long ago. "Thou art the Christ, the Son of the living God!" To most of his listeners to say, "Jesus is the Christ," was folly, and to say, "Jesus is the Lord," was blasphemy.

The three names are names of the same Person, but they proclaim altogether different aspects of His work and His character. The name "Jesus" is the name of the Man, and brings to us a brother; the name "Christ" is the name of office, and brings to us a Redeemer; the name "Lord" is the name of dignity, and brings to us a King.

I. First, then, the name Jesus is the name of the Man, which tells us of a Brother.

There were many men in Palestine who bore the name of Jesus when He bore it. We find that one of the early Christians had it, and it comes upon us with almost a shock when we read that one "Jesus, called Justus," was the name of one of the friends of the

Apostle Paul (Col. 4:11). But, through reverence on the part of Christians, and through horror on the part of Jews, the name ceased to be a common one. And its disappearance from familiar use has hid from us the fact of its common employment at the time when our Lord bore it. Though it was given to Him as indicative of His office of saving His people from their sins, yet none of all the crowds who knew Him as Jesus of Nazareth supposed that in His name there was any greater significance than in those of the "Simons," "Johns," and "Judahs," in the circle of His disciples.

Now the use of Jesus as the proper name of our Lord is very noticeable. In the Gospels, as a rule, it stands alone hundreds of times, while in combination with any other of the titles it is rare. "Jesus Christ," for instance, only occurs, if I count right, twice in Matthew, once in Mark, twice in John. But if you turn to the Epistles and the latter books of the Scriptures, the proportions are reversed. There you have hundreds of instances of the occurrence of such combinations as "Jesus Christ," "Christ Jesus," "The Lord Jesus," "Christ the Lord," and not frequently the full solemn title, "The Lord Jesus Christ." But the occurrence of the proper name "Jesus" alone is the exception. So far as I know, there are only some thirty or forty instances of its use singly in the whole of the books of the New Testament outside of the four Evangelists. The occasions where it is used are all of them occasions in which one may see that the writer's intention is to put strong emphasis, for some reason or other, on the Manhood of our Lord Jesus, and to assert as broadly as may be, His entire participation with us in the common conditions of our human nature, corporeal and mental.

And I think I shall best bring out the meaning and worth of the name by putting a few of these instances before you.

For example, we find more than once phrases like this: "we believe that *Jesus* died," "having therefore boldness to enter into the holiest by the blood of *Jesus*," and the like, which emphasize His death as the death of a man like ourselves, and bring us close to the historical reality of His human pains and agonies for us. "*Christ* died" is the statement which makes the purpose and efficacy of His death more plain, but "*Jesus* died" shows us His death as not only the work of the appointed Messiah, but as the act of our brother man, the outcome of His human love, and never rightly to be understood if His work be thought of apart from His personality.

There is brought into view, too, prominently, the side of Christ's sufferings which we are all apt to forget—the common human side of His agonies and His pains. I know that a certain school of preachers and of unctuous religious hymns and other forms of composition dwell, a great deal too much for reverence, upon the mere physical aspect of Christ's sufferings. But the temptation, I believe, with most of us is to dwell too little upon that, to argue about the death of Christ, to think about it as a matter of speculation, to regard it as a mysterious power, to look upon it as an official act of the Messiah who was sent into the world for us; and to forget that He bore a manhood like our own, a body that was impatient of pains and wounds and sufferings, and a human life which, like all human lives, naturally recoiled and shrank from the agony of death.

And while, therefore, the great message, "It is Christ that died," is ever to be pondered, we have also to think with sympathy and gratitude on the homelier representation coming nearer to our hearts, which proclaims that "Jesus died." Let us not forget the Brother's manhood that had to agonize, and to suffer, and to die as the price of our salvation.

Again, when the Scripture would set our Lord before us, as in His humanity, our pattern and example, it sometimes uses this name in order to give emphasis to the thought of His Manhood, as, for example, in the words of the Epistle to the Hebrews, "looking unto Jesus, the Author and Perfector of faith." That is to say, a mighty stimulus to all brave perseverance in our efforts after higher Christian nobleness lies in the vivid and constant realization of the true manhood of our Lord, as the type of all goodness, as having Himself lived by faith, and that in a perfect degree and manner. We are to turn away our eyes from contemplating all other lives and motives, and to "look off" from them to Him. In all our struggles, let us think of Him. Do not take poor human creatures for your ideal of excellence, nor tune your harps to their keynotes. To imitate men is degradation, and is sure to lead to deformity; none of them is a safe guide. Black veins are in the purest marble, and flaws in the most lustrous diamonds, but to imitate Jesus is freedom, and to be like Him is perfection. Our code of morals is His life. He is the Ideal incarnate. The secret of all progress is, "Run, looking unto Jesus."

Then, again, we have His manhood emphasized when His sympathy is to be commended to our hearts. "The great High Priest, who is passed into the heavens" is *"Jesus"* . . . "who was in all points tempted like as we are." To every sorrowing soul, to all men burdened with heavy tasks, unwelcome duties, pains and sorrows of the imagination, or of the heart, or of the memory, or of physical life, or of the circumstances—to all there comes the thought, "Every ill that flesh is heir to" He knows by experience and in the Man Jesus we find not only the pity of a God but the sympathy of a Brother.

The Prince of Wales, a fortnight ago, went for an afternoon into the slums in Holborn, and everybody said, and said deservedly, "right" and "princely." *This* Prince has "learned pity in the huts where poor men lie," and knows by experience all their squalor and misery. The Man Jesus is the sympathetic Priest. The Rabbis, who did not usually see very far into the depth of things, yet caught a wonderful glimpse when they said, "Messiah will be found sitting outside the gate of the city *amongst the lepers."* That *is* where He sits, and the perfectness of His sympathy, and the completeness of His identification of Himself with all our tears and our sorrows, is taught us when we learn that our High Priest is not merely Christ the official, but Jesus the Man.

And then you read such words as these: "If we believe that *Jesus* died and rose again, even so them also which sleep in Jesus will God bring with Him." I think anybody who reads with sympathy must feel how very much closer to our hearts that consolation comes, "Jesus rose again," than even the mighty word which the Apostle uses on another occasion, "Christ is risen from the dead." The one tells us of the risen Redeemer, the other tells us of the risen Brother. And wherever there are sorrowing souls, learning loss and following their dear ones into the darkness with yearning hearts, there, too, the consolation comes; they lie down beside their Brother and with their Brother they shall rise again.

So, again, most strikingly, and yet somewhat singularly, in the words of Scripture which paint most loftily the exaltation of the risen Savior to the right hand of God, and His wielding of absolute power and authority, it is the old human name that is used; as if the writers would bind together the humiliation and the exaltation, and were holding up hands of wonder at the thought that a Man had risen thus to the Throne of the Universe. What an emphasis and glow of hope there is in such words as these, "We see not yet all things put under Him, but we see *Jesus*," the very Man who was here with us, "crowned with glory and honor." So in the Book of Revelation the chosen name for Him that sits amid the glories of the heavens, and settles the destinies of the universe, and orders the course of history, is Jesus. As if the Apostle would assure us that the face which looked down upon him from amid the blaze of the glory was indeed the face that he knew long ago upon earth, and the breast that "was girded with a golden girdle" was the breast upon which he so often had leaned his happy head.

. So the ties that bind us to the Man Jesus should be the human bonds that knit us to one another, transferred to Him and purified and strengthened. All that we have failed to find in men we can find in Him.

Human wisdom has its limits, but here is a Man whose word is truth, who is Himself the truth. Human love is sometimes hollow, often impotent; it looks down upon us, as a great thinker has said, like the Venus of Milo, that lovely statue, smiling in pity, but it has no arms. But here is a love that is mighty to help, and on which we can rely without disappointment or loss. Human excellence is always limited and imperfect, but here is One whom we may imitate and be pure. So let us do like that poor woman in the Gospel story—bring the precious alabaster box of ointment, the love of these hearts of ours, which is the most precious thing we have to give. The box of ointment that we have so often squandered upon unworthy heads, let us come and pour it upon His, not unmingled with our tears, and anoint Him, our beloved and our King. This Man has loved each of us with a brother's heart; let us love Him with all our hearts.

II. So much for the first name. The second, "Christ," is the name of office, and brings to us a Redeemer. I need not dwell at any length upon the original significance and force of the name; it is familiar, of course, to us all. It stands as a transference into Greek of the Hebrew Messiah, the one and the other meaning, as we all know, the Anointed.

But what is the meaning of claiming for Christ that He is anointed? A sentence will answer the question. It means that He fulfills all which the inspired imagination of the great ones of the past had seen in that dim Figure that rose before the prophet and psalmist. It means that He is anointed or inspired by the Divine indwelling to be Prophet, Priest, and King all over the world. It means that He is, though the belief had faded away from the minds of His generation, a sufferer while a Prince, and to "turn away unrighteousness" from the world, and not from "Jacob" only, by a sacrifice and a death.

I cannot see less in the contents of the Jewish idea, the prophetic idea of the Messiah, than these points: Divine inspiration or anointing; a sufferer who is to redeem; the fulfiller of all the rapturous visions of psalmist and of prophet in the past.

And so, when Peter stood up among that congregation of wondering strangers and scowling Pharisees and said: "The Man that died on the Cross, the Rabbi-peasant from half-heathen Galilee, is the Person Whom all the generations have been looking forward to," no wonder that nobody believed him except those whose hearts were touched, for it is never possible for the common mind at any epoch to believe that the man who stands beside them is very much bigger than themselves. Great men have always to die and get a halo of distance around them before their true stature can be seen.

And now two remarks are all I can afford myself upon that, and one is this: the hearty recognition of His Messiahship is the center of all discipleship. The earliest and the simplest Christian creed, which yet, like the little brown roll in which the infant beech leaves lie folded up, contains in itself all the rest, was this: "Jesus is Christ," and although it is no part of my business to say how much imperfection and confusion of head comprehension may exist with a heart acceptance of Jesus that saves a soul from sin, yet I cannot in faithfulness to my own convictions conceal the belief that he who contents himself with "Jesus" and does not grasp "Christ" has cast away the most valuable and characteristic part of the Christianity which he professes. Surely the most simple inference is that a *Christian* is at least a man who recognizes the Christship of Jesus. And I press that upon you, my friends; it is not enough for the sustenance of your own souls and for the cultivation of a vigorous religious life that men should admire, however profoundly and deeply the humanity of the Lord, unless that humanity leads them on to see the office of the Messiah to whom their whole hearts cleave. "Jesus is the Christ" is the minimum Christian creed.

And then, still further, let me remind you how the recognition of Jesus as Christ is essential to giving its full value to the facts of the manhood. Jesus died! Yes! What then? What is that to me? Is that all I have to say? If that is simply a human death, like all the rest, I want to know what makes it a Gospel. I want to know what more interest I have in it than I have in the death of Socrates, or in the death of any men or women whose names were in the obituary column of yesterday's newspaper. "Jesus died." That is the fact. What is wanted to turn the fact into a Gospel? That I shall know Who it was who died, and why He died. "I declare unto you the Gospel which I preach," Paul says, "how that *Christ* died for our sins, according to the Scriptures." The belief that the death of Jesus was the death of the Christ is needful to make that death the means of my deliverance from the burden of sin. If it be only the death of Jesus, it is beautiful, pathetic, as many another martyr's has been, but if it be the death of Christ, then "my faith can lay her hand" on that great sacrifice and know "her guilt was there."

So in regard to His perfect example. If we only see His manhood when we are "looking unto Jesus," the contemplation of His perfection would be as paralyzing as spectacles of supreme excellence usually are. But when we can say, "*Christ* also suffered for us, leaving us an example," and so can deepen the thought of His Manhood into that of His Messiahship and the conception of His work as example into that of His work as sacrifice, we can hope that His Divine power will dwell in us to mold our lives to the likeness of His human life of perfect obedience.

So in regard to His resurrection and glorious ascension at the right hand of God. We have not only to think of the solitary man raised from the grave and caught up to the throne. If it were only "Jesus" Who rose and ascended, His resurrection and ascension might be as much to us as the raising of Lazarus, or the rapture of Elijah; namely, a demonstration that death did not destroy conscious being and that a man could rise to Heaven, but they would be no more. But if "*Christ* is risen from the dead," He is "become the first-fruits of them that slept." If *Jesus* has gone up on high, others may or may not follow in His train. It may show that manhood is not incapable of elevation to heaven, but it has no power to draw others up after it. But if *Christ* is gone up, He is gone to prepare a place for us, not to fill a solitary throne, and His ascension is the assurance that He will lift us, too, to dwell with him and share His triumph over death and sin.

Most of the blessedness and beauty of His example, all the mystery and meaning of His death, and all the power of His resurrection depend on the fact that "it is *Christ* that died, yea rather, that is risen again, who is even at the right hand of God."

III. "The Lord" is the name of dignity and brings before us the King. There are three grades, so to speak, of dignity expressed by this one word "Lord" in the New Testament. The lowest is that in which it is almost the equivalent of our own English title of respectful courtesy, "Sir," in which sense it is often used in the Gospels, and refers to our Lord as to many others of the persons there. The second is that in which it expresses dignity and authority, and in that sense it is frequently applied to Christ. The third highest is that in which it is the equivalent of the Old Testament "Lord," as a Divine name; in which sense also it is applied to Christ in the New Testament.

The first and last of these may be left out of consideration now; the central one is the meaning of the word here. I have only time to touch upon two thoughts: to connect this name of dignity first with one and then with the other of the two names that we have already considered.

"Jesus is Lord"; that is to say, wonderful as it is, the manhood is exalted to supreme dignity. It is the teaching of the New Testament, that our nature in Jesus, the Child of Mary, sits on the throne of the universe and rules over all things. Those rude herdsmen, brothers of Joseph, came into Pharaoh's palace (strange contrast to their tents) and there found their brother ruling over that ancient and highly civilized land! We have the Man Jesus for the Lord over all. Trust His dominion and rejoice in His rule, and bow before His authority. Jesus is Lord.

Christ is Lord. That is to say, His sovereign authority and dominion are built upon the fact of His being Deliverer, Redeemer, Sacrifice. His Kingdom is a Kingdom that rests upon His suffering. "Wherefore God also hath exalted Him, and given Him a name that is above every name."

It is because He wears a vesture dipped in blood that on the vesture is the name written, "King of kings, and Lord of lords." It is "because He shall deliver the needy when he crieth," as the prophetic psalm has it, that "all kings shall fall down before Him and all nations shall serve Him." Because He has given His life for the world He is the Master of the world. His humanity is raised to the throne because His humanity stooped to the cross. As long as men's hearts can be touched by absolute unselfish surrender, and as long as men can know the blessedness of responsive surrender, so long will He who gave Himself for the world be the Sovereign of the world, and the Firstborn from the dead be the Prince of all the kings of the earth.

And so, dear friends, our thoughts today all point to this lesson. Do not you content yourselves with a maimed Christ. Do not tarry in the Manhood; do not be content with an adoring reverence for the nobility of His soul, the gentle wisdom of His words, the beauty of His character, the tenderness of His compassion. All that will be of small help for your needs. There is more in His mission than that; even His death for you and for all men. Take Him for your Christ, but do not lose the Person in the Work, any more than you lose the Work in the Person. And be not content with an intellectual recognition of Him, but bring Him the faith which cleaves to Him and His work as its only hope and peace, and the love which, because of His work as Christ, flows out to the beloved Person Who has done it all. Thus loving Jesus and trusting Christ, you will bring obedience to your Lord and homage to your King, and learn the sweetness and power of the name that is above every name, the name of the Lord Jesus Christ.

May we all be able, with clear and unfaltering conviction of the understanding and loving affiance of our whole souls, to repeat as our own the grand words in which so many centuries have proclaimed their faith—words which shed a spell of peacefulness over stormy lives, and fling a great light of hope into the black jaws of the grave. "I believe in Jesus Christ, His only Son, our Lord!"

22

The Son of Man

Who is this Son of Man?—John 12:34

Last Sunday, as you may remember, we were considering the names given in Scripture to our Lord Jesus Christ. I have thought that a suitable sequel to that sermon may be one devoted to the consideration of the remarkable name which our Lord gives to Himself: the Son of Man. And I have selected this instance of its occurrence rather than any other because it brings out a point which is too frequently overlooked; viz., that the name was an entirely strange and enigmatical one to the people who heard it.

This question of utter bewilderment distinctly shows us that, and negates, as it seems to me, the supposition which is often made that the name "Son of Man" upon the lips of Jesus Christ was equivalent to Messiah. Obviously there is no such significance attached to it by those who put this question. As obviously, for another reason, the two names do not cover the same ground; for our Lord sedulously avoided calling Himself the Christ, and habitually called Himself the Son of Man.

Now one thing to observe about this name is that it is never found upon the lips of any but Jesus Christ. No man ever called Him the Son of Man while He was upon earth, and only once do we find it applied to Him in the rest of Scripture; and that is on the occasion on which the first martyr, Stephen, dying at the foot of the old wall, saw "the heavens opened, and the Son of Man standing at the right hand of God." Two other apparent instances of the use of the expression occur, both of them in the Book of Revelation, both of them quotations from the Old Testament, and in both the more probable reading gives, *A* Son of Man, not "*the* Son of man."

One more preliminary remark and I will pass to the title itself. The name has been often supposed to be taken from the remarkable prophecy in the Book of Daniel, of one "like a Son of man," who receives from the Ancient of Days an everlasting kingdom which triumphs over those kindgdoms of brute force which the prophet had seen. No doubt there is a connection between the prophecy and our Lord's use of the name, and it is to be observed that what the prophet speaks of is not "the Son," but "one *like a* Son of man," or, in other words, that what the prophecy dwells upon is simply the manhood of the future King in contradistinction to the bestial forms of Lion and Leopard and Bear, whose kingdoms go down before him. Of course Christ fulfills that prediction and is the "One like a Son of man," but we cannot say that the title is derived from the prophecy, in which, strictly speaking it does not occur.

What, then, is the force of this name, as applied to Himself by our Lord?

First, we have in it Christ putting out His hand, if I may say so, to draw us to Himself, identifying Himself with us. Then we have, just as distinctly, Christ, by the use of this name, in a very real sense distinguishing Himself from us, and claiming to hold a unique and solitary relation to mankind. And then we have Christ, by the use of this name in its connection with the ancient prophecy, pointing us onward to a wonderful future.

I. First then, Christ thereby identifies Himself with us. The name Son of Man, whatever more it means, declares the historical fact of His Incarnation and the reality and genuineness, the completeness and fullness of His assumption of humanity. And so it is significant to notice that the name is employed continually in the places in Scripture where special emphasis is to be placed, for some reason or other, upon our Lord's manhood. As, for instance, when He would bring into view the depth of His humiliation. It is this name that He uses when He says, "Foxes have holes and the birds of the air have nests, but the Son of Man hath not where to lay His head." The use of the term there is very significant and profound;

He contrasts His homelessness not with the homes of men who dwell in palaces, but with the homes of the inferior creatures. As if He would say, "Not merely am I individually homeless and shelterless, but I am so because I am truly a man, the only creature that builds houses and the only creature that has not a home. Foxes have holes, anywhere they can rest; the birds of the air have," not as our Bible gives it, "nests," but "roosting places; any bough will do for them. All living creatures are at home in this material universe; I, as a Representative of humanity, wander a pilgrim and a sojourner." We are all restless and homeless; the creatures correspond to their environment. We have desires and longings, wild yearnings, and deep-seated needs, that "wander through eternity"; the Son of Man, the representative of manhood, "hath not where to lay His head."

Then the same expression is employed on occasions when our Lord desires to emphasize the completeness of His participation in all our conditions. As, for instance, "the Son of Man came eating and drinking," knowing the ordinary limitations and necessities of corporeal humanity, having the ordinary dependence upon external things, nor unwilling to taste, with pure and thankful lip, whatever gladnesses may be found in man's path through the supply of natural appetites.

And the name is employed habitually on occasions when He desires to emphasize His manhood as having truly taken upon itself the whole weight and weariness of man's sin, and the whole burden of man's guilt, and the whole tragicalness of the penalties thereof. As in the familiar passages, so numerous that I need only refer to them and need not attempt to quote them, in which we read of the Son of Man being betrayed into the hands of sinners; in those words, for instance, which so marvelously blend the lowliness of the Man and the lofty consciousness of the mysterious relation which He bears to the whole world: "The Son of Man came not to be ministered unto, but to minister, and to give His life a ransom for the many."

Now if we gather all these instances (and they are only specimens culled almost at random) together and meditate for a moment on the name as illuminated by such words as these, they suggest to us, first, how truly and how blessedly He is "bone of our bone, and flesh of our flesh." All our human joys were His. He knew all human sorrow. The ordinary wants of human nature belonged to Him; He hungered, He thirsted and was weary; He ate and drank and slept. The ordinary wants of the human heart He knew; He was hurt by hatred, stung by ingratitude, yearned for love; His spirit expanded among friends and was pained when they fell away. He fought and toiled, and sorrowed and enjoyed. He had to pray, to trust and to weep. He was a Son of Man, a true man among men. His life was brief; we have but fragmentary records of it for three short years. In outward form it covers but a narrow area of human experience, and large tracts of human life seem to be unrepresented in it. Yet all ages and classes of men, in all circumstances, however unlike those of the peasant Rabbi who died when He was just entering mature manhood, may feel that this Man comes closer to them than all beside. Whether for stimulus for duty, or for grace and patience in sorrow, or for restraint in enjoyment, or for the hallowing of all circumstances and all tasks, the presence and example of the Son of Man are sufficient. Wherever we go, we may track His footsteps by the drops of His blood upon the sharp flints that we have to tread. In all narrow passes, where the briars tear the wool of the flock, we may see, left there on the thorns, what they rent from the pure fleece of the Lamb of God that went before. The Son of Man is our Brother and our Example.

And is it not beautiful, and does it not speak to us touchingly and sweetly of our Lord's earnest desire to get very near us and to bring us very near to Him, that this name, which emphasizes humiliation and weakness, and the likeness to ourselves, should be the name that is always upon His lips? Just as, if I may compare great things with small, some teacher or philanthropist who went away from civilized into savage life might leave behind him the name by which he was known in Europe, and adopt some barbarous designation that was significant in the language of the savage tribe to whom he was sent, and say to them, "That is my name now, call me by that"—so this great Leader of our souls who has landed upon our coasts with His hands full of blessings, His heart full of love, has taken a name that makes Him one of ourselves, and is never wearied of speaking to our hearts and telling us that it is that by which He chooses to be known. It is a touch of the same infinite condescension which prompted His coming, that makes Him choose as His favorite and habitual designation the name of weakness and identification, the name "Son of Man."

II. But, now, turn to what is equally distinct and clear in this title. Here we have our Lord distinguishing Himself from us and plainly claiming a unique relationship to the whole world.

Just fancy how absurd it would be for one of us to be perpetually insisting on the fact that he was a man, to be taking that as his continual description of himself, and pressing it upon people's attention as if there was something strange about it! The idea is preposterous, and the very frequency and emphasis with which the name comes from our Lord's lips lead one to suspect that there is something lying behind it more than appears on the surface. That impression is confirmed and made a conviction if you mark the article which is prefixed, *the* Son of Man. *A* son of man is a very different idea. When He says, "*the* Son of man," He seems to declare that in Himself there are gathered up all the qualities that constitute humanity; that He is, to use modern language, the realized Ideal of manhood, the typical Man, in Whom is everything that belongs to manhood, and Who stands forth as complete and perfect.

Appropriately, then, the name is continually used with suggestions of authority and dignity contrasting with those of humiliation. "The Son of Man is Lord of the Sabbath." "The Son of Man hath power on earth to forgive sins," and the like. So that you cannot get away from this, that this Man Whom the whole world has conspired to profess to admire for His gentleness, and His meekness, and His lowliness, and His religious sanity, stood forward and said, "I am complete and perfect, and everyything that belongs to manhood you will find in Me."

And it is very significant in this connection that the designation occurs more frequently in the first three Gospels than in the fourth; which is alleged to present higher notions of the nature and personality of Jesus Christ than are found in the other three. There are more instances in Matthew's Gospel in which our Lord calls Himself the Son of Man, with all the implication of uniqueness and completeness which that name carries, there are more even in the Gospel of the Servant, the Gospel according to Mark, than in the Gospel of the Word of God, the Gospel according to John. And so I think we are entitled to say that by this name, which the testimony of all four Gospels makes it certain, even to the most suspicious reader, that Christ applied to Himself, He declared His humanity, His absolutely perfect and complete humanity.

In substance He is claiming the same thing for Himself that Paul claimed for Him when he called Him the second Adam. There have been two men in the world, says Paul: the fallen Adam, with his infantile and undeveloped perfections, and the Christ, with His full and complete humanity. All other men are fragments, He is the "entire and perfect chrysolite." As one of our epigrammatic seventeenth century divines has it, "Aristotle is but the rubbish of an Adam," and Adam is but the dim outline sketch of a Jesus. Between these two there have been none. The one Man as God meant him, the type of man, the perfect humanity, the realized ideal, the home of all the powers of manhood, is He who Himself claimed that place for Himself, and stepped into it with the strange words upon His lips: "I am meek and lowly of heart."

"Who is this Son of Man?" Ah! brethren, "who can bring a clean thing out of an unclean? Not one." A perfect Son of Man, born of a woman, "bone of our bone and flesh of our flesh," must be more than a Son of Man. And that moral completeness and that ideal perfection in all the faculties and parts of His nature which drove the betrayer to clash down the thirty pieces of silver in the sanctuary in despair that "he had betrayed innocent blood"; which made Pilate wash his hands "of the blood of this just person"; which stopped the mouths of the adversaries when He challenged them to convince Him of sin, and which all the world ever since has recognized and honored, ought surely to lead us to ask the question, "Who is this Son of Man?" and to answer it, as I pray we all may answer it, "Thou art the Christ, the Son of the living God."

This fact of absolute completeness invests His work with an altogether unique relationship to the rest of mankind. And so we find the name employed upon His own lips in connections in which He desires to set Himself forth as the single and solitary medium of all blessing and salvation to the word. As, for instance, "The Son of Man came to give His life a ransom for the many"; "Ye shall see the Heavens opened, and the angels of God ascending and descending on the Son of Man." He is what the ladder was in the vision to the patriarch, with his head upon the stone and the Syrian sky over him, the Medium of all communication between earth and Heaven. And that ladder which joins Heaven to earth, and brings all angels down on the solitary watchers comes straight down, as the sunbeams do, to every man wherever he is. Each of us sees the shortest line from his own standing place to the central light, and its beams come straight to the apple of each man's eye. So because Christ is more than a man, because He is *the* Man, His blessings come to each of us direct and straight, as if they had been launched from the throne with a purpose and a message to us alone. Thus He who is in Himself perfect manhood touches all men, and all men touch Him, and the Son of Man, whom God hath sealed, will give to every one of us the bread from heaven. The unique relationship which brings Him into connection with every soul of man upon earth, and makes Him the Savior, Helper, and Friend of us all, is expressed when He calls Himself the Son of Man.

III. And now one last word in regard to the predictive character of this designation. Even if we cannot regard it as being actually a quotation of the prophecy in the Book of Daniel, there is an evident allusion to that prophecy, and to the whole circle of ideas presented by it of an everlasting dominion, which shall destroy all antagonistic power, and of a solemn coming for judgment of one like a Son of Man.

We find, then, the name occurring on our Lord's lips very frequently in that class of passages with which we are so familiar, and which are so numerous that I need not quote them to you, in which he speaks of the second coming of the Son of Man. As, for instance, that one which connects itself most distinctly with the Book of Daniel, the words of high solemn import before the tribunal of the High Priest. "Hereafter shall ye see the Son of Man sitting at the right hand of power and coming in the glories of heaven." Or, as when He says, "He hath given Him authority to execute judgment also because He is the Son of Man." Or as when the proto-martyr, with his last words declared in sudden burst of surprise and thrill of gladness, "I see the heavens opened, and the Son of Man standing at the right hand of God."

Two thoughts are all that I can touch on here. The name carries with it a blessed message of the present activity and perpetual manhood of the risen Lord. Stephen does not see Him, as all the rest of Scripture paints Him, *sitting* at the right hand of God, but *standing* there. The emblem of His sitting at the right hand of God represents triumphant calmness in the undisturbed confidence of victory. It declares the completeness of the work that He has done upon earth, and that all the history of the future is but the unfolding of the consequences of that work which by His own testimony was finished when He bowed His head and died. But the dying martyr sees Him *standing*, as if He had sprung to His feet in response to the cry of faith from the first of the long train of sufferers. As if the Emperor upon His seat looking down upon the arena where the gladiators are contending to the death, could not sit quiet among the flashing axes of the lictors and the purple curtains of His throne and see their death-struggles, but must spring to His feet to help them, or at least bend down with the look and with the reality of sympathy. So Christ, the Son of Man, bearing His manhood with Him,

> Still bends on earth a brother's eye;

and is the ever-present Helper of all struggling souls who put their trust in Him.

Then, as to the other and main thought here in view, the second coming of that perfect Manhood to be our Judge. It is too solemn a subject for human lips to say much about. It has been vulgarized, and the power taken out of it by many well-meant attempts to impress it upon men's hearts. But that *coming is certain*. That manhood could not end its relationship to us with the Cross, nor yet with the slow, solemn, upward progress which bore Him, pouring down blessings, up into the same bright cloud that had dwelt between the cherubim and had received Him into its mysterious recesses at the Transfiguration. That He should come again is the only possible completion of His work.

That Judge is our brother. So in the deepest sense we are tried by our Peer. Man's knowledge at its highest cannot tell the moral desert of anything that any man does. You may judge action, you may sentence for breaches of law, you may declare a man clear of any blame for such, but for any man to read the secrets of another man's heart is beyond human power; and if he were only a man who is the Judge, there will be wild work and many a blunder in the sentences that are given. But when we think that it is the Son of Man who is our Judge, then we know that the Omniscience of Divinity that ponders the hearts and reads the motives will be all blended with the tenderness and sympathy of Humanity; that we shall be judged by One who knows all our frame, not only with the knowledge of a Maker, if I may so say, as from outside, but with the knowledge of a possessor, as from within; that we shall be judged by One who has fought and conquered in all temptations, and, most blessed of all, that we shall be judged by One with whom we have only to plead His own work and His own love and His Cross that we may stand acquitted before His throne.

So, brethren, in that one mighty name all the past, present, and future are gathered and blended together. In the past, His Cross fills the retrospect; for the future, there rises up, white and solemn, His Judgment throne "The Son of Man *is* come to give His life a ransom for the many." That is the center point of all history. The Son of man *shall* come to judge the world. That is the one thought that fills the future. Let us lay hold by true faith on the mighty work which He has done on the Cross; then we shall rejoice to see our Brother on the throne when the "judgment is set and the books are opened." Oh, friends, cleave to Him ever in trust and love, in communion and imitation, in obedience and confession, that ye may be accounted worthy "to stand before the Son of Man" in that day.

23

Two Fortresses

The name of the Lord is a strong tower; the righteous runneth into it, and is safe. The rich man's wealth is his strong city, and as a high wall in his own conceit
—Proverbs 18:10, 11.

The mere reading of these two verses shows that, contrary to the usual rule in the Book of Proverbs, they have a bearing on each other. They are intended to suggest a very strong contrast, and that contrast is even more emphatic in the original than in our translation because, as the margin of your Bibles will tell you, the last word of the former verse might be more correctly rendered, "the righteous runneth into it and is set on high." It is the same word which is employed in the next verse: "a high wall."

So we have "the strong tower" and the "the strong city"; the man lifted up above danger on the battlements of the one, and the man fancying himself to be high above it (and only fancying himself) in the imaginary safety of the other.

I. Consider then, first, the two fortresses.

One need only name them side by side to feel the full force of the intended contrast. On the one hand, the Name of the Lord with all its depths and glories, with its blaze of lustrous purity, and infinitudes of inexhaustible power; and on the other, "the rich man's wealth." What contempt is expressed in putting the two side by side! It is as if the author had said, Look on this picture and on this! Two fortresses! Yes! The one is like Gibraltar, inexpugnable on its rock; and the other is like a painted castle on the stage, flimsy canvas that you could put your foot through—solidity by the side of nothingness. For even the poor appearance of solidity is an illusion, as our text says with bitter emphasis, "a high wall in his own conceit."

"The name of the Lord," of course, is the Biblical expression for the whole character of God, as He has made it known to us, or, in other words, for God Himself, as He has been pleased to reveal Himself to mankind. The syllables of that name are all the needs of which He has taught us what He is; every act of power, of wisdom, of tenderness, of grace that has manifested these qualities and led us to believe that they are all infinite. In the name, in its narrower sense, the name of *Jehovah,* there is much of "the name" in its wider sense. For that name "Jehovah," both by its significance and by the circumstances under which it was originally employed, tells us a great deal about God. It tells us, for instance, by virtue of its signification, that He is self-existent, depending upon no other creature. "I AM THAT I AM!" No other being can say that. All the rest of us have to say, "I am that which God made me." Circumstances and a hundred other things have made me; God finds the law of His being and the fountain of His being within Himself.

> He sits on no precarious throne,
> Nor borrows leave to be.

His name proclaims Him to be self-existent, and as self-existent, eternal; and as eternal, changeless; and as self-existent, eternal, changeless, infinite in all the qualities by which He makes Himself known. This boundless Being, all full of wisdom, power, and tenderness, with whom we can enter into relations of amity and concord, surely He is "a strong tower into which we may run and be safe."

But far beyond even the sweep of that great name, Jehovah, is the knowledge of God's deepest heart and character which we learn in Him who said, "I have declared Thy name unto My brethren, and will declare it." Christ in His life and death, in His meekness, sweetness, gentleness, calm wisdom, infinite patience, attractiveness; yearning over sinful hearts, weeping over rebels, in the graciousness of His life, in the sacredness and the power of His Cross, is the Revealer to our hearts of the heart of God. If I may so say, He has built "the strong tower" broader, has expanded its area and widened its gate, and lifted its summit yet nearer the heavens, and made the name of God a wider name and a mightier name, and a name of surer defense and blessing than ever it was before.

And so, dear brethren, it all comes to this, the name that is "the strong tower" is the name "My Father!" A Father of infinite tenderness and wisdom and power. Oh! Where can the child rest more quietly than on the mother's breast, where can the child be safer than in the circle of the father's arms? "The name of the Lord is a strong tower."

Now turn to the other for a moment: "The rich man's wealth is" (with great emphasis on the next little word) "*his* strong city, and as a high wall in his own conceit." Of course we have not to deal here only with wealth in the shape of money, but all external and material goods, the whole mass of the "things seen and temporal," are gathered together here in this phrase.

Men use their imaginations in very strange fashion, and make, or fancy they make, for themselves out of the things of the present life a defense and a strength. Like some poor lunatic out upon a moor, who fancies himself ensconced in a castle; like some barbarous tribes behind their stockades or crowding at the back of a little turf wall, or in some old tumbledown fort that the first shot will bring rattling down about their ears, fancying themselves perfectly secure and defended, so do men deal with these outward things that are given them for another purpose altogether: they make of them defenses and fortresses.

It is difficult for a man to have them and not to trust them. So Jesus said to His disciples once, "How hardly shall they that have riches enter into the Kingdom"; and when they were astonished at His words, He repeated them with the significant variation, "How hard is it for them that trust in riches to enter into the Kingdom of God." So He would teach that the misuse and not the possession of wealth is the barrier, but so, too, He would warn us that, nine times out of ten, the possession of them in more than a very modest measure, tempts a man into confidence in them.

The illusion is one that besets us all. We are all tempted to make a defense of the things that we can see and handle. Is it not strange, and is it not sad, that most of us just turn the truth round about and suppose that the real defense is the imaginary, and that the imaginary one is the real? How many men are there in this chapel who, if they spoke out of their deepest convictions, would say, "Oh yes! the promises of God are all very well, but I would rather have the cash down. I suppose that I may trust that He will provide bread and water, and all the things that I need, but I would rather have a good solid balance at the banker's." How many of you would rather honestly, and at the bottom of your hearts, have that than God's word for your defense? How many of you think that to trust in a living God is but grasping at a very airy and unsubstantial kind of support, and that the real solid defense is the defense made of the things that you can see?

My brother! It is exactly the opposite way. Turn it clean round and you get the truth. The unsubstantial shadows are the material things that you can see and handle; illusory as a dream, and as little able to ward off the blows of fate as a soap bubble. The real is the unseen beyond—"the things that *are*," and He who alone really is, and in His boundless and absolute Being is our only defense.

In one aspect or another, that false imagination with which my last text deals is the besetting sin of Manchester. Not the rich man only, but the poor man just as much, is in danger of it. The poor man who thinks that everything would be right if only he were rich, and the rich man who thinks that everything is right because he is rich, are exactly the same man. The circumstances differ, but the one man is but the other turned inside out. And all round about us we see the fierce fight to get more and more of these things, the tight grip of them when we have got them, the overestimate of the value of them, the contempt for the people who have less of them than ourselves. Our aristocracy is an aristocracy of wealth, in some respects, one by no means to be despised, because there often go a great many good qualities to the making and the stewardship of wealth; but still it is an evil that men should be so largely estimated by their money as they are here. It is not a sound state of opinion which has made "what is he *worth*?" mean "how much of *it* has he?" We are taught here to look upon the prizes of life as being mainly wealth. To win that is "success," "prosperity," and it is very hard for us all not to be influenced by the prevailing tone.

I would urge you young men, especially, to lay this to heart: that of all delusions that can beset you in your course, none will work more disastrously than the notion that the summum bonum, the shield and stay of a man, is the "abundance of the things that he possesses." I fancy I see more listless, discontented, unhappy faces looking out of carriages than I see upon the pavement. And I am sure of this, at any rate, that all which is noble and sweet and good in life can be wrought out and possessed upon as much bread and water as will keep body and soul together, and as much furniture as will enable a man to sit at his meal and lie down at night. And as for the rest, it has many advantages and blessings, but oh! It is all illusory as a defense against the evils that will come, sooner or later, to every life.

II. Consider next how to get into the true Refuge.

"The righteous runneth into it and is safe," says my text. You may get into the illusory one very easily. Imagination will take you there. There is no difficulty at all about that. And yet the way by which a man makes this world his defense may teach you a lesson as to how you can make God your defense. How does a man make this world his defense? By trusting to it. He who says to the fine gold, "Thou art my confidence," has made it his fortress; and that is how you will make God your fortress, by trusting to Him. The very same emotion, the very same act of mind, heart, and will, may be turned either upwards or downwards, as you can turn the beam from a lantern which way you please. Direct it earthwards and you "trust in the uncertainty of riches." Flash it heavenwards and you "trust in the living God."

And that same lesson is taught by the words of our text, "The righteous runneth into it." I do not dwell upon the word "righteous." That is the Old Testament point of view, which could not conceive it possible that any man could have deep and close communion with God except on condition of a pure character. I will not speak of that at present, but point to the picturesque metaphor which will tell us a great deal more about what faith is than many a philosophical dissertation. Many a man who would be perplexed by a theologian's talk will understand this: "The righteous runneth into the name of the Lord."

The metaphor brings out the idea of eager haste in betaking one-self to the shelter, as when an invading army comes into a country, and the unarmed peasants take their portable belongings and their cattle, and catch up their children in their arms and set their wives upon their mules and make all haste to some fortified place; or as when the manslayer in Israel fled to the city of refuge, or as when Lot hurried for his life out of Sodom. There would be no dawdling then, but with every muscle strained, men would run into the stronghold, counting every minute a year till they were inside its walls, and heard the heavy door close between them and the pursuer. No matter how rough the road, or how overpowering the heat—no time to stop to gather flowers or even diamonds on the road, when a moment's delay might mean the enemy's sword in your heart!

Now that metaphor is frequently used to express the resolved and swift act by which, recognizing in Jesus Christ, who declares the name of the Lord, our hidingplace, we shelter ourselves in Him and rest secure. One of the picturesque words by which the Old Testament expressed "trust" means literally "to flee to a refuge." The Old Testament *trust* is the New Testament *faith,* even as the Old Testament *"Name of the Lord"* answers to the New Testament *"Name of Jesus."* And so we run into this sure hidingplace and strong fortress of the name of the Lord, when we betake ourselves to Jesus and put our trust in Him as our defense.

Such a faith—the trust of mind, heart, and will—laying hold of the name of the Lord, makes us "righteous," and so capable of "dwelling with the devouring fire" of God's perfect purity. The Old Testament point of view was righteousness, in order to abide in God. The New Testament begins, as it were, at an earlier stage in the religious life and tells us how to get the righteousness, without which, it holds as strongly as the Old Testament, "no man shall see the Lord." It shows us that our faith, by which we run into that fortress, fits us to enter the fortress because it makes us partakers of Christ's purity.

So my earnest question to you all is, Have you "fled for refuge to lay hold" on that Savior in whom God has set His name? Like Lot out of Sodom, like the manslayer to the city of refuge, like the unwarlike peasants to the baron's tower, before the border thieves, have you gone thither for shelter from all the sorrows and guilt and dangers that are marching terrible against you? Can you take up as yours the old grand words of exuberant trust in which the Psalmist heaps together the names of the Lord, as if walking about the city of his defense, and telling the towers thereof, "The Lord is my rock, and my fortress, and my deliverer; my God, my strength, in whom I will trust; my buckler, and the horn of my salvation, and my high tower"? If you have, then "because you have made the Lord your refuge, there shall no evil befall you."

III. So we have, lastly, what comes of sheltering in these two refuges.

As to the former of them, I said at the beginning of these remarks that the words "is safe" were more accurately as well as picturesquely rendered by "is set aloft." They remind us of the psalm which has many points of resemblance with this text, and which gives the very same thought when it says, "I will set him on high, because he hath known My name." The fugitive is taken within the safe walls of the strong tower, and is set up high on the battlements, looking down upon the baffled pursuers, and far beyond the reach of their arrows. To stand upon that tower lifts a man above the region where temptations fly, above the region where sorrow strikes; lifts him above sin and guilt and condemnation and fear, and calumny and slander, and sickness, and separation and loneliness and death; "and all the ills that flesh is heir to."

Or, as one of the old Puritan commentators has it: "The tower is so deep that no pioneer can undermine it, so thick that no cannon can breach it, so high that no ladder can scale it." "The righteous runneth into it," and is perched up there; and can look down like Lear from his cliff and all the troubles that afflict the lower levels shall "show scarce so gross as beetles" from the height where he stands, safe and high, hidden in the name of the Lord.

I say little about the other side. Brethren, the world in any of its forms, the good things of this life in any shape, whether that of money or any other, can do a great deal for us. They can keep a great many inconveniences from us, they can keep a great many cares and pains and sorrows from us. I was going to say, to carry out the metaphor, they can keep the rifle bullets from us. But, ah! When the big siege guns get into position and begin to play, when the great trials that every life must have sooner or later come to open fire at us, then the defense that anything in this outer world can give comes rattling about our ears very quickly. It is like the pasteboard helmet which looked as good as if it had been steel, and did admirably as long as no sword struck it.

There is ony one thing that will keep us peaceful and unharmed, and that is to trust our poor shelterless lives and sinful souls to the Savior who has died for us. In Him we find the hidingplace, in which, secure, as beneath the shadow of a great rock, dreaded evils will pass us by, as impotent to hurt as savages before a castle fortified by modern skill. All the bitterness of outward calamities will be taken from them before they reach us. Their arrows will still wound, but He will have wiped the poison off before He lets them be shot at us. The force of temptation will be weakened, for if we live near Him we shall have other tastes and desires. The bony fingers of the skeleton Death, who drags men from all other homes, will not dislodge us from our fortress dwelling. Hid in Him we shall neither fear going down to the grave or coming up from it, nor judgment, nor eternity. Then, I beseech you, make no delay, Escape! Flee for your life! A growing host of evil marches swift against you. Take Christ for your defense and cry to Him,

> Lo! from sin and grief and shame,
> Hide me, Jesus! in Thy name.

24

The Sacrifice of the Body

I beseech you, therefore, brethren, by the mercies of God, that ye present your bodies a living sacrifice, holy, acceptable unto God, which is your reasonable service—Romans 12:1.

In the former part of this letter, the Apostle has been building up a massive fabric of doctrine, which has stood the waste of centuries and the assaults of enemies, and has been the home of devout souls. He now passes to speak of practice, and he binds the two halves of his letter indissolubly together by that significant "therefore," which does not only look back to the thing last said but to the whole of the preceding portion of the letter. "What God hath joined together let no man put asunder." Christian living is inseparably connected with Christian believing. Possibly the error of our forefathers was in cutting faith too much loose from practice and supposing that an orthodox creed was sufficient, though I think the extent to which they did suppose that has been very much exaggerated. The temptation of this day is precisely the opposite. "Conduct is three-fourths of life," says one of our teachers. Yes. But what about the fourth fourth which underlies conduct? Paul's way is the right way. Lay broad and deep the foundation of God's facts revealed to us, and then build upon that the fabric of a noble life. This generation superficially tends to cut practice loose from faith, and so to look for grapes from thorns and figs from thistles. Wrong thinking will not lead to right doing. "I beseech you, therefore brethren, that ye present your bodies a living sacrifice."

The Apostle, in beginning his practical exhortations, lays as the foundations of them all two companion precepts: one, with

221

which we have to deal, affecting mainly the outward life; its twin sister, which follows in the next verse, affecting mainly the inward life. He who has drunk-in the spirit of Paul's doctrinal teaching will present his body a living sacrifice, and be renewed in the spirit of his mind; and thus, outwardly and inwardly, will be approximating to God's ideal and all specific virtues will be his in germ. Those two precepts lay down the broad outline, and all that follow in the way of specific commandments is but filling in its details.

I. We observe that we have here, first, an all-inclusive directory for the outward life.

Now it is to be noticed that the metaphor of sacrifice runs through the whole of the phraseology of my text. The word rendered "present" is a technical expression for the sacerdotal action of offering. A tacit contrast is drawn between the sacrificial ritual, which was familiar to Romans as well as Jews, and the true Christian sacrifice and service. In the former, a large portion of the sacrifices consisted of animals which were slain. Ours is to be "a living sacrifice." In the former, the offering was presented to the Deity, and became His property. In the Christian service, the gift passes, in like manner, from the possession of the worshiper and is set apart for the uses of God, for that is the proper meaning of the word "holy." The outward sacrifice gave an odor of a sweet smell, which, by a strong metaphor, was declared to be fragrant in the nostrils of Deity. In like manner, the Christian sacrifices were purely outward and derived no efficacy from the disposition of the worshiper. Our sacrifice, though the material of the offering be corporeal, is the act of the inner man, and so is called "rational" rather than "reasonable," as our Version has it, or as in other parts of Scripture, "spiritual." And the last word of my text, "service," retains the sacerdotal allusion, because it does not mean the service of a slave or domestic, but that of a priest.

And so the sum of the whole is that the master word for the outward life of a Christian is sacrifice. That, again, includes two things: self-surrender and surrender to God.

Now Paul was not such a superficial moralist as to begin at the wrong end and talk about the surrender of the outward life unless as the result of the prior surrender of the inward, and that priority of the consecration of the man to his offering of the body is contained in the very metaphor. For a priest needs to be consecrated before he can offer, and we in our innermost wills, in the depths of our nature, must be surrendered and set apart to God ere any of our outward activities can be laid upon His altar. The Apostle, then, does not make the mistake of substituting external for internal surrender, but he presupposes that the latter has preceded. He puts the sequence more fully in the parallel passage in this very letter: "Yield yourselves unto God, and your bodies as instruments of righteousness unto Him." So, then, first of all, we must be priests by our inward consecration, and then, since "a priest must have somewhat to offer," we must bring the outward life and lay it upon His altar.

Now of the two thoughts which I have said are involved in this great keyword, the former is common to Christianity, with all noble systems of morality, whether religious or irreligious. It is a commonplace, on which I do not need to dwell, that every man who will live a man's life and not that of a beast must sacrifice the flesh, and rigidly keep it down. But that commonplace is lifted into an altogether new region, assumes a new solemnity, and finds new power for its fulfillment when we add to the moralist's duty of control of the animal and outward nature the other thought, that the surrender must be to God.

There is no need for my dwelling at any length on the various practical directions in which this great exhortation must be wrought out. It is of more importance, by far, to have well fixed in our minds and hearts the one dominant thought that sacrifice is the keyword of the Christian life than to explain the directions in which it applies. But still, just a word or two about these. There are three ways in which we may look at the body, which the Apostle here says is to be yielded up unto God.

It is the recipient of impressions from without. *There* is a field for consecration. The eye that looks upon evil, and by the look has rebellious, lustful, sensuous, foul desires excited in the heart, breaks this solemn law. The eye that among the things seen dwells with complacency on the pure, and turns from the impure as if a hot iron had been thrust into its pupil; that in the things seen discerns shimmering behind them, and manifested through them, the things unseen and eternal, is the consecrated eye. "Art for art's sake," to quote the cant of the day, has too often meant art for the flesh's sake. And there are pictures and books, and sights of various sorts, flashed before the eyes of you young men and women which it is pollution to dwell upon, and should be pain to remember. I beseech you all to have guard over these gates of the heart and to pray, "Turn away mine eyes from viewing vanity." And the other senses, in like manner, have need to be closely connected with God if they are not to rush us down to the devil.

The body is not only the recipient of impressions. It is the possessor of appetites and necessities. See to it that these are indulged with constant reference to God. It is no small attainment of the Christian life "to eat our meat with gladness and singleness of heart, praising God." In a hundred directions, this characteristic of our corporeal lives tends to lead us all away from supreme consecration to Him. There is the senseless luxury of this generation. There is the exaggerated care for physical strength and completeness among the young; there is the intemperance in eating and drinking which is the curse and the shame of England. There is the provision for the flesh, the absorbing care for the procuring of material comforts, which drowns the spirit in miserable anxieties, and makes men bondslaves. There is the corruption which comes from drunkenness and from lust. There is the indolence which checks lofty aspirations and stops a man in the middle of noble work. And there are many other forms of evil on which I need not dwell, all of which are swept clean out of the way when we lay to heart this injunction: "I beseech you present your bodies a living sacrifice," and let appetites and tastes and corporeal needs be kept in rigid subordination and in conscious connection with Him. I remember a quaint old saying of a German schoolmaster, who apostrophized his body thus: "I go with you three times a day to eat; you must come with me three times a day to pray." Subjugate the body, and let it be the servant and companion of the devout spirit.

It is also, besides being the recipient of impressions and the possessor of needs and appetites, our instrument for working in the world. And so the exhortation of my text comes to include this, that all our activities done by means of brain and eye and tongue and hand and foot shall be consciously devoted to Him, and laid as a sacrifice upon His altar. That pervasive, universally-diffused reference to God in all the details of daily life is the thing that Christian men and women need most of all to try to cultivate. "Pray without ceasing," says the Apostle. This exhortation can only be obeyed if our work is indeed worship, being done by God's help, for God's sake, in communion with God.

So, dear friends, sacrifice is the keynote—meaning thereby surrender, control, and stimulus of the corporeal frame, surrender to God, in regard to the impressions which we allow to be made upon our senses, to the indulgence which we grant to our appetites, and the satisfaction which we seek for our needs, and to the activities which we engage in by means of this wondrous instrument with which God has trusted us. These are the plain principles involved in the exhortation of my text. "He that soweth to the flesh shall of the flesh reap corruption." "I keep under my body and bring it into subjection." It is a good servant; it is a bad master.

II. Note, secondly, the relation between this priestly service and other kinds of worship.

I need only say a word about that. Paul is not meaning to depreciate the sacrificial ritual from which he drew his emblem. But he is meaning to assert that the devotion of a life manifested through bodily activity is higher in its nature than the symbolical worship of any altar and of any sacrifice. And that falls in with prevailing tendencies in this day, which has laid such a firm hold on the principle that daily conduct is better than formal worship, that it has forgotten to ask the question whether the daily conduct is likely to be satisfactory if the formal worship is altogether neglected. I believe, as profoundly as any man can, that the true worship is distinguishable from and higher than the more sensuous forms of the Catholic or other sacramentarian churches, or the more simple of the Puritan and Nonconformist, or the altogether formless of the Quaker. I believe that the best worship is the manifold activities of daily life laid upon God's altar, so that the division between things secular and things sacred is to a large extent misleading and irrelevant. But at the same time, I believe that you have very little chance of getting this diffused and all-pervasive reference of all a man's doings to God unless there are, all through his life, recurring with daily regularity, reservoirs of power, stations where he may rest, kneeling-places where the attitude of service is exchanged for the attitude of supplication; times of quiet communion with God which shall feed the worshiper's activities as the white snowfields on the high summits feed the brooks that sparkle by the way, and bring fertility wherever they run. So, dear brethren, remember that while life is the field of worship, there must be the inward worship within the shrine if there is to be the outward service.

III. Lastly, note the equally comprehensive motive and ground of this all-inclusive directory for conduct.

"I beseech you, by the mercies of God." That plural does not mean that the Apostle is extending his view over the whole wide field of the divine beneficence, but rather that he is contemplating the one all-inclusive mercy about which the former part of his letter has been elequent—viz., the gift of Christ—and contemplating it in the manifoldness of the blessings which flow from it. The mercies of God which move a man to yield himself as a sacrifice are not the diffused beneficenses of His providence, but the concentrated love that lies in the person and work of His Son.

And there, as I believe, is the one motive to which we can appeal with any prospect of its being powerful enough to give the needful impetus all through a life. The sacrifice of Christ is the ground on which our sacrifices can be offered and accepted, for it was the sacrifice of a death propitiatory and cleansing, and on it, as the ancient ritual taught us, may be reared the enthusiastic sacrifice of a life—a thankoffering for it.

Nor is it only the ground on which our sacrifice is accepted, but it is the great motive by which our sacrifice is impelled. *There* is the difference between the Christian teaching, "present your bodies a sacrifice," and the highest and noblest of similar teaching elsewhere. One of the purest and loftiest of the ancient moralists was a contemporary of Paul's. He would have re-echoed from his heart the Apostle's directory, but he knew nothing of the Apostle's motive. So his exhortations were powerless. He had no spell to work on men's hearts, and his lofty teachings were as the voice of one crying in the wilderness. While Seneca taught, Rome was a cesspool of moral putridity and Nero butchered. So it always is. There may be noble teachings about self-control, purity, and the like, but an evil and adulterous generation is slow to dance to such piping.

Our poet has bid us

> Move upwards, casting out the beast,
> And let the ape and tiger die.

But how is this heavy bulk of ours to "move upwards"; how is the beast to be "cast out"; how are the "ape and tiger" in us to be slain? Paul has told us, "By the mercies of God." Christ's gift, meditated on, accepted, introduced into will and heart, is the one power that will melt our obstinacy, the one magnet that will draw us after it.

Nothing else, brethren, as your own experience has taught you, and as the experience of the world confirms, nothing else will bind Behemoth and put a hook in his nose. Apart from the constraining motive of the love of Christ, all the cords of prudence, conscience, advantage, by which men try to bind their unruly passions and manacle the insisting flesh, are like the chains on the demoniac's wrists: "And he had oftentimes been bound by chains, and the chains were snapped asunder." But the silken leash with which the fair Una in the poem leads the lion, the silken leash of love will bind the strong man and enable us to rule ourselves. If we will open our hearts to the sacrifice of Christ, we shall be able to offer ourselves as thankofferings. If we will let His love sway our wills and consciences, He will give our wills and consciences power to master and to offer up our flesh. And the great change, according to which He will one day change the body of our humiliation into the likeness of the body of His glory, will be begun in us if we live under the influence of the motive and the commandment which this Apostle bound together in our text and in his other great words, "Ye are not your own, ye are bought with a price; therefore, glorify God in your body and spirit, which are His."

25

What Faith Makes of Death†

*An entrance ministered abundantly. Shortly I must
put off this my tabernacle. My decease*—2 Peter 1:11,
14, 15.

We are all mourners here this morning. A life of practical godliness, of bright Christian service, and, latterly, of wonderfully
brave endurance, has come at last to the end to which we slowly
learned to know it must come. The loving wife, who was a helper
and a counselor as well, the staunch loyal friend, the diligent worker,
with her open hand, her frank cordiality, her clear insight, her resolute will, has passed from our sight, but never from our love nor
our memory. The empty place in the home can only be filled by
Him who has made it empty, and we all pray that He may be near.
Every member of this congregation must feel that a strong stay
has gone. A wider circle, for whom I may presume to speak, mourns
the loss of a dear friend; a far wider one, covering the whole country, offers through my lips this morning affectionate and earnest
sympathy to the stricken hearts here today.

But, dear brethren, the pulpit is not the place for personal eu-
logium, and I think I shall best discharge my duty if I try to turn our
common sorrow to account by setting before you some general considerations drawn from these three fragments, which I have ventured
to isolate from their connection because they have a certain unity
as being all euphemisms for one thing. The Bible very seldom
speaks of death by its own ugly name. It rather chooses to use ex-

---

† Delivered at Myrtle Street Chapel, Liverpool (on occasion of the death of
Mrs. Stowell Brown).

pressions which veil its pain and its terror; and so does common speech. But the reason in the two cases is exactly opposite. The Bible will not call death "death" because it is not a bit afraid of it; the world will not call death "death" because it is so much afraid of it.

The Christian view has robbed it for all its pain and its terror. It has limited its power to the mere outside of the man, and the conviction that death can no more touch me than a sword can hack a sunbeam, reduces it to insignificance. These thoughts are brought out in these fragmentary words which I ask you to consider now. I think you will see that they lend us some very valuable and gladdening thoughts as to the aspect in which Christian faith should regard the act of death.

I have ventured to alter their order for the sake of bringing together the two which are most closely connected.

I. I ask you, then, to look with me first at that representation of death as putting off the tabernacle.

"Knowing that shortly I must put off this, my tabernacle, even as our Lord Christ hath showed." There is, of course, a reference here to the warning which the Apostle received from his Lord, "signifying what death he should die." He had learned that in his old age he should be seized and bound and led "whither he would not." In all probability, the language of our verse would be more accurately represented if we read for "shortly" *suddenly*—the Apostle's anticipation not being so much that his dissolution was impending as that his death, when it came, would be sudden; that is to say violent. And therefore he seeks to warn and prepare his brethren beforehand.

The expressions seem to blend the two figures: that of a tabernacle, or tent, and that of a vesture. As the Apostle Paul, in like manner, blends the same two ideas when he talks of being "clothed upon with our house which is from heaven" and unclothed from "our earthly house of this tabernacle."

To such small dimensions has Christian faith dwindled down the ugly thing, death. It has come to be nothing more than a change of vesture, a change of dwelling.

Now what lies in that metaphor? Three things that I touch upon for a moment. First of all, the rigid limitation of the region within which death has any power at all. It affects a man's vesture, his dwelling place, something that belongs to him, something that wraps him, but nothing that is himself. This enemy may seem to come in and capture the whole fortress, but it is only the outworks that are thrown down—the citadel stands. The organ is one thing, the player on it is another; and whatever befalls that has nothing to do with what touches him. Instead of an all-mastering conqueror, then, as sense tells us that death is, and as a great deal of modern science is telling us that death is, it is only a power that touches the fringe and circumference, the wrappage and investiture of my being, and has nothing to do with that being itself. The "foolish senses" may declare that death is lord because they "see no motion in the dead." But in spite of sense and anatomist's scalpels, organization is not life. Mind and conscience, will and love, are something more than functions of the brain, and no scalpel can ever cut into *self*. I live, and may live—and blessed be God! I can say—*shall* live, apart altogether from this bodily organization. Whatever befalls it is only like changing a dress or removing into another house. The man is untouched.

Another thing implied in this figure, and, indeed, in all three metaphors of our text, is that life runs on unbroken and the same through and after death.

If the Apostle be right in his conviction that the change only affects the circumference, then of course that follows naturally. Unbroken and the same! The gulf looks deep and black to us on this side, but, depend upon it, it looks a mere chink which a step can cross when seen from the other. Like some of those rivers that disappear in a subterranean tunnel and then emerge into the light again, the life that sinks out of sight in the dark valley of the shadow of death will come up into a brighter sunshine beyond the mountains, and it will be running in the same direction that it followed when it was lost to mortal eye. For just as the dying Stephen knew his Master again when he saw Him standing in the glory, we should know our dear ones after they had passed through this change, for all the sweetness and all the love would be there still, and nothing would be gone but the weakness that encompassed them and the imperfection that sometimes masked their true beauty.

The same in direction, the same in essence, uninterrupted through the midst of the darkness, the life goes on. A man is the same whatever dress he wears. Though we know that much will be changed and that new powers may come, and old wants and weaknesses fall away with new environment, still the essential self will be unchanged and the life will run on with a break and with scarcely a deflection. There is no magic in the act of death which changes the set of a character, or the tendencies and desires of a nature. As you die so you live, and you live in your death and after your death the same man and woman that you were when the blow fell.

So, my brother, if you need it, take the warning that lies in this truth, and see to it that the right character is begun to be formed here, for if it be not, there is no power in death to change its direction.

The last idea that is here in this first of our metaphors is that of a step in advance. "I must put off this, my tabernacle." Yes! In order that instead of the nomad tent, the ragged canvas, I may put on the building, the permanent house; in order that, instead of the "vesture of decay," I may put on the fine linen, clean and white, which is the righteousness of saints, and the body which is a fit organ for the perfected spirit.

True! That does not come at once, but still the stripping off of the one is the preparation for the investiture with the other, and there is advance in the change. Death is as truly a step forward in a life's history as birth is. Though the full "redemption" of the body be not yet received by them who sleep in Jesus, they wait in peace. They are blessed, conscious, lapped in the rest of God, and surely taught by Him Who knows all things, all that it would gladden or help them to know of us whom they surely love still. They dwell out of the body but they dwell in the Lord, and He will be to them their means of communication and the outer universe, eyes to the blind and hearing to the deaf.

Of course the process of divesting goes on at different rates. Elijah had his chariot of fire, Elisha is not less favored when he falls sick of the lingering sickness wherewith he should die. The one has larger means of ministering than the other, and up to the last moment may teach lessons and give impulses. Some have the privilege given them, like our dear friend, of putting off the garments slowly and teaching, as she did, lessons of brave patience and of how to bear pain and weariness with undimmed spirit and unflagging interest in others, which those who learned them will keep as precious memories. But however the end comes, whether the wind rises and beats upon the house and it falls in one sudden ruin, or whether it is slowly unroofed and dismantled until it is no longer habitable, let us thank God that we know for our dear ones and for ourselves that whatever becomes of the clay hovel, the tenant is safe and has gone to live in a fair house in a "distant City glorious."

II. And now we may turn to the remaining two metaphors here, which have a more close connection with each other and yet are capable of being dealt with separately. Death is further spoken of as a departure.

"I will endeavor," says the Apostle, "That we may be able after my decease." The word for "decease" here is a very unusual one, as no doubt many of you know. It is employed with reference to death only twice in the New Testament: once in the text and once in the account of our Lord's Transfiguration, where Moses and Elias are represented as speaking with Him "of the decease that He should accomplish at Jerusalem." You may observe that immediately after the last of my texts, the Apostle begins to speak about that Transfiguration and makes definite reference to what he had heard there; so that it is, at all events, possible that he selects the unusual word with some reference to, or some remembrance of, its use upon that occasion in the narrative of one of the Evangelists. Again, it is the word which has been transferred into English as Exodus and may possibly be here employed with some allusion to the departure of the children of Israel from the land of bondage. Now looking at these three points: the literal meaning of this word, its employment in reference to the deliverance from Egypt; and its employment in reference to the death of Christ, we gather from them valuable considerations.

This aspect of death shows it to us as seen from this side. Like the former, it minimizes its importance by making it merely a change of place—another stage in a journey. We have had many changes already, only this is the last stage, the last day's march, and it takes us *home*. But yet the sad thoughts of separation and withdrawal are here. These show us the saddest aspect of death, which no reflection and no consolations of religion will ever make less sad. Death, the separator, is, and must always be, an unwelcome messenger. He comes and lays his bony hand upon us, and unties the closest embraces, and draws us away from all the habitudes and associations of our lives, and bans us into a lonely land.

But even in this aspect there is alleviation if we will think about this departure in connection with the two uses of the word which I have mentioned.

A change of place, yes! An Exodus from bondage, as true a deliverance from captivity as that old Exodus was. Life has its chains and limitations, which are largely due to the bodily life hemming in and shackling the spirit. It is a prison house, though it be full of God's goodness. We cannot but feel that, even in health and much more in sickness, the bondage of flesh and sense, of habits rooted in the body, and of wants which it feels, weighs heavily upon us. By one swift stroke of Death's hammer, the fetters are struck off. Death is a Liberator in the profoundest sense; the Moses that leads the bondmen into a desert it may be, but to liberty and towards their own land, to their rest. It is the angel who comes in the night to God's prisoned servant, striking the fetters from his limbs, and leading him through the iron gate into the city. And so we do not need to shiver and fear for ourselves or to mourn for our dear ones, if they have passed out of the bondage of "corruption into the liberty of the glory of the children of God." Death is a departure which is an emancipation.

Again, it is a departure which is conformed to Christ's "decease," and is guided and companioned by Him.

Ah! There you touch the deepest source of all comfort and all strength.

> We can go through no darker rooms
> Than He has gone before.

And the memory of His presence is comfort and light. What would it be, for instance, to a man stumbling in the polar regions, amidst eternal ice and trackless wastes, to come across the footprints of a man? What would it be if he found out that they were the footprints of his own brother? And you and I have a Brother's steps to tread in when we take that last weary journey from which flesh and sense shrink and fail.

Nor have we only the memory of a past companionship, but, blessed be God—the reality of a present Friend. When all other ties snap, that holds. There is an awful solitude in death into which no human affection can find its way. It comes and wraps a man in a cloud through which love and sympathy cannot pass, but its thickest and mistiest folds are not too dense for Christ to enter. We may fear when we enter into the cloud, and when our dear ones go into it we may wring our hands in sorrow that our help avails to little; but be sure they have found, and shall find, Christ in the heart of it, and He will say to us, "When thou passest through the waters I will be with thee, and through the floods they shall not overwhelm thee." The departure is not all pain if we travel in the company of Jesus Christ.

III. The last aspect of these metaphors is that one contained in the words of our first text, "An entrance ministered abundantly." The going out is a going in; the journey has two ends, only the two ends are so very near each other that the same act is described by the two terms. Looked at from this side it is a going out; looked at from the other side it is a coming in.

"There is but a step betwixt me and *life.*" One moment, while we are saying, "Is he gone?" is enough to lead the dying into the presence chamber of the King. To awake is the work of a moment. We but open our eyes, and the realm of dreams falls to pieces and we see realities. One step crosses the frontier.

If I had time I might dwell upon the thought which is plainly taught us in this last of our texts, of the close connection and entire correspondence between the abundance of the entrance and the character of the life. "*So* an entrance," says my text, "shall be ministered," and that "so" carries you back to the forcible exhortations in the early part of the chapter. The connection between keeping them and the abundance of "the entrance" is still more emphasized when we know that the same word in a different form occurs in the precept, "*Add* to your faith," and in the promise, "An entrance shall be *ministered.*" Which is to say, in other words, if we

236 • *What Faith Makes of Death*

take care to provide that our faith is enriched and increased with these graces and excellencies of Christian character, then, and then only, shall be abundant entrance be ours.

No question whatever, then, but that there is distinctly laid down here the principle that it is not all the same what *sort* of a Christian a Christian man or woman may be, but that the kind of Christian they are will tell in the kind of entrance they have in the Heaven above.

The smallest faith that unites a man's heart with Jesus Christ makes him capable of receiving so much of salvation as is contained in the bare entrance into the Kingdom; but every degree of faith's increase, and every degree of faith's enrichment, makes him more capable of receiving more of God in Christ, and he will get all he can hold. So every deed here on earth of Christian conduct, and every grace here on earth of Christian character, has its issue and its representative in a new influx of the glory, and a more intimate possession of the bliss, and a more abundant entrance into the everlasting Kingdom.

We all enter at the same gate, but we are set at the banqueting table in due order. We all pass into the same Kingdom, but some of us may at once advance further into the land. Be sure, then, of this: that as our faith is enriched by conduct and character, so our Heaven will be enlarged with raptures and brilliancies.

So, when we see a life of which Christian faith has been the underlying motive, and in which many graces of the Christian character have been plainly manifested, passing from among us, let not our love look only at the empty place on earth, but let our faith rise to the thought of the filled place in Heaven. Let us not look down to grave, but up to the skies. Let us not dwell on the departure, but on the abundant entrance. Let us not only remember, but also hope. And as love and faith, memory and hope, follow our friend as she passes "within the veil," let us thank God that we are sure:

> *She*, when the bridegroom with his feastful friends
> Passes to bliss, at the mid hour of night
> Has gained HER entrance.

My friends! This day's services speak to each of you. Cannot you hear the "great Voice saying, Come up hither!" Is your life rooted in Jesus Christ? Have you given your life's service to Him? Is this world a fleeting show to you because He is the reality that you love and trust? Is it so?

If it is, you may be always confident. Life will be full of power for work and gladness. A present Christ will comfort you concerning your dear ones gone, and when it comes to your turn to go, all the grim features of Death will be softened down into solemn beauty, and he, as God's messenger, will lead you for a moment into the wilderness, and there speak to your heart, and "so an entrance shall be ministered abundantly unto you into the everlasting Kingdom of our Lord and Savior Jesus Christ."

May it be so with us all! Amen!

26

How the Little May Be Used to Get the Great

He that is faithful in that which is least is faithful also in much, and he that is unjust in the least is unjust also in much. If, therefore, ye have not been faithful in the unrighteous mammon, who will commit to your trust the true riches? And if ye have not been faithful in that which is another man's, who shall give you that which is your own?—Luke 16:10–12

These are very revolutionary words in more than one respect. There are two things remarkable about them. One is the contrast which is run in all three verses between what our Lord calls "mammon" (that is, simply outward good) and the inward riches of a heart devoted to, and filled with, God and Christ. The former, the material good, "is that which is least," "unrighteous," "another man's," or, leaving out the word "man's" as conveying a false idea, "another's." The inward good is "that which is much," "the true riches," "your own." Christ upsets the world's standard of value as one might do who went among savages whose only medium of currency was cowrie-shells, and putting these aside, let them see gold and silver in the stones that were kicked about by their feet. All that is least in their eyes is greatest, all that is greatest in their eyes is trash.

But another striking thing about the words is the broad, bold statement that a man's use of the lower goods determines, or is at least an element in determining, his possession of the highest. That is a thing that Protestant Christians are shy of saying; they seem to think that somehow or other it militates against the plain teaching of Scripture that *faith* is the condition of salvation. But it is distinctly a part of our Lord's teaching here, and the sooner we make room for it in our creeds, the better for our practice and for ourselves.

I. First, then, I desire to consider briefly that strange, new standard of value which is set up here. On the one side is placed the whole glittering heap of all material good that man can touch or handle, all that wealth can buy of this perishable world; and on the other hand, there are the modest and unseen riches of pure thoughts and high desires of a noble heart, of a life assimilated to Jesus Christ. The two are compared in three points as to their intrinsic magnitude, as to their quality, as to our ownership of them.

Of the great glittering heap our Lord says: "It is nothing, at its greatest it is small"; and of the other our Lord says: "At its smallest it is great." Just a word or two about these antitheses. "Small" and "great" of course are relative terms; they imply a comparison with each other, and imply also a reference of both to a common standard of value. They not only assert that earth's good is small by the side of, and in comparison with, the other class of good, but they refer both the one and the other class of good to a standard.

And what is the standard? If you have enough of a thing to fill the vessel which is meant to contain it, you will call that quantity great; if not, it will be estimated as little. What are these two classes of good measured by but their respective power of filling the heart? Outward good at its greatest is small if so measured; inward good at its smallest is great. The smallest soul towers above the biggest fortune. Dives' riches are all too small to satisfy Lazarus. All the wealth of all the Rothschilds is too little to fill the soul of the poorest beggar that stands by their carriage door with hungry eyes. The least degree of truth, of love, of goodness, is bigger in its power to fill the heart than all the externals that human avarice can gather about it.

Now do we believe that? Do we order our lives as if we did believe it? Do we regulate our desires and wishes as if it were an axiom with us that the least of God is more than the most of the world? Can we thus enter into the understanding of Christ's scale and standard and think of all the external as "That which is least," and of the inward as "that which is much"?

The world looks at worldly wealth through a microscope which magnifies the infinitesimally small, and then it looks at "the land that is very far off" through a telescope turned the wrong way, which diminishes all that is great. But if we can get up by the side of Jesus Christ and see things with His eyes and from His station, it will be as when a man climbs a mountain and the little black line, as it seemed to him when looked at from the plain, has risen up into a giant cliff and all the big things down below, as they seemed when he was among them, have dwindled. That white speck is a palace; that bit of a green patch there, over which the skylark flies in a minute, is a great lord's estate. Oh, dear brethren, we do not need to wait to get to Heaven to learn Heaven's tables of weights and measures! One grain of true love to God is greater in its power to enrich than a California of gold. Manchester men and women, who are tempted to the opposite heresy, do you fix it in your mind that all this visible is trivial, and all the unseen is the great!

Take, again, the second antithesis, the "unrighteous mammon" and "the true riches." That word, "unrighteous" in its application to material good is somewhat difficult. I do not think that it means only a certain class of outward good; namely, that which is unjustly gotten, but that it is the designation of the whole. If we keep strictly to the antithesis, "unrighteous" must be the opposite of "true." The word would then come to mean very nearly the same as *deceitful, that which betrays*. One can see that these two ideas are closely related and that the meaning of "unrighteous" may easily slide into that of "deceptive," and probably it is best to take that as the meaning of the word here. If anyone were to contend, however, that the expression pointed to the fact that all material wealth has evil so mixed up with it that, though not in itself bad, it leads to all sorts of unrighteousness, so that it may be called in a somewhat popular way of speaking, "the unrighteous mammon," I should not dispute it, though preferring the other sense which makes the word the exact contrast of the *true* riches.

And so we have presented to us the old familiar thought that external good of all sorts looks to be a great deal better than it is. It promises a great many things that it never fulfills, tempting us as a fish is tempted to the hook by a bait which hides the hook. It is "a juggling fiend" that "keeps the word of promise to our ear and breaks it to our hope." No man ever found in any outward good, when he got it, that which he fancied was in it when he was chasing after it.

It has always been and ever will be a delusion and a lie to the man who trusts it. But the inward riches of faith, true holiness, lofty aspirations, Christ-directed purposes, all these are true. They promise no more than they perform. They bring more than they said they would. No man ever goes to that well and lets down his bucket and brings it up empty. No man ever leans upon that staff and it breaks beneath his weight. No man ever said, "I have tasted Thy love, and lo! It does not satisfy me! I have realized Thy help and lo! It has not been enough!" What we have to say is, "The little I have tasted rebukes me that I have not longed for and possessed more, for it is sweet beyond all other sweetnesses, and strong beyond all other strengths!" The riches within are "*true* riches." The outward are like the fairy gold in the old legends that is given into a man's palm and when the morning comes it is a handful of withered beech leaves. You get it and you are not happier than you were before you got it. That is the experience of every man who makes the world his confidence. On one hand is the "unrighteous mammon" that does not keep its promises, that does not deal fairly with the people who give themselves up to it and trust to it; and on the other hand, the "true riches."

And then the last contrast is between "another's" and "your own." Another's? Well, that may mean God's, and therefore you are stewards, as the whole parable that precedes the text has been teaching. But I am not sure that that is the only, or indeed the principal, reference of the word here. And I think when our Lord speaks of all outward possessions as being, even while mine, another's, He means to point there not only to the fact of stewardship, but also to the fact of the limitations and defects of all outward possessions of outward good. That is to say, there is no real contact between the outward things that a man has and himself. The only things that you really have, paradox as it sounds, are the things that you *are*. All the rest you hold by a very slight tie, like the pearls that are sewn upon some half-barbarious Eastern magnate's jacket, which he shakes off as he walks. So men say, "This is mine!" and it only means, "it is not yours." There is no real possession, even while there is an apparent one, and just because there is no real contact, because there is always a gap between the man and his goods, because he has not, as it were, gathered them into himself, therefore the possession is transient as well as incomplete. It slips away from the hand even while you hold it. And just as we may say, "There is no present, but everything is past or future, and what we call the present is only the meeting point of these two times," so we may say there is no possession because everything is either coming into my hands or going out of them, and my apparent ownership is only for a moment. I simply transmit,

'Twas mine, 'tis his, and has been slave to thousands.

And so it passes.

And then consider the common accidents of life which rob men of their goods, and the waste by the very act of use, which gnaws them away as the sea does the cliffs; and, last of all, death's separation. What can be taken out of a man's hands by death has no right to be called his. Other men will stand in this pulpit that I call mine, other men will sit in those pews that you call yours. I have got books on my shelves that have dead men's names in them; what of truth and wisdom they draw from the books is in them today, wherever they are, and is theirs, but the book that was theirs was never theirs really. It is mine today, it will be somebody else's tomorrow. Each, for the moment, says "Mine!" and Christ says "No! No! Another's!" That which is your own is that which you can gather into your heart and keep there, and which death cannot take away from you.

So let us learn how to compare the worth of these two kinds of riches, and to make our own that from which "neither life, nor death, nor things present, nor things to come, nor any creature shall be able to separate us."

II. Notice for a moment the other broad principle that is laid down in these three verses, as to the highest use of the lower good.

Our Lord, as I have said in my introductory remarks, distinctly asserts here, as a principle, that our manner of employing the lesser goods of outward possession is an element in determining the amount of our possession of the highest blessing. And as I said, good people are sometimes chary of asserting that with the plain emphasis with which it is here asserted, for fear they should damage the central truth that God's mercy and the gifts of His grace come to men through faith, not through their conduct. I believe that, of course, as being the fundamental principle on which all other of these statements of Scripture must be explained, with which they must be harmonized; and nothing I have to say and nothing, I am sure, that Jesus Christ wished to say, militates in the slightest degree against that truth, that a man receives into his heart "the true riches" simply on condition of his desiring them and of his trusting Jesus Christ to give them.

If I had to speak to a man who had no Christian character about him and no Christian faith in him, I should not begin by saying to him, "Use your outward goods faithfully and well, and then you will get the highest good," If for no other reason yet for this, that I do not suppose he *could* use them faithfully and well unless he *had* the highest good, which comes to him by faith.

But that being understood, to say that a man's conduct may help or hinder him towards the possession and in the exercise of the faith which is the condition of his possessing the true riches and highest good, is no contradiction to the central truth of the Gospel. And that is what Jesus Christ says here. Whether you are a Christian man or whether you are not, this is true about you, that the way in which you deal with your outward goods, your wealth, your capacity of all sorts, may become a barrier to your possessing the higher, or it may become a mighty help.

There are plenty of people, and some of them listening to me now, who are kept from being Christians because they love the world so much. They have no desires after God or goodness because their desires are engrossed and absorbed in the earthly and visible. They so handle that "which is least" that it has taken from them all the wish for that which is greatest. They have lived upon sweetmeats until their appetite is so entirely vitiated that they do not want bread. Like some sea anemone that gathers-in its tentacles and shuts itself up over its prey, so that you cannot shove a bristle into the lips, your hearts may close over your earthly good in such a fashion, so tight, and desperate, and obstinate, that God's grace and His proffered gifts have no chance of finding their way into your hearts at all. There are some of you of whom that is true today.

And is it not true about many Christians that their too-high estimate of, and too-great carefulness about, and too-niggardly disposal of, the things that perish, the goods of this lower life, are hindering their Christian career? "Ye did run well, what did hinder you?" I will tell you what is hindering a great many of you: what hindered the runners in that old Grecian legend, when she whom they were pursuing cast down in the path a golden apple, and they turned aside and slackened their pace to catch at that. Old men, who, as Christians, are almost dead and who can remember that, as young men, before they had got on in the world, they were full of earnest desires and self-sacrificing love to Jesus Christ—are there any of that sort here this morning? Christian men and women who do not use their wealth for the highest purposes and under the highest responsibilities, are there any of that sort here? Have you loaded your souls with thick clay and held the world so close to your eyes that, though it be "that which is least," it is big enough to shut out that which is most, and which lies beyond? Oh! my brother! It is a very solemn truth, and you had better find room for it in your creed, that a great many Christians are hindered in their possession of the highest good by their unfaithful use of the lowest.

The world thinks that the highest use of the highest things is to gain possession of the lowest thereby, and that truth and genius and poetry are given to select spirits and are wasted unless they make money out of them. Christ's notion of the relationship is exactly the opposite: that all the outward is then lifted to its noblest purpose when it is made rigidly subordinate to the highest; and that is the best thing that any man can do with his money is so to spend it as to "purchase for himself a good degree," "laying up for himself in store a good foundation that he may lay hold on eternal life."

III. And now let me say one last word as to the faithfulness which thus utilizes the lowest as a means of possessing more fully the highest.

We are not at all left in doubt as to what is the manner of thus employing the lowest gifts. Our text is our Lord's pointing the lesson of the striking parable of the unjust steward. I gather from it, as well as from other general considerations, these three words which I desire to leave with you as being the principles upon which this faithful use of the lowest class of goods is to be carried out.

You will be "faithful" if, through all your administration of your possessions, there runs, first, the principle of stewardship; you will be "faithful" if, through all your administration of your earthly possessions there runs, second, the principle of sacrifice; you will be "faithful" if, through all your administration of your earthly possessions, there runs, third, the principle of brotherhood.

Stewardship. The consciousness of having nothing that we have not received, of having received nothing for our very own to be used according to our own will, the ever-present sense of obligation to administer our master's goods as he would, and for his purposes, must be clear and active in us if we are to be "faithful." "Of Thine own have we given Thee" is to be always our conviction, for all is God's—His before it was ours, His while it seems ours, and His by a new right when we give it back to Him.

One of the plainest duties of stewardship is that we bring conscience and deliberate consideration to bear upon our administration of this world's goods. We are not faithful stewards if we spend according to our own whim and fancy, and let our "charity" depend, as it so often does, on little better than accident or habit. We are stewards in regard to what we spend on ourselves and our families, as well as in what we spend for purposes beyond ourselves; our personal and domestic expenditure, our savings and our gifts, and the proportion between them should all equally pass under the inspection of deliberate conscience. If that were once thoroughly understood and practiced by us, we should be very different people, and there would be very different results from many an appeal that is made to us. Stewardship means deliberation, and intelligent consideration, and conscientious disposal and administration as of a fund that is not mine, but is put into my hand.

Sacrifice. That is the fundamental law of the Christian life and it must be applied especially in this region of outward possessions, where the opposite law of selfishness works most strongly. How much owest thou unto thy Lord? All things, and "thine own self besides." So, touched by the mercies of God, we should bring in glad surrender ourselves and our all as thank offerings to Him by Whose bitter sacrifice we are reconciled to God, and put in possession of ourselves and of all else. "Worthy is the Lamb that was slain to receive riches."

Brotherhood. Christianity is not communism, but it will do all that communism tries to do. Property is not theft, but property selfishly administered is theft. We are but distributing agents and we have a right to take a commission and to support ourselves and families, but we have no right to do anything more. What we call our own is in this sense, too, another's, and belongs to our brethren because it, and they, and we all belong to God. We get everything in order that we may transmit it to others. We are all bound together by such subtle and close ties that each is laid under obligation to share his portion with his neighbor. Whether it be outward goods or faculties of the mind or heart, wisdom, or sympathy, or the yet-higher gifts of the Gospel that redeems, we receive that we may impart—

> The least flower with a brimming cup may stand
> And share its dewdrop with another near.

These three principles of stewardship, sacrifice and brotherhood, honestly applied, will make us "faithful," and will make us capable of fuller possession of the true riches which God ever gives as largely as we can receive. Here and now we may win a greater possession of the love and likeness of God and may have our spirits widened to receive more of all that makes us noble and calm, hopeful and strong, by our Christian administration of earthly goods. And on the other hand, we may so mis-spend, mis-love, and mis-administer them as that they shall be a clog to keep us down and a mist to blind our eyes, that we may not rise to behold the "King in His beauty, and the land that is very far off."

Nor does the effect end with earth. Faithful stewardship, like all other true conduct based upon the love of Jesus Christ, will make us more capable of a larger possession of the life and the glory of God hereafter. It may have been some earnest Christian worker who, like one that some of us mourn today, with little of this world's goods to give, has gone into some neglected neighborhood, and there, with sympathy and effort and prayer, has labored; and has been laid in his grave amidst the weeping of those he had helped and of the drunkards he had reformed. Or it may have been a prince, who, like one that all England is morning today, did the duties of his high station, as we have reason to hope, from high motive and under the influence of Christian principle. It may have been a poor workman who spent his fifteen shillings a week for God's glory and as a steward; or it may have been a millionaire who gave largely out of his abundance to God's cause. But whoever they were, "Blessed are the dead which die in the Lord, for they rest from their labors and their works do follow them."

> Their works and alms, and all their good endeavor,
> Stayed not behind nor in the grave were trod,
> But as Faith pointed with her golden rod,
> Followed them up to bliss and joy forever.

27

The Gifts of Christ as Witness, Risen and Crowned

Grace be unto you and peace from. . . . Jesus Christ,
Who is the faithful Witness and the first begotten of
the dead, and the Prince of the kings of the earth
—Revelation 1:4, 5.

So loftily did John in his old age come to think of his Lord. The former days of blessed nearness had not faded from his memory; rather he understood their meaning better than when he was in the midst of their sweetness. Years and experience, and the teaching of God's Spirit, had taught him to understand what the Master meant when He said: "It is expedient for you that I go away"; for when He had departed John saw Him a great deal more clearly than ever he had done when he beheld Him with his eyes. He sees Him now invested with these lofty attributes, and, so to speak, involved in the brightness of the Throne of God. For the words of my text are not only remarkable in themselves, and in the order in which they give these three aspects of our Lord's character, but remarkable also in that they occur in an invocation in which the Apostle is calling down blessings from Heaven on the heads of his brethren. The fact that they do so occur points a question: Is it possible to conceive that the writer of these words thought of Jesus Christ as less than Divine? Could he have asked for "grace and peace" to come down on the Asiatic Christians from the Divine Father, and an Abstraction and a Man? A strange Trinity that would be, most certainly. Rightly or wrongly, the man that said "Grace and peace be unto you, from Him which is, and which was, and which is to come, and from the seven spirits which are before His Throne, and from Jesus Christ," believed that the name of the One God was Father, Son, and Holy Spirit.

But it is not so much to this as to the connection of these three clauses with one another, and to the bearing of all three on our Lord's power of giving grace and peace to men's hearts, that I want to turn your attention now. I take the words simply as they lie here, asking you to consider, first, how grace and peace come to us "from the faithful Witness"; how, secondly, they come "from the first begotten from the dead"; and how, lastly, they come "from the Prince of the kings of the earth."

I. Now as to the first of these, "the faithful Witness." All of you who have any familiarity with the language of Scripture will know that a characteristic of all the writings which are ascribed to the Apostle John, viz., his Gospel, his Epistles, and the book of the Revelation, is their free and remarkable use of that expression, "Witness." It runs through all of them, and is one of the many threads of connection which tie them all together, and which constitute a very strong argument for the common authorship of the three sets of writings, vehemently as that has of late been denied.

But where did John get this word? According to his own teaching he got it from the lips of the Master, Who began His career with these words, "We speak that we do know, and bear witness to that we have seen," and who all but ended it with these royal words, "Thou sayest that I am a King! For this cause came I into the world, that I should bear witness unto the Truth." Christ Himself, then, claimed to be in an eminent and special sense the witness to the world.

The witness of what? What was the substance of His testimony? It was a testimony mainly about God. The words of my text substantially cover the same ground as His own words, "I have declared Thy name unto my brethren," and as those of the Apostle: "The only begotten Son which is in the bosom of the Father, He hath declared Him." And they involve the same ideas as lie in the great name by which He is called in John's Gospel, "the Word of God."

That is to say, all our highest and purest and best knowledge of God comes from the life and conduct and character of Jesus Christ. His revelation is no mere revelation by words. Plenty of men have talked about God, and said noble and true and blessed things about Him. Scattered through the darkness of heathenism, and embedded in the sinfulness of every man's heart, there are great and lofty and pure thoughts about Him, which to cleave to and follow out would bring strength and purity. It is one thing to speak about God in words, maxims, precepts; it is another thing to show us God in act and life. The one is theology, the other is Gospel. The one is the work of man, the other is the exclusive prerogative of God manifested in the flesh.

It is not Christ's words only that make Him the "Amen," the "faithful and true Witness," but in addition to these, He witnesses by all His deeds of grace, and truth, and gentleness, and pity; by all His yearnings over wickedness, and sorrow, and sinfulness; by all His drawings of the profligate and the outcast and the guilty to Himself, His life of loneliness, His death of shame. In all these, He is showing us not only the sweetness of a perfect human character, but *in* the sweetness of a perfect human character, the sweeter sweetness of our Father, God. The substance of His testimony is the Name, the revelation of the character of His Father and our Father.

This name of "witness" bears likewise strongly upon the characteristic and remarkable *manner* of our Lord's testimony. The task of a witness is to affirm; his business is to tell his story—not to argue about it, simply to state it. And there is nothing more characteristic of our Lord's words than the way in which, without attempt at proof or argumentation, He makes them stand on their own evidence; or, rather, depend upon His veracity. All His teaching is characterized by what would be insane presumption in any of us, and would at once rule us out of court as unfit to be listened to on any grave subject, most of all on religious truth. For His method is this: "Verily, verily, I say to you! Take it on My word. You ask Me for proof of My saying: I am the proof of it; I assert it. That is enough for you!" Not so do men speak. So does the faithful Witness speak; and instead of the conscience and common sense of the world rising up and saying, "This is the presumption of a religious madman and dictator," they have bowed before Him and said, "Thou art fairer than the children of men! Grace is poured into Thy lips." He is the "faithful Witness," Who lays His own character and veracity as the basis of what He has to say, and has no mightier word by which to back His testimony than His own sovereign "Verily! verily!"

The name bears, too, on the *ground* of His testimony. A faithful witness is an eye-witness. And that is what Christ claims when He witnesses about God. "We speak that we do know, we testify that we have seen." "I speak that which I have seen with My Father!" There is nothing more remarkable about the oral portion of our Lord's witness than the absence of any appearance, such as marks all the wisest words of great men, of having come to them as the result of patient thought. We never see Him in the act of arriving at a truth, nor detect any traces of the process of forming opinions in Him. He speaks as if He had seen, and His tone is that of one who is not thinking out truth or grasping at it, but simply narrating that which lies plain and clear ever before His eyes. I do not ask you what that involves, but I quote His own statement of what it involves: "No man hath ascended up into Heaven save He that came down from Heaven, even the Son of Man which is in Heaven."

There have been plenty of great and gracious words about God, and there have been plenty of black and blasphemous thoughts of Him. They rise in our own hearts, and they come from our brothers' tongues. Men have worshiped gods gracious, gods loving, gods angry, gods petulant, gods capricious; but God after the fashion of the God whom Jesus Christ avouches to us, we have nowhere else, a God of absolute love, Who "so loved the world"—that is, you and me—"that He gave His only begotten Son, that whosoever believeth on Him should not perish."

And now I ask, is there not grace and peace brought to us all from that faithful Witness, and from His credible testimony? Surely the one thing that the world wants is to have the question answered whether there really is a God in Heaven that cares anything about me, and to Whom I can trust myself wholly; believing that He will lift me out of all my meannesses and sins, and make me clean and pure and blessed like Himself. Surely that is the deepest of all human needs, howsoever little men may know it. And sure I am that none of us can find the certitude of such a Father unless we give credence to the message of Jesus Christ our Lord.

This day needs that witness as much as any other; sometimes in our unbelieving moments, we think *more* than any other. There is a wave—I believe it is only a wave—passing over the cultivated

thought of Europe at present which will make short work of all belief in a God that does not grip fast to Jesus Christ. As far as I can
read the signs of the times, and the tendency of modern thinking,
it is this: either an absolute Silence, a Heaven stretching above us,
blue and clear, and cold, and far away, and *dumb;* or else a Christ
that speaks—He or none! The Theism that has shaken itself loose
from Him will be crushed, I am sure, in the encounter with the ag-
nosticism and the materialism of this day. And the one refuge is to
lay fast hold of the old truth: "The only begotten Son, which is in
the bosom of the Father, He hath declared Him."

Oh! You orphan children that have forgotten your Father, and
have turned prodigals and rebels; you that have begun to doubt if
there is anyone above this low earth that cares for you; you that have
got bewildered and befogged amidst the manifold denials and con-
troversies of this day, come back to the one voice that speaks to us
in tones of confident certainty as from personal knowledge of a Father. "He that hath seen Me hath seen the Father," says Jesus to us
all: "hearken unto Me, and know God, Whom to know in Me is
eternal life." Listen to Him. Without His testimony you will be the
sport of fears, and doubts, and errors. With it in your hearts you will
be at rest. Grace and peace come from the faithful Witness.

II. We have grace and peace from the Conqueror of Death.

The "first *begotten* from the dead" does not precisely convey the
idea of the original, which would be more accurately represented by
"the first *born* from the dead"—the resurrection being looked upon
as a kind of birth into a higher order of life. It is, perhaps, scarcely
necessary to observe that the accuracy of this designation, "the first
born from the dead," as applied to our Lord is not made questionable because of the mere fact that there were others who rose from
the dead before His resurrection, for all of these died again. What a
strange feeling that must have been for Lazarus and the others, to go
twice through the gates of death; twice to know the pain and the pang
of separation! But these all have been gathered to the dust, and lie
now waiting "the adoption, that is the resurrection of the body." But
this Man, being raised, dieth no more, death hath no more dominion over Him. And how is it that grace and peace come to us from
the risen Witness? Two or three words may be said about that.

Think how, first of all, the resurrection of Jesus Christ is the confirmation of His testimony. In it the Father, to whom He hath borne witness in His life and death, bears witness to Christ, that His claims were true and His work well-pleasing. He is "declared to be the Son of God by the resurrection from the dead." If our Lord did not rise from the dead, as all Christendom today (Easter Sunday) has been declaring its faith that He did, then, as it seems to me, there is an end to His claims to be Son of God, and Son of Man, or any thing other than a man like the rest of us. If He be no more and naught else than a man, altogether like the rest of us, then there is an end to any special revelation of the Divine nature, heart, purposes, and will, in His works and character. They may still be beautiful, they may still reveal God in the same sense in which the doings of any good man suggest a fontal source of goodness from which they flow, but beyond that they are nothing. So all the truth, and all the peace, all the grace and hope which flow to us from the witness of Jesus Christ to the Father, are neutralized and destroyed unless we believe in the resurrection from the dead. His words may still remain gracious, and true in a measure, only all dashed with the terrible mistake that He asserted that He would rise again, and rose not. But as for His life, it ceases to be in any real sense, because it ceases to be in any unique sense, the revelation to the world of the character of God.

And, therefore, as I take it, it is no exaggeration to say the whole fabric of Christianity, and all Christ's worth as a witness to God, stand or fall with the fact of His resurrection. If you pull out that keystone, down comes the arch. There may still be fair carving on some of the fallen fragments, but it is no longer an arch that spans the great gulf, and has a firm pier on the other side. Strike away the resurrection and you fatally damage the witness of Jesus. You cannot strike the supernatural out of Christianity, and keep the natural. The two are inextricably woven together that to wrench away the one lacerates the other, and makes it bleed, even to death. If Christ be not risen we have nothing to preach, and you have nothing to believe. Our preaching and your faith are alike vain: ye are yet in your sins. Grace and peace come from faith in the "first begotten from the dead."

And that is true in another way too. Faith in the resurrection gives us a living Lord to confide in—not a dead Lord. Whose work we may look back upon with thankfulness; but a living one, Who works now upon us, and by Whose true companionship and real affection, strength and help are granted to us every day. The cold frost of death has not congealed that stream of love that poured from His heart while He lived on earth; it flows yet for each of us, for all of us, for the whole world.

My brother, we cannot do without a living Christ to stand beside us, to sympathize, to help, to love. We cannot do without a living Christ with Whom we may speak, Who will speak to us. And that communion which is blessedness, that communication of power and righteousness which is life, are only possible if it be true that His death was not the end of His relationship to us, or of His work in the world, but was only a transition from one stage of that work to another. We have to look to Christ, the "faithful Witness," the Witness Who witnessed when He died; but we have to look to Him that is risen again and takes His place at the right hand of God. And the grace and peace flow to us not only from the contemplation of the past witness of the Lord, but are showered upon us from the open hands of the risen and living Christ.

In still another way do grace and peace reach us, from the "first begotten from the dead," inasmuch as in Him and in His resurrection—life we are armed for victory over that foe whom He has conquered. If He be the firstborn, He will have "many brethren." The "first" implies a second. He has been raised from the dead, therefore death is not the destruction of conscious life. He has been raised from the dead, therefore any other man may be. Like another Samson, He has come forth from the prison-house, with the bars and gates upon His mighty shoulders, and has carried them away up there to the hill-top where He is. And the prison-house door stands gaping wide, and none so weak but he can pass out through the ever open portals. Christ has risen, and therefore if we will trust Him we have conquered that last and grimmest foe. And so for ourselves, when we are trembling, as we all do with the natural shrinking of flesh from the thought of that certain death; for ourselves, in our hours of lonely sorrow, when the tears come or the heart is numbed with pain; for ourselves when we lay ourselves down in our beds to die, grace and peace, like the dove that fell on His sacred head as it rose from the water of the baptism—will come from His hands Who is not only "the faithful Witness," but the "first begotten from the dead."

III. Lastly, we have grace and peace from the King of kings.

The series of aspects of Christ's work here is ranged in order of time, insofar as the second follows the first, and the third flows from both, though we are not to suppose that our Lord has ceased to be the faithful Witness when He has ascended His Sovereign Throne. His own saying, "I have declared Thy name, and will declare it," shows us that His witness is perpetual, and carried on from His seat at the right hand of God.

He is the "Prince of the kings of the earth," just because He is "the faithful Witness." That is to say: His dominion is the dominion of the truth; His dominion is a kingdom over men's wills and spirits. Does He rule by force? No! Does He rule by outward means? No! By terror? No! But because, as He said to the astonished Pilate, He came "to bear witness to the truth"; therefore is He the King not of the Jews only but of the whole world. A kingdom over heart and conscience, will and spirit, is the kingdom which Christ has founded, and His rule rests upon His witness.

And not only so, He is "the Prince of the kings of the earth" because in that witness He dies, and so becomes a "martyr" to the truth—the word in the original conveying both ideas. That is to say, His dominion rests not only upon truth. That would be a dominion grand as compared with the kingdom of this world, but still cold. His dominion rests upon love and sacrifice. And so His Kingdom is a kingdom of blessing and of gentleness; and He is crowned with the crowns of the universe, because He was first crowned with the crown of thorns. His first regal title was written upon His Cross, and from the Cross His Royalty ever flows. He is the King because He is the sacrifice.

And He is the Prince of the kings of the earth because, witnessing and slain, He has risen again; His resurrection has been the step midway, as it were, between the humiliation of earth and death, and the loftiness of the Throne. By it He has climbed to

His place at the right hand of God. He is King and Prince, then, by right of truth, love, sacrifice, death, resurrection.

And King to what end! That He may send grace and peace. Is there no peace for a man's heart in feeling that the Brother that loves him and died for him rules over all the perplexities of life, the confusions of Providence, the sorrows of a world, and the corruptions of his own nature? Is it not enough to drive away fears, to anodyne cares, to disentangle perplexities, to quiet disturbances, to make the coward brave, and the feeble strong, and the foolish wise, and the querulous patient, to think that my Christ is King; and that the hands which were nailed to the Cross wield the scepter, and that He who died for me rules the universe and rules me?

Oh, brethren! There is no tranquility for a man anywhere else but in the humble, hearty recognition of that Lord as his Lord. Crown Him with your reverence, with your loyal obedience, with your constant desires; crown him with your love, the most precious of all the crowns that He wears, and you will find that grace and peace come to you from Him.

Such, then, is the vision that this seer in Patmos had of this Lord. It was to him a momentary opening of the heavens, which showed him his throned Lord; but the fact which was made visible to his inward eye for a moment is an eternal fact. Today as then, tomorrow as today, for Asiatic Greeks and for modern Englishmen, for past centuries, for the present, and for all the future, for the whole world forever, Jesus Christ is the only witness whose voice breaks the awful silence and tells us of a Father; the only Conqueror of Death Who makes the life beyond a firm, certain fact; the King Whose dominion it is life to obey. We all need Him. Your hearts have wants which only His grace can supply, your lives have troubles which only His peace can still. Sin and sorrow, change and trial, separation and death, are facts in every man's experience. They are ranked against us in serried battalions. You can conquer them all if you will seek shelter and strength from Him who has died for you, and lives to succor and to save. Trust Him! Let your faith grasp the past fact of the cross whose virtue never grows old, and the present fact of the Throne from which He bends down with hands full of grace; and on His lips the tender old words: "Peace I leave with you, My peace give I unto you!"

28

The Christian Life a Transfiguration

*Be not conformed to this world, but be ye trans-
formed by the renewing of your minds*—Romans 12:2.

In the preceding verse the Apostle begins the hortatory or practical
part of the Epistle, and gathers the whole sum of Christian duty
into one word—Sacrifice. In like manner, in this verse another general idea from which all Christian morality may be deduced, is put
forth. As all is to be sacrifice, so all is to be transformation. Self-
denying surrender is the one principle; continued change into another likeness is the other, which, taken together may be regarded
as the all-sufficient rules of all Christian conduct and character.

There are three things that strike me in these words—where Paul
begins, namely with an inward change; what he expects from the inward change, a life transfigured; and what he is sure will be the result of such a transfigured life, a growing unlikeness to the fleeting
fashion of this world. So we have to look together briefly at these
three things.

I. Where Paul begins, with an inward renewal, "the renewing of
your minds." He goes deep down, because he had learned in his
Master's school who said: "Make the tree good and the fruit good."
To tinker at the outside with a host of anxious rules about conduct,
and red-tape restrictions, and prescriptions, is all wasted time and
vain effort. You may wrap a man up in the swaddling bands of specific precepts until you can scarcely see him, and he cannot move,
and you have not done a bit of good. We have to go deeper than
that, down to the "hidden man of the heart" to touch the inward

259

springs of action. The inner man must be dealt with first, and then the outward will come right in due time. How many of the plans for the social and moral renovation of the world, come under the lash of this condemnation, and are at once declared to be inadequate because they only skim the surface of the evil! They are as superficial as a doctor's treatment would be, who would direct all his attention to curing pimples when the patient is dying of consumption. They wipe away the matter of a sore, and leave the sore itself untouched. We shall have to go deeper than that, as Paul, echoing his Master, reminds us and to begin right in the middle if we intend to influence to any purpose the circumference and the outside. First of all must come the renewing of the mind and, after that, the transfiguration of the life.

Still further, not only have we to begin in the middle—but there has to be a radical change in the middle—the renewing of the mind, the making of the mind over again. "The mind," I suppose, is here taken in a somewhat popular sense, for Paul is not teaching psychology, but practical morality. The word seems to be equivalent to the thinking faculty, the "intellect" as we say, but, possibly, to be used in a somewhat wider sense as including the whole inner man, with feelings, and desires, as well as thoughts. That inner man has got a wrong twist somehow; it needs to be recreated, made anew, molded over again. For in all of us, apart from this renovating and ennobling influence, it is what Paul calls "the mind of the flesh," or human nature unredeemed and unregenerate. It is held in slavery and submission to the external—to the material; it is a mass of affections fixed upon the transient of low thoughts. A predominant self-regard characterizes it and its actions. That is a sad stern picture.

Ah! dear brethren, what man that knows himself, and has ever tried fairly to judge his own inner history and life, but will say: "It is all true"? Nature's sternest painter is her best. The teaching that a man, apart from God and the renovating influences of Christianity, has a mind that needs to be shaped all over again before it is capable of nobility and purity and true holiness, and wisdom, is a teaching to which, if you will strip it of the mere, hard shell of theological language, by which it has often been made repulsive to men, everybody's conscience, when once it is fairly appealed to, gives in its "Amen!" And when I come to a miscellaneous congregation like this, and bring the message to each heart—"Thou art the man!"—there is not one of us, if he is honest with himself, but will say, "Yes! I know it all; I am!" Apart from God we have minds enslaved, that need to be emancipated.

Then another step here is—this new creation of the inner man is only possible as the result of the communication of a life from without. That communicated life from without is the life of Jesus Christ Himself, put into your heart, on condition of your simply opening the door of your heart by faith, and saying to Him "Come in, Thou blessed of the Lord." And He comes in, bearing in His hands this gift most chiefly, the gift of a germ of life which will mold and shape our "mind" after His own blessed pattern.

But that renewal, beginning in the center, absolutely essential for all lofty and pure living, which is in itself the result of the communication of the gift of Jesus Christ, which gift is the result of our simple faith—that new life, when given, needs to be fostered and cherished. It is only a little spark that has to kindle a great heap of green wood, and to turn it into its own ruddy likeness. We have to keep our two hands round it, for fear it should be blown out by the rough gusts and tempests of passion and of circumstance. It is only a little seed that is sown in our hearts; we have to cherish and cultivate it, to water it by our prayers, and to watch over it, lest either the fowls of the air with light wings should carry it away, or the heavy wains of the world's business and the world's pleasures should crush it to death, or the thorns of earthly desires should spring up and choke it. We must cherish it and care for it, that it may bring forth fruit abundantly in our life.

II. So much for the first point that is here. Now a word or two about the second; the transfigured life which follows upon that inward renewal. Many of you know, I have no doubt, that the word in our text—"Be ye *transformed* by the renewal of your minds," is the same as is employed in two of the Evangelist's accounts of our Lord's transfiguration. And it is never employed except there, and here, and once besides.

I daresay it would be going too far to say that in selecting this word the Apostle had in his mind any allusion to that incident, but the coincidence is, at all events, remarkable; and we may, I think, fairly take that event as illustrating very beautifully the nature of the change which should pass over us. In the transfiguration, our Lord's indwelling divinity seems as it were, to have come floating up to the surface for once, and to have been made visible. So in like manner from within to the outward edge of the being, this renewed mind shall work, irradiating our faces with a diviner beauty, and turning even this "muddy vesture of decay" into snowy whiteness, "so as no fuller on earth shall be able to white" it. "A transfigured life" suggests to us, in the light of the story, even nobler and loftier aspirations and hopes than the phrase, "a transformed life." There lie in it, and in the context, some important thoughts. It suggests that the inward life, if it is healthy and true and strong, will certainly shape the outward conduct and character. Just as truly as the physical life molds the infant's limbs, just as truly as every periwinkle shell on the beach is shaped into the convolutions that will fit the inhabitant, by the power of the life that lies within, so the renewed mind will make a fit dwelling for itself. To a large extent a man's spirit shapes his body. Did you never see some homely face, perhaps that of a gray-haired, wrinkled old woman, perhaps that of some pallid invalid, that had in it the very radiance of Heaven, and of which it might be said without exaggeration that it "was as the face of an angel"? Did you never see goodness making men and women beautiful? Did you never see some noble emotion stamp its own nobility on the countenance, and seem to dilate a man's very form and figure, and make the weakest like an angel of God? Have not there been other faces besides the face of Moses, that shone as men came down from the Mount of Communion with God? Or as Milton puts it:

> Oft converse with heavenly habitants
> Begins to cast a beam on the outward shape,
> The unpolluted temple of the mind.

Even as the fashion of His countenance was altered, so the inner life of Christ deep and true in a man's heart will write its presence in his countenance, and show how awful and how blessed goodness is.

But apart from that, which of course is not immediately in the Apostle's mind here, surely it does not need many words to remind you that the inward change of the mind, of which I have been speaking, will manifest itself in conduct and character. What about the Christianity that does not show itself as such? What about men that look exactly as if they were not Christians? What about the inward life that never comes up to the surface?

A certain kind of seaweeds that lie at the bottom of the sea, when their flowering time comes, elongate their stalks and reach the light and float upon the top, and then, when they have flowered and fruited, they sink again into the depths. Our Christian life should come up to the surface and open out its flowers there, and show them to the heavens and to all eyes that look. Does your Christianity do that! It is no use talking about the inward change unless there is the outward transfiguration. Ask yourselves the question whether that is visible or not in your lives.

And then, still further, this image of our text suggests to us that the essential character of our transfiguration is the molding of us into the likeness of Jesus Christ. Christ's life is in you if you are in Him. If you are a Christian man or woman you have got a bit of Jesus Christ in you. And just as every leaf that you take off some plants and stick into a flower-pot will in time become a little plant exactly like the parent from which it was taken, so the Christ-life that is in you, if it is worth anything—that is to say, if it is really in you at all—will be shaping you into His likeness, and growing into a copy of its source and origin. The least little tiny speck of musk, invisibly taken from a cake of it, and carried away ever so far, will diffuse the same fragrance as the mass from which it came; and the little almost imperceptible slice, if I may so say, of Jesus Christ's life that is in you and me, if it be in us at all, will smell as sweet if not as strong as the great life from which it came. The life of Christ in us will mold us, in the measure of its power, into the likeness of Christ, from Whom it comes. What a blessed thought that we may move among men, as copies of Jesus Christ, with like visible consecration, and making men feel as they look at us that the gospel has power to evoke a rare beauty of character which witnesses for His transforming grace!

But, as I said before, in reference to the inward renewal, so I say in reference to the outward transfiguration, the life within will not work up to the surface and manifest itself in our conduct and character except upon condition of our continual effort, and our own honest endeavor. No doubt it is His life that molds us, no doubt it is the gift of His Divine Spirit, whereby our characters are refined and hallowed, are ennobled and elevated, are delivered from self-ishness, are lifted from their low creeping along the ground, and taught to aspire to the heavens. But all that will not come without our cooperation, earnest and prayerful and perpetual. We must be fellow-workers with God, in the task of building up our characters into the likeness of our Master. The fact that His Spirit is given to us is not a reason for our indolence, but it *is* a reason for our work, because it supplies us with the material with which we can work with some hope of success, and gives us the power by which we can do the thing that we desire.

So instead of a man saying, "It is Christ's life in me that must mold me, and therefore I need do nothing," he should say, "I have Christ's life within me to mold me, and therefore I must work." What would you think of a man that said, "It is the steam that drives the spindles, so I need not put the belting on!" And just as wise is he who makes the thought of the renovation and transfiguration being all the work of Christ a pillow for his indolence, and an excuse for his selfish sloth. "Work out your own salvation, for it is God that worketh in you."

III. Lastly, let us consider the ultimate consequence which the Apostle regards as certain, from this central inward change; viz., the unlikeness to the world around. "Be not conformed to this world."

I need not spend time in discussing the notion to be attached to the expression, "this world." Suffice it for our present purpose to say it stands for the whole mass of men and things apart from God. And the "fashion of this world" is the whole set of maxims, opinions, thoughts, theories, views of life, pursuits, the like, of such men.

We all know well enough what the world is, by the specimen of it that we have inside of ourselves, but the principle that I want to insist upon for a moment is this: that the more we get like Jesus Christ, the more certainly we get unlike the world.

For the two theories of life are clean contrary, the one is all-limited by this "bank and shoal of time," the other stretches out through the transient to lay hold on the Infinite and Eternal. The one is all for self, the other is all for God, with His will for law, and His love for motive. The two theories, I say, are contrary the one to the other, so that likeness to and adherence to the one must needs be dead in the teeth of the other.

And that contrariety is as real today as ever it was. Paul's "world" was a grim, heathen, persecuting world; our "world" has got christened, and goes to church and chapel, like a respectable gentleman. But for all that it is still the world all the same, and you and I have to shake our hands free of it as thoroughly as ever it was a Christian man's duty to do so. No doubt there is a great deal of world in the Church, and, thank God, there is a little of the Church in the world, so that the gulf does not seem quite as deep as once it was. But when you come down to fundamentals, and the underlying principles of life, the antagonism is as great and real as ever it was. So let no man fancy that this generation has less need for this commandment than any generation that has gone before.

How is the commandment to be obeyed? Well, of course there are large tracts of human life where the saint and the sinner have to do exactly the same things; where the holiest and the most selfish have to perform the same functions, be touched by the same emotions, feel the same anxieties, weep the same tears, and smile the same smiles, attend to the same tasks, and gather together the same treasures. No doubt! And yet "there shall be two women grinding at a mill," the one of them at that side shall be a Christian, the other of them on that side shall not. They push the handle round, and the push that carries the handle round half of the circumference of the millstone may be a bit of religious worship, and the push that carries it round the other half the circumference may be a bit of serving the world and the flesh and the devil. Two men shall be sitting at the same desk, two boys at the same bench at school, two servants in the same kitchen, two students at the same class at Owen's College, and the one shall be serving God and glorifying His name, and the other shall be serving self and Satan. The one may be immersed in and the other may be antagonistic to the world, to the very depths of his soul. Not the things done, but the motive, makes the difference.

And yet that is not all that has to be said. There are a great many things which it is not my business, standing here, to enumerate *seriatim*, in which not to be "conformed to the world" means to be outwardly different, and to have nothing to do with certain acts and certain people. Have nothing to do with things for instance, which in themselves are unmistakably wrong; nor with things which, not being in themselves unmistakably wrong, have got evil inextricably mixed up with them, like, as I believe, the English stage; nor with things which, not being in themselves unmistakably wrong, and not having evil inextricably mixed up with them, are yet, as experience shows you, bad for *you*. This generation of the Church seems in business and in daily life, and most of all in its amusements, to be trying how near it can go to the world, which is to me a suspicious sign that much of it is only a christened world after all. Do not you try, my brother, if you want your Christian life to be vigorous and strong, how near to the world you can go. It is a dangerous game. It is like children trying how far they can stretch out of the nursery window without tumbling into the street; you will go over some day when you miscalculate a little bit.

Rather "be ye transfigured," and then you will find that when the inner mind is changed, many of the things that attracted tempt no more, and many of the people that wanted to have you do not care to have you, for you spoil their sport and are a wet blanket to their amusements and enjoyments. Do you deepen the life of Christ in your hearts, and see to it that day by day the influence of His sweet love is more and more manifest in your nature, and then of itself this nonconformity to the world's maxims and the world's fashion will certainly come.

Unless our unlikeness to the world is the result of our growing likeness to Christ, it is of little value. It is useless to preach unworldliness to men unless they have Christ in their hearts. The great means of becoming unlike the world is becoming like Him, and the great means of becoming like Him is living near Him and drinking in His life and Spirit. So we shall be delivered from the world's tyranny.

So, dear brethren, a great hope is offered to every man; even the foolishest, the weakest, the most vile and degraded. There is nobody so deeply stamped with the mark and superscription of the Beast, but that it may be erased from his forehead, and printed there the sign and the token of the Lamb. We cannot, by any effort, mold our natures afresh. But we can open our hearts to the entrance of Christ's transforming life. That will change all the hard, obstinate nature, as a furnace conquers the masses of ore cast into it until they become fluid in proportion as they absorb the heat. So we may be melted by the love and molded into the likeness of our Lord.

We should widen our expectations to the magnificent sweep of His promise. "As we have borne the image of the earthly, we shall also bear the image of the heavenly." But we must begin by opening our hearts to the leaven which shall work onward and outwards till it has changed all. Let us gaze on Him in love and faith, till, looking, we become like Him. The sun when it shines upon a mirror makes the mirror shine like a little sun. "We all with open face, reflecting as a mirror does the glory of the Lord, shall be changed into the same image."

29

*From the Depths
to the Heights*

*1. Out of the depths have I cried unto Thee, O Lord. 2. Lord
hear my voice; let Thine ears be attentive to the voice of my supplications. 3. If Thou, Lord shouldst mark iniquities, O Lord!
who shall stand? 4. But there is forgiveness with Thee, that
Thou mayest be feared. 5. I wait for the Lord, my soul doth wait,
and in His word do I hope. 6. My soul waiteth for the Lord
more than they that watch for the morning: I say, more than they
that watch for the morning. 7. Let Israel hope in the Lord; for
with the Lord there is mercy, and with Him is plenteous redemption. 8. And he shall redeem Israel from all his iniquities*
—Psalm 130.

This psalm gives us what we may call the ascent of the soul
from the depths to the heights.

It is "a song of degrees," as the heading tells us, that is, a "song
of *goings up.*" Whatever that very enigmatical phrase may mean,
there is a sense in which this Psalm, at any rate, is distinctly a song
of ascent, in that it starts from the very lowest point of self-abase-
ment and consciousness of evil, and rises steadily and, though it may
be slowly, yet surely, up to the tranquil summit, led by a consciousness of the Divine Presence and grace.

Let us, then, read the Psalm over this morning, and try to bring
out some little of its depth and beauty. It falls very clearly into
four portions, of a couple of verses each. The first of them is a cry
from the depths. Then in the second and third verses we have the
second rung of the ladder, as it were, or stage of ascent. That great
yearning for God is for a moment checked by a dark thought,
which, however, being overcome, issues into a blessed bright assurance. The man has been crying to God, and he stops; his voice
is, as it were, blown back into his own throat when he thinks this—

269

"If thou, Lord, shouldest mark iniquities, O Lord! who shall stand?" And then we must insert a thought that is not expressed in the Psalm. "But Thou *dost not* so mark iniquity." "*For,*" as the little word at the beginning of verse 4 would be more accurately rendered, "there is forgiveness with Thee, that thou mayest be feared." So the dark thought is overwhelmed and drowned, as it were, in the great, glad confidence—"There is forgiveness with Thee, that Thou mayest be feared."

And then, after the appropriation, in this great act of confidence and faith, of the great truth of God's forgiving mercy, there comes the third step in the ladder, also expressed in a couple of verses: "I wait for the Lord, my soul doth wait, and in His word do I hope. My soul waiteth for the Lord more than they that watch for the morning: I say, more than they that watch for the morning." That is to say, there we get the permanent, peaceful dependence upon God, of the spirit that has tasted His forgiving mercy. Conscious dependence, blessed tranquillity, fixed reliance upon God's faithful Word, and an absorbing desire for more and more of the light which alone can scatter the darkness of fear and guilt and sin—these are the third step on the ladder.

And then the fourth, likewise expressed in a couple of verses, is what I may call the missionary call from the depths of personal experience of God's forgiving mercy: "Let Israel hope in the Lord, for with the Lord there is mercy, and with Him is plenteous redemption. And he shall redeem Israel from all his transgressions." Up on the summit of that great hope, which belongs to all Israel, of a complete, an all-embracing deliverance and redemption, the Psalmist stands with the sunshine about him, having climbed steadily from that low, abject condition of consciousness of his sin and evil.

So much, then, for the outline of the course of thought that lies here. And now let me just say a word or two about each of these steps.

I. We have the cry from the depths.

What depths? The psalmist thinks of himself as of a man at the bottom of a pit, sending up to the surface a faint call which may easily be unheard. He has some sense of the height to which his voice must rise, and as he catches a glimpse of the exalted Lord, he feels how far below he is. Measured by the height of that throne "high from the beginning," all men are in the depths. But he does not merely mean to express his sense of human insignificance, nor even his sorrows, nor his despondency. There are deeper pits than these, so deep that these are by comparison but dimples on the surface, and a man never truly cries to God till he has been down into the deepest of them.

The depths which the Psalmist here means are away down far below these shallow ones. They are the depths into which the spirit feels itself going down, sick and giddy, when there comes the thought, "I am a sinful man, O Lord, in the presence of Thy great purity." Out of these depths does he cry to God.

Now, three remarks are all I have time to make on this matter:

First, the depths are the place for us all. Every man amongst us has to go down there, if we take the place that belongs to us.

The next thing is—Unless you have cried to God out of these depths you have never cried to Him at all. Unless you come to Him as a penitent sinful man, with the consciousness of transgression awakened within you, your prayers are shallow.

Or, to put it into other words, the beginning of all true personal religion lies in the sense of my own sin and my lost condition. Why, the difference between the tepid, superficial religion that so many of you have—and true religion consists a great deal more in this than in anything else—that in the one case a sense of sin has been awakened, and in the other it has not. The reason why multitudes of people who formally call themselves Christians have such a slight hold of Christian truth, and why the Gospel has so small a power over them, is because they have never found out, in any real sense of the word, that they are sinful men.

You *say* it no doubt. You breathe out formal confessions. Have you ever been down into the depths, brother? If you have not, this psalm may teach you that you have never cried to God. It is a very easy-going kind of religion, and so it is a very fashionable kind, which diminishes the importance of the fact of sin; and it is not only a very easy-going one, but a very impotent one. I believe, for my part, that as far as creed is concerned, one main reason of the larger number of the misapprehensions and waterings-down of the full-toned Christian truth which we see round us, is that men have not appreciated the importance, as a factor in their theology, of the doctrine of sin. And so far as practice is concerned, one main reason why the prevalent religion is such a poor, flabby, impotent thing is the same. If a man does not think much about sin, he does not think much about a Divine Savior. And wherever you find a conception of Christianity which makes light of the Divinity or of the sacrifice of Jesus Christ, the reason for that error lies very largely in this other one—an under-estimate of the importance of the fact of sin.

Wherever you find men and women with a Christianity that sits very lightly upon them, that does not impel them to any acts of service and devotion, that seldom breaks out into any heroisms of self-surrender, and never rises into the heights of communion with God, depend upon it that the roots of it are to be found here, that the man has never been down into the abyss and never sent his voice up from it as some man that had tumbled down a coalpit might fling a despairing call up to the surface, in the hope that somebody wandering past the mouth of it might hear the cry. "Out of the depths" he has not cried unto God.

And the third thought about this first part is that you want nothing more than a cry to draw you from the pit. If out of the depths you cry, you will cry yourself out of the depths. Here is a man at the foot of a cliff that rises beetling like a black wall behind him, the sea in front, the bare, upright rock at his back, not a foothold for a mouse between the tide at the bottom and the grass at the top. What is he to do? There is only one thing—he can shout. Perchance somebody will hear him, a rope may come dangling down in front of him; and if he has nerve, he may shut his eyes and make a spring and catch it.

There is no way for you up out of the pit, brother, but to cry to God, and that will bring a rope down. Nay, rather, the rope is there. Your grasping the rope and your cry are one. "Ask, and ye shall receive!" God has let down the fullness of His forgiving love in Jesus Christ our Lord, and all that we need is the call, which is likewise faith, which accepts while it desires, and desires in its acceptance; and then we are lifted up "out of the horrible pit and the miry clay," and our feet are set upon a rock, and our goings established.

We have all to go down into the depths if we would understand ourselves. If we have not cried out of the depths we have never cried at all. Religion begins with penitence. A cry is all that is needed to bring us out of the depths. That is the first step on this ladder.

II. And now as to the second. We have here a dark fear and a bright assurance. As I said, the man's prayer is, as it were, blown back into his throat by the thought, "If Thou, Lord, shouldst mark iniquities, O Lord! who shall stand?" And then—as if he *would not* be swept away from his confidence even by this great blast of cold air from out of the North, that comes like ice and threatens to chill his hope to death—"But," says he, "there is forgiveness with Thee, that Thou mightest be feared." So these two halves represent the struggle in the man's mind. They are like a sky, one half of which is piled with thunder-clouds, and the other serenely blue. To "mark iniquities" is to impute them to us. The word, in the original, means to *watch,* that is to say, to remember in order to punish. If a man be regarded by God's eye through the mist of his sins, they turn the bright sun of God's own light into a red-hot, flaming ball of fire. "If Thou, Lord, shouldest mark iniquities,"—that is, shouldest take them into account in Thy thoughts and dispositions and dealings towards us—"O Lord! who shall stand?" Here, then, we have expressed the profound sense of the impossibility of any man's sustaining the righteous judgment of God. "Who shall stand," exclaimed a prophet, "when He appeareth?" "Who may stand in Thy sight," cried a psalmist, "when once Thou art angry?" Like a man having to yield ground to an eager enemy, or to bend before the blast, every man has to bow before that flashing brightness and to own that retribution would be destruction.

I do not wish to bring exaggerated charges. But has not every man moments in which he knows that remorse is not too strong a word to apply to what should be his feelings about his past? I do not charge you with vices or with crimes. I do not say there are no moral distinctions amongst men outside the pale of Christianity. I would not say, as St. Augustine said, "That the virtues of the heathen were splendid vices." At least I should want to talk a page and a half of commentary if I did adopt the phrase; but I ask you, Is not this true, that you know that there is an awful difference between what you ought to be and what you are?

Do we not all know that our characters and our lives have been, as it were, distorted, that our moral nature has been marred with animal lusts, and that ambitions and worldly desires have come in and prevented us from following the law of conscience? Is not that very conscience, more or less distorted, drugged and dormant? And is not all this largely voluntary? Do we not feel, in spite of all pleas about circumstances and "heredity," that we could have helped being what we are? And do we not feel that, after all, if there be such a thing as God's judgment and retribution, it must come down on us with terrible force? That is what our psalm means when it says that if God be strict to mark iniquities there is not one of us that can stand before Him; and we know it is true. You may be a very respectable man; that is not the question. You may have kept your hands clear from anything that would bring you within the sweep of the law; that has nothing to do with this matter. You may have subdued animal passions, been sober, temperate, chaste, generous—a hundred other things. Our congregations are not made up, as a rule, of reprobates, but they *are* made up, as a rule, of two classes—one of sinful men that have a little found out how sinful they are, and who are trying to trust in God's mercy in Jesus Christ, and so to get better, and the other of Pharisees, who have never been down into the depths of their own hearts, nor caught a glimpse of their own evil; but who listen to all the warnings and pleadings of the Gospel and never think that they have any personal interest in them, but are actually coated over with a water-proofing from their very knowledge of the truth which prevents the truth telling on them, and think themselves all right because they come to church or chapel on a Sunday, and do not go for a walk in the fields with a dog at their heels.

Ah! Dear friends, gross, palpable sin slays its thousands, and that clean, respectable, ghastly purity of a godless, self-complacent morality, I do believe, slays it tens of thousands. "The publicans and the harlots shall go into the Kingdom of God before you!" Not because they are better, but because—poor wretches! God help them!

They know that there is nothing in their lives that they can plume themselves upon. And you, not because your goodness is not goodness of a sort, but because you are building upon it, and think that such words as those of my text go clean over your heads—you are in this perilous position.

Oh! Dear friends! Will you go home today and take ten minutes at your own home quietly to think over that verse of my psalm, "If Thou, Lord, shouldest mark iniquities, O Lord who shall stand!" Can I? CAN I?

That is the thundery side of the sky, and it makes all the more tender the sapphire blue of the other side: "But there is forgiveness with Thee, that Thou mayest be feared." No man ever comes to that confidence that has not sprung to it, as it were, by a rebound from the other thought. It needs, first of all, that the heart should have tremblingly entertained the contrary hypothesis, in order that the heart should spring to the relief and the gladness of the counter truth. It must first have felt the shudder of the thought, "If thou, Lord, shouldst mark iniquities" in order to come to the gladness of the thought, "But there is forgiveness with Thee!"

"Forgiveness!" The word so translated here in my text has for its literal meaning, "cutting-off," "excision." And so it suggests the notion of taking a man's sin, that great black deformity that has grown upon his soul, and cutting it clean out with a merciful amputating knife. You know that doctors sometimes say, "Well, the only salvation of him would be an operation, but the tumor has got so implicated with the vital tissues that it would scarcely be possible to apply the knife." That is what the world says, and that is what philosophy says, and modern pessimism says, about my sin, and your sin, and the world's sin. "No! We cannot operate; we cannot cut out the cankerous tumor." Christianity says, "Miserable physicians are ye all; stand aside!" and it removes the malignant growth by a mighty and wondrous act of God's Divine mercy and Infinite power and love, in the Cross of Jesus Christ, which separates between man and his disease, and cuts it out, leaving him the more living after the amputation of that which was killing him. The world thinks the disease to be a bit of the man that cannot be got rid of. No, says the Gospel; it can all be swept away through God's forgiveness.

Men may say, "There cannot be forgiveness; you cannot alter consequences." But forgiveness has not to do only with consequences; but also and chiefly with the personal relation between me and God, and that can be altered. A judge pardons when he remits penalties. A father forgives though he sometimes chastises.

If a man has sinned, his whole life thereafter will be different from what it would have been if he had not sinned. I know that well enough. You cannot, by any pardon, alter the past, and make it not to be. I know that well enough. The New Testament doctrine and the Old Testament hope of forgiveness do not assert that you can, but say that you and God can get right with one another. A *person* can pardon. We have not merely to do with impersonal laws; we have not only to do with "the mill of God—" "that grinds slowly," but with God Himself. There is such a thing as the pardon of God. His love will come to a man free, unembittered, and will not be dammed back by transgressions, if the man will go and say, "Father! I have sinned! Forgive for Thy dear Son's sake. There is forgiveness with Thee!"

And that forgiveness lies at the root of all true godliness. No man reverences, and loves, and draws near to God so rapturously, so humbly, as the man that has learned pardon through Jesus Christ. My dear friend believe this; your religion must have for its foundation the assurance of God's pardoning mercy in Christ, or it will have no firm and deep foundation at all. I press that upon you, and ask you this one question: Is the basis of your religion the sense that God has forgiven you freely all your iniquities? "There is forgiveness with Thee, *that Thou mayest be feared.*" That is the second step of this song of ascents.

III. And now about the third stage of this ladder. "My soul waiteth for the Lord more than they that watch for the morning: I say, more than they that watch for the morning. I wait for the Lord, my soul doth wait, and in His word do I hope." There is the permanent, peaceful attitude of the spirit that has tasted the consciousness of forgiving love—a continual dependence upon God.

Like a man that has just recovered from some illness, but still leans upon the care, and feels his need of seeing the face of that skillful physician that has helped him through, there will be still, and always, the necessity for the continual application of that pardoning love. But they that have tasted that the Lord is gracious can sit very quietly at His feet and trust themselves to His kindly dealings, resting their souls upon His strong word, and looking for the fuller communication of light from Himself. This is a beautiful picture of a tranquil, continuous, ever-rewarded, and ever-fresh waiting upon Him, and reliance upon His mercy.

"More than they that watch for the morning." That is beautiful! The consciousness of sin was the dark night. The coming of His forgiving love flushed all the eastern Heaven with diffused brightness that grew into perfect day. And so the man waits quietly for the dawn, and his whole soul is one absorbing desire that God may dwell with him, and brighten and gladden him.

IV. I must not dwell upon these words, for I wish to say just a word about the last of the rounds of this ladder, in which the personal experience becomes general, and an evangel, a call upon the man's lips to all his brethren. "Let Israel hope in the Lord." There was no room for anything in his heart when he began this psalm except his own self in his misery, and that Great One high above him there. There was nobody in all the universe to him but himself and God, at his first cry from the depths.

There is nothing which isolates a man so awfully as a consciousness of sin and of his relation to God. But there is nothing that so knits him to all his fellows, and brings him into such wide-reaching bonds of amity and benevolence, as the sense of God's forgiving mercy for his own soul. So the call bursts from the lips of the pardoned man, inviting all to taste the experience and exercise the trust which have made him glad: "Let Israel hope in the Lord."

And then look at the broad Gospel that he has attained to know and to preach. "For with the Lord there is mercy, and with Him is redemption." Not only forgiveness, but redemption—and that from every form of sin. It is "plenteous"—multiplied, as the word might be rendered. Our Lord has taught us to what a sum that Divine multiplication amounts. Not once, nor twice, but "seventy times seven" is the prescribed measure of human forgiveness, and shall men be more placable than God! The perfect numbers, seven and ten are multiplied together, and that again increased seven fold, to make a numerical symbol for the Innumerable, and to bring the Infinite within the terms of the Finite. It is inexhaustible redemption, not to be provoked, not to be overcome by any obstinacy of evil—available for all, available for every grade and every repetition of transgression. "Mine iniquities are more than the hairs of my head," confesses another Psalmist, but almost in the same breath he tells us of God's loving thoughts, which are still more numerous than the hairs of his head—"If I would declare and speak of *them,* they are more than can be numbered." That forgiving grace is older and mightier than all sins, and is able to conquer them all. As when an American prairie for hundreds of miles is smoking in the autumn fires, nothing that man can do can cope with it. But the clouds gather and down comes the rain, and there is water enough in the sky to put out the fire. And so God's inexhaustible mercy, streaming down upon the lurid smoke-pillars of man's transgression, and that alone is enough to quench the flame of a man's and of a world's transgression, though heated from the lowest hell.

"With Him is plenteous redemption; He shall redeem Israel from *all* his iniquities." That is the Old Testament prophecy. Let me leave on your hearts the New Testament fulfillment of it. The Psalmist said, "He shall redeem Israel from all his iniquities." He was sure of that, and his soul was at "peace in believing" it. But there were mysteries about it which he could not understand. He lived in the twilight dawn, and he and all his fellows had to watch for the morning, of which they saw but the faint promise in the Eastern sky. The sun is risen for us—"Thou shalt call his name Jesus, for He shall save His people from their sins." That is the fulfillment, the vindication, and explanation of the Psalmist's hope. Lay hold on Christ, and He will lift you out of the depths, and set you upon the sunny heights of the Mountain of God.

30

Simon the Cyrenian

They compelled one Simon, a Cyrenian, who passed by, coming out of the country, the father of Alexander and Rufus, to bear His Cross—Mark 15:21.

How little these people knew that they were making this man immortal! What a strange fate that is which has befallen those persons in the Gospel narrative, who for an instant came into contact with Jesus Christ. Like ships passing athwart the white ghost-like splendor of the moonlight on the sea, they gleam silvery pure for a moment as they cross its broad belt and then are swallowed up again in the darkness.

This man Simon, fortuitously, as men say, meeting the little procession at the gate of the city, for an instant is caught in the radiance of the light, and stands out visible forevermore to all the world; and then sinks into the blackness, and we know no more about him. This brief glimpse tells us very little, and yet the man and his act and its consequences may be worth thinking about.

He was a Cyrenian; that is, he was a Jew by descent, probably born, and certainly resident, for purposes of commerce, in Cyrene, on the North African coast of the Mediterranean. No doubt he had come up to Jerusalem for the Passover; and like very many of the strangers who flocked to the Holy City for the feast, met some difficulty in finding accommodation in the city, and so was obliged to go and lodge in one of the outlying villages. From this lodging he is coming in, in the morning, knowing nothing about Christ nor His trial, knowing nothing of what he is about to meet, and happens to see the procession as it is passing out of the gate. He is, by the centurion impressed to help the fainting Christ to carry the heavy Cross. He probably thought Christ a common criminal, and would resent the task laid upon him by the rough authority of the officer in command. But he was gradually touched into some kind of sympathy; drawn closer and closer, as we suppose, as he looked upon this dying meekness; and at last, yielding to the soul-conquering power of Christ.

Tradition says so, and the reasons for supposing that it may be so may be very simply stated. The description of him in our text as "the father of Alexander and Rufus" shows that, by the time when Mark wrote, his two sons were members of the Christian community, and had attained some eminence in it. A Rufus is mentioned in the salutations in Paul's Epistle to the Romans, as being "elect in the Lord," that is to say, "eminent," and his mother is associated in the greeting, and commended as having been motherly to Paul as well as to Rufus. Now, if we remember that Mark's Gospel was probably written in Rome, and for Roman Christians, the conjecture seems a very reasonable one that the Rufus here was the Rufus of the Epistle to the Romans. If so, it would seem that the family had been gathered into the fold of the Church, and in all probability, therefore, the father with them.

Then there is another little morsel of possible evidence which may just be noticed. We find in the Acts of the Apostles, in the list of the prophets and teachers in the Church at Antioch, a "Simon, who is called Niger," and side by side with him one "Lucius of Cyrene," from which place we know that several of the original brave preachers to the Gentiles in Antioch came. It is *possible* that this may be our Simon, and that he who was the last to join the band of disciples during the Master's life and learned courage at the Cross was among the first to apprehend the worldwide destination of the Gospel, and to bear it beyond the narrow bounds of his nation.

At all events, I think we may, with something like confidence, believe that his glimpse of Christ on that morning and his contact with the suffering Savior ended in his acceptance of Him as his Christ, and in his bearing in a truer sense the Cross after Him.

And so I seek now to gather some of the lessons that seem to me to arise from this incident.

I. First, the greatness of trifles. If that man had started from the little village where he lived five minutes earlier or later, if he had walked a little faster or slower, if he had happened to be lodging on the other side of Jerusalem, or if the whim had taken him to go in at another gate, or if the centurion's eye had not chanced to alight on him in the crowd, or if the centurion's fancy had picked out somebody else to carry the cross, then all his life would have been different.

And so it is always. You go down one turning rather than another, and your whole career is colored thereby. You miss a train, and you escape death. Our lives are like the Cornish rocking stones, pivoted on little points. The most apparently insignificant things have a strange knack of suddenly developing unexpected consequences, and turning out to be, not small things at all, but great and decisive and fruitful.

Let us then look with ever fresh wonder on this marvelous contexture of human life, and on Him that molds it all to His own perfect purposes. Let us bring the highest and largest principles to bear on the smallest events and circumstances, for you can never tell which of these is going to turn out a revolutionary and formative influence in your life. And if the highest Christian principle is not brought to bear upon the trifles, depend upon it it will never be brought to bear upon the mighty things. The most part of every life is made up of trifles, and unless these are ruled by the highest motives, life, which is divided into grains like the sand, will have gone by, while we are preparing for the big events which we think worthy of being regulated by lofty principles. Take care of the pennies and the pounds will take care of themselves.

Look after the trifles, for the law of life is like that which is laid down by the Psalmist about the Kingdom of Jesus Christ: "There shall be a handful of corn in the earth," a little seed sown in an apparently ungenial place "on the top of the mountains." Ay! But this will come of it, "The fruit thereof shall shake like Lebanon," and the great harvest of benediction or of curse, of joy or of sorrow, will come from the minute seeds that are sown in the *great* trifles of your daily life.

Let us learn the lesson, too, of quiet confidence in Him in Whose hands the whole puzzling, overwhelming mystery lies. If a

man once begins to think of how utterly incalculable the consequences of the smallest and most commonplace of his deeds may be,
how they may run out into all eternity, and like divergent lines, may
enclose a space that gets larger and wider the further they travel; if,
I say, a man once begins to indulge in thoughts like these, it is difficult for him to keep himself calm and sane at all, unless he believes
in the great living Providence that lies above all, and shapes the vi-
cissitude and mystery of life. We can leave all in His hands—and if
we are wise we shall do so—to Whom *great* and *small* are terms that
have no meaning; and Who looks upon men's lives, not according
to the apparent magnitude of the deeds with which they are filled,
but simply according to the motive from which, and the purpose towards which, these deeds were done.

II. Then, still further, take this other lesson, which lies very
plainly here—the blessedness and honor of helping Jesus Christ. If
you turn to the story of the Crucifixion, in John's Gospel, you
will find that the narratives of the three other Gospels are, in some
points supplemented by it. In reference to our Lord's bearing of the
Cross, we are informed by John that when He left the Judgment
Hall He was carrying it Himself, as was the custom with criminals
under the Roman law. The heavy cross was laid on the shoulder, at
the intersection of its arms and stem, one of the arms hanging
down in front of the bearer's body, and the long upright trailing behind.

Apparently our Lord's physical strength, sorely tried by a night
of excitement and the hearings in the High Priest's Palace, and before Pilate, as well as by the scourging, was unequal to the task of
carrying, albeit for that short passage, the heavy weight. And there
is a little hint of that sort in the context. In the verse before my text
we read, "they led Jesus out to crucify Him," and in the verse
after, "they bring," or *bear* "Him to the place Golgotha," as if
when the procession began, they led Him, and before it ended
they had to carry Him, His weakness having become such that
He Himself could not sustain the weight of His cross or of His own
enfeebled limbs. So, with some touch of pity in their rude hearts, or
more likely with professional impatience of delay, and wanting to
get their task over, the soldiers lay hold of this stranger, press him

into the service and make him carry the heavy upright, which trailed on the ground behind Jesus. And so they pass on to the place of execution.

Very reverently, and with few words, one would touch upon the physical weakness of the Master. Still, it does not do us any harm to try to realize how very marked was the collapse of His physical nature, and to remember that that collapse was not entirely owing to the pressure upon Him of the mere fact of physical death; and that it was still less a failure of His will, or like the abject cowardice of some criminals who have had to be dragged to the scaffold, and helped up its steps; but that the reason why His flesh failed was very largely because there was laid upon Him the mysterious burden of the world's sin.

Christ's demeanor in the act of death, in such singular contrast to the calm heroism and strength of hundreds who have drawn all their heroism and strength from Him, suggests to us that, looking upon His sufferings, we look upon something the significance of which does not lie on the surface; and the extreme pressure of which is to be accounted for by that blessed and yet solemn truth of prophecy and Gospel alike—"The Lord hath laid on Him the iniquity of us all."

But, apart from that, which does not enter properly into my present contemplations, let us remember that though changed in form, very truly and really in substance, this blessedness and honor of helping Jesus Christ is given to us; and is demanded from us, too, if we are His disciples. He is despised and set at nought still. He is crucified afresh still. There are plenty of men in this day who scoff at Him, mock Him, deny His claims, seek to cast Him down from His throne, rebel against His dominion. It is an easy thing to be a disciple when all the crowd is crying "Hosanna!" It is a much harder thing to be a disciple when the crowd, or even when the influential cultivated opinion of a generation is crying "Crucify Him! Crucify Him!" And some of you Christian men and women have to learn the lesson that if you are to be Christians you must be Christ's companions when His back is at the wall as well as when men are exalting and honoring Him; that it is your business to confess Him when men deny Him, to stand by Him when men forsake Him, to avow Him when the avowal is likely to bring contempt upon you from some people; and thus, in a very real sense, to bear His Cross after Him. "Let us go forth unto Him without the camp, bearing His reproach"; the tail-end of His Cross. It is the lightest! He has borne the heaviest end on His own shoulders; but we have to ally ourselves with that suffering and despised Christ if we are to be His disciples.

I do not dwell upon the lesson often drawn from this story, as if it taught us to "take up *our* cross daily and follow Him." That is another matter, and yet is closely connected with that about which I speak, but what I say is, Christ's Cross has to be carried today; and if we have not found out that it has, let us ask ourselves if we are Christians at all. There will be hostility, alienation, a comparative coolness, and absence of a full sense of sympathy with you, in many people, if you are a true Christian. You will come in for a share of contempt from the wise and the cultivated of this genera-tion, as in all generations. The mud that is thrown after the Master will spatter your faces too, to some extent; and if we are walking with Him we shall share, to the extent of our communion with Him, in the feelings with which many men regard Him. Stand to your col-ors! Do not be ashamed of Him in the midst of a crooked and perverse generation.

And there is yet another way too, in which this honor of help-ing the Lord is given to us. As in His weakness He needed some-one to aid Him to bear His Cross, so in His glory He needs our help to carry out the purposes for which the Cross was borne. The paradox of a man carrying the Cross of Him Who carried the world's burden is repeated in another form too. He needs nothing, and yet He needs us. He needs nothing, and yet He needed that ass which was tethered at the place where two ways met, in order to ride into Jerusalem upon it. He does not need man's help, and yet He does need it, and He asks for it. And though He bore Simon the Cyrenian's sins "in His own body on the tree," He needed Simon the Cyrenian to help Him to bear the tree. He needs us to help Him to spread throughout the world the blessed consequences of that Cross and bitter Passion. So to us all is granted the honor, and from us all are required the sacrifice and the service of helping the suffering Savior.

III. Another of the lessons which may very briefly be drawn from this story is that of the perpetual recompense and record of the humblest Christian work. There were different degrees of criminality, and different degrees of sympathy with Him, if I may use the word, in that crowd that stood round the Master. The criminality varied from the highest degree of violent malignity in the Scribes and Pharisees, down to the lowest point of ignorance, and therefore all but entire innocence on the part of the Roman legionaries, who were merely the mechanical instruments of the order given, and stolidly "watched Him there," with eyes which saw nothing.

On the other hand, there were all grades of service, and help and sympathy, from the vague emotions of the crowd who beat their breasts, and the pity of the daughters of Jerusalem, the kindly-meant help of the soldiers, who would have moistened the parched lips, to the heroic love of the women at the Cross, whose ministry was not ended even with His life. But surely the most blessed share in that day's tragedy was reserved for Simon, whose bearing of the Cross may have been compulsory at first, but became, ere it was ended, willing service. But whatever were the degrees of recognition of Christ's character, and of sympathy with the meaning of His sufferings, yet the smallest and most transient impulse of loving gratitude that went out towards Him was rewarded then, and is rewarded forever, by blessed results in the heart that feels it.

Besides these, service for Christ is recompensed, as in the instance before us, by a perpetual memorial. How little Simon knew that "wherever in the whole world this Gospel was preached, there also, this that *he* had done should be told for a memorial of him!" How little he understood when he went back to his rural lodging that night, that he had written his name high up on the tablet of the world's memory, to be legible forever. Why, men have fretted their whole lives away to get what this man got, and knew nothing of— one line is a chronicle of fame.

So we may say, it shall be always, "I will never forget any of their works." We may not leave them inscribed in any records that men can read. What of that, if they are written in letters of light in the "Lamb's Book of Life," to be read out by Him before His Father, and the holy angels in that last great day? We may not leave any separable traces of our services, any more than the little brook that comes down some gulley on the hillside flows separate from its sisters, with whom it has coalesced, in the bed of the great river or in the rolling, boundless ocean. What of that so long as the work, in its consequences, shall last? Men that sow some great prairie broadcast cannot go into the harvest field and say, "I sowed the seed from which that ear came, and you the seed from which this one sprang." But the waving abundance belongs to them all, and each may be sure that his work survives and is glorified there; "that he that soweth and he that reapeth may rejoice together." So a perpetual remembrance is sure for the smallest Christian service.

IV. The last thing that I would say is, let us learn from this incident the blessed results of contact with the suffering Christ. Simon the Cyrenian apparently knew nothing about Jesus Christ when the Cross was laid on his shoulders. He would be reluctant to undertake the humiliating task, and would plod along behind Him for a while, sullen and discontented; but by degrees be touched by more of sympathy, and get closer and closer to the Sufferer. And if he stood by the Cross when it was fixed, and saw all that transpired there, no wonder if, at last, after more or less protracted thought and search, he came to understand Who He was that he had helped, and to yield himself to Him wholly.

Yes! Dear brethren, Christ's great saying, "I, if I be lifted up, will draw all men unto Me," began to be fulfilled when He began to be lifted up. The centurion, the thief, this man Simon, by looking on the Cross, learned the Crucified.

And it is the only way by which any of us will ever learn the true mystery and miracle of Christ's great and loving Being and work. I beseech you, take your places there behind Him, near His Cross; gazing upon Him till your hearts melt, and you, too, learn that He is your Lord, and your Savior, and your God. The Cross of Jesus Christ divides men into classes as the Last Day will. It, too, parts men—sheep to the right hand, goats to the left. If there was a penitent, there was an impenitent thief; if there was a convinced centurion, there were gambling soldiers; if there were hearts touched with compassion, there were mockers who took His very agonies and flung them in His face as a refutation of His claims. On the day when that Cross was raised on Calvary it began to be what it has been ever since, and is at this moment to every soul who hears the gospel, "a savor of life unto life, or of death unto death." Contact with the suffering Christ will either bind you to His service, and fill you with His Spirit, or it will harden your hearts, and make you ten-fold more selfish—that is to say, "tenfold more a child of hell," than you were before you saw and heard of that Divine meekness of the suffering Christ. Look to Him, I beseech you, who bears what none can help Him to carry, the burden of the world's sin. Let Him bear yours, and yield to Him your grateful obedience, and then take up your cross daily, and bear the light burden of self-denying service to Him, who has borne the heavy load of sin for you and all mankind.

31

The Patient Master and the Slow Scholars

Jesus saith unto him, Have I been so long time with you, and yet hast thou not known Me, Philip?—John 14:9

The Apostle Philip, like some others of the less important of the Apostolic band, appears only in this Gospel. The little that we know of him shows us his character with considerable clearness. He was the first whom Christ Himself called, and immediately on his obeying that call, he found Nathanael. You remember that his answer to Nathanael's doubt, "Can any good thing come out of Nazareth?" was "Come and see!" Sight was to him the great satisfying experience. He held fast by the maxim: "seeing is believing."

The same simple, matter of fact character comes out in the second reference to him, in connection with our Lord's miraculous feeding of the multitude with the "five barley loaves and the two small fishes." He singles out Philip to put to him the question, "Where are we to buy bread that these may eat?" The answer keeps close within the limits of the visible. He has no thought beyond a quick, practical calculation, "So many people, so much bread, and so little money in our purses." A solid, steady, practical man, who was in the way of trusting his senses more than anything else, and who was not very familiar with any loftier region.

Then we find him put to perplexity by the desire of the heathen Greeks to see Christ, and not venturing to say anything about it to the Master, so dim was his conception of Him, until he had plucked up heart of grace by taking counsel with his fellow townsman Simon.

In the text, in precise harmony with all these indications of character, we get him breaking in upon our Lord's discourse with a request in which good and evil, right and wrong, are strangely blended: "Show us the Father, and it sufficeth us." He was right to the heart's core in believing that Jesus Christ could do that, and he was right, through and through, in believing that that would be enough for any man; but he was wrong in fancying that an outward, visible manifestation—which was what was running in his head—such as had been granted to prophets and lawgivers, was better, or more, than he had had for three years already. The thing that he was asking, in its highest form was there before him, and, while he thought so much of seeing, he had not been able to see it, though he had been staring at it for three years!

"Have I been so long with you, and yet thou hast not known Me?" That is the question which may well touch all our hearts, and bring us to our knees before Him. I purpose to look at this question, then, of our Lord's this morning in three ways: First of all, as teaching us what ignorance of Christ is; second, as a wonderful glimpse into His pained and loving heart; and lastly, as a piercing question for us all.

I. First, this question of our Lord's seems to me to carry in it a great lesson as to what ignorance of Christ is. Why does our Lord charge Philip here with not knowing Him? Because Philip had said "Lord! show us the Father and it sufficeth us." And why was that question a betrayal of Philip's ignorance of Christ? Because it showed that he had not discerned Him as being "the only Begotten of the Father, full of grace and truth," and had not understood that "He that hath seen Me hath seen the Father." Not knowing that, all his knowledge of Christ, howsoever tender and sweet it may have been, howsoever full of love, and reverence, and blind admiration—is but twilight knowledge, which may well be called ignorance.

I would press that one thought upon you, dear brethren, as plainly coming out of this question and underlying it—that not to know Christ as the manifest God is practically to be ignorant of Him altogether. This man asked for some visible manifestation, such as their old books told them had been granted to Moses on the mountain, to Isaiah in the temple, and to many another one besides.

But if such revelation had been given—and Christ could have given it if He would—what a poor thing it would have been when put side by side with that mild and lambent light that was ever streaming from Him, making God visible to every sensitive and responsive nature! For these external manifestations for which Philip is here hungering, what could they show? They could show certain majestic, splendid, pompous, outside characteristics of God, but they could never show *God*, much less could they show "the Father." The revelation of Righteousness and Love could be entrusted to no flashing brightnesses, and to no thunders and lightnings. There can be no revelation of these things to the outward eye, but only to the heart, through the medium of a human life. For not the power which knows no weariness, not the eye which never closes, not the omniscience which holds all things, great and small, in its grasp, are the divinest glories in God. These are but the fringe, the outermost parts of the circumference; the living Center is a Righteous Love, which cannot be revealed by any means but by showing it in action; nor shown in action by any means so clearly as by a human life. Therefore, above all other forms of manifestations of God stands the Person of Jesus Christ, God manifest in the flesh.

And let me remind you that this is His own claim, not once nor twice, not in this Gospel alone, but in a hundred other places. Some people tell us that the conception of our Lord Jesus Christ proper to John's Gospel as being the revelation of the Father, is peculiar to John's Gospel. Did you ever read these words in one of the others: "No man knoweth the Father but the Son, and he to whomsoever the Son will reveal Him"? It seems to me that if there is anything certain about Jesus Christ at all, it is certain that, while upon earth, He claimed habitually to be the visible manifestation of God, in a degree and in a manner wholly unlike that in which a pure, good, wise, righteous man may claim to shine with some reflected beams of Divine brightness. And we have to reckon and make our account with that, and shape our theology accordingly.

So we have to look upon all Christ's life as showing men the Father. His gentle compassion, His meek wisdom, His patience with contumely and wrong, His long-suffering yearning over men, His continual efforts to draw them to Himself—all these are the full revelation of God to the world. They all reach their climax on the cross. As we look on Him, faint and bleeding, yet to the end pitying and saving, we see the full, final revelation of the very heart of God, and with adoring wonder, exclaim "Low, this is our God, we have waited for Him, and He will save us."

There are some of you who admire and reverence this great Teacher, this pure Humanity, who know much of Him, who seek to follow in His footsteps in some measure, but who stand outside that innermost circle wherein He manifests Himself as the God Incarnate, the Sacrifice, and the Savior of the sins of the world. While I thankfully admit that a man's relation to Christ may be a great deal deeper and more vital and blessed than his articulate creed, I am bound to say that not to know Him in this His very deepest and most essential character is little different from being ignorant of Him altogether.

Here is a great thinker or teacher, whose fame has filled the world, whose books are upon every student's shelf; he lives in a little remote country hamlet; the cottagers beside him know him as a kind neighbor, and a sympathetic friend. They have never heard of his books, they have never heard of his thoughts, they do not know anything of his worldwide reputation, all over the world. Do you call that knowing him? You do not know a man if you only know the surface, and not the secrets of his being.

You do not know a man if you only know the subordinate characteristics of his nature, but not the essential ones. The very inmost secret of Christ is this, that he is the Incarnate God, the sacrifice for the sins of the whole world.

You may be disciples, in the imperfect sense in which these Apostles were disciples before the Cross, and the Resurrection, and the Ascension, imperfect disciples like them, but without their excuse for it. But oh! Brethren, you will never know Him until you know Him as the Eternal Word, and until you can say "We beheld His glory, the glory as of the only Begotten of the Father, full of grace and truth." Not seeing that, you see but as a dim speck, or a star a little brighter than its brethren that hang in the heavens of history, Him Who really is the Central Sun, for Whom all light comes, to Whom the whole creation moves. If you know Him for the Incarnate Word and Lamb who bears the world's sin, you know Him for what He is. All the rest is most precious, most fair; but without that central truth, you have but a fragmentary Christ, and nothing less than the whole Christ is enough for you.

II. Now, secondly, I take these words as giving us a glimpse into the pained and loving heart of our Lord. We very seldom hear Him speak about His own feelings or experience, and when He does it is always in some such incidental way as this. So that these glimpses, like little windows opening out upon some great prospect, are the more precious to us.

I think we shall not misunderstand the tone of this question if we see in it wonder, pained love, and tender remonstrance. "Have I been so long with you, and yet hast thou not known Me?" In another place we read: "He marvelled at their unbelief." And here there is almost a surprise that He should have been shining so long and so near, and yet the purblind eyes should have seen so little.

But there is more than that, there is complaint and pain in the question—the pain of vainly endeavoring to teach, vainly endeavoring to help, vainly endeavoring to love. And there are few pains like that. All men that have tried to help and bless their fellows have known what it is to have their compassion and their efforts thrown back upon themselves. And there are few sorrows heavier to carry than this, the burden of a heart that would fain pour its love into another heart if that heart would only let it, but is repelled, and obliged to bear away its treasures unimparted. The slowness of the pupil is the sorrow of the honest teacher. The ingratitude and non-receptiveness of some churlish nature that you have tried to lavish good upon, have they not often brought a bitterness to your hearts?

If ever you have had a child, or a friend, or a dear one that you have tried to get by all means to love you, and to take your love, and who has thrown it all back in your face, you may know in some faint measure what was at least one of the elements which made Him the "Man of Sorrows and acquainted with grief."

But this question reveals not only the pain caused by slow apprehension and unrequited love, but also the depth and patience of a clinging love that was not turned away by the pain. How tenderly the name "Philip" comes in at the end! It recalls that other instance when a whole world of feeling and appeal was compressed into the one word to the weeping woman, "Mary," and when another world of unutterable rapture of surprise and joy was in her one answering word, "Rabboni." It bids us think of that patient love of His which will not be soured by any slowness or scantiness of response. Dammed back by our sullen rejection, it still flows on, seeking to conquer by long-suffering. Refused, it still lingers round the closed door of the heart, and knocks for entrance. Misunderstood, it still meekly manifests itself. Surely in that gentle compassion, in that patience with man's wrong and contumely, and imperfect apprehension and inadequate affection, we see the manifested God.

Let us remember, too, that the same pained and patient love is in the heart of the throned Christ today. Mystery and paradox as it may be, I suppose that there still passes over even His victorious and serene repose in the Heavens some shadow of pain and sorrow when we turn away from Him, or so slowly apprehend His character and His work. And I may, I think, fairly bring to you this question, "Do ye thus requite the Lord?" and urge this appeal of His pitying, tender love on each of us—Grieve not the heart that has died for you.

We cannot understand how anything like pain should, however slightly, darken that glory; but if it be true that He in the Heavens has yet "a fellow-feeling of our pains," it is not less true that His love is still wounded by our lovelessness, and His manifestation of Himself made sad by the slowness of our reception of Him.

III. Let us look at this question as being a piercing question addressed to each of us. It is the great wonder of human history that, after eighteen hundred years, the world knows so little of Jesus Christ. The leaders of opinion, the leaders of the literature of England, for instance, today, the men that profess to guide the thoughts of this generation, how little they know, really, about this Master! What profound misconceptions of the whole genius of Christianity, and of Him who is Christianity, we see among teachers who pay Him high homage and conventional respect, as well as among those who profess to reject Him and His mission. Some people take a great

deal more trouble to understand Buddha than they do to understand
Christ. How little, too, the mass of men know about Him! It is
enough to break one's heart to look round one, and think that He
has been so long time with the world, and that this is all which has
come of it. The Light has been shining for all these eighteen hundred
years, and yet the mist is so little cleared away, and the ice is so little melted. The great proof that the world is bad is that it does not
believe in Jesus Christ, the Son of God, and that He has stood before it for nearly nineteen centuries now, and so few have been led
to turn to Him with the adoring cry, "My Lord and my God."

But let us narrow our thoughts to ourselves. This question
comes to many of you in a very pointed way. You have known
about Jesus Christ all your lives, and yet, in a real, deep sense you
do not know Him at this moment. For the knowledge of which my
text speaks is the knowledge by acquaintance with a person rather
than the knowledge that a man may have of a book. And it is the
knowledge by experience. Have you that? Do you know Christ as
a man knows his friend, or do you know Him as you know about
Julius Caesar? Do you know Christ because you live with Him and
He with you, or do you know about Him in that fashion in which
a man in a great city knows about his neighbor across the street, that
has lived beside him for five and twenty years and never spoken to
him once all the time? Is that your knowledge of Christ? If so, it is
no knowledge at all. "I have heard of Him by the hearing of the ear,"
describes all the acquaintance which a great many of my friends here
have with Him. Oh! My brother! The very fact that He has been so
long with you is the reason why you know so little about Him. People that live close by something, which men come from the ends of
the earth to see, have often never seen it. A man may have lived all
his life within sound of Niagara, and perhaps never have gone to
look at the rush of the waters. Is that what you do with Jesus
Christ? Are you so accustomed to hear about Him that you do not
know Him? have so long heard of Him that you never come to see
Him? "Have I been so long with you, and yet hast thou not known
Me?"

And, dear friends, you who do know Him a little, this question
comes to you with a very pathetic appeal. In Him are infinite depths

to be experienced and to become acquainted with, and if we know Him at all as we ought to do, our knowledge of Him will be growing day by day. But how many of us stand at the same spot that we did when we first said that we were Christians!

We are like the Indians who live in rich gold countries and could only gather the ore that happened to lie upon the surface or could be washed out of the sands of the river. In this great Christ there are depths of gold, great reefs and veins of it, that will enrich us all if we dig, and we shall not get it unless we do. He is the boundless ocean. We have contented ourselves with coasting along the shore, and making timid excursions from one headland to another. Let us strike out into the middle deep, and see all the wonders that are there. This great Christ is like the infinite sky with its unresolved nebula. We have but looked with our poor, dim eyes. Let us take the telescope that will reveal to us suns blazing where now we only see darkness.

If we have any true knowledge of Jesus Christ at all it ought to be growing every day; and why does it not? You know a man because you are much with him. As the old proverb says: "If you want to know anybody you must summer and winter with them"; and if you want to know Jesus Christ, there must be a great deal more meditative thoughtfulness, and honest study of His life and work than most of us have put forth. We know people, too, by sympathy, and by love, and by keeping near them. Keep near your Master, Christian men! Oh, it is a wonder, and a shame, and a sin for us professing Christians, that, having tasted the sweetness of His love, we should come down so low as to long for the garbage of earth. Who is fool enough to prefer vinegar to wine, bitter herbs to grapes, dross to gold? Who is there that, having consorted with the King, would gladly herd with ragged rebels? And yet that is what we do. We love one another, our families, people round about us. We labor to surround ourselves with friends, and to fill our hearts from these many fountains. All right and well! But let us seek to know Christ more, and to know Him most chiefly in this aspect, that He is for us the manifest God and the Savior of the world. "For this is life eternal, to know Thee the only true God, and Jesus Christ, Whom Thou hast sent."

Then let us keep near Him, and love Him, that we may know him better as the Lamb of God that taketh away the sin of the world. So we shall be filled with all the fullness of God, and not need to ask for any other vision of the Father, beyond the all-sufficing sight of God in Christ, reconciling the world to Himself.

32

"See Thou to That"

I have sinned in that I have betrayed the innocent blood, And they said, What is that to us? See thou to that.
I am innocent of the blood of this just person; See ye to it—Matthew 27:4–24.

So, what the priests said to Judas, Pilate said to the priests. They contemptuously bade their wretched instrument bear the burden of his own treachery. They had condescended to use his services, but he presumed too far if he thought that that gave him a claim upon their sympathies. The tools of more respectable and bolder sinners are flung aside as soon as they are done with. What were the agonies or the tears of a hundred such as he to these high-placed and heartless transgressors? Priests though they were, and therefore bound by their office to help any poor creature that was struggling with a wounded conscience, they had nothing better to say to him than this scornful gibe: "What is that to us? See thou to that."

Pilate, on the other hand, metes to them the measure which they had meted to Judas. With curious verbal correspondence, he repeats the very words of Judas and of the priests. "Innocent blood," said Judas. "I am innocent of the blood of this just person," said Pilate. "See thou to that," answered they. "See ye to it," says he. He tries to shove off his responsibility upon them, and they are quite willing to take it. Their consciences are not easily touched. Fanatical hatred which thinks itself influenced by religious motives is the blindest and cruelest of all passions, knowing no compunction, and utterly unperceptive of the innocence of its victim.

And so these three, Judas, the priests, and Pilate, suggest to us, I think, a threefold way in which conscience is perverted. Judas represents the agony of conscience, Pilate represents the shuffling sophistications of a half-awakened conscience, and those priests and people represent the torpor of an altogether misdirected conscience.

I. Judas—the agony of conscience. "I have sinned in that I have betrayed the innocent blood." We do not need to enter at any length upon the difficult question as to what were the motives of Judas in his treachery. For my part I do not see that there is anything in the Scripture narrative, simply interpreted, to bear out the hypothesis that his motives were mistaken zeal and affection for Christ; and a desire to force Him to the avowal of His Messiahship. One can scarcely suppose zeal so strangely perverted as to begin by betrayal, and if the object was to make our Lord speak out His claims, the means adopted were singularly ill-chosen. The story, as it stands, naturally suggests a much less far-fetched explanation.

Judas was simply a man of a low earthly nature, who became a follower of Christ, thinking that he was to prove a Messiah of the vulgar type, or another Judas Maccabaeus. He was not attracted by Christ's character and teaching. As the true nature of Christ's work and kingdom became more obvious, he became more weary of Him and it. The closest proximity to Jesus Christ made eleven enthusiastic disciples, but it made one traitor. No man could live near Him for three years without coming to hate Him if he did not love Him. Then, as ever, He was set for the fall and for the rise of many. He was the savor of life unto life, or of death unto death.

But be this as it may, we have here to do with the sudden revulsion of feeling which followed upon the accomplished act. This burst of confession does not sound like the words of a man who had been actuated by motives of mistaken affection. He knows himself a traitor, and that fair, perfect character rises before him in its purity, as he had never seen it before—to rebuke and confound him.

So this exclamation of his puts into a vivid shape, which may help it to stick in our memories and hearts, this thought—what an awful difference there is in the look of a sin before you do it and afterwards! Before we do it the thing to be gained seems so attractive, and the transgression that gains it seems so comparatively insignificant. Yes! And when we have done it the two alter places; the thing that we win by it seems so contemptible—thirty pieces of silver! pitch them over the Temple enclosure and get rid of them— the things that we win by it seem so insignificant, and the thing that we did to win them dilates into such awful magnitude!

For instance, suppose we do anything that we know to be wrong, being tempted to it by a momentary indulgence of some mere animal impulse. By the very nature of the case, that dies in its sat- isfaction and the desire dies along with it. We do not want the thing any more when once we have got it. It lasts but a moment and is past. Then we are left alone with the thought of the sin that we have done. When we get the prize of our wrong-doing, we find out that it is not as all-satisfying as we expected it would be. Most of our earthly aims are like that. The chase is a great deal more than the hare. Or, as George Herbert has it, "Nothing between two dishes," a splendid service of silver plate, and when you take the cover off there is no food to eat. "Such are the pleasures here."

Universally, this is true, that sooner or later, when the delirium of passion and the rush of temptation are over and we wake to consciousness, we find that we are none the richer for the thing gained, and oh! so infinitely the poorer for the means by which we gained it. It is that old story of the Veiled Prophet that wooed and won the hearts of foolish maidens, and, when he had them in his power in the inner chamber, removed the silver veil which they had thought hid dazzling glory and showed hideous features that struck despair into their hearts. Every man's sin does that for him. And to you I come now with this message: every wrong thing that you do, great or small, will be like some of those hollow images of the gods that one hears of in barbarian temples—looked at in front, fair, but when you get behind them you find a hollow, full of dust and spiders' webs and unclean things. Be sure of this, every sin is a blunder.

That is the first lesson that lies in these words of this wretched traitor; but again, here is an awful picture for us of the hell upon earth, of a conscience which has no hope of pardon.

I do not suppose that Judas was lost, if he were lost, because he betrayed Jesus Christ, but because, having betrayed Jesus Christ, he never asked to be forgiven. And I suppose that the difference between the traitor who betrayed Him and the other traitor who denied Him, was this, that the one, when "he went out and wept bitterly," had the thought of a loving Master with him, and the other when "he went out and hanged himself" had the thought of nothing but that foul deed glaring before him. I pray you to learn this lesson—you cannot think too much, too blackly, of your own sins, but you may think too exclusively of them, and if you do, they will drive you to madness of despair.

My dear friend, there is no penitence or remorse which is deep enough for the smallest transgression; but there is no transgression which is so great but that forgiveness for it may come. And we may have it for the asking if we will go to that dear Christ that died for us. The consciousness of sinfulness is a wholesome consciousness. I would that every man and woman listening to me now had it deep in their consciences, and then I would that it might lead us all to that one Lord in whom there is forgiveness and peace. Be sure of this, that if Judas Iscariot, when his "soul flared forth in the dark," died without hope and without pardon, it was not because his crime was too great for forgiveness, but because the forgiveness had never been asked. There is no unpardonable sin except that of refusing the pardon that avails for all sin.

II. So much, then, for this first picture and the lessons that come out of it. In the next place we take Pilate, as the representative of what I have ventured to call the shufflings of a half-awakened conscience.

"I am innocent of the blood of this just person," says he, "see ye to it." He is very willing to shuffle off his responsibility upon the priests and people, and they, for their part, are quite as willing to accept it; but the responsibility can neither be shuffled off by him nor accepted by them. His motive in surrendering Jesus to them was probably nothing more than the low and cowardly wish to humor his turbulent subjects, and so to secure an easy tenure of office. For such an end what did one poor man's life matter? He had a great contempt for the accusers, which he is scarcely at the pains to conceal. It breaks out in half-veiled sarcasms, by which he cynically indemnifies himself for his ignoble yielding to the constraint which they put upon him. He knows perfectly well that the Roman power has nothing to fear from this King, whose Kingdom rested on His witness to the Truth. He knows perfectly well that unavowed motives of personal enmity lie at the bottom of the whole business. In the words of our text he acquits Christ, and thereby condemns himself. If Pilate knew that Jesus was innocent, he knew that he, as governor, was guilty of prostituting Roman justice, which was Rome's best gift to her subject nations, and of giving up an innocent man to death, in order to save himself trouble and to conciliate a howling mob. No washing of his hands will cleanse them. "All the perfumes of Arabia will not sweeten" that hand. But his words let us see how a man may sophisticate his conscience and quibble about his guilt.

Here, then, we get once more a vivid picture that may remind us of what, alas! we all know in our own experience, how a man's conscience may be clear-sighted enough to discern, and vocal enough to declare, that a certain thing is wrong, but not strong enough to restrain from doing it. Conscience has a voice and an eye; alas! it has no hands. It shares the weakness of all law, it cannot get itself executed. Men will climb over a fence, although the board that says, "Trespassers will be prosecuted," is staring them in the face in capital letters at the very place where they jump. Your conscience is a king without an army, a judge without officers. "If it had authority, as it has the power, it would govern the world," but as things are, it is reduced to issuing vain edicts and to saying, "Thou shalt not!" And if you turn around and say "I will, though," then conscience has no more that it can do.

And then here, too, is an illustration of one of the most common of the ways by which we try to slip our necks out of the collar, and to get rid of the responsibilities that really belong to us. "See ye to it" does not avail to put Pilate's crime on the priests' shoulders. Men take part in evil, and each thinks himself innocent, because he has companions. Half-a-dozen men carry a burden together; none of them fancies that he is carrying it. It is like the case of turning out a platoon of soldiers to shoot a mutineer—nobody knows whose bullet killed him, and nobody feels himself guilty; but there the man lies dead, and it was somebody that did it. So corporations, churches, societies, and nations do things that individuals would not do, and each man of them wipes his mouth and says, "I have done no harm." And even when we sin alone we are clever at finding scapegoats. "The woman tempted me and I did eat," is the formula universally used yet. The school-boy's excuse: "Please, sir! It was not me! It was the other boy!" is what we are all ready to say.

Now, I pray you, brethren, to remember that, whether our consciences try to shuffle off responsibility for united action upon the other members of the firm, or whether we try to excuse our individual actions by laying blame on our tempers, or whether we adopt the modern slang, and talk about circumstances, and heredity and the like, as being reasons for the diminution or the extinction of the notion of guilt, it is sophistical trifling; and down at the bottom the most of us know that I alone am responsible for the volition which leads to my act. I could have helped it if I had liked. Nobody compelled me to keep in the partnership of evil, or to yield to the tempter. Pilate was not forced by his subjects to give the commandment that "it should be as they required." They had their own burden to carry. Each man has to bear the consequences of his actions. There are many "burdens" which we can "bear for one another, and so fulfill the law of Christ"; but every man has to bear as his own burden of the fruits of his deeds. In that harvest, he that soweth and he that reapeth are one, and each of us has to drink as we ourselves have brewed. "God will send the bill to you," and you have to pay for your share, however many companions you may have had in the act.

So do not you sophisticate your consciences with the delusion that your responsibility may be shifted to any other person or thing. These may diminish, or may modify your responsibility, and God takes all that into account. But after all these have been taken into account, there is this left—that you yourselves have done the act, which you need not have done unless you had so willed, and that having done it, you have to carry it on your back forevermore. "See thou to that," was a heartless word, but it was a true one. "Every one of us shall give an account of himself to God," and as the old Book of Proverbs has it, "If thou be wise thou shalt be wise for thyself, and if thou scornest thou alone shalt bear it."

III. And so, lastly, we have here another group still—the priests and people. They represent for us the torpor and misdirection of conscience. "Then answered all the people and said, His blood be on us and on our children." They were perfectly ready to take the burden upon themselves. They thought that they were "doing God service" when they slew God's Messenger. They had no perception of the beauty and gentleness of Christ's character. They believed Him to be a blasphemer, and they believed it to be a solemn religious duty to slay Him then and there. Were they to blame because they slew a blasphemer? According to Jewish law—no! They were to blame because they had brought themselves in such a moral condition that that was all they thought of and saw in Jesus Christ. With their awful words they stand before us, as perhaps the crowning instances in Scripture history of the possible torpor which may paralyze consciences.

I need not dwell, I suppose, even for a moment, upon the thought of how the highest and noblest sentiments may be perverted into becoming the allies of the lowest crime. You remember one of the victims of the guillotine said, as her last words, "O Liberty! What crimes have been done in thy name!" O Religion! What crimes have been done in *thy* name! This is one of the lessons to be gathered from Calvary.

But, passing that, to come to the thing that is of more consequence to each of us, let us take this thought, dear brethren, as to the awful possibility of a conscience going fast asleep in the midst of the wildest storm of passion, like that unfaithful prophet Jonah, down in the hold of the heathen ship. You can lull your consciences into dead slumber. You can stifle them so that they shall not speak a word against the worst of your sins. You can do it by simply neglecting them, by habitually refusing to listen to them. If you keep picking all the leaves and buds off the tree before they open, it will stop flowering. You can do it by gathering round yourself always, and only, evil associations and evil deeds. The habit of sinning will lull a conscience faster than almost anything else. We do not know how hot this chapel is, or how much the air is exhausted, because we have been sitting in it for an hour and a half. But if we came into it from outside now, we should feel the difference. Styrian peasants thrive and fatten upon arsenic, and men may flourish upon all iniquity and evil, and conscience will say never a word. Take care of that delicate balance within you, and see that you do not tamper with it nor twist it.

Conscience may be misguided as well as lulled. It may call evil good, and good evil; it may take honey for gall, and gall for honey. And so we need something outside of ourselves to be our guide, our standard. We are not to be contented that our consciences acquit us. "I know nothing against myself, yet I am not hereby justified," says the Apostle, "he that judgeth me is the Lord." And it is quite possible that a man may have no prick of conscience and yet have done a very wrong thing. So we want, as it seems to me, something outside of ourselves that shall not be affected by our variations. Conscience is like the light on the binnacle of a ship. It tosses up and down along with the vessel. We want a steady light yonder on that headland, on the fixed solid earth, which shall not heave with the heaving wave, nor vary at all. Conscience speaks lowest when it ought to speak loudest. The worst man is least troubled by his conscience. It is like a lamp that goes out in the thickest darkness. Therefore we need, as I believe, a revelation of truth and goodness and beauty outside of ourselves to which we may bring our consciences that they may be enlightened and set right. We want a standard like the standard weights and measures that are kept in the Tower of London, to which all the people in the little country villages may send up their yard measures, and their pound weights, and find out if they are just and true. We want a *Bible*, and we want a *Christ* to tell us what is duty, as well as to make it possible for us to do it.

These groups which we have been looking at now, show us how very little help and sympathy a wounded conscience can get from its fellows. The conspirators turn upon each other as soon as the detectives are amongst them, and there is always one of them ready to go into the witness box and swear away the lives of the others to save his own neck. Wolves tear sick wolves to pieces.

Round us there stands Society, pitiless and stern, and Nature, rigid and implacable; not to be besought, not to be turned. And when we, in the midst of this universe of fixed law and cause and consequence, wail out, "I have sinned," a thousand voices say to us, "What is that to us? See thou to that." And so I am left with my guilt —it and I together. There comes One with outstretched, wounded hands, and says, "Cast all thy burden upon Me, and I will free thee from it all." "Surely He hath borne our griefs and carried our sorrows!" Trust in Him, in His great sacrifice, and you will find that His "innocent blood" has a power that will liberate your conscience from its torpor, its vain excuses, its agony and despair.

33

How to Dwell
in the Fire of God

Who among us shall dwell with the devouring fire? Who among us shall dwell with everlasting burnings? He that walketh righteously, and speaketh uprightly; he that depiseth the gain of oppressions, that shaketh his hands from holding of bribes, that stoppeth his ears from hearing of blood, and shutteth his eyes from seeing evil—Isaiah 33:14, 15.
He that dwelleth in love dwelleth in God—1 John 4:16.

I have put these two verses together because, striking as is at first sight, the contrast in their tone, they refer to the same subject, and they substantially preach the same truth. A hasty reader, who is more influenced by sound than by sense, is apt to suppose that the solemn expressions in my first text: "the devouring fire" and "everlasting burnings" mean *hell*. They mean *God,* as is quite obvious from the context. The man who is to "dwell in the devouring fire" is the *good* man. He that is able to abide "the everlasting burnings" is "the man that walketh righteously and speaketh uprightly," that "despiseth the gain of oppression, that shaketh his hands from holding of bribes, that stoppeth his ears from hearing of blood, and shutteth his eyes from seeing evil." The prophet has been calling all men, far and near, to behold a great act of Divine judgment in which God has been manifested in flaming glory, consuming evil; now he represents the "sinners in Sion," the unworthy members of the nation, as seized with sudden terror, and anxiously asking this question, which in effect means: "Who among us can abide peacefully, joyfully, fed and brightened, not consumed and annihilated, by that flashing brightness and purity?" The prophet's answer is the answer of common sense—like draws to like. A holy God must have holy companions.

But that is not all. The fire of God is the fire of love as well as the fire of purity; a fire that blesses and quickens, as well as a fire that destroys and consumes. So the Apostle John comes with his answer, not contradicting the other one, but deepening it, expanding it, letting us see the foundations of it, and proclaiming that as a holy God must be surrounded by holy hearts, which will open themselves to the flame as flowers to the sonshine, so a loving God must be clustered about by loving hearts, who alone can enter into deep and true friendship with Him.

The two answers, then, of these texts are one at bottom; and when Isaiah asks, "Who shall dwell with the everlasting fire?"—the perpetual fire, burning and unconsumed, of that Divine righteousness—the deepest answer, which is no stern requirement but a merciful promise, is John's answer, "He that dwelleth in love dwelleth in God."

The simplest way, I think, of bringing out the force of the words before us will be just to take these three points which I have already suggested—the world's question, the partial answer of the prophet, the complete answer of the Apostle.

I. The world's question.

I need only remind you how frequently in the Old Testament the emblem of fire is employed to express the Divine nature. In many places, though by no means in all, the prominent idea in the emblem is that of the purity of the Divine nature, which flashes and flames as against all which is evil and sinful. So we read in one grand passage in this very book, "the Light of Israel shall become a fire." As if the lambent beauty of the highest manifestation of God gathered itself together, intensified itself, was forced back upon itself; and from merciful, illuminating light turned itself into destructive and consuming fire. And we read, you may remember, too, in the description of the symbolical manifestation of the Divine nature which accompanied the giving of the Law on Sinai that "the glory of the Lord was like devouring fire on the top of the mountain," and yet into that blaze and brightness the Law-giver went, and lived and moved in it.

There is, then, in the Divine nature a side of antagonism and opposition to evil, which flames against it, and labors to consume it.

I would speak with all respect for the motives of many men in this day who dread to entertain the idea of the Divine wrath against evil lest they should in any manner trench upon the purity and perfectness of the Divine love. I respect and sympathize with the motive altogether; and I neither respect nor sympathize with the many ferocious pictures of that which is called the wrath of God against sin, which much so-called orthodox teaching has indulged in. But if you will only remove from that word "anger" the mere human associations which cleave to it, of passion on the one hand, and of a wish to hurt its object on the other, then you cannot, I think, deny to the Divine nature the possession of that passionless and unmalignant wrath, without striking a fatal blow at the perfect purity of God. A God that does not hate evil, that does not flame out against it, using all the energies of His being to destroy it, is a God to whose character there cleaves a fatal suspicion of indifference to good, of moral apathy. If I have not a God to trust in that hates evil because He loveth righteousness, then "the pillared firmament itself were rottenness, and earth's base built on stubble"; nor were there any hope that this damnable thing that is killing and sucking the life-blood out of our spirits should ever be destroyed and cast aside. Oh! It is short-sighted wisdom, and it is cruel kindness, to tamper with the thought of the wrath of God, the "everlasting burnings" of that eternally pure nature wherewith it wages war against all sin!

But then let us remember that, on the other side, the fire which is the destructive fire of perfect purity is also the fire that quickens and blesses. God is love, says John, and love is fire, too. We speak of "the flame of love," of "warm affections," and the like. The symbol of fire does not mean destructive energy only. And these two are one. God's wrath is a form of God's love; God hates because He loves.

And the "wrath" and the "love" differ much more in the difference of the eye that looks, than they do in themselves. Here are two bits of glass, one of them catches and retains all the fiery-red rays, the other all the yellow. It is the one, same, pure, white beam that passes through them both, but one is only capable of receiving the fiery-red beams of the wrath, and the other is capable of receiving the golden light of the love. Let us take heed lest, by destroying the wrath, we maim the love; and let us take heed lest, by exaggerating the wrath, we empty the love of its sweetness and its preciousness; and let us accept the teaching that these are one, and that the deepest of all the things that the world can know about God lies in that double saying, which does not contradict its second half by its first, but completes its first by its second—God is Righteousness, God is Love.

Well, then, that being so, the question rises to every mind of ordinary thoughtfulness: "Who among us shall dwell with the devouring fire? Who among us shall dwell with everlasting burnings?" A God fighting against evil; can you and I hope to hold familiar fellowship with Him? A God fighting against evil; if He rises up to exercise His judging and His punishing energies, can we meet Him? "Can thy heart endure and thy hands be strong, in the day that I shall deal with thee?" is the question that comes to each of us if we are reasonable people. I do not dwell upon it; but I ask you to take it, and entertain it for yourselves.

To "dwell with everlasting burnings" means two things. First, it means to hold a familiar intercourse and communion with God. The question which presents itself to thoughtful minds is—what sort of man must I be if I am to dwell near God? The lowliest bush may be lit by the Divine fire, and not be consumed by it; and the poorest heart may be all aflame with an indwelling God, if only it yield itself to Him, and long for His likeness. Electricity only flames into consuming fire when its swift passage is resisted. The question for us all is, how can I receive this Holy fire into my bosom, and not be burned? Is any communion possible, and if it be, on what conditions? It is the question which the heart of man is really asking, though it knows not the meaning of its own unrest.

"To dwell with everlasting burnings" means, secondly, to bear the action of the fire, the judgment of the present and the judgment of the future. The question for each of us is, can we face that judicial and punitive action of that Divine Providence which works even here, and how can we face the judicial and punitive action in the future?

I suppose you all believe, or at least say that you believe, that there is such a future judgment. Have you ever asked yourselves the question, and rested not until you got a reasonable answer to it, on which, like a man leaning on a pillar, you can lean the whole weight of your expectations—how am I to come into the presence of that devouring fire? Have you got any fireproof dress that will enable you to go into that furnace like the Hebrew youths, and walk up and down in the midst of it, well and at liberty? Have you? "Who shall dwell amidst the everlasting fires?"

That question has stirred sometimes, I know, in the consciences of every man and woman that is listening to me. Some of you have tampered with it, and tried to throttle it, and laughed at it, and shuffled it out of your mind by the engrossments of business, and tried to get rid of it in all sorts of ways: and here it has met you again today. Let us have it settled, in the name of common sense (to invoke nothing higher) once for all, upon reasonable principles that will stand; and do you see that you settle it today.

II. And now, look next at the prophet's answer. It is simple. He says that if a man is to hold fellowship with, or to face the judgment of, the pure and righteous God, the plainest dictate of reason and common sense is that he himself must be pure and righteous to match. The details into which his answer to the question runs out are all very homely, prosaic, pedestrian kind of virtues, nothing at all out of the way, nothing that people would call splendid or heroic. Here they are: "He that walks righteously,"—a short injunction, easily spoken, but how hard!—"and speaketh uprightly, he that despiseth the gain of oppression, that shaketh his hands from holding of bribes, that stoppeth his ears from hearing of blood, that shutteth his eyes from seeing evil." Righteous action, righteous speech, inward hatred of possessions gotten at my neighbor's cost, and a vehement resistance to all the seductions of sense; shutting his hands, stopping his ears, fastening his eyes up tight so that he may not handle, nor hear, nor see the evil—there is the outline of a homely, everyday sort of morality which is to mark the man who, as Isaiah says, can "dwell amongst the everlasting fires."

Now, if at your leisure you will turn to the Psalms 15 and 24 you will find there two other versions of the same questions and the same answer, both of which were obviously in our prophet's mind when he spoke. In the one you have the question put: "Who shall abide in Thy tabernacle?" In the other you have the same question put: "Who shall ascend into the hill of the Lord?" And these two psalms answer the question and sketch the outline (and it is only an outline) of a righteous man, from the Old Testament point of view, substantially in the same fashion that Isaiah does here.

I do not need to remark upon the altogether unscientific and non-exhaustive nature of the description of righteousness that is set forth here. There are a great many virtues, plain and obvious, that are left out of the picture. But I want you to notice one very special defect, as it might seem. There is not the slightest reference to anything that we call religion. It is all purely pedestrian, worldly morality; do righteous things; do not tell lies; do not cheat your neighbor; stop your ears if people say foul things in your hearing; shut your eyes if evil comes before you. These are the kind of duties enjoined, and these only. The answer of my text moves altogether on the surface, dealing only with conduct, not with character, and dealing with conduct only in reference to this world. There is not a word about the inner nature, not a word about the inner relation of a man to God. It is the minimum of possible qualifications for dwelling with God.

Well, now, do you achieve that minimum? Suppose we waive for the moment all reference to God; suppose we waive for the moment all reference to motive and inward nature; suppose we keep ourselves only on the outside of things, and ask what sort of *conduct* a man must have that is able to walk with God? We have heard the answer.

Now, then, is that *me*? Is this sketch here, admittedly imperfect, a mere black-and-white swift outline, not intended to be shaded or colored, or brought up to the round; is this mere outline of what a good man ought to be, at all like me? Yes or no? I think we must all say No! to the question, and acknowledge our failure to attain to this homely ideal of conduct. The requirement pared down to its lowest possible degree, and kept as superficial as ever you can keep it, is still miles above me, and all I have to say when I listen to such words is, "God be merciful to me a sinner."

My dear friends! Take this one thought away with you today: the requirements of the most moderate conscience are such as no man among us is able to comply with. And what then? Am I to be shut up to despair? Am I to say—then nobody can dwell within that bright flame? Am I to say—then when God meets man, man must crumble away into nothing and disappear? Am I to say, for myself— then, alas! for me, when I stand at His judgment bar?

III. Let us take the Apostle's answer: "God is love, and he that dwelleth in love dwelleth in God."

Now, to begin with, let us distinctly understand that the New Testament answer, represented by John's great words, entirely endorses Isaiah's; and that the difference between the two is not that the Old Testament, as represented by Psalmist and Prophet, said: "You must be righteous in order to dwell with God," and that the New Testament says: "You need not be!" Not at all! John is just as vehement in saying that nothing but purity can bind a man in thoroughly friendly and familiar conjunction with God as David or Isaiah was. He insists as much as anybody can insist upon this great principle, that if we are to dwell with God we must be like God, and that we are like God when we are like Him in righteousness and love, "He that saith he hath fellowship with Him, and walketh in darkness, is a liar!" That is John's short way of gathering it all up. Righteousness is as essential in the Gospel scheme for all communion and fellowship with God as ever it was declared to be by the most rigid of legalists; and if any of you have got the notion that Christianity has any other terms to lay down than the old terms— that righteousness is essential to communion—you do not understand Christianity. If any of you are building upon the notion that a man can come into loving and familiar friendship with God as long as he loves and cleaves to any sin, you have got hold of a delusion that will wreck your souls yet—is, indeed, harming, wrecking them now, and will finally destroy them if you do not get rid of it. Let us always remember that the declaration of my first text lies at the very foundation of the declaration of my second.

What, then, is the difference between them? Why for one thing it is this—Isaiah tells us that we must be righteousness, John tells us how we may be. The one says "There are the conditions," the other says, "Here are the means by which you can have the conditions." Love is the productive germ of all righteousness; it is the fulfilling of the law. Get that into your hearts, and all these relative and personal duties will come. If the deepest, inmost life is right, all the surface of life will come right. Conduct will follow character, character will follow love.

The efforts of men to make themselves pure, and so to come into the position of holding fellowship with God are like the wise efforts of children in their gardens. They stick in their little bits of rootless flowers, and they water them, but, being rootless, the flowers are all withered tomorrow and flung over the hedge the day after. But if we have the love of God in our hearts, we have not rootless flowers, but the seed which will spring up and bear fruit of holiness.

But that is not all. Isaiah says: "Righteousness," John says "Love," which makes righteousness. And then he tells us how we may get love, having first told us how we may get righteousness: We love Him because He first loved us. It is just as impossible for a man to work himself into loving God as it is for a man to work himself into righteous actions. There is no difference between the impossibilities in the two cases. But what we can do is, we can go and gaze at the thing that kindles the love; we can contemplate the Cross on which the great Lover of our souls died, and thereby we can come to love Him. John's answer goes down to the depths, for his notion of love is the response of the believing soul to the love of God which was manifested on the Cross of Calvary. To have righteousness we must have love; to have love we must look to the love that God has for us; to look rightly to the love that God has for us we must have faith. Now you have got to the very bottom of the matter. That is the first step of the ladder—faith; and the second step is love, and the third step is righteousness.

And so the New Testament, in its highest and most blessed declarations, rests itself firmly upon these rigid requirements of the old law. You and I, dear brethren, have but one way by which we can walk in the midst of that fire, rejoicing and unconsumed, namely that we shall know and believe the love which God hath for us, love Him back again "with pure hearts fervently," and in the might of that receptive faith and productive love, become like Him in holiness, and ourselves be "baptized with the Holy Ghost and with fire." Thus, fire-born and fiery, we shall dwell as in our native home, in God Himself.

34

The Fourfold Symbols of the Spirit

A rushing mighty wind. . . . Cloven tongues like as fire. . . . I will pour out My Spirit upon all flesh—Acts 2:2, 3, 17.

Ye have an unction from the Holy One—1 John 2:20.

Wind, fire, water, oil—these four are constant Scriptural symbols for the Spirit of God. We have them all in these fragments of verses which I have taken for my text this morning, and which I have isolated from their context for the purpose of bringing out simply these symbolical references. I think that perhaps we may get some force and freshness to the thoughts proper to this day (Whit Sunday) by looking at these rather than by treating the subject in some more abstract form. We have then the Breath of the Spirit, the Fire of the Spirit, the Water of the Spirit, the Anointing Oil of the Spirit. And the consideration of these four will bring out a great many of the principal Scriptural ideas about the gift of the Spirit of God which belongs to all Christian souls.

I. First, "a rushing mighty wind."

Of course, the symbol is but the putting into picturesque form of the idea that lies in the name. Spirit is breath. Wind is but air in motion. Breath is the synonym for life. Spirit and life are two words for one thing. So then, in the symbol, the "rushing mighty wind," we have set forth the highest work of the Spirit—the communication of a new and supernatural life.

We are carried back to that grand vision of the prophet who saw the bones lying, very many and very dry, sapless and disintegrated, a heap dead and ready to rot. The question comes to him: "Son of man! Can these bones live?" The only possible answer, if he consult experience, is, "O Lord God! Thou knowest." Then follows the great invocation: "Come from the four winds, O breath, and breathe upon these bones that they may live." And the breath comes and "they stand up, an exceeding great army." It is the Spirit that quickeneth. The Scripture treats us all as dead, being separated from God, unless we are united to Him by faith in Jesus Christ. According to the saying of the Evangelist, "They which believe on Him receive" the Spirit, and thereby receive the life which He gives, or, as our Lord Himself speaks, are "born of the Spirit." The highest and most characteristic office of the Spirit of God is to enkindle this new life, and hence His noblest name, among the many by which He is called, is the Spirit of life.

Again, remember, "that which is born of the Spirit is spirit." If there be life given it must be kindred with the life which is its source. Reflect upon these profound words of our Lord: "The wind bloweth where it listeth, and thou hearest the sound thereof, and canst not tell whence it cometh nor whither it goeth. So is every one that is born of the Spirit." They describe first the operation of the life-giving Spirit, but they describe also the characteristics of the resulting life.

"The wind bloweth where it listeth." That spiritual life, both in the Divine source and in the human recipient, is its own law. Of course the wind has its laws, as every physical agent has; but these are so complicated and undiscovered that it has always been the very symbol of freedom, and poets have spoken of these "chartered libertines," the winds, and "free as the air" has become a proverb. So that Divine Spirit is limited by no human conditions or laws, but dispenses its gifts in superb disregard of conventionalities and externalisms. Just as the lower gift of what we call "genius" is above all limits of culture or education or position, and falls on a wool-stapler in Stratford-on-Avon, or on a plowman in Ayrshire, so, in a similar manner, the altogether different gift of the Divine, life-giving Spirit follows no lines that Churches or institutions draw. It falls upon an Augustinian monk in a convent, and he shakes Europe. It falls upon a tinker in Bedford jail, and he writes *Pilgrim's Progress*. It falls upon a cobbler in Kettering, and he founds modern Christian missions. It blows "where it listeth," sovereignly indifferent to the expectations and limitations and the externalisms, even of organized Christianity, and touching this man and that man, not arbitrarily but according to "the good pleasure" that is a law to itself, because it is perfect in wisdom and in goodness.

And as thus the life-giving Spirit imparts Himself according to higher laws than we can grasp, so in like manner the life that is derived from it is a life which is its own law. The Christian conscience, touched by the Spirit of God, owes allegiance to no regulations or external commandments laid down by man. The Christian conscience, enlightened by the Spirit of God, at its peril will take its beliefs from any other than from that Divine Spirit. All authority over conduct, all authority over belief is burned up and disappears in the presence of the grand democracy of the true Christian principle: "Ye are all the children of God by faith in Jesus Christ": and every one of you possesses the Spirit which teaches, the Spirit which inspires, the Spirit which enlightens, the Spirit which is the guide to all truth. So "the wind bloweth where it listeth," and the voice of that Divine Quickener is,

> Myself shall to My darling be
> Both law and impulse.

Under the impulse derived from the Divine Spirit, the human spirit "listeth" what is right, and is bound to follow the promptings of its highest desires. Those men only are free as the air we breathe, who are vitalized by the Spirit of the Lord, for where the Spirit of the Lord is, there, and there alone, is liberty.

In this symbol there lies not only the thought of a life derived, kindred with the life bestowed, and free like the life which is given, but there lies also the idea of power. The wind which filled the house was not only mighty but "borne onward"—fitting type of the strong impulse by which in olden times "holy men spake as they were 'borne onward' " (the word is the same) "by the Holy Ghost." There are diversities of operations, but it is the same breath of God, which sometimes blows in the softest pianissimo that scarcely rustles the summer woods in the leafy month of June, and sometimes storms in wild tempest that dashes the seas against the rocks. So this mighty life-giving Agent moves in gentleness and yet in power, and sometimes swells and rises almost to tempest, but is ever the impelling force of all that is strong and true and fair in Christian hearts and lives.

The history of the world since that day of Pentecost has been a commentary upon the words of my text. With viewless, impalpable energy the mighty breath of God swept across the ancient world and "laid the lofty city" of paganism "low; even to the ground, and brought it even to the dust." A breath passed over the whole civilized world, like the breath of the west wind upon the glaciers in the spring, melting the thick-ribbed ice, and wooing forth the flowers, and the world was made over again. In our own hearts and lives this is the one power that will make us strong and good. The question is all-important for each of us, "Have I this life, and does it move me, as the ships are borne along by the wind?" "As many as are impelled by the Spirit of God, they"—*They*—"are the sons of God." Is that the breath that swells all the sails of your lives, and drives you upon your course? If it be, you are Christians; if it is not, you are not.

II. And now a word as to the second of these symbols: "Cloven tongues as of fire"—the fire of the Spirit.

I need not do more than remind you how frequently that emblem is employed both in the Old and in the New Testament. John the Baptist contrasted the cold negative efficiency of his baptism, which, at its best, was but a baptism of repentance, with the quickening power of the baptism of Him that was to follow him; when he said "I indeed baptize you with water, but he that cometh after me is mightier than I. He shall baptize you with the Holy Ghost and with fire." The two mean but one, the fire being the emblem of the Spirit.

You will remember, too, how our Lord Himself employs the same metaphor when He speaks about His coming to bring fire on the earth, and His longing to see it kindled into a beneficent blaze. In this connection, the fire is a symbol of a quick, triumphant energy, which will transform us into its own likeness. There are two sides to that emblem, as we saw in our last sermon, one destructive, one creative; one wrathful, one loving. There are the fire of love, and the fire of anger. There is the fire of the sunshine which is the condition of life, as well as the fire of the lightning which burns and consumes. The emblem of fire is selected to express the work of the Spirit of God, by reason of its leaping, triumphant, transforming energy. See, for instance, how, when you kindle a pile of dead green wood, the tongues of fire spring from point to point until they have conquered the whole mass, and turned it all into a ruddy likeness of the parent flame. And so here, this fire of God, if it falls upon you, will burn up all your coldness, and will make you glow with enthusiasm, working your intellectual convictions in fire, not in frost, making your creed a living power in your lives, and kindling you into a flame of earnest consecration.

The same idea is expressed by the common phrases of every language. We talk about the fervor of love, the warmth of affection, the blaze of enthusiasm, the fire of emotion, the coldness of indifference. Christians are to be set on fire of God. If the Spirit dwell in us, it will make us fiery like itself, even as fire makes the wettest green wood into fire. We have more than enough of cold Christians who are afraid of nothing so much as of being betrayed into warm emotion.

I believe, dear brethren, and I am bound to express the belief, that one of the chief wants of the Christian Church of this generation, the Christian Church of this city, the Christian Church of this chapel, is more of the fire of God! We are all icebergs compared with what we ought to be. Look at yourselves; never mind about your brethren. Let each of us look at his own heart, and say whether there is any trace in his Christianity of the power of that Spirit Who is fire. Is our religion flame or ice? Where among us are to be found lives blazing with enthusiastic devotion and earnest love? Do not such words sound like mockery when applied to us? Have we not to listen to that solemn old warning that never loses its power, and, alas! seems never to lose its appropriateness; "because thou art neither cold nor hot I will spue thee out of my mouth." We ought to be like the burning beings before God's throne, the seraphim, the spirits that blaze and serve. We ought to be like God Himself, all aflame with love. Let us seek penitently for that Spirit of fire who will dwell in us all if we will.

The metaphor of fire suggests also—purifying. "The spirit of burning" will burn the filth out of us. That is the only way by which a man can ever be made clean. You may wash and wash and wash with the cold water of moral reformation; you will never get the dirt out with it. No washing and no rubbing will ever clear sin. The way to cleanse a soul is to do with it as they do with foul clay—thrust it into the fire and that will burn all the blackness out of it. Get the love of God into your hearts, and the fire of His Divine Spirit into your spirits to melt you down, as it were, and then the scum and the dross will come to the top, and you can skim them off. Two things conquer my sin; the one is the blood of Jesus Christ, which washes me from all the guilt of the past; the other is the fiery influence of that Divine Spirit which makes me pure and clean for all the time to come. Pray to be kindled with the fire of God!

III. Then once more, take that other metaphor, "I will pour out of My Spirit."

That implies an emblem which is very frequently used, both in the Old and in the New Testament, viz., the Spirit as water. As our Lord said to Nicodemus: "Except a man be born of water and of the Spirit, he cannot enter into the Kingdom of God." The "water" stands in the same relation to the "Spirit" as the "fire" does in the saying of John the Baptist already referred to—that is to say, it is simply a symbol or material emblem of the Spirit. I suppose nobody would say that there were two baptisms spoken of by John, one of the Holy Ghost and one of fire—and I suppose that just in the same way, there are not two agents of regeneration pointed at in our Lord's words, nor even two conditions, but that the Spirit is the sole agent, and "water" is but a figure to express some aspect of His operations. So that there is no reference to the water of baptism in the words, and to see such a reference is to be led astray by sound, and out of a metaphor to manufacture a miracle.

There are other passages where, in like manner, the Spirit is compared to a flowing stream, such as, for instance, when our Lord said, "He that believeth on Me, out of his belly shall flow rivers of living water," and when John saw a "river of water of life proceeding from the throne." The expressions, too, of "pouring out" and "shedding forth" the Spirit, point in the same direction, and are drawn from more than one passage of Old Testament prophecy.

What, then, is the significance of comparing that Divine Spirit with a river of water? First, cleansing, of which I need not say any more, because I have already spoken about it in the previous part of my sermon. Then, further, refreshing, and satisfying. Ah! Dear brethren, there is only one thing that will slake the immortal thirst in your souls. The world will never do it; love or ambition gratified and wealth possessed, will never do it. You will be as thirsty after you have drunk of these streams as ever you were before. There is one spring "of which if a man drink, he shall never thirst" with unsatisfied, painful longings, but shall never cease to thirst with the longing which is blessedness, because it is fruition. Our thirst can be slaked by the deep draught of the river of the Water of Life, which proceeds from the Throne of God and the Lamb. The Spirit of God, drunk in by my spirit, will still and satisfy my whole nature, and with it I shall be glad. Drink of this! "Ho! Everyone that thirsteth, come ye to the waters!"

The Spirit is not only refreshing and satisfying, but also productive and fertilizing. In Eastern lands a rill of water is all that is needed to make the wilderness rejoice. Turn that stream on to the barrenness of your hearts, and fair flowers will grow that would never grow without it. The one means of lofty and fruitful Christian living is a deep, inward possession of the Spirit of God. The one way to fertilize barren souls is to let that stream flood them all over, and then the flush of green will soon come, and that which was else a desert will "rejoice and blossom as the rose."

So this water will cleanse, it will satisfy and refresh, it will be productive and will fertilize, and "everything shall live whithersoever that river cometh."

IV. Then, lastly, we have the oil of the Spirit. "Ye have an unction," says John, in our last text, "from the Holy One."

I need not remind you, I suppose, of how in the old system, prophets, priests, and kings were anointed with consecrating oil, as a symbol of their calling, and of their fitness for their special offices. The reason for the use of such a symbol, I presume, would lie in the invigorating and in the supposed, and possibly real, health-giving effect of the use of oil in those climates. Whatever may have been the reason for the use of oil in official anointings, the meaning of the act was plain. It was a preparation for a specific and distinct service. And so, when we read of the oil of the Spirit, we are to think that it is that which fits us for being prophets, priests, and kings, and which calls us because it fits us for these functions.

You are anointed to be prophets that you may make known Him Who has loved and saved you; and may go about the world evidently inspired to show forth His praise, and make His Name glorious. That anointing calls and fits you to be priests, mediators between God and man; bringing God to men, and by pleading and persuasion, and the presentation of the truth, drawing men to God. That unction calls and fits you to be kings, exercising authority over the little monarchy of your own natures, and over the men round you, who will bow in submission whenever they come in contact with a man all evidently aflame with the love of Jesus Christ, and filled with His Spirit. The world is hard and rude; the world is blind and stupid; the world often fails to know its best friends and its truest benefactors; but there is no crust of stupidity so crass and dense but that through it there will pass the penetrating shafts of light that ray from the face of a man who walks in fellowship with Jesus. The whole Israel of old were honored with these sacred names. They were a kingdom of priests; and the Divine voice said of the nation "Touch not Mine anointed, and do My prophets no harm." How much more are all Christian men, by the anointing of the Holy Spirit, made prophets, priests, and kings to God! Alas for the difference between what they ought to be and what they are!

And then do not forget also that when the Scriptures speak about Christian men as being anointed, it really speaks of them as being Messiahs. "Christ" means *anointed,* does it not? "Messiah" means *anointed.* And when we read in such a passage as that of my text, "Ye have an unction from the Holy One," we cannot but feel that the words point in the same direction as the great words of our Master Himself, "As My Father hath sent Me, even so send I you." By derived authority, no doubt, and in a subordinate and secondary sense, of course, we are Messiahs, anointed with that Spirit which was given to Him not by measure, and which has passed from Him to us. "If any man have not the Spirit of Christ, he is none of His."

So, dear brethren, all these things being certainly so, what are we to say about the present state of Christendom? What are we to say about the present state of English Christianity, Church and Dissent alike? Is Pentecost a vanished glory, then? Has that rushing mighty wind blown itself out, and a dead calm followed? Has that leaping fire died down into gray ashes? Has the great river that burst out then, like the stream from the foot of the glaciers of Mont Blanc, full-grown in its birth, been all swallowed up in the sand, like some of those rivers in the East? Has the oil dried in the cruse? People tell us that Christianity is on its death-bed; and to look at a great many professing Christians seems to confirm the statement. But let us thankfully recognize that we are not straitened in God, but in ourselves. To how many of us the question might be put: "Did you receive the Holy Ghost when you believed?" And how many of us by our lives answer: "We have not so much as heard whether there be any Holy Ghost." Let us go where we can get it; and remember the blessed words: "If ye, being evil, know how to give good gifts to your children, how much more will your Heavenly Father give the Holy Spirit to them that ask Him."

35

Sorrow According to God

Godly sorrow worketh repentance to salvation not to be repented of, but the sorrow of the world worketh death—2 Corinthians 7:10.

Very near the close of his missionary career the Apostle Paul summed up his preaching as being all directed to enforcing two points, "Repentance towards God, and faith in our Lord Jesus Christ." These two, repentance and faith, ought never to be separated in thought, as they are inseparable in fact. True repentance is impossible without faith, true faith cannot exist without repentance.

Yet the two are separated very often, even by earnest Christian teachers. The tendency of this day is to say a great deal about faith, and not nearly enough in proportion about repentance; and the effect is to obscure the very idea of faith, and not seldom to preach, "Peace! peace! when there is no peace." A Gospel which is always talking about faith, and scarcely ever talking about sin and repentance, is denuded, indeed, of some of its most unwelcome characteristics, but is also deprived of most of its power, and it may very easily become an ally of unrighteousness, and an indulgence to sin. The reproach that the Christian doctrine of salvation through faith is immoral in its substance derives most of its force from forgetting that "repentance towards God" is as real a condition of salvation as is "faith in our Lord Jesus Christ." We have here the Apostle's deliverance about one of these twin thoughts. We have three stages—the root, the stem, the fruit; sorrow, repentance, salvation. But there is a right and a wrong kind of sorrow for sin. The right kind breeds repentance, and thence reaches salvation; the wrong kind breeds nothing, and so ends in death.

Let us, then, trace these stages, not forgetting that this is not a complete statement of the case, and needs to be supplemented in the spirit of the words which I have already quoted, by the other part of the inseparable whole, "faith toward our Lord Jesus Christ."

I. First, then, consider the true and the false sorrow for sin.

The Apostle takes it for granted that a recognition of our own evil, and a consequent penitent regretfulness, lie at the foundation of all true Christianity. Now, I do not insist upon any uniformity of experience in people, any more than I should insist that all their bodies should be of one shape or of one proportion. Human lives are infinitely different, human dispositions are subtly varied, and because neither the one nor the other are ever reproduced exactly in any two people, therefore the religious experience of no two souls can ever be precisely alike.

We have no right to ask—and much harm has been done by asking—for an impossible uniformity of religious experience, no more than we have a right to expect that all voices shall be pitched in one key, or all plants flower in the same month, or after the same fashion. You can print off as many copies as you like, for instance, of a drawing of a flower, on a printing-press, and they shall all be alike, petal for petal, leaf for leaf, shade for shade; but no two hand-drawn copies will be so precisely alike, still less will any two of the real buds that blow on the bush. Life produces resemblance with differences; it is machinery that makes facsimiles.

So we insist on no pedantic or unreal uniformity; and yet, while leaving the widest scope for divergencies of individual character and experience, and not asking that a man all diseased and blotched with the leprosy of sin for half a life-time, and a little child that has grown up at its mother's knee, "in the nurture and admonition of the Lord," and so has been kept "innocent of much transgression," shall have the same experience; yet Scripture, as it seems to me, and the nature of the case do unite in asserting that there are certain elements which, in varying proportions indeed, will be found in all true Christian experience, and of these an indispensable one—and in a very large number, if not in the majority of cases, a fundamental one—is this which my text calls "godly sorrow."

Dear brethren, surely a reasonable consideration of the facts of our conduct and character point to that as the attitude that becomes us. Does it not? I do not charge you with crimes in the eye of the law. I do not suppose that many of you are living in flagrant disregard of the elementary principles of common everyday morality. There are some, no doubt. There are, no doubt, unclean men here; there are some who eat and drink more than is good for them, habitually; there are, no doubt, men and women who are living in avarice and worldliness, and doing things which the ordinary conscience of the populace point to as faults and blemishes. But I come to you respectable people that can say: "I am not as other men are, unjust, adulterers, or even as this publican"; and pray you, dear friends, to look at your character all round, in the light of the righteousness and love of God, and to plead to the indictment which charges you with neglect of many a duty and with sin against Him. How do you plead, "guilty or not guilty, sinful or not sinful?" Be honest with yourselves, and the answer will not be far to seek.

Notice how my text draws a broad distinction between the right and the wrong kind of sorrow for sin. "Godly sorrow" is, literally rendered, *sorrow according to God,"* which may either mean sorrow which has reference to God, or sorrow which is in accordance with His will; that is to say, which is pleasing to Him. If it is the former, it will be the latter. I prefer to suppose that it is the former—that is, sorrow which has reference to God. And then, there is another kind of sorrow, which the Apostle calls the "sorrow of the world," which is devoid of that reference to God. Here we have the characteristic difference between the Christian way of looking at our own faults and shortcomings, and the sorrow of the world, which has got no blessing in it, and will never lead to anything like righteousness and peace. It is just this—one has reference to God, puts its sin by His side, sees its blackness relieved against the "fierce light" of the Great White Throne, and the other has not that reference.

To expand that for a moment, there are plenty of us who, when our sin is behind us, and its bitter fruits are in our hands, are sorry enough for our faults. A man that is lying in the hospital, a wreck, with the sins of his youth gnawing the flesh off his bones, is often enough sorry that he did not live more soberly and chastely and temperately in the past days. That fraudulent bankrupt that has not got his discharge and has lost his reputation, and can get nobody to lend him money enough to start him in business again, as he hangs about the streets, slouching in his rags, is sorry enough that he did not keep the straight road. The "sorrow of the world" has no thought about God in it at all. The consequences of sin set many a man's teeth on edge who does not feel any compunction for the wrong that he did. My brethren, is that the position of any that are listening to me now?

Again, men are often sorry for their conduct without thinking of it as sin against God. Crime means the transgression of man's law, wrong means the transgression of conscience's law. Sin is the transgression of God's law. Some of us would perhaps have to say—"I have done crime." We are all of us quite ready to say: "I have done wrong many a time"; but there are some of us that hesitate to take the other step, and say: "I have done sin." Sin has, for its correlative, God. If there is no God, there is no sin. There may be faults, there may be failures, there may be transgression, breaches of the moral law, things done inconsistent with man's nature and constitution, and so on; but if there be a God, then we have personal relations to that person and His law; and when we break His law it is more than crime; it is more than fault; it is more than transgression; it is more than wrong; it is sin. It is when you lift the shutter off conscience, and let the light of God rush in upon your hearts and consciences, that you have the wholesome sorrow that worketh repentance and salvation and life.

Oh, dear friends, I do beseech you to lay these simple thoughts to heart. Remember, I urge no rigid uniformity of experience or character, but I do say that unless a man has learned to see his sin in the light of God, and in the light of God to weep over it, he has yet to know "the strait gate that leadeth unto life."

I believe that a very large amount of the superficiality and easy-goingness of the Christianity of today comes just from this, that so many who call themselves Christians have never once got a glimpse of themselves as they really are. I remember once peering over the edge of the crater of Vesuvius, and looking down into the pit, all swirling with sulphurous fumes. Have you ever looked into your hearts, in that fashion, and seen the wreathing smoke and the flashing fire there? If you have, you will cleave to that Christ, Who is your sole deliverance from sin.

But, remember, there is no prescription about depth or amount or length of time during which this sorrow shall be felt. If, on the one hand, it is essential, on the other hand there are a great many people who ought to be walking in the light and the liberty of God's Gospel who bring darkness and clouds over themselves by the anxious scrutinizing question: "Is my sorrow deep enough?" Deep enough! What for? What is the use of sorrow for sin? To lead a man to repentance and to faith. If you have as much sorrow as leads you to penitence and trust, you have enough. It is not your sorrow that is going to wash away your sin, it is Christ's blood. So let no man trouble himself about the question, Have I sorrow enough? The one question is: "Has my sorrow led me to cast myself on Christ?"

II. Still further, look now for a moment at the next stage here. "Godly sorrow worketh repentance."

What is repentance? No doubt many of you would answer that it is "sorrow for sin," but clearly this text of ours draws a distinction between the two. There are very few of the great key words of Christianity which have suffered more violent and unkind treatment, and have been more obscured by misunderstandings, than this great word. It has been weakened down into penitence, which in the ordinary acceptation, means simply the emotion that I have already been speaking about, viz. a regretful sense of my own evil. And it has been still further docked and degraded, both in syllables and in its substance, into *penance*. But the "repentance" of the New Testament and of the Old Testament—one of the twin conditions of salvation—is neither sorrow for sin nor works of restitution and satisfaction, but it is, as the word distinctly expresses, a change of purpose in regard to the sin for which man mourns. I have no time to expand and to elaborate this idea as I should like, but let me remind you of one or two passages in Scripture which may show that the right notion of the word is not sorrow but changed attitude and purpose in regard to my sin.

We find passages, some of which ascribe and some deny repentance to the Divine nature. But if there be a repentance which is possible for the Divine nature, it obviously cannot mean sorrow for sin, but must signify a change of purpose. In the Epistle to the Romans we read, "The gifts and calling of God are without repentance," which clearly means without change of purpose on His part. And I read in the story of the mission of the Prophet Jonah, that, "The Lord repented of the evil which He had said He would do unto them, and He did it not." Here, again, the idea of repentance is clearly and distinctly that of a change of purpose. So fix this on your minds, and lay it on your hearts, dear friends, that the repentance of the New Testament is not idle tears nor the twitchings of a vain regret, but the resolute turning away of the sinful heart from its sins. It is "repentance toward God," the turning from the sin to the Father, and that is what leads to salvation. The sorrow is separated from the repentance in idea, however closely they may be intertwined in fact. The sorrow is one thing, and the repentance which it works is another.

Then, notice that this change of purpose and breaking off from sin is produced by the sorrow for sin, of which I have been speaking; and that the production of this repentance is the main characteristic difference between the godly sorrow and the sorrow of the world. A man may have his paroxysms of regret, but the question is: Does it make any difference in his attitude? Is he standing after the tempest of sorrow has swept over him, with his face in the same direction as before; or has it whirled him clean round, and set him in the other direction? The one kind of sorrow, which measures my sin by the side of the brightness and purity of God, vindicates itself as true, because it makes me hate my evil and turn away from it. The other, which is of the world, passes over me like the empty wind through an archway, it whistles for a moment and is gone, and there is nothing left to show that it was ever there. The one comes like one of those brooks in tropical countries, dry and white for half the year, and then there is a rush of muddy waters, fierce but transient and leaving no results behind. My brother! When your conscience pricks, which of these two things does it do? After the prick, is the word of command that your Will issues. "Right about face!" or is it, "As you were?" Godly sorrow worketh a change of attitude, purpose, mind; the sorrow of the world leaves a man standing where he was. Ask yourselves the question: Which of the two are you familiar with?

Again, the true means of evoking true repentance is the contemplation of the Cross. Law and the fear of hell may startle into sorrow, and even lead to some kind of repentance. But it is the great power of Christ's love and sacrifice which will really melt the heart into true repentance. You may hammer ice to pieces, but it is ice still. You may bray a fool in a mortar, and his folly will not depart from him. Dread of punishment may pulverize the heart, but not change it; and each fragment, like the smallest bits of a magnet, will have the same characteristics as the whole mass. But "the goodness of God leads to repentance," as the prodigal is conquered and sees the true hideousness of the swine's trough, when he bethinks himself of the father's love. I beseech you to put yourselves under the influence of that great love, and look on that Cross till your hearts melt.

III. We come to the last stage here. Salvation is the issue of repentance. "Godly sorrow worketh repentance unto salvation not to be repented of."

What is the connection between repentance and salvation? Two sentences will answer the question. You cannot get salvation without repentance. You do not get salvation by repentance.

You cannot get the salvation of God unless you shake off your sin. It is no use preaching to a man, "Faith, Faith! Faith!!" unless you preach along with it, "Break off your iniquities." "Let the wicked forsake his way and the unrighteous man his thoughts, and let him turn unto the Lord." The nature of the case forbids it. It is a clear contradiction in terms, and an absolute impossibility in fact, that God should save a man with the salvation which consists in the deliverance from sin, while that man is holding to his sin. Unless, therefore, you have not merely sorrow, but repentance, which is turning away from sin with resolute purpose, as a man would turn from a serpent, you cannot enter into the Kingdom of Heaven.

But you do not get salvation for your repentance. It is no case of barter, it is no case of salvation by works, that work being repentance:

> Could my zeal no respite know,
> Could my tears forever flow,
> All for sin could not atone,
> Thou must save, and Thou alone.

Not my penitence, but Christ's death, is the ground of the salvation of everyone that is saved at all. Yet repentance is an indispensable condition of salvation.

What is the connection between repentance and faith? There can be no true repentance without trust in Christ. There can be no true trust in Christ without the forsaking of my sin. Repentance without faith, insofar as it is possible, is one long misery; like the pains of those poor Hindu devotees that will go all the way from Cape Comorin to the shrine of Juggernaut, and measure every foot of the road with the length of their own bodies in the dust. Men will do anything, and willingly make any sacrifice, rather than open their eyes to see this, that repentance, clasped hand in hand with faith, leads the guiltiest soul into the forgiving presence of the crucified Christ, from whom Peace flows into the darkest heart.

On the other hand, faith without repentance is not possible, in any deep sense. But insofar as it is possible, it produces a superficial Christianity which vaguely trusts to Christ without knowing exactly what it is trusting Him for, or why it needs Him; and which has a great deal to say about what I may call the less important parts of the Christian system, and nothing to say about its vital center, which preaches a morality which is not a living power to create, which practices a religion which is neither a joy nor a security. The old word of the Master has a deep truth in it: "These are they which heard the word, and anon with joy received it." Having no sorrow, no penitence, no deep consciousness of sin, "they have no root in themselves, and in time of temptation they fall away." If there is to be a profound, an all-pervading, life-transforming sin and devil-conquering faith, it must be a faith rooted deep in penitence and sorrow for sin.

Dear brethren, if, by God's grace, my poor words have touched your consciences at all, I beseech you, do not trifle with the budding conviction! Do not seek to have the wound skinned over. Take care that you do not let it all pass in idle sorrow or impotent regret.

If you do, you will be hardened, and the worse for it, and come nearer to that condition which the sorrow of the world worketh, the awful death of the soul. Do not wince from the knife before the roots of the cancer are cut out. The pain is merciful. Better the wound than the malignant growth. Yield yourselves to the Spirit that would convince you of sin, and listen to the voice that calls to you to forsake your unrighteous ways and thoughts. But do not trust to any tears, do not trust to any resolves, do not trust to any reformation. Trust only to the Lord that died on the Cross for you, Whose death for you, Whose life in you, will be deliverance from your sin. Then you will have a salvation which, in the striking language of my text, "is not to be repented of," which will leave no regrets in your hearts in the day when all else shall have faded, and the sinful sweets of this world shall have turned to ashes and bitterness on the lips of the men that feed on them.

"The sorrow of the world works death." There are men and women listening to me now who are half-conscious of their sin, and are resisting the pleading voice that comes to them, who at the last will open their eyes upon the realities of their lives, and in a wild passion of remorse, exclaim: "I have played the fool, and have erred exceedingly." Better to make thorough work of the sorrow, and by it to be led to repentance toward God and faith in Christ, and so secure for our own that salvation for which no man will ever regret having given even the whole world, that he might gain his own soul.

36

The First Disciples:
I. John and Andrew

And the two disciples heard Him speak, and they fol-
lowed Jesus. Then Jesus turned and saw them following,
and saith unto them, What seek ye? They said unto Him;
Rabbi (which is to say, being interpreted, Master), where
dwellest Thou? He saith unto them, Come and see. They
came and saw where He dwelt, and abode with Him that
day, for it was about the tenth hour—John 1:37–39.

In these verses we see the head waters of a great river; for we
have before us nothing less than the beginnings of the Christian
Church. So simply were the first disciples made. The great society
of believers was born like its Master, unostentatiously and in a
corner.

Jesus has come back from His six weeks in the wilderness after
His baptism, and has presented Himself before John the Baptist for
his final attestation. It was a great historical moment when the
Last of the Prophets stood face to face with the Fulfillment of all
prophecy. In his words: "Behold the Lamb of God Which taketh
away the sin of the world!" Jewish prophecy sang its swan-song, ut-
tered its last rejoicing "Eureka! I have found Him!" and died as it
spoke.

We do not sufficiently estimate the magnificent self-suppression
and unselfishness of the Baptist, in that he, with his own lips, here
repeats his testimony in order to point his disciples away from
himself, and to attach them to Jesus. If he could have been touched
by envy, he would not so gladly have recognized it as his lot to de-
crease while Jesus increased. Rare magnanimity that in a teacher! The
two who hear John's words are Andrew, Simon Peter's brother,
and an anonymous man; the latter is probably the Evangelist. For

it is remarkable that we never find the names of James and John in this Gospel (though from the other Gospels we know how closely they were associated with our Lord), and that we only find them referred to as "the sons of Zebedee," once near the close of the book. That fact points, I think, in the direction of John's authorship of this Gospel.

These two, then, follow Jesus behind, fancying themselves unobserved, not wanting to speak to Him, and probably with some notion of tracking Him to His home, in order that they may seek and interview at a later period. But He Who notices the first beginnings of return to Him, and always comes to meet men, and is better to them than their wishes, will not let them steal behind Him uncheered, nor leave them to struggle with diffidence and delay. So He turns to them, and the events which I have read in the verses that follow as my text for this morning, ensue.

We have, I think, three things especially to notice here. First, the Master's question to the whole world, "What seek ye?" Second, the Master's invitation to the whole world, "Come and see!" Lastly, the personal communion which brings men's hearts to Him, "They came and saw where he dwelt, and abode with Him that day."

I. So, then, first look at this question of Christ to the whole world, "What seek ye?" As it stands, on its surface, and in its primary application, it is the most natural of questions. Our Lord hears footsteps behind Him, and, as anyone would do, turns about, with the question which anyone would ask, "What is it that you want?" That question would derive all its meaning from the look with which it was accompanied, and the tone in which it was spoken. It might mean either annoyance and rude repulsion of the request, even before it was presented, or it might mean a glad wish to draw out the petition, and more than half a pledge to bestow it. All depends on the smile with which it was asked, and the intonation of voice which carried it to their ears. And if we had been there we should have felt, as they evidently felt, that though in form a question, it was in reality a promise, and that it drew out their shy wishes, made them conscious to themselves of what they desired, and gave them confidence that their desire would be granted. Clearly it had sunk very deep into the Evangelist's mind; and now, at the end of his life, when his course is nearly run, the never-to-be-forgotten voice sounds still in his memory, and he sees again, in sunny clearness, all the scenes that had transpired on that day by the fords of the Jordan. The first words and the last words of those whom we have learned to love are cut deep on our hearts.

It was not an accident that the first words which the Master spoke in His Messianic office were this profoundly significant question, "What seek ye?" He asks it of us all, He asks it of us today. Well for them who can answer, "Rabbi! where dwellest *Thou?*" "It is Thou Whom we seek!" So, venturing to take the words in that somewhat wider application, let me just suggest to you two or three directions in which they seem to point.

I. First, the question suggests to us this: the need of having a clear consciousness of what is our object in life. The most of men have never answered that question. They live from hand to mouth, driven by circumstances, guided by accidents, impelled by unreflecting passions and desires, knowing what they want for the moment, but never having tried to shape the whole of their lives into one consistent theory, so as to stand up before God in Christ when He puts the question to them, "What seek ye?" and to answer the question.

These incoherent, instinctive, unreflective lives that so many of you are living are a shame to your manhood, to say nothing more. God has made us for something else than that we should thus be the sport of circumstances. It is a disgrace to any of us that our lives should be like some little fishing boat, with an unskillful or feeble hand at the tiller, yawing from one point of the compass to another, and not keeping a straight and direct course. I pray you, dear brethren, to front this question: "After all, and at bottom, what is it I am living for? Can I formulate the aims and purposes of my life in any intelligible statement of which I should not be ashamed?" Some of you are not ashamed to *do* what you would be very much ashamed to say, and you practically answer the question, "What are you seeking?" by pursuits that you dare not call by their own ugly names.

There may be people in this congregation this morning that are living for their lusts, for their passions, for their ambitions, for avarice, that are living in all uncleanness and godlessness. I do not know. There are plenty of shabby, low aims in all of us, which do not bear being dragged out into the light of day. I beseech you to try and get hold of the ugly things and bring them up to the surface, however much they may seek to hide in the congenial obscurity, and twist their slimy coils round something in the dark. If you dare not put your life's object into words, bethink yourselves whether it ought to be your life's object at all.

Ah, brethren! If we would ask ourselves this question, and answer it with any thoroughness, we should not make so many mistakes as to the places where we look for the things for which we are seeking. If we knew what we were really seeking, we should know where to go to look for it. Let me tell you what you are seeking, whether you know it or not. You are seeking for rest for your heart, a home for your spirits; you are seeking for perfect truth for your understandings, perfect beauty for your affections, perfect goodness for your conscience. You are seeking for all these three, gathered into one white beam of light, and you are seeking for it all in a person. Many of you do not know this, and so you go hunting in all manner of impossible places for that which you can only find in one. To the question, "What seek ye?" the deepest of all answers, the only real answer is, "My soul thirsteth for God, for the living God." If you know that, you know where to look for what you need! "Do men gather grapes of thorns?" If these are really the things that you are seeking after, in all your mistaken search—oh! how mistaken is the search! Do men look for pearls in cockleshells, or for gold in coal-pits; and why should you look for rest of heart, mind, conscience, spirit, anywhere and in anything short of God? "What seek ye?" The only answer is, "We seek *Thee!*"

And then, still further, let me remind you how these words are not only a question, but are really a veiled and implied promise. The question, "What do you want of Me?" may either strike an intending suppliant like a blow, and drive him away with his prayer sticking in his throat unspoken, or it may sound like a merciful invitation, "What is thy petition, and what is thy request, and it shall be granted unto thee?" We know which of the two it was here. Christ asks all such questions as this (and there are many of them in the New Testament), not for His information, but for our strengthening. He asks people, not because He does not know before they answer, but that, on the one hand, their own minds may be clear as to their wishes, and so they may wish the more earnestly because of the clearness; and that on the other hand, their desires being expressed, they may be the more able to receive the gift which He is willing to bestow. So He here turns to these men, whose purpose He knew well enough, and says to them, "What seek ye?" Herein He is doing the very same thing on a lower level, and in an outer sphere, as is done when He appoints that we shall pray for the blessings which He is yearning to bestow, but which He makes conditional on our supplications, only because by these supplications our hearts are opened into a capacity for receiving them.

We have, then, in the words before us, thus understood, our Lord's gracious promise to give what is desired on the simple condition that the suppliant is conscious of his own wants, and turns to Him for the supply of them. "What seek ye?" It is a blank check that He puts into their hands to fill up. It is the key of His treasure-house which He offers to us all, with the assured confidence that if we open it we shall find all that we need.

Who is He that thus stands up before a whole world of seeking, restless spirits, and fronts them with the question which is a pledge, conscious of His capacity to give to each of them what each of them requires? Who is this that professes to be able to give all these men and women and children bread here in the wilderness? There is only one answer—the Christ of God.

And He has done what He has promised. No man or woman ever went to Him, and answered this question, and presented their petition for any real good, and was refused. No man can ask from Christ what Christ cannot bestow. No man can ask from Christ what Christ will not bestow. In the loftiest region, the region of inward and spiritual gifts, which are the best gifts, we can get everything that we want, and our only limit is, not His boundless Omnipotence and willingness, but our own poor, narrow, and shriveled desires. "Ask, and ye shall receive; seek, and ye shall find."

He stands before us, if I may so say, like some of those fountains erected at some great national festival, out of which pour for all the multitude every variety of draught which they desire, and each man that goes with his empty cup gets it filled, and gets it filled with that which he wishes. "What seek ye?" Wisdom? You students, you thinkers, you young men that are fighting with intellectual difficulties and perplexities, "What seek ye?" Truth? He gives us that. You others, "What seek ye?" Love, peace, victory, self-control, hope, anodyne for sorrow? Whatever you desire, you will find in Jesus Christ. The first words with which He broke the silence when He spoke to men as the Messiah, were at once a searching question, probing their aims and purposes, and a gracious promise pledging Him to a task not beyond His power, however far beyond that of all others, even the task of giving to each man his heart's desire. "What seek ye?" "Seek, and ye shall find."

II. Then, still further, notice how, in a similar fashion, we may regard here the second words which our Lord speaks as being His merciful invitation to the world. "Come and see."

The disciples' answer was simple and timid. They did not venture to say, "May we talk to You?" "Will You take us to be Your disciples?" All they can muster courage to ask now is, "Where dwellest Thou?" At another time, perhaps, we will go to this Rabbi and speak with him. His answer is, "Come! Come now! Come, and by intercourse with Me, learn to know Me." His temporary home was probably nothing more than some selected place on the river's bank, for He had not where to lay His head; but such as it was He welcomes them to it. "Come and see!"

Take a plain, simple truth out of that. Christ is always glad when people resort to Him. When He was here in the world, no hour was inconvenient or inopportune; no moment was too much occupied; no physical wants of hunger, or thirst, or slumber were ever permitted to come between Him and seeking hearts. He was never impatient. He was never wearied of speaking, though He was often wearied in speaking. He never denied Himself to anybody, or said, "I have something else to do than to attend to you." And just as in literal fact, while He was here upon earth, nothing was ever permitted to hinder His drawing near to anybody that wanted to draw near to Him, so nothing now hinders it; and He is glad when any of us resort to Him and ask Him to let us speak to Him and be with Him.

His weariness or occupation never shut men out from Him then. His glory does not shut them out now.

Then there is another thought here. This invitation of the Master is also a very distinct call to a first-hand knowledge of Jesus Christ. Andrew and John had heard from the Baptist about Him, and now what He bids them to do is to come and hear Himself. That is what he calls you, dear brethren, to do. Do not listen to us, let the Master Himself speak to you. Many who reject Christianity reject it through not having listened to Jesus Himself teaching them, but only to theologians and other human representations of the truth. Go and ask Christ to speak to you with His own lips of truth, and take Him as the expositor of His own system. Do not be contented with traditional talk and second-hand information. Go to Christ, and hear what He Himself has to say to you.

Then, still further, in this "come and see" there is a distinct call to the personal act of faith. Both of these words, *"Come,"* and *"see,"* are used in the New Testament as standing emblems of faith. Coming to Christ is trusting Him; trusting Him is seeing Him, looking unto Him. "Come unto Me, and I will give you rest." "Look unto Me, and be ye saved, all ye ends of the earth." There are two metaphors, both of them pointing to one thing, and that one thing is the invitation from the dear lips of the loving Lord to every man, woman, and child in this congregation. "Come and see!" "Put your trust in Me, draw near to Me by desire and penitence, draw near to Me in the fixed thought of your mind, in the devotion of your will, in the trust of your whole being. Come to Me, and see Me by faith; and then—and then—your hearts will have found what they seek, and your weary quest will be over, and like the dove you will fold your wings and nestle at the foot of the Cross, and rest forevermore. Come! Come and see!"

III. So, lastly, we have in these words a parable of the blessed experience which binds men's hearts to Jesus forever. "They came and saw where He dwelt, and abode with Him that day, for it was about the tenth hour." "Dwelt" and "abode" are the same words in the original. It is one of John's favorite words, and in its deepest meaning expresses the close, still communion which the soul may have with Jesus Christ, which communion, on that never-to-be-forgotten day, when he and Andrew sat with Him in the quiet, confidential fellowship that disclosed Christ's glory full of grace and truth to their hearts, made them His forever.

If the reckoning of time here is made according to the Hebrew fashion, the "tenth hour" will be ten o'clock in the morning. So, one long day of talk! If it be according to the Roman legal fashion, the hour will be four o'clock in the afternoon, which would only give time for a brief conversation before nightfall. But, in any case, sacred reserve is observed as to what passed in that interview. A lesson for a great deal of blatant talk, in this present day, about conversion and the details thereof!

> Not easily forgiven are those who, setting wide the doors
> That bar the secret bridal chambers of the heart,
> Let in the day.

John had nothing to say to the world about what the Master said to him and his brother in that long day of communion.

One plain conclusion from this last part of our narrative is that the impression of Christ's own personality is the strongest force to make disciples. The character of Jesus Christ is, after all, the center and the standing evidence, and the mightiest credential of Christianity. It bears upon its face the proof of its own truthfulness. If such a character was not lived, how did it ever come to be described, and described by such people? And if it was lived, how did it come to be? The historical veracity of the character of Jesus Christ is guaranteed by its very uniqueness. And the Divine origin of Jesus Christ is forced upon us as the only adequate explanation of His historical character. "Truly this man was the Son of God."

I believe that to lift Him up is the work of all Christian preachers and teachers; as far as they can to hide themselves behind Jesus Christ, or at the most to let themselves appear, just as the old painters used to let their own likenesses appear in the great altarpieces—a little kneeling figure there, away in a dark corner of the background. Present Christ, and He will vindicate His own character; He will vindicate His own nature; He will vindicate His own Gospel. "They came and saw where He dwelt, and abode with Him." And the end of it was that they abode with Him forevermore. And so it will always be.

Once more, personal experience of the grace and sweetness of this Savior binds men to Him as nothing else will:

> He must be loved ere that to you
> He will seem worthy of your love.

The deepest and sweetest, and most precious part of His character and of His gifts can only be known on condition of possessing Him and them, and they can be possessed only on condition of holding fellowship with Him. I do not say to any man—"try Trust in order to be sure that Jesus Christ is worthy to be trusted," for by its very nature faith cannot be an experiment or provisional.

I do not say that my experience is evidence to you, but at the same time I do say that it is worth any man's while to reflect upon this, that none who ever trusted in Him have been put to shame. No man has looked to Jesus and has said: "Ah! I have found Him out! His help is vain, His promises empty." Many men have fallen away from Him, I know, but not because they have proved Him a liar, but because they have become unfaithful.

And so, dear brethren, I come to you with the old message: "Oh! taste," and thus you will "see that the Lord is good." There must be the faith first, and then there will be the experience, which will make anything seem to you more credible than that He Whom you have loved and trusted, and Who has answered your love and your trust should be anything else than the Son of God, the Savior of mankind. Come to Him, and you will see. The impregnable argument will be put into your mouth, "Whether this man be a sinner or not, I know not. One thing I know, that whereas I was blind, now I see." Look to Him, listen to Him, and when He asks you, "What seek ye?" answer "Rabbi, where dwellest Thou? It is Thou Whom we seek." He will welcome you to close blessed intercourse with Him, which will knit you to Him with cords that cannot be broken, and with His loving voice making music in memory and heart, you will be able triumphantly to confess—"Now we believe, not because of any man's saying, for we have heard Him ourselves, and know that this is indeed the Christ, the Savior of the world."

37

The First Disciples:
II. Simon Peter

One of the two which heard John speak, and followed Him, was Andrew, Simon Peter's brother. He first findeth his own brother, Simon, and saith unto him, We have found the Messiah, which is, being interpreted, the Christ. And he brought him to Jesus, and when Jesus beheld him, He said, Thou art Simon, the son of Jona, thou shalt be called Cephas, which is by interpretation a stone —John 1:40–42.

There are many ways by which souls are brought to their Savior. Sometimes, like the merchantman seeking goodly pearls, men seek Him earnestly and find Him. Sometimes, by the intervention of another, the knowledge of Him is kindled in dark hearts. Sometimes He Himself takes the initiative, and finds those that seek Him not. We have illustrations of all these various methods in these simple records of the gathering in of the first disciples. Andrew and his friend, with whom we were occupied in our last sermon, looked for Christ and found Him. Peter, with whom we have to do now, was brought to Christ by his brother; and the third of the group, consisting of Philip, was sought by Christ while he was not thinking of Him, and found an unsought treasure. And then Philip, again, like Andrew, finds a friend, and brings him to Christ.

Each of the incidents has its own lesson, and each of them adds something to the elucidation of John's two great subjects, the revelation of Jesus as the Son of God and the development of that faith in Him which gives us life. It may be profitable to consider each group in succession, and mark the various aspects of these two subjects presented by each.

In this incident, then, we have two things mainly to consider, first, the witness of the disciple; second, the self-revelation of the Master.

I. The witness of the disciple. We have seen that the unknown companion of Andrew was probably the Evangelist himself, who, in accordance with his uniform habit, suppresses his own name, and that that omission points to John's authorship of this Gospel. Another morsel of evidence as to the date and purpose of the Gospel lies in the mention here of Andrew as "Simon Peter's brother." We have not yet heard anything about Simon Peter. The Evangelist has never mentioned his name, and yet he takes it for granted that his hearers knew all about Peter, and knew him better than they did Andrew. That presupposes a considerable familiarity with the incidents of the Gospel story, and is in harmony with the theory that this fourth Gospel is the latest of the four, and was written for the purpose of supplementing, not of repeating, their narrative. Hence a number of the phenomena of the Gospel, which have troubled critics, are simply and sufficiently explained.

But that by the way. Passing that, notice first the illustration that we get here of how instinctive and natural the impulse is, when a man has found Jesus Christ, to tell someone else about Him. Nobody said to Andrew, "Go and look for your brother!" And yet, as soon as he had fairly realized the fact that this Man standing before him was the Messiah, though the evening seems to have come, he hurries away to find his brother, and share with him the glad conviction.

Now, that is always the case. If a man has any real depth of conviction, he cannot rest till he tries to share it with somebody else. Why, even a dog that has had its leg mended, will bring other limping dogs to the man that was kind to it. Whoever really believes anything becomes a propagandist.

Look round about us today! And hearken to the Babel, the wholesome Babel of noises, where every sort of opinion is trying to make itself heard. It sounds like a country fair where every huckster is shouting his loudest. That shows that the men believe the things that they profess. Thank God that there is so much earnestness in the world! And now are Christians to be dumb while all this vociferous crowd is calling its wares, and quacks are standing on their platforms shouting out their specifics, which are mostly delusions? Have you not a medicine that will cure everything, a real heal-all, a veritable pain-killer? If you believe that you have, certainly you will never rest till you share your boon with your brethren.

If the natural effect of all earnest conviction, viz., a yearning and an absolute necessity to speak it out, is no part of your Christian experience, very grave inferences ought to be drawn from that. This man, before he was yet twenty-four hours a disciple, had made another. Some of you have been disciples for as many years, and have never even tried to make one. Whence comes that silence which is, alas, so common among us?

It is very plain that, making all allowance for changed manners, for social difficulties, for timidity, for the embarrassment that besets people when they talk to other people about religion, which is "such an awkward subject to introduce into mixed company," and the like; making all allowance for that, there is a deplorable number of Christian people who ought to be, in their own circles, evangelists and missionaries, who are, if I may venture to quote very rude words which the Bible uses, "Dumb dogs lying down, and loving to slumber." "He first findeth his own brother, Simon!"

Now, take another lesson out of this witness of the disciple, as to the channel in which such effort naturally runs. "He *first* findeth *his own brother*." Well, then, there was a second that found somebody or other. The language of the text suggests that the Evangelist's tendency to the suppression of himself, of which I have spoken, hides away, if I may so say, in this singular expression, the fact that he too went to look for a brother, but that Andrew found his brother before John found his. If so, each of the original pair of disciples went to look for one who was knit to him by close ties of kindred and affection, and found him and brought him to Christ; and before the day was over the Christian Church was doubled, because each member of it, by God's grace, added another. Home, then, and those who are nearest to us, present the natural channels for Christian work. Many a very earnest and busy preacher, or Sunday-school teacher, or missionary, has brothers and sisters, husband or wife, children or parents at home to whom he has never said a word about Christ. There is an old proverb: "The shoemaker's wife is always the worst shod." The families of many very busy Christian teachers suffer woefully for want of remembering "he first findeth his own brother." It is a poor affair if all your philanthropy and Christian energy go off noisily in Sunday-schools and mission-stations, and if your own vineyard, the people at your own fireside, never hear anything from you about the Master whom you say you love. Some of you want that hint; will you take it?

But, then, the principle is one that might be fairly expanded beyond the home circle. The natural relationships into which we are brought by neighborhood and by ordinary associations prescribe the direction of our efforts. What, for instance, are we set down in this swarming population of Lancashire for? For business and personal ends? Yes, partly. But is that all? Surely, if we believe that there is a Divinity that shapes our ends and determines the bounds of our habitation, we must believe that other purposes affecting other people are also meant by God to be accomplished through us, and that where a man who knows and loves Christ Jesus is brought into neighborly contact with thousands who do not, he is thereby constituted his brethren's keeper, and is as plainly called to tell them of Christ as if a voice from Heaven had bid him do it. What is to be said of the depth and vital energy of the Christianity that neither hears the call nor feels the impulse to share its blessing with the famishing Lazarus at its gate? What will be the fate of such a church? Why, if you live in luxury in your own well-drained and ventilated house, and take no heed to the typhoid fever or cholera in the slums at the back, the chances are that seeds of the disease will find their way to you, and kill your wife, or child, or yourself. And if you Christian people, living in the midst of godless people, do not try to heal them, they will infect you. If you do not seek to impress your conviction that Christ is the Messiah upon an unbelieving generation, the unbelieving generation will impress upon you its doubts whether He is; and your lips will falter, and a pallor will come over the complexion of your love, and your faith will become congealed, and turn into ice.

Notice again the simple word which is the most powerful means of influencing most men. Andrew did not begin to argue with his brother. Some of us can do that and some of us cannot. Some of us are influenced by argument and some of us are not. You may pound a man's mistaken creed to atoms with sledgehammers of reasoning, and he is not much the nearer being a Christian than he was before; just as you may pound ice to pieces and it is pounded ice after all. The mightiest argument that we can use, and the argument that we can all use, if we have got any religion in us at all, is that of Andrew, "We have found the Messiah."

I was reading the other day a story in some newspaper or other about a minister that preached a very elaborate course of lectures in refutation of some form of infidelity, for the special benefit of a man that attended his place of worship. Soon after the man came and declared himself a Christian. The minister said to him, "Which of my discourses was it that removed your doubts?" The reply was, "Oh! It was not any of your sermons that influenced me. The thing that set me thinking was that a poor woman came out of the chapel beside me, and stumbled on the steps, and I stretched out my hand to help her, and she said, 'Thank you!' Then she looked at me and said: 'Do you love Jesus Christ, my blessed Savior?' And I did not, and I went home and thought about it; and now I can say *I* love Jesus." The poor woman's word, and her frank confession of her experience, was all the transforming power.

If you have found Christ, you can say you have. Never mind about the how! Any how! Only say it! A boy that is sent on an errand by his father has only one duty to perform, and that is to repeat what he was told. Whether we have any eloquence or not, whether we have any logic or not, whether we can speak persuasively and gracefully or not, if we have got hold of Christ at all we can say that we have; and it is at our peril that we do not. We can say it to somebody. There is surely someone who will listen to you more readily than to anybody else. Surely you have not lived all your life and bound nobody to you by kindness and love, so that they will gladly attend to what you say. Well, then, *use* the power that is given to you.

Remember the beginnings of the Christian Church—two men; each of whom found his brother. Two and two make four; and if every one of us would go, according to the old law of warfare, and each of us slay our man, or rather each of us give life by God's grace to someone, or try to do it, our congregations and our churches would grow as fast as, according to the old problem, the money grew that was paid down for the nails in the horse's shoes. Two snowflakes on the top of a mountain are an avalanche by the time they reach the valley. "He first findeth his brother, Simon."

II. And now I turn to the second part of this text, the self-revelation of the Master. The bond which knit these men to Christ at first was by no means the perfect Christian faith which they afterwards attained. They recognized Him as the Messiah, they were personally attached to Him, they were ready to accept His teaching and to obey His commandments. That was about as far as they had gotten. But they were scholars. They had entered the school. The rest will come. We had not, then, to expect that Christ would begin by preaching to them faith in His Divinity and atoning work. He binds them to *Himself*. That is lesson enough for a beginner for one day.

It was the impression which Christ Himself made on Simon which completed the work begun by his brother. What, then, was the impression? He comes all full of wonder and awe, and he is met by a look and a sentence.

The look, which is described by an unusual word, was a penetrating gaze which regarded Peter with fixed attention. It must have been remarkable, to have lived in John's memory for all these years. Evidently, as I think, a more-than-natural insight is implied. So, also, the saying with which our Lord received Peter seems to me to be meant to show more-than-natural knowledge: "Thou art Simon, the son of Jonas." Christ may, no doubt, have learned the Apostle's name and lineage from his brother, or in some other ordinary way. But if you observe the similar incident which follows in the conversation with Nicodemus, and the emphatic declaration of the next chapter that Jesus knew both "all men," and "what was in man"—both human nature as a whole, and each individual—it is more natural to see here superhuman knowledge.

So, then, the first point in our Lord's self-revelation here is that He shows Himself possessed of supernatural and thorough knowledge. One remembers the many instances where our Lord read men's hearts, and the prayer addressed to him, probably by Peter, "Thou, Lord, which knowest the hearts of all men," and the vision which John saw of eyes like a flame of fire, and the sevenfold "I know thy works."

It may be a very awful thought, "Thou, God, seest me." It is a very unwelcome thought to a great many men, and it will be so to us unless we can give it the modification which it receives from the belief in the Divinity of Jesus Christ, and feel sure that the eyes which are blazing with Divine Omniscience are dewy with Divine and human love.

Do you believe it? Do you feel that Christ is looking at you, and searching you altogether? Do you rejoice in it? Do you carry it about with you as a consolation and a strength in moments of weakness, and it times of temptation? Is it as blessed to you to feel "Thou Christ beholdest me now," as it is for a child to feel that when it is playing in the garden its mother is sitting up at the window watching it, and that no harm can come? There have been men driven mad in prisons because they knew that somewhere in the wall there was a little pinhole, through which a jailer's eye was always, or might be always, glaring down at them. And the thought of an absolute Omniscience up there, searching me to the depths of my nature, may become one from which I recoil shudderingly, and will not be altogether a blessed one unless it comes to me in this shape: "My Christ knows me altogether and loves me better than He knows. And so I will spread myself out before Him, and though I feel that there is much in which I dare not tell to men, I will rejoice that there is nothing which I need to tell to Him. He knows me through and through. He knew me when He died for me. He knew me when He forgave me. He knew me when He undertook to cleanse me. Like this very Peter I will say: 'Lord thou knowest all things,' and, like him, I will cling the closer to His feet, because I know, and He knows, my weakness and my sin."

Another revelation of our Lord's relation to His disciples is given in the fact that he changes Simon's name. Jehovah, in the Old Testament, changes the names of Abraham and of Jacob. Babylonian kings in the Old Testament change the names of their vassal princes. Masters impose names on their slaves; and I suppose that even the marriage custom of the wife's assuming the name of her husband rests originally upon the same idea of absolute authority. That idea is conveyed in the fact that our Lord changes Peter's name, and so takes absolute possession of him, and asserts His mastery over him. We belong to Him altogether, because He has given Himself altogether for us. His absolute authority is the correlative of His utter self-surrender. He Who can come to me and say: "I have spared not my life for thee," and He only, has the right to come to me and say: "yield yourself wholly to Me." So, Christian friends, your Master wants all your service; do you give yourselves up to Him out and out, not by half and half.

Lastly, that change of name implies Christ's power and promise to bestow a new character and new functions and honors. Peter was by no means a "Peter" then. The name no doubt mainly implies official function, but that official function was prepared for by personal character; and insofar as the name refers to character, it means firmness. At that epoch Peter was rash, impulsive, head-strong, self-confident, vain, and, therefore, necessarily changeable. Like the granite, all fluid and hot, and fluid because it was hot, he needed to cool in order to solidify into rock. And not until his self-confidence had been knocked out of him, and he had learned humility by falling; not until he had been beaten from all his presumption, and tamed down, and sobered and steadied by years of difficulty and responsibilities did he become the rock that Christ meant him to be. All *that* lay concealed in the future, but in the change of his name, while he stood on the very threshold of his Christian career, there was preached to him, and there is preached to us, this great truth, that if you will go to Jesus Christ He will make a new man of you. No man's character is so obstinately rooted in evil but Christ can change its set and direction. No man's natural dispositions are so faulty and low but that Christ can develop counterbalancing virtues, and out of the evil and weakness make strength. He will not make a Peter into a John, or a John into a Paul, but He will deliver Peter from the "defects of his qualities," and lead them up into a higher and a nobler region. There are no outcasts in the view of the transforming Christ. He dismisses no people out of His hospital as incurable, because anybody, everybody, the blackest, the most rooted in evil, those who have longest indulged in any given form of transgression, may all come to Him; with the certainty that if they will cleave to Him; He will read all their character and all its weaknesses, and then with a glad smile of welcome and assured confidence on His face, will ensure to them a new nature, and new dignities. "Thou art Simon—thou shalt be Peter."

The process will be long. It will be painful. There will be a great deal pared off. The sculptor makes the marble image by chipping away the superfluous marble. Ah! and when you have to chip away superfluous flesh and blood it is bitter work, and the chisel is often deeply dyed in gore, and the mallet seems to be very cruel. Simon did not know all that had to be done to make a Peter of him. We have to thank His providence that we do not know all the sorrows and trials of the process of making us what He wills us to be. But we may be sure of this, that if only we keep near our Master, and let Him have His way with us, and work His will upon us, and if only we will not wince from the blows of the Great Artist's chisel, then out of the roughest block He will carve the fairest statue; and He will fulfill for us at last His great promise: "I will give unto him a white stone, and in the stone a new name written, which no man knoweth save he that receiveth it."

38

The First Disciples: III. Philip

The day following, Jesus would go forth into Galilee, and findeth Philip, and saith unto him: Follow Me
—John 1:43.

The day following"—We have a diary in this chapter, and the next, extending from the day when John the Baptist gives his official testimony to Jesus up till our Lord's first journey to Jerusalem. The order of events is this. The deputation from the Sanhedrim to John occupied the first day. On the second Jesus comes back to John after his temptation, and receives his solemn attestation. On the third day, John repeats his testimony, and three disciples, probably four, make the nucleus of the church. These are the two pairs of brothers, James and John, Andrew and Peter, who stand first in every catalogue of the Apostles, and were evidently nearest to Christ.

"The day following" of our text is the fourth day. On it our Lord determines to return to Galilee. His objects in His visit to John were accomplished—to receive his public attestation, and to gather the first little knot of His followers. Thus launched upon His course, He desired to return to His native district.

These events had occurred where John was baptizing, in a place called in the English version Bethabara, which means "The house of crossing," or as we might say, Ferry-house. The traditional site for John's baptism is near Jericho, but the next chapter (verse 1) shows that it was only a day's journey from Cana of Galilee, and must therefore have been much further north than Jericho. A ford, still bearing the name Abarah, a few miles south of the lake of Gennesaret has lately been discovered. Our Lord then, and His

357

disciples had a day's walking to take them back to Galilee. But apparently before they set out on that morning, Philip and Nathanael were added to the little band. So these two days saw six disciples gathered round Jesus.

Andrew and John sought Christ and found Him. To them He revealed Himself as very willing to be approached, and glad to welcome any to His side. Peter, who comes next, was brought to Christ by his brother, and to him Christ revealed Himself as reading his heart, and promising and giving him higher functions and a more noble character.

Now I come to the third case, "Jesus findeth Philip," who was not seeking Jesus, and who was brought by no one. To him Christ reveals Himself as drawing near to many a heart that has not thought of Him, and laying a masterful hand of gracious authority on the springs of life and character in that autocratic word "Follow Me." So we have a gradually heightening revelation of the Master's graciousness to all souls, to them that seek and to them that seek Him not. It is only to the working out of these simple thoughts that I ask your attention now.

I. First, then, let us deal with the revelation that is given us here of the seeking Christ.

Everyone who reads this chapter with even the slightest attention must observe how "seeking" and "finding" are repeated over and over again. Christ turns to Andrew and John with the question, "What *seek* ye?" Andrew, as the narrative says, "*findeth* his own brother, Simon, and saith unto him; 'We have *found* the Messiah!' " Then, again, Jesus *finds* Philip; and again, Philip, as soon as he has been won to Jesus, goes off to *find* Nathanael; and his glad word to him is, once more, "We have found the *Messiah.*" It is a reciprocal play of finding and seeking all through these verses.

There are two kinds of finding. There is a casual stumbling upon a thing that you were not looking for, and there is a finding as the result of seeking. It is the latter which is here. Christ did not casually stumble upon Philip, upon that morning, before they departed from the fords of the Jordan on their short journey to Cana of Galilee. He went to look for this other Galilean, one who was connected with Andrew and Peter, a native of the same little village.

He went and found him; and while Philip was all unexpectant and undesirous, the Master came to him and laid His hand upon him, and drew him to Himself.

Now that is what Christ often does. There are men like the merchantman who went all over the world seeking goodly pearls, who with some eager longing to possess light, or truth, or goodness, or rest, search up and down and find it nowhere, because they are looking for it in a hundred different places. They are expecting to find a little here and a little there, and to piece all together to make of the fragments one all-sufficing restfulness. Then when they are most eager in their search, or, when perhaps it has all died down into despair and apathy, the veil, seems to be withdrawn, and they see Him Whom they have been seeking all the time and knew not that He was there beside them. All, and more than all, that they sought for in the many pearls is stored for them in the one Pearl of great price. The ancient covenant stands firm today as forever. "Seek and ye shall find, knock and it shall be opened unto you."

But then there are others, like Paul on the road to Damascus; like Matthew the publican, sitting at the receipt of custom, on whom there is laid a sudden hand, to whom there comes a sudden conviction, on whose eyes, not looking to the east, there dawns the light of Christ's presence. Such cases occur all through the ages, for He is not to be confined, bless His name! within the narrow limits of answering seeking souls, or of showing Himself to people that are brought to Him by human instrumentality; but far beyond these bounds He goes, and many a time discloses His beauty, and His sweetness to hearts that knew not of Him, and who can only say, "Lo! God was in this place, and I knew it not." "Thou wast found of them that sought Thee not."

As it was in His miracles upon earth, so it has been in the sweet and gracious works of His grace ever since. Sometimes He healed in response to the yearning desire that looked out of sick eyes, or that spoke from parched lips, and no man that ever came to Him and said, "Heal me!" was sent away beggared of His blessing. Sometimes He healed in response to the beseeching of those who with loving hearts, carried their dear ones and laid them at His feet. But sometimes to magnify the spontaneity and the completeness of His own love, and to show us that He is bound and limited by no human co-operation, and that He is His own motive, He reached out the blessing to a hand that was not extended to grasp it; and by His question, "Wilt thou be made whole?" kindled desires that else had lain dormant forever.

And so in this story before us; He will welcome and over-answer Andrew and John when they come seeking; He will turn round to them with a smile on His face, that converts the question, "What seek ye?" into an invitation, "Come and see." And when Andrew brings his brother to Him, He will go more than half-way to meet him. But when these are won, there still remains another way by which He will have disciples brought into His Kingdom, and that is by Himself going out and laying His hand on the man and drawing him to His heart by the revelation of his Love.

But further, and in a deeper sense He really seeks us all, and unasked bestows His love upon us.

Whether we seek Him or not, there is not heart upon earth which Christ does not desire; and no man or woman within the sound of His Gospel whom He is not in a very real sense seeking that He may draw them to Himself. His own word is a wonderful one: "The Father *seeketh* such to worship Him"; as if God went all up and down the world looking for hearts to love Him and to turn to Him with reverent thankfulness. And as the Father so the Son—who is for us the revelation of the Father: "The Son of Man is come to *seek* and to save that which was lost." Nobody on earth wanted Him, or dreamed of His coming. When He bowed the heavens and gathered Himself into the narrow space of the manger in Bethlehem and took upon Him the limitations and the burdens, and the weaknesses of manhood, it was not in response to any petition, it was in reply to no seeking; but He came spontaneously, unmoved, obeying but the impulse of His own heart, and because He would have mercy. He Who is the Beginning, and will be first in all things, was first in this. Before they called, He answered, and came upon earth unbesought and unexpected, because His own infinite love brought Him hither. Christ's mercy to a world does not come like water in a well that has to be pumped up, by our petitions, by our search, but like water in some fountain, rising sparkling into the sunlight by its own inward impulse. He is His own motive; and came to a forgetful and careless world, like a shepherd who goes after his flock in the wilderness, not because they bleat for him, while they crop the herbage which tempts them ever further from the fold and remember him and it no more, but because he cannot have them lost. Men are not conscious of needing Christ till He comes. The supply creates the demand. He is like the "dew which tarrieth not for man, nor waiteth for the sons of men."

But not only does Christ seek us all, inasmuch as the whole conception and execution of His great work are independent of man's desires, but He seeks us each in a thousand ways. He longs to have each of us for His disciples. He seeks each of us for His disciples, by the motion of His Spirit on our spirits, by stirring conviction in our consciences, by pricking us often with a sense of our own evil, by all our restlessness and dissatisfaction, by the disappointments and the losses, as by the brightnesses and the goodness of earthly providences, and often through such agencies as my lips and the lips of other men. The Master Himself, Who seeks all mankind, has sought and is seeking you at this moment. Oh! Yield to His search. The shepherd goes out on the mountainside, for all the storm and the snow, and wades knee-deep through the drifts until he finds the sheep. And your Shepherd, Who is also your Brother, has come looking for you, and at this moment is putting out His hand and laying hold of some of you through my poor words, and saying to you, as He said to Philip, "Follow Me!"

II. And now let us next consider that word of authority, which, spoken to the one man in our text is really spoken to us all. "Jesus findeth Philip, and said unto him: 'Follow Me!' " No doubt a great deal more passed, but no doubt, what more passed was less significant and less important for the development of faith in this man than what is recorded. The word of authority, the invitation which was a demand, the demand which was an invitation, and the personal impression which He produced upon Philip's heart, were the things that bound him to Jesus Christ forever. "Follow me," spoken at the beginning of the journey of Christ and His disciples back to Galilee, might have meant merely, on the surface, "Come back with us." But the words have, of course, a much deeper meaning. They mean—be

My disciple. Think what is implied in them, and ask yourself whether the demand that Christ makes in these words is an unreasonable one, and then ask yourselves whether you have yielded to it or not.

We lose the force of the image by much repetition. Sheep follow a shepherd. Travelers follow a guide. Here is a man upon some dangerous cornice of the Alps, with a ledge of limestone as broad as the palm of your hand for him, and perhaps a couple of feet of snow above that for him to walk upon, a precipice on either side; and his guide says, as he ropes himself to him, "Now, tread where I tread!" Travelers follow their guides. Soldiers follow their commanders. There is the hell of the battlefield; here a line of wavering, timid, raw recruits. Their commander rushes to the front and throws himself upon the advancing enemy with one word, "Follow!" And the weakest becomes a hero. Soldiers follow their captains.

Your shepherd comes to you and calls, "Follow me."

Your Captain and Commander comes to you and calls, "Follow Me." In all the dreary wilderness, in all the difficult contingencies and conjunctions, in all the conflicts of life, this Man strides in front of us and proposes Himself to us as Guide, Example, Consoler, Friend, Companion, everything; and gathers up all duty, all blessedness, in the majestic and simple words, "Follow Me."

It is a call at the least to accept Him as a Teacher, but the whole gist of the context here is to show us that from the beginning Christ's disciples did not look upon Him as a Rabbi's disciples did, as being simply a teacher, but recognized Him as the Messiah, the Son of God, the King of Israel. So that they were called upon by this command to accept His teaching in a very special way, not merely as Hillel or Gamaliel asked their disciples to accept theirs. Do you do that? Do you take Him as your illumination about all matters of theoretical truth, and of practical wisdom? Is His declaration of God your theology? Is His declaration of His own Person your creed? Do you think about His Cross as He did when He elected to be remembered in all the world by the broken body and the shed blood, which were the symbols of His reconciling death? Is His teaching, that the Son of Man comes to give His life a ransom for many, the ground of your hope? Do you follow Him in your belief, and following Him in your belief, do you accept Him, as, by His death and passion, the Savior of your soul? That is the first step—to follow Him, to trust him wholly for what He is, the Incarnate Son of God, the Sacrifice for the sins of the whole world, and therefore for your sins and mine. This is a call to faith.

It is also a call to obedience. "Follow Me" certainly means, "Do as I bid you," but softens all the harshness of that command. Sedulously plant your little feet in His firm footsteps. Where you see His track going across the bog be not afraid to walk after Him, though it may seem to lead you into the deepest and the blackest of it. Follow Him, and you will be right. "Follow Him" and you will be blessed. Do as Christ did, or as according to the best of your judgment it seems to you that Christ would have done if He had been in your circumstances; and you will not go far wrong. "The Imitation of Christ," which the old anonymous monk wrote his book about, is the sum of all practical Christianity. "Follow Me!" makes discipleship to be something more than intellectual acceptance of His teaching, something more than even reliance for my salvation upon His work. It makes discipleship—springing out of these two—the acceptance of His teaching and the consequent reliance, by faith, upon His word—to be a practical reproduction of His character and conduct in mine.

It is a call to communion. If a man follows Christ, he will walk close behind Him, and near enough to Him to hear Him speak, and to be "guided by His eye." He will be separated from other people, and from other things. In these four things, then—Faith, Obedience, Imitation, Communion—lies the essence of discipleship. No man is a Christian who has not in some measure all four. Have you got them?

What right has Jesus Christ to ask me to follow Him? Why should I? Who is He that He should set Himself up as being the perfect Example and the Guide for all the world? What has He done to bind me to Him, that I should take Him for my Master, and yield myself to Him in a subjection that I refuse to the mightiest names in literature, and thought, and practical benevolence? Who is this that assumes thus to dominate over us all? Ah! Brethren, there is only one answer. This is none other than the Son of God Who has given Himself a Ransom for me, and therefore, has the right, and only therefore has the right, to say to me, 'Follow Me.' "

III. And now one last word. Think for a moment about this silently and swiftly obedient disciple. Philip says nothing. Of course the narrative is a mere sketchy outline. He is silent but he yields.

Ah! Brethren, how quickly a soul may be won or lost! That moment, when Philip's decision was trembling in the balance, was but a moment. It might have gone the other way, for Christ has no pressed men in His army; they are all volunteers. It might have gone the other way. A moment may settle for you whether you will be His disciple or not. People tell us that the belief in instantaneous conversions is unphilosophical. It seems to me that the objections to them are unphilosophical. All decisions are matters of an instant. Hesitation may be long, weighing and balancing may be a protracted process, but the decision is always a moment's work, a knife-edge. And there is no reason whatever why anyone listening to me now may not now, if he or she will, do as this man Philip did on the spot, and when Christ says, "Follow Me," turn to Him and answer, "I will follow Thee whithersoever Thou goest."

There is an old Church tradition which says that the disciple who, at a subsequent period answered Christ: "Lord! suffer me first to go and bury my father," was this same Apostle. I do not think that is at all likely, but the tradition suggests to us one last thought about the reasons, why people are kept back from yielding this obedience to Christ's invitation. Many of you are kept back as that procrastinating follower was, because there are some other duties, which you feel, or make to be, more important. "I will think about Christianity, and turning religious when this, that, or the other thing has been got over. I have my position in life to make. I have a great many things to do that must be done at once, and really, I have not time to think about it."

Then there are some of you that are kept from following Christ because you have never found out yet that you need a guide at all. Then there are some of you that are kept back because you like very much better to go your way, and to follow your own inclination;

and dislike the idea of following the will of another. There are a host of other reasons that I do not need to deal with now; but oh, brethren, none of them are worth pleading. They are excuses, they are not reasons. "They all with one consent began to make excuse." Excuses, not reasons; and manufactured excuses, in order to cover a decision which has been taken before, and on other grounds altogether, which it is not convenient to bring up to the surface. I am not going to deal with these in detail, but I beseech you, do not let what I venture to call Christ's seeking of you once more, even by my poor words now, be in vain.

Follow Him! Trust, obey, imitate, hold fellowship with Him. You will always have a Companion, you will always have a Protector. "He that followeth Me," saith He, "shall not walk in darkness, but shall have the light of life." And if you will listen to the Shepherd's voice and follow Him, that sweet old promise will be true, in its Divinest and sweetest sense about your life, in time; and about your life in the moment of death, the isthmus between two worlds, and about your life in eternity—"They shall not hunger nor thirst, neither shall the sun nor heat smite them; for He that hath mercy on them shall lead them, even by the springs of water shall He guide them." Follow thou Me.

39

The First Disciples: IV. Nathanael

Philip findeth Nathanael, and saith unto him, We have found Him of Whom Moses in the law, and in the prophets, did write, Jesus of Nazareth, the Son of Joseph. And Nathanael said unto him, Can there any good thing come out of Nazareth? Philip saith unto him, Come and see. Jesus saw Nathanael coming to Him, and saith of him, Behold an Israelite indeed, in whom is no guile! Nathanael saith unto Him, Whence knowest Thou me? Jesus answered and said unto him, Before that Philip called thee, when thou wast under the fig tree, I saw thee. Nathanael answered and saith unto Him, Rabbi, Thou art the Son of God; Thou art the King of Israel—John 1:45–49.

The words are often the least part of a conversation. The Evangelist can tell us what Nathanael said to Jesus, and what Jesus said to Nathanael, but no evangelist can reproduce the look, the tone, the magnetic influence which streamed out from Christ, and, we may believe, more than anything He said, riveted these men to Him.

It looks as if Nathanael and his companions were very easily convinced, as if their adhesion to such tremendous claims as those of Jesus Christ was much too facile a thing to be a very deep one. But what can be put down in black and white goes a very short way to solve the secret of the power which drew them to Himself.

The incident which is before us now runs substantially on the same lines as the previous bringing of Peter to Jesus Christ. In both cases the man is brought by a friend, in both cases the friend's weapon is simply the expression of his own personal experience, "We have found the Messiah," although Philip has a little more to say about Christ's correspondence with the prophetic word. In both cases the work is finished by our Lord Himself manifesting His own supernatural knowledge to the inquiring spirit, though in the case of Nathanael that process is a little more lengthened out than in the case of Peter, because there was a little ice of hesitation and of doubt to be melted away. And Nathanael, starting from a lower point than Peter, having questions and hesitations which the other had not, rises to a higher point of faith and certitude, and from his lips first of all comes the full, articulate confession, beyond which the Apostles never went as long as our Lord was upon earth: "Rabbi, Thou art the Son of God; Thou art the King of Israel." So that both in regard of the revelation that is given of the character of our Lord, and in regard of the teaching that is given of the development and process of faith in a soul, this last narrative fitly crowns the whole series. In looking at it with you now, I think I shall best bring out its force by asking you to take it as falling into these three portions: first, the preparation—a soul brought to Christ by a brother; then the conversation—a soul fastened to Christ by Himself; and then the rapturous confession—"Rabbi, Thou art the Son of God; Thou art the King of Israel."

I. Look, then, first of all, at the preparation—a soul brought to Christ by a brother. "Philip findeth Nathanael." Nathanael, in all probability, as commentators will tell you is the Apostle Bartholomew; and in the catalogues of the Apostles in the Gospels, Philip and he are always associated together. So that the two men, friends before, had their friendship riveted and made more close by this sacredest of all bonds, that the one had been to the other the means of bringing him to Jesus Christ. There is nothing that ties men to each other like that. If you want to know the full sweetness of association with friends, and of human love, get some heart knit to yours by this sacred and eternal bond that it owes to you its first knowledge of the Savior. So all human ties will be sweetened, ennobled, elevated, and made perpetual.

"We have found Him of Whom Moses, in the law, and the prophets did write: Jesus of Nazareth, the Son of Joseph." Philip knows nothing about Christ's supernatural birth, nor about its having been in Bethlehem; to him He is the son of a Nazarene peasant. But, notwithstanding that, He is the great, significant, mysterious Person for Whom the whole sacred literature of Israel had been one long yearning for centuries; and he has come to believe that this Man standing beside him is the Person on Whom all previous Divine communications for a millennium past focused and centered.

I need not dwell upon these words, because to do so would be to repeat substantially what I said in a former sermon on these first disciples, about the value of personal conviction as a means of producing conviction in the minds of others, and about the necessity and the possibility of all who have found Christ for themselves saying so to others, and thereby becoming His missionaries and evangelists.

I do not need to repeat what I said on that occasion; therefore, I pass on to the very natural hesitation and question of Nathanael: "Can there any good thing come out of Nazareth?" A prejudice, no doubt, but a very harmless one; a very thin ice which melted as soon as Christ's smile beamed upon him. And a most natural prejudice. Nathanael came from Cana of Galilee, a little hill village, three or four miles from Nazareth. We all know the bitter feuds and jealousies of neighboring villages, and how nothing is so pleasant to the inhabitants of one as a gibe about the inhabitants of another. And in Nathanael's words there simply speaks the rustic jealousy of Cana against Nazareth.

It is easy to blame him, but do you think that you or I, if we had been in his place, would have been likely to have said anything very different? Suppose you were told that a peasant out of Rossshire was a man on whom the whole history of this nation hung. Do you think you would be likely to believe it without first saying, "That is a strange place for such a person to be born in." Galilee was the despised part of Palestine, and Nazareth obviously was a proverbially despised village of Galilee; and this Jesus was a carpenter's son that nobody had ever heard of. It seemed to be a strange head on which the Divine Dove should flutter down, passing by all the Pharisees and the Scribes, all the great people and wise people. Nathanael's prejudice was but the giving voice to a fault that is as wide as humanity, and which we have, every day of our lives, to fight with; not only in regard of religious matters but in regard of all others—namely, the habit of estimating people, and their work, and their wisdom, and their power to teach us, by the class to which they are supposed to belong, or even by the place from which they come.

"Can any good thing come out of Nazareth?" "Can a German teach an Englishman anything that he does not know?" "Is a Protestant to owe anything of spiritual illumination to a Roman Catholic?" "Are we Dissenters to receive any wisdom or example from Churchmen?" "Will a Conservative be able to give any lessons in politics to a Liberal?" "Is there any other bit of England that can teach Lancashire?" Take care that while you are holding up your hands in horror against the prejudices of our Lord's contemporaries, who stumbled at His origin, you are not doing the same thing in regard to all manner of subjects twenty times a day.

That is one very plain lesson, and not at all too secular for a sermon. Take another. This three-parts innocent prejudice of Nathanael brings into clear relief for us what a very real obstacle to the recognition of our Lord's Messianic authority His apparent lowly origin was. We have got over it, and it is no difficulty to us; but it was so then. When Jesus Christ came into this world, Judea was ruled by the most heartless of aristocracies, an aristocracy of cultured pedants. Wherever you get such a class you get people who think that there can be nobody worth looking at, or worth attending to, outside the little limits of their own supercilious superiority. Why did Jesus Christ come from "the men of the earth," as the rabbis called all who had not learned to cover every plain precept with spider's webs of casuistry? Why, for one thing, in accordance with the general law that the great reformers and innovators always come from outside these classes, that the Spirit of the Lord shall come on a herdsman like Amos, and fishermen and peasants spread the Gospel through the world; and that in politics, in literature, in science, as well as in religion, it is always true that "not many wise men after the flesh, not many mighty, not many noble are called." To the cultivated classes you have to look for a great deal that is precious and good, but for fresh impulse, in unbroken fields, you have to look outside them. And so the highest of all lives is conformed to the general law.

More than that, "Jesus of Nazareth, the Son of Joseph," came thus because He was the poor man's Christ, because He was the ignorant man's Christ, because His word was not for any class, but as broad as the world. He came poor, obscure, unlettered, that all who, like Him, were poor and untouched by the finger of earthly culture, might in Him find their Brother, their Helper, and their Friend.

"Philip saith unto him, Come and see." He is not going to argue the question. He gives the only possible answer to it—"You ask me, can any good thing come out of Nazareth?" "Come and see whether it is a good thing or not; and if it is, and came out of Nazareth, well then, the question has answered itself." The quality of a thing cannot be settled by the origin of the thing.

As it so happened, this Man did not come out of Nazareth at all, though neither Philip nor Nathanael knew it but if He had, it would have been all the same. The right answer was "Come and see."

Now, although, of course, there is no kind of correspondence between the mere prejudice of this man Nathanael and the rooted intellectual doubts of other generations, yet "Come and see" carries in it the essence of all Christian apologetics. By far the wisest thing that any man who has to plead the cause of Christianity can do is to put Christ well-forward, and let people look at Him, and trust Him to produce His own impression. We may argue round, and round, and round about Him forevermore, and we shall never convince as surely as by simply holding Him forth. "I, if I be lifted up, will draw all men unto Me." Yet we are so busy proving Christianity that we sometimes have no time to preach it; so busy demonstrating that Jesus Christ is this, that, and the other thing, or contradicting the notion that He is not this, that, and the other thing, that we forget simply to present Him for men to look at. Depend upon it, while argument has its function, and there are men that must be approached thereby; on the whole, and for the general, the true way of propagating Christianity is to proclaim it, and the second best way is to prove it. Our arguments do fare very often very much as did that elaborate discourse that a bishop once preached to prove the existence of a God, at the end of which a simple old woman who had not followed his reasoning very intelligently, exclaimed, "Well, for all he says, I can't help thinking there is a God after all." The errors that are quoted to be confuted often remain more clear in the hearers' minds than the attempted confutations. Hold forth Christ—cry aloud to men, "Come and see!" and some eyes will turn and some hearts cleave to Him.

And, on the other side, dear brethren, you have not done fairly by Christianity until you have complied with this invitation, and submitted your mind and heart honestly to the influence and the impression that Christ Himself would make upon it.

II. We come now to the second stage—the conversation between Christ and Nathanael, where we see a soul fastened to Christ by Himself.

In general terms, as I remarked, the method by which our Lord manifests his Messiahship to this single soul is a revelation of His supernatural knowledge of him.

But a word or two may be said about the details. Mark the emphasis with which the Evangelist shows us that our Lord speaks this discriminating characterization of Nathanael before Nathanael had come to Him: "He saw him coming." So it was not with a swift, penetrating glance of intuition that He read his character in his face. It was not that He generalized rapidly from one action which He had seen him do. It was not from any previous personal knowledge of him, for, obviously, from the words of Philip to Nathanael, the latter had never seen Jesus Christ. As Nathanael was drawing near Him, before he had done anything to show himself, our Lord speaks the words which show that He had read his very heart. "Behold an Israelite indeed, in whom is no guile."

That is to say, here is a man who truly represents that which was the ideal of the whole nation. The reference is, no doubt, to the old story of the occasion on which Jacob's name was changed to Israel. And we shall see a further reference to the same story in the subsequent verses. Jacob had wrestled with God in that mysterious scene by the brook Jabbok, and had overcome, and had received instead of the name Jacob, "a supplanter," the name of Israel, "for as a Prince hast thou power with God and hast prevailed." And, says Christ: This man also is a son of Israel, one of God's warriors, who has prevailed with Him by prayer. "In whom is no guile"— Jacob in his early life had been marked and marred by selfish craft.

Subtlety and guile had been the very key-note of his character. To drive that out of him years of discipline and pain and sorrow had been needed. And not until it had been driven out of him could his name be altered, and he become Israel. This man has had the guile driven out of him. By what process? The words are a verbal quotation from Psalm 32: "Blessed is he whose transgression is forgiven, whose sin is covered. Blessed is the man unto whom the Lord imputeth not iniquity, and in whose spirit there is no guile." Clear, candid openness of spirit, and the freedom of soul from all that corruption which the Psalmist calls "guile," is the property of him only who has received it, by confession, by pardon, and by cleansing, from God. Thus, Nathanael, in his wrestling, had won the great gift. His transgression had been forgiven; his iniquity had been covered; to him God had not imputed his sin; and in his spirit, therefore, there was no guile. Ah, brother! If that black drop is to be cleansed out of your heart, it must be by the same means— confession to God and pardon from God. And then you too, will be a prince with Him, and your spirit will be frank and free, and open and candid.

Nathanael, with astonishment, says, "Lord, whence knowest Thou me?" Not that he appropriates the description to himself, or recognizes the truthfulness of it, but he is surprised that Christ should have means of forming any judgment with reference to him, and so he asks Him, half expecting an answer which will show the natural origin of our Lord's knowledge: "Whence knowest Thou me?" Then comes the answer, which, to supernatural insight into Nathanael's character, adds supernatural knowledge of Nathanael's secret actions; "Before that Philip called thee, when thou wast under the fig tree, I saw thee." And it is because I saw thee under the fig tree that I knew thee to be "an Israelite indeed, in whom there is no guile." So then, under the fig tree, Nathanael must have been wrestling in prayer; under the fig tree must have been confessing his sins; under the fig tree must have been longing and looking for the Deliverer who was to "turn away ungodliness from Jacob." So solitary had been that vigil, and so little would any human eye that had looked upon it have known what had been passing in his mind, that Christ's knowledge of it and of its significance at once lights up in Nathanael's heart the fire of the glad conviction, "Thou art the son of God." If we had seen Nathanael, we should only have seen a man sitting, sunk in thought, under a fig tree; but Jesus had seen the spiritual struggle which had no outward marks, and to have known which He must have exercised the Divine prerogative of reading the heart.

I ask you to consider whether Nathanael's conclusion was not right, and whether that woman of Samaria was not right when she hurried back to the city, leaving her water-pot, and said: "Come and see a man that told me *all* that ever I did." That "all" was a little stretch of facts, but still it was true in spirit. And her inference was absolutely true: "Is not this the Christ, the Son of God?" This is the first miracle that Jesus Christ wrought. His supernatural knowledge which cannot be struck out from the New Testament representations of His character, is as much a mark of Divinity as any of the other of His earthly manifestations. It is not the highest; it does not appeal to our sympathies as some of the others do, but it is irrefragable. Here is a man to whom all men with whom He came in contact were like those clocks with a crystal face, which shows us all the works. How does he come to have this perfect and absolute knowledge?

That omniscience, as manifested here, shows us how glad Christ is when He sees anything good, anything that He can praise in any of us. "Behold an Israelite indeed, in whom there is no guile." Not a word about Nathanael's prejudice, not a word about any of his faults, (though no doubt he had plenty of them) but the cordial praise that he was an honest, a sincere man, following after God and after truth. There is nothing which so gladdens Christ as to see in us any faint traces of longing for, and love towards, and likeness to, His own self. His omniscience is never so pleased as when beneath heaps and mountains of vanity and sin it discerns in a man's heart some poor germ of goodness and longing for His grace.

And then, again, notice how we have here our Lord's omniscience set forth as cognizant of all our inward crises and struggles. "When thou wast under the fig tree, I saw thee." I suppose all of us could look back to some place or other, under some hawthorn hedge, or some boulder by the seashore, or some mountaintop, perhaps in some back-parlor, or in some crowded street, where some never-to-be-forgotten epoch in our soul's history passed, unseen by all eyes, and which would have shown no trace to any onlooker, except perhaps a tightly compressed lip. Let us rejoice to feel that Christ sees all these moments which no other eye can see. In our hours of crisis, and in our monotonous, uneventful moments, in the rush of the furious waters, when the stream of our lives is caught among rocks, and in the long, languid reaches of its smoothest flow, when we are fighting with our fears or yearning for His light, or even when sitting dumb and stolid, like snowmen, apathetic and frozen in our indifference, He sees us, and pities, and will help the need which He beholds.

> Think not thou canst sigh a sigh,
> And thy Savior is not by;
> Think not thou canst weep a tear,
> And thy Savior is not near.

"When thou wast under the fig tree, I saw thee."

III. One word more about this rapturous confession, which crowns the whole: "Rabbi, thou art the Son of God; Thou art the King of Israel."

Where had Nathanael learned these great names? He was a disciple of John the Baptist, and he had no doubt heard John's testimony as recorded in this same chapter, when he told us how the voice from Heaven had bid him recognize the Messiah by the token of the descending Dove, and how he "saw and bare record that this is the Son of God." John's testimony was echoed in Nathanael's confession. Undoubtedly, he attached but vague ideas to the name, far less articulate and doctrinal than we have the privilege of doing. To him "Son of God" could not have meant all that it ought to mean to us, but it meant something that he saw clearly, and a great deal beyond that he saw but dimly. It meant that God had sent, and was in some special sense the Father of, this Jesus of Nazareth.

"Thou art the King of Israel." John had been preaching, "The Kingdom of Heaven is at hand." The Messiah was to be the theocratic King, the King, not of "Judah," nor of "the Jews," but of Israel, the nation that had entered into covenant with God. So the substance of the confession was the Messiahship of Jesus, as resting upon His special Divine relationship and leading to His Kingly sway.

Notice also the enthusiasm of the confession; one's ear hears clearly a tone of rapture in it. The joy bells of the man's heart are all a-ringing. It is no mere intellectual acknowledgment of Christ as Messiah. The difference between mere head-belief and heart-faith lies precisely in the presence of these elements of confidence, of enthusiastic loyalty, and absolute submission.

So the great question for each of us is, not, Do I believe as a piece of my intellectual creed that Christ is "the Messiah, the Son of God, the King of Israel?" I suppose almost all my hearers here now do that. That will not make you a Christian, my friend. That will neither save your soul nor quiet your heart, nor bring you peace and strength in life, nor open the gates of the Kingdom of Heaven to you. A man may be miserable, wholly sunk in all manner of wickedness and evil, die the death of a dog, and go to punishment hereafter, though he believe that Jesus Christ is the Son of God and the King of Israel. You want something more than that. You want just this element of rapturous acknowledgment, of loyal submission, absolute obedience, of unfaltering trust.

Look at these first disciples, six brave men that had all that loyalty and love to Him; though there was not a soul in the world but themselves to share their convictions. Do they not shame you? When He comes to you, as He does come, with this question, "Whom do ye say that I am?" may God give you grace to answer. "Thou art the Christ, the Son of the living God." And not only to answer it with your lips, but to trust Him wholly with your hearts, and with enthusiastic devotion to bow your whole being in adoring wonder and glad submission at His feet. If we are "Israelites indeed," our hearts will crown Him as the "King of Israel."

40

The First Disciples: V. Believing and Seeing

> *Jesus answered and said unto him, Because I said unto thee, I saw thee under the fig tree, believest thou? Thou shalt see greater things than these. And He said unto him, Verily, verily I say unto you, Hereafter ye shall see Heaven open, and the angels of God ascending and descending upon the Son of Man*—John 1:50, 51.

Here we have the end of the narrative of the gathering together of the first disciples, which has occupied several sermons. We have had occasion to point out how each incident in the series has thrown some fresh light upon two main subjects, namely, upon some phase or other of the character and work of Jesus Christ, and upon the various ways by which faith, which is the condition of discipleship, is kindled in men's souls. These closing words may be taken as the crowning thoughts on both these matters.

Our Lord recognizes and accepts the faith of Nathanael and his fellows, but like a wise Teacher, lets His pupils at the very beginning get a glimpse of how much lies ahead for them to learn; and in the act of accepting the faith gives just one hint of the great tract of yet uncomprehended knowledge of Him which lies before them; "Because I said unto thee, I saw thee under the fig tree, believest thou? Thou shalt see greater things than these." He accepts Nathanael's confession and the confession of his fellows. Human lips have given Him many great and wonderful titles in this chapter. John called Him the Lamb of God; the first disciples hailed Him as the "Messiah, which is the Christ"; Nathanael fell before Him with the rapturous exclamation, "Thou art the Son of God; Thou art the King of Israel." All these crowns had been put on His head by human hands, but here He crowns Himself. He makes a mightier claim than any that they had dreamed of, and proclaims Himself to be the medium of all communication and intercourse between Heaven and earth. "Hereafter ye shall see the heavens opened, and the angels of God ascending and descending upon the Son of Man."

So, then, there are two great principles that lie in these verses, and are contained in, first, our Lord's mighty promise to His new disciples, and second, in our Lord's witness to Himself. Let me say a word or two about each of these.

I. Our Lord's promise to His new disciples.

Christ's words here may either be translated as a question or as an affirmation. It makes comparatively little difference to the substantial meaning whether we read "believest thou" or "thou believest." In the former case there will be a little more vivid expression of surprise and admiration at the swiftness of Nathanael's faith, but in neither case are we to find anything of the nature of blame or of doubt as to the reality of his belief. The question, if it be a question, is no question as to whether Nathanael's faith was a genuine thing or not. There is no hint that he has been too quick with his confession, and has climbed too rapidly to the point that he has attained. But in either case, whether the word be a question or an affirmation, we are to see in it the solemn and glad recognition of the reality of Nathanael's confession and belief.

Here is the first time that that word "belief" came from Christ's lips; and when we remember all the importance that has been attached to it in the subsequent history of the Church, and the revolution in human thought which followed upon our Lord's demand of our faith, there is an interest in noticing the first appearance of the word. It was an epoch in the history of the world when Christ first claimed and accepted a man's faith.

Of course the second part of this verse, "Thou shalt see greater things than these"; has it proper fulfillment in the gradual manifestation of His person and character, which followed through the events recorded in the Gospels. His life of service, His words of wisdom, His deeds of power, and of pity, His death of shame and of glory, His resurrection and His ascension, these are the "greater things" which Nathanael is promised. They all lay unrevealed yet, and what our Lord means is simply this: "If you will continue to trust in Me, as you have trusted Me, and stand beside Me, you will see unrolled before your eyes and comprehended by your faith the great facts which will make the manifestation of God to the world." But though that be the original application of the words, yet I think we may fairly draw from them some lessons that are of importance to ourselves; and I ask you to look at the hint that they give us about three things—faith and discipleship, faith and sight, faith and progress. "Believest thou? Thou shalt see great things than these."

First, here is light thrown upon the relation between faith and discipleship. It is clear that our Lord here uses the word for the first time in the full Christian sense, that He regards the exercise of faith as being practically synonymous with being a disciple, that from the very first, believers were disciples, and disciples were believers.

Then, notice still further that our Lord here employs the word "belief" without any definition of what or who it is that they were to believe. He Himself, and not certain thoughts about Him, is the true object of a man's faith. We may believe a proposition, but faith must grasp a person. Even when the person is made known to us by a proposition which we have to believe before we can trust the person, still the essence of faith is not the intellectual process of laying hold upon a certain thought, and acquiescing in it, but the moral process of casting myself in full confidence upon the Being that is revealed to me by the thought of laying my hand and leaning my weight on the Man Whom the truth tells me about. And so faith, which is discipleship, has in it for its very essence the personal element of trust in Jesus Christ.

Then, further, notice how widely different from our creed Nathanael's creed was, and yet how identical with our faith, if we are Christians, Nathanael's faith was. He knew nothing about the very heart of Christ's work, His atoning death. He knew nothing about the highest glory of Christ's character, His Divine Sonship, in an unique and lofty sense. These lay unrevealed, and were amongst the greater things which he was yet to see; but though thus his knowledge was imperfect, and his creed incomplete as compared with ours, his faith was the very same. He laid hold upon Christ, he cleaved to Him with all his heart, he was ready to accept His teaching, he was willing to do His will, and as for the rest—"Thou shalt see greater things than these." So, dear brethren, from these words of my text here, from the unhesitating attribution of the lofty notion of faith to this man, from the way in which our Lord uses the word, are gathered these three points that I beseech you to ponder. No discipleship without faith. Faith is the personal grasp of Christ Himself. The contents of creeds may differ while the element of faith remains the same. I beseech you let Christ come to you with the question of my text, and as He looks you in the eyes, hear Him say to you "Believest *thou?*"

Secondly, notice how in this great promise to the new disciples, there is light thrown upon another subject, viz., the connection between faith and sight. There is a great deal about seeing in this context. Christ said to the first two that followed Him, "Come and see." Philip met Nathanael's thin film of prejudice with the same words, "Come and see." Christ greeted the approaching Nathanael with "When thou wast under the fig-tree I saw thee." And now His promise is cast into the same metaphor: "Thou shalt see greater things than these."

There is a double antithesis here: "I saw thee," "Thou shalt see Me." "Thou wast convinced because thou didst feel that thou wert the passive object of My vision. Thou shalt be still more convinced when illuminated by Me. Thou shalt see even as thou art seen. I saw thee, and that bound thee to Me; thou shalt see Me, and that will confirm the bond."

There is another antithesis, namely—between believing and seeing. "Thou believest—that is thy present; thou shalt see, that is thy hope for the future." Now I have already explained that, in the proper primary meaning and application of the words, the sight which they promise is simply the observance with the outward eye of the historical facts of our Lord's life which were yet to be learned. But still we may gather a truth from this antithesis which will be of use to us. "Thou believest—thou shalt see." That is to say, in the loftiest region of spiritual experience you must believe first, in order that you may see.

I do not mean, as is sometimes meant, by that statement that a man has to try to force his understanding into the attitude of accepting religious truth in order that he may have an experience which will convince him that it is true. I mean a very much simpler thing than that, and a very much truer one, viz., this, that unless we trust to Christ and take our illumination from Him, we shall never behold a whole set of truths which, when once we trust Him, are all plain and clear to us. It is no mysticism to say that. What do you *know* about God?—I put emphasis upon the word "know."— What do you know about Him, however much you may argue and speculate and think probable, and fear, and hope, and question, about Him? What do you know about Him apart from Jesus Christ? What do you know about human duty, apart from Him? What do you know of all that dim region that lies beyond the grave, apart from Him? If you trust Him, if you fall at His feet and say "Rabbi! Thou art my teacher and mine illumination," then you will see. You will see God, man, yourselves, duty; you will see light upon a thousand complications and perplexities; and you will have a brightness above that of the noon-day sun, streaming into the thickest darkness of death and the grave and the awful Hereafter. Christ is the light. In that "light shall we see light." And just as it needs the sun to rise in order that my eye may behold the outer world, so it needs that I shall have Christ shining in my Heaven to illuminate the whole Universe, in order that I may see clearly. "Believe and thou shalt see." For only when we trust Him do the mightiest truths that affect humanity stand plain and clear before us.

And besides that, if we trust Christ, we get a living experience of a multitude of facts and principles which are all mist and darkness to men except through their faith; an experience which is so vivid and brings such certitude as that it may well be called vision. The world says, "Seeing is believing." So it is about the coarse things that you can handle, but about everything that is higher than these invert the proverb, and you get the truth. "Seeing is believing." Yes, in regard to outward things. Believing is seeing in regard to God and spiritual truth. "Believest thou? Thou shalt see."

Then, thirdly, there is light here about another matter, the connection between faith and progress. "Thou shalt see greater things than these." A wise teacher stimulates his scholars from the beginning, by giving them glimpses of how much there is ahead to be learned. That does not drive them to despair; it braces all their powers. And so Christ, as His first lesson to these men, substantially says, "You have learned nothing yet, you are only beginning." That is true about us all. Faith at first, both in regard of its contents and its quality, is very rudimentary and infantile. A man when he is first converted—perhaps suddenly—knows after a fashion that he himself is a very sinful, wretched, poor creature, and he knows that Jesus Christ has died for him, and is his Savior, and his heart goes out to Him, in confidence, and love, and obedience. But he is only standing at the door and peeping in yet. He has only mastered the alphabet. He is but on the frontier of the promised land. His faith has brought him into contact with Infinite power, and what will be the end of that? He will indefinitely grow. His faith has started him on a course to which there is no natural end. As long as it keeps alive he will be growing and growing, and getting nearer and nearer to the great center of all.

So here is a grand possibility opened out in these simple words, a possibility which alone meets what you need, and what you are craving for, whether you know it or not, namely, something that will give you ever new powers and acquirements; something which will ensure your closer and ever closer approach to an absolute object of joy and truth; something that will ensure you against stagnation and guarantee unceasing progress. Everything else gets worn out, sooner or later; if not in this world, then in another. There is one course on which a man can enter with the certainty that there is no end to it, that it will open out, and out, and out as he advances—with the certainty that come life, come death, it is all the same.

When the tree grows too tall for the greenhouse, they lift the roof, and it grows higher still. Whether you have your growth in this lower world, or whether you have your top up in the brightness and the blue of Heaven, the growth is in one direction. There is a way that secures endless progress, and here lies the secret of it: "Thou believest! Thou shalt see greater things than these."

Now, brethren, that is a grand possibility, and it is a solemn lesson for some of you. You professing Christian people, are you any taller than you were when you were born? Have you grown at all? Are you growing now? Have you seen any further into the depths of Jesus Christ than you did on that first day when you fell at His feet and said, "Thou art the Son of God, Thou art the King of Israel!" His promise to you then was, "Thou believest! Thou shalt see greater things." If you have not seen greater things it is because your faith has broken down, if it has not expired.

II. Now let me turn to the second thought which lies in these great words. We have here, as I said, our Lord crowning Himself by His own witness to His own dignity. "Hereafter ye shall see the Heavens opened." Mark how, with superbly autocratic lips, He bases this great utterance upon nothing else but His own word. Prophets ever said, "Thus saith the Lord." Christ ever said: "Verily, verily, I say unto you." "Because He could swear by no greater, He swore by Himself." He puts His own assurance instead of all argument and of all support to His words.

"Hereafter." A word which is possibly not genuine, and is omitted, as you will observe, in the Revised Version. If it is to be retained, it must be translated, no "hereafter," as if it were pointing to some indefinite period in the future, but "from henceforth," as if asserting that the opening heavens and the descending angels began to be manifested from that first hour of His official work. "Ye shall see Heaven open, and the angels of God ascending and descending." That is a quotation from the story of Jacob at Bethel. We have found reference to Jacob's history already in the conversation with Nathanael, "An Israelite indeed, in whom is no guile." And here is an unmistakable reference to that story, when the fugitive, with his head on the stony pillow, and the blue Syrian sky, with all its stars, rounding itself above him, beheld the ladder on which the angels of God ascended and descended. So says Christ, you shall see, in no vision of the night, in no transitory appearance, but in a practical waking reality, that ladder come down again, and the angels of God moving upon it in their errands of mercy.

And who, or what, is this ladder? Christ. Do not read these words as if they meant that the angels of God were to come down on Him to help, and to honor, and to succor Him as they did once or twice in His life, but as meaning that they are to ascend and descend by Him for the help and blessing of the whole world.

That is to say, to put it into short words, Christ is the sole medium of communication between Heaven and earth, the ladder with its foot upon the earth, in His humanity, and its top in the Heavens. "No man hath ascended up into Heaven save He Which came down from Heaven, even the Son of Man Which is in Heaven."

My time will not allow me to expand these thoughts as I meant to have done; let me put them in the briefest outline. Christ is the medium of all communication between Heaven and earth, inasmuch as He is the medium of all revelation. I have spoken incidentally about that in the former part of this sermon, so I do not dwell on it now.

Christ is the ladder between Heaven and earth, inasmuch as in Him the sense of separation, and the reality of separation, are swept away. Sin has shut Heaven; there comes down from it many a blessing upon unthankful heads, but between it in its purity and the earth in its muddy foulness "there is a great gulf fixed." It is not because God is great and I am small, or because He is Infinite and I am a mere pin-point as against a great continent; it is not because He lives forever, and my life is but a hand-breadth; it is not because of the difference between His Omniscience and my ignorance, His strength and my weakness, that I am parted from Him: "Your sins have separated between you and your God." And no man, build he Babels ever so high, can reach thither. There is one means by which the separation is at an end, and by which all objective hindrances to union, and all subjective hindrances, are alike swept away. Christ has come, and in Him the Heavens have bended down to touch, and touching to bless, this low earth, and man and God are at one once more.

He is the ladder, or sole medium of communication, inasmuch as by Him all Divine blessings, grace, helps, and favors, come down angel-like, into our weak and needy hearts. Every strength, every mercy, every spiritual power, consolation in every sorrow, fitness for duty, illumination in darkness, all gifts that any of us can need, come to us down that one shining way, the mediation and the work of the Divine-Human Christ, the Lord.

He is the ladder, the sole medium of communication between Heaven and earth, inasmuch as by Him my poor desires, and prayers, and intercessions, my wishes, my sighs, my confessions rise to God. "No man cometh to the Father but by Me." He is the ladder, the means of all communication between Heaven and earth, inasmuch as at the last, if ever we enter there at all, we shall enter through Him and through Him alone, Who is "the Way, the Truth, and the Life."

Ah! Dear brethren, men are telling us now that there is no connection between earth and Heaven except such as telescopes and spectroscopes can make out. We are told that there is no ladder, that there are no angels, that possibly there is no God, or if that there be, we have nothing to do with Him nor He with us; that our prayers cannot get to His ears, if He have ears, nor His hand be stretched out to help us, if He have a hand. I do not know how this cultivated generation is to be brought back again to faith in God and delivered from that ghastly doubt which empties Heaven and saddens earth to its victims, but by giving heed to the Word which Christ spoke to the whole race while he addressed Nathanael, "Ye shall see the Heavens opened and the angels of God ascending and descending upon the Son of Man." If He be the Son of God, then all these Heavenly messengers reach the earth by Him. If He be the Son of Man, then every man may share in the gifts which through Him are brought into the world, and in His Manhood, which evermore dwelt in Heaven, even while on earth, and was ever girt about by angel presences, is at once the measure of what each of us may become, and the power by which we may become it.

One thing is needful for this wonderful consummation, even our faith. And oh! How blessed it will be if in waste solitudes we can see the open Heavens, and in the blackest night the blaze of the glory of a present Christ, and hear the soft rustle of angels' wings filling the air, and find in every place a house of God and a gate of Heaven, because He is there. All that may be yours on one condition: "Believest thou? Thou shalt see the Heavens opened, and the angels of God ascending and descending upon the Son of Man."

41

Christic and His Captors

*As soon then as He had said unto them, I am He, they
went backward, and fell to the ground. Then asked He
them again, Whom seek ye? And they said, Jesus of Nazareth. Jesus answered, I have told you that I am He; if therefore, ye seek Me, let these go their way. That the saying
might be fulfilled which He spake, of them which Thou
gavest Me have I lost none—John 18:4–9.*

This remarkable incident is narrated by John only. It fits in with
the purpose which he himself tells us governed his selection of
the incidents which he records. "These things are written," says he,
near the end of the Gospel, "That ye might believe that Jesus is the
Son of God, and that, believing, ye might have life in His name."
The whole of the peculiarities of the substance of John's Gospel are
to be explained on the two grounds that he was writing a supplement to, and not a substitute for, or a correction of, the Gospels already in existence, and that his special business was to narrate such
facts and words as set forth the glory of Christ as the Only Begotten of the Father.

The incident before us is, as I think, one of these. The Evangelist would have us see in it, as I gather from his manner of narrating it, mainly three things. He emphasizes that strange recoil of the
would-be captors before Christ's majestic, calm "I am He." That
was a manifestation of Christ's glory. He emphasizes our Lord's patient standing there, in the midst of the awe-struck crowd, and
even inciting them, as it would seem, to do the work for which they
had come out. That was a manifestation of the voluntariness of
Christ's sufferings. And He emphasizes the self-forgetting care
with which at that supreme moment He steps between His faithless,

weak friends and danger with the wonderful words, "If ye seek Me, let these go their way." To the Evangelist that little incident is an illustration, on a very low level, and in regard to a comparatively trivial matter, of the very same principle by which salvation from all evil in time and in eternity, is guaranteed to all that believe on Him:

I. First, then, consider this remarkable momentary manifestation of our Lord's glory.

"I am He!" When they were thus doubly assured by the traitor's kiss and by His own confession, why did they not lay hands upon Him? There He stood in the midst of them, alone, defenseless; there was nothing to hinder their binding Him on the spot. Instead of that they recoil, and fall in a huddled heap before Him. Some strange awe and terror, of which they themselves could have given no account, was upon their spirits. How came it about? Many things may have conspired to produce it. I am by no means anxious to insist that this was a miracle. Things of the same sort, though much less in degree, have been often seen when some innocent and illustrious victim has for a moment paralyzed the hands of his would-be captors, and made them feel, though it were but transiently, "how awful goodness is." There must have been many in that band who had heard Him, though, in the uncertain light of quivering moonbeams and smoking torches, they failed to recognize Him till He spoke. There must have been many more who had heard of Him, and many who suspected that they were about to lay hands on a holy man, perhaps on a prophet. There must have been reluctant tools among the inferiors, and no doubt some among the leaders, whose conscience needed but a touch to be roused to action. To all His calmness and dignity would appeal, and the manifest freedom from fear or desire to flee would tend to deepen the strange thoughts which began to stir in their hearts.

But the impression which the narrative seems to leave appears to me to be of something more than this. It looks as if there were something more than human in Christ's look and tone. It may have been the same in kind as the ascendancy which a pure and calm nature has over rude and inferior ones. It may have been the same in kind as has sometimes made the headsman on the scaffold pause before he struck, and has bowed rude jailers into converts before some grayhaired saint or virgin martyr; yet the difference is so great in degree as practically to become quite another thing. Though I do not want to insist upon any "miraculous" explanation of the cause of this cure, yet I would ask, may it not be that here we see, perhaps apart from Christ's will altogether, rising up for one moment to the surface, the indwelling majesty which was always there?

We do not know the laws that regulated the dwelling of the Godhead bodily within that human frame, but we do know that at one other time there came upon His features a transfiguration, and over His very garments a luster which was not thrown upon them from without, but rose up from within. And I am inclined to think that here, as there, though under such widely different circumstances and to such various issues, there was for a moment a little rending of the veil of His flesh, and an emission of some flash of the brightness that always tabernacled within Him; and that, therefore, just as Isaiah, when He saw the King in His glory, said, "Woe is me, for I am undone!" And just as Moses could not look upon the Face, but could only see the back parts, so here the one stray beam of manifest Divinity that shot through the crevice, as it were, for an instant, was enough to prostrate with a strange awe even those rude and insensitive men. When He had said "I am He," there was something that made them feel, "This is One before whom violence cowers abashed, and in Whose presence impurity has to hide its face." I do not assert that this is the explanation of that panic terror. I only ask, may it not be?

But, whatever we may think was the reason, at all events the incident brings out very strikingly the elevation and dignity of Christ, and the powerful impressions made by His personality, even at such a time of humiliation. This Evangelist is always careful to bring out the glory of Christ, especially when that glory lies side by side with His lowliness. The blending of these two is one of the remarkable features in the New Testament portrait of Jesus Christ. Wherever in our Lord's life any incident indicates more emphatically than usual the lowliness of His humiliation, there, by the side of it, you get something that indicates the majesty of His glory. For instance, He is born a weak infant, but angels herald His birth; He lies in a manger, but a star hangs trembling above it, and leads sages from afar, with their myrrh, and incense, and gold. He submits Himself to the baptism of repentance, but the Heavens open and a voice proclaims, "This is My beloved Son!" He sits wearied on the stone-coping of the well, and craves for water from a peasant woman; but He gives her the Water of Life. He lies down and sleeps, from pure exhaustion, in the stern of the little fishing boat, but He wakes to command the storm, and it is still. He weeps beside the grave, but He flings His voice into its inmost recesses, and the sheeted dead come forth. He well-nigh faints under the agony in the garden, but an angel from Heaven strengthens Him. He stands a prisoner at a human bar, but He judges and condemns His judges. He dies, and that hour of defeat is His hour of triumph, and the union of shame and glory is most conspicuous in that hour when on the Cross the "Son of Man is *glorified,* and God is glorified in Him."

This strange blending of opposites—the glory in the lowliness, and the abasement in the glory—is the keynote of this singular event. He will be delivered into the hands of men. Yes, but ere He is delivered He pauses for an instant, and in that instant comes a flash above the brightness of the noonday sun to tell of the hidden glory.

Do not forget that we may well look upon that incident as a prophecy of what shall be. As one of the suggestive, old commentators on this verse says: "He will say 'I am He' again, a third time. What will He do coming to reign, when He did this coming to die? And what will His manifestation be as a Judge when this was the effect of the manifestation as He went to be judged?" "Every eye shall see Him"; and they that loved not His appearing shall fall before Him when He cometh to be our Judge; and shall call on the rocks and the hills to cover them.

II. There is here, secondly, a manifestation of the voluntariness of our Lord's suffering. When that terrified mob recoiled from Him, why did He stand there so patiently? The time was propitious for flight, if He had cared to fly. He might have passed through the midst of them and gone his way, as He did once before, if He had chosen. He comes from the garden; there shall be no difficulty in finding Him. He tells who He is; there shall be no need for the traitor's kiss. He lays them low for a moment, but He will not flee. When Peter draws his sword, He rebukes his ill-advised appeal to force, and then He holds out His hands and lets them bind Him. It was not their fetters, but the cords of love which held Him prisoner. It was not their power, but His own pity which drew Him to the judgment hall and the Cross.

Let us dwell upon that thought for a moment. The whole story of the Gospels is constructed upon the principle, and illustrates the fact, that our Lord's life, as our Lord's death, was a voluntary surrender of Himself for man's sin, and that nothing led Him to, and fastened Him on, the Cross but His own will. He willed to be born. He "came into the world" by His own choice. He "took upon Him the form of a servant." He "took part" of the children's flesh and blood. His birth was His own act, the first of the long series of the acts, by which for the sake of the love which He bore us, He "humbled Himself." Step by step He voluntarily journeyed toward the Cross, which stood clear before Him from the very beginning as the necessary end, made necessary by His love.

As we get nearer and nearer to the close of the history, we see more and more distinctly that He willingly went toward the Cross. Take, for instance, the whole account of the last portion of our Lord's life, and you see in the whole of it a deliberate intention to precipitate the final conflict. Hence the last journey to Jerusalem when "His face was set," and His disciples followed Him amazed. Hence the studied publicity of His triumphal entry into Jerusalem. Hence the studied, growing severity of His rebukes to the priests and rulers. The same impression is given, though in a somewhat different way, by His momentary retreat from the from the city and by the precautions taken against premature arrest, that He might not die before the Passover. In both, the hastening toward the city and in the retreating from it, there is apparent the same design: that He Himself shall lay down His life, and shall determine the how, and the when, and the where as seems good to Him.

If we look at the act of death itself, Jesus did not die because He must. It was not the nails of the Cross, the physical exhaustion, the nervous shock of crucifixion that killed Him. He died because He would. "I have power to lay down My life," He said, "and I have power"—of course—"to take it again." At that last moment, He was Lord and Master of death when He bowed His head to death. And, if I might so say, He summoned that grim servant with a "Come!" and he came, and He set him his task with a "Do this," and he did it. He was manifested as the Lord of death, having its keys in His hands when He died upon the Cross.

Now I pray you to ask yourselves the question, if it be true that Christ died because He would, why was it that He would die? If because He chose, what was it that determined His choice? And there are but two answers, which two are one. The Divine motive that ruled His life is doubly expressed: "I must do the will of My Father," and "I must save the world."

The taunt that those Jewish rulers threw at Him had a deeper truth than they dreamed, and was an encomium, and not a taunt. "He saved others." Yes, and *therefore*, "Himself He cannot save." He cannot, because His choice and will to die are determined by His free love to us and to all the world. His fixed will bore His body to the Tree, and His love was the strong spring which kept His will fixed.

You and I have our share in these voluntary sufferings, and our place in that loving heart which underwent them for us. Oh! Should not that thought speak to all our hearts, and bind us in grateful service and lifelong surrender to Him Who gave Himself for us; and *must* die because He loved us all so much that He *could* not leave us unsaved.

III. We have, lastly, here, a symbol, or, perhaps, more accurately, an instance, on a small scale, of Christ's self-sacrificing care for us. His words: "If ye seek Me, let these go their way," sound more like the command of a prince than the intercession of a prisoner. The calm dignity of them strikes one just as much as the perfect self-forgetfulness of them.

It was a very small matter which He was securing thereby. These men would have to die for Him some day, but they were not ready for it yet. And so He casts the shield of His protection round them for a moment, and interposes Himself between them and the band of soldiers in order that their weakness may have a little more time to grow strong. And though it was wrong and cowardly for them to forsake Him and flee, yet these words of my text more than half gave them permission and warrant for their departure: "Let these go their way."

Now, John did not think that this small deliverance was all that Christ meant by these great words: "Of them which Thou gavest Me have I lost none!" He saw that it was one case, a very trifling one, a merely transitory one, yet ruled by the same principles which are at work in the immensely higher region to which the words properly refer. Of course, they have their proper fulfillment in the spiritual realm, and are not fulfilled, in the highest sense, till all who have loved and followed Christ are presented faultless before the Father in the home above.

But the little incident may be a result of the same cause as the final deliverance is. A dew-drop is shaped by the same laws which mold the mightiest of the planets. The old divines used to say that God was greatest in the smallest things, and the self-sacrificing care of Jesus Christ, as He gives Himself a prisoner that His disciples may go free, comes from the same deep heart of pitying love, which led Him to die the just for the unjust. It may then well stand for a partial fulfillment of His mighty words, even though these wait for their complete accomplishments till the hour when all the sheep are gathered into the one fold, and no evil beasts, nor weary journeys, nor barren pastures can harass them any more.

This trivial incident, then, becomes an exposition of highest truth. Let us learn from such a use of such an event to look upon all common and transitory circumstances as governed by the same loving hands, and working to the same ends as the most purely spiritual. The visible is the veil which drapes the invisible and clings so closely to it as to reveal its outline. The common events of life are all parables to the devout heart, which is the wise heart. They speak mystic meanings to ears that can hear. The redeeming love of Jesus is proclaimed by every mercy which perishes in the using; and all things should tell us of His self-forgetting, self-sacrificing care.

Thus, then, we may see in that picture of our Lord's surrendering Himself that His trembling disciples might go free, an emblem of what He does for us, in regard to all our foes. He stands between us and them, receives their arrows into His own bosom, and says, "Let these go their way." God's law comes with its terrors, with its penalties, to us who have broken it a thousand times. The consciousness of guilt and sin threatens us all more or less, and with varying intensity in different minds. The weariness of the world, "the ills that flesh is heir to," the last grim enemy, Death, and that which lies beyond them all, ring you round, my friends!— What are you going to do in order to escape from them?

You are a sinful man, you have broken God's law. That law goes on crashing its way and crushing down all that is opposed to it. You have a weary life before you, however joyful it may sometimes be. Cares and troubles, and sorrows, and tears, and losses, and disappointments, and hard duties that you will not be able to perform, and dark days in which you will be able to see but very little light, are all certain to come sooner or later; and the last moment will draw near when the King of Terrors will be at your side; and beyond death there is a life of retribution in which men reap the things that they have sown here. All that is true, much of it is true about you at this moment, and it will all be true someday. In view of that, what are you going to do?

I preach to you a Savior Who has endured all for us. As a mother might fling herself out of the sleigh that her child might escape the wolves in full chase, here is One that comes and fronts all your foes, and says to them "Let these go their way. Take Me." "By His stripes we are healed." "On Him was laid the iniquity of us all."

He died because He chose; He chose because He loved. His love had to die in order that His death might be our life, and that in it we should find our forgiveness and peace. He stands between our foes and us. No evil can strike us unless it strike Him first. He takes into His own heart the sharpest of all the darts which can pierce ours. He has borne the guilt and punishment of a world's sin. These solemn penalties have fallen upon Him that we, trusting in Him, "may go our way," and that there may be no condemnation to us if we are in Christ Jesus. And if there be no condemnation, we can stand whatever other blows may fall upon us. They are easier to bear, and their whole character is different, when we know that Christ has borne them already. Two of the three whom Christ protected in the garden died a martyr's death; but do you not think that James bowed his neck to Herod's sword, and Peter let them gird him and lead him to his cross more joyfully and with a different heart when they thought of Him that had died before them? The darkest prison cell will not be so very dark if we remember that Christ has been there before us, and death itself will be softened into sleep because our Lord has died. "If therefore," says He, to the whole pack of evils baying round us, with their cruel eyes and their hungry mouths, "ye seek Me, let these go their way." So, brother, if you will fix your trust, as a poor, sinful soul in that dear Christ, and get behind Him, and put Him between you and your enemies, then, in time and in eternity, that saying will be fulfilled in you which He spoke, "Of them which Thou gavest Me, I have lost none."

42

Sky, Earth, and Sea: A Parable of God

Thy mercy, O Lord, is in the heavens; and thy faithfulness reacheth unto the clouds. Thy righteousness is like the great mountains; Thy judgments are a great deep; O Lord, Thou preservest man and beast. How excellent is Thy lovingkindness, O Lord! therefore the children of men put their trust under the shadow of thy wings—Psalm 36:5–7.

This wonderful description of the manifold brightness of the Divine nature is introduced in this psalm with singular abruptness. It is set side by side with a vivid picture of an evildoer, a man who mutters in his own heart his godlessness, and with obstinate determination plans and plots in forgetfulness of God. Without a word to break the violence of the transition, side by side with that picture, the Psalmist sets before us these thoughts of the character of God. He seems to feel that that was the only relief in the contemplation of the miserable sights of which the earth is only too full. We should go mad when we think of man's wickedness unless we could look up and see, with one quick turn of the eye, the Heaven opened and the throned Love that sits up there gazing on all the chaos, and working to soothe sorrow, and to purify evil.

Perhaps there is another reason for this dramatic and striking swiftness of contrast between the godless man and the revealed God. The true test of a life is its power to bear the light of God being suddenly let in upon it. How would yours look, my friend, if all at once a window in Heaven was opened, and God glared in upon you? Set your lives side by side with Him. They always are side by side with Him whether you know it or not; but you had better bring your "deeds to the light that they may be made manifest" now, rather than to have to do it so suddenly, and a great deal more sorrowfully, when you are dragged out of the shows and illusions of time, and He meets you on the threshold of another world. Would a beam of light from God, coming in upon your life, be like a light falling upon a gang of conspirators, that would make them huddle all their implements under their cloaks, and scuttle out of the way as fast as possible? Or would it be like a gleam of sunshine upon the flowers, opening out their petals and wooing from them fragrance? Which?

But I turn from such considerations as these to the more immediate subject of my contemplations this morning. I have ventured to take so great words for my text, though each clause would be more than enough for many a sermon, because my aim now is a very modest one. I desire simply to give, in the briefest way, the connection and mutual relation of these wonderful words; not to attempt any adequate treatment of the great thoughts which they contain, but only to set forth the meaning and interdependence of these manifold names for the beams of the Divine light, which are presented here. The chief part of our text sets before us God in the variety and boundlessness of His loving nature, and the close of it shows us man sheltering beneath God's wings. These are the two main themes for our present consideration.

I. We have, first, God in the boundlessness of His loving nature.

The one pure light of the Divine nature is broken up, in the prism of the psalm, into various rays, which theologians call, in their hard, abstract way, Divine attributes. These are "mercy, faithfulness, righteousness." Then we have two sets of Divine acts—judgments, and the preservation of man and beast; and finally we have again "lovingkindness," as our version has unfortunately been misled, by its love for varying its translation, to render the same word which begins the series and is there called "mercy."

Now that "mercy" or "lovingkindness" of which my text thus speaks, is very nearly equivalent to the New Testament "love"; or, perhaps, still more nearly equivalent to the New Testament "grace." Both the one and the other mean substantially this—active love communicating itself to creatures that are inferior and that might have expected something else to befall them. Mercy is a modification of love, inasmuch as it is love to an inferior. The hand is laid gently upon the man, because if it were laid with all its weight it would crush him. It is the stooping goodness of a king to a beggar. And mercy is likewise love in its exercise to persons that might expect something else, being guilty. As a general coming to a body of mutineers with pardon and favor upon his lips, instead of with condemnation and death; so God comes to us forgiving and blessing. All His goodness is forbearance, and His love is mercy, because of the weakness, the lowliness, and the ill-desert of us on whom the love falls.

Now notice that this same "quality of mercy" stands here at the beginning and at the end. All the attributes of the Divine nature, all the operations of the Divine hand lie within the circle of His mercy—like diamonds set in a golden ring. Mercy, or love flowing out in blessings to inferior and guilty creatures, is the root and ground of all God's character; it is the foundation and impulse of all His acts. Modern science reduces all modes of physical energy to one, for which it has no name but—energy. We are taught by God's own revelation of Himself—and most especially by His final and perfect revelation of Himself in Jesus Christ—to trace all forms of Divine energy back to one which David calls mercy, which John calls love.

It is last as well as first, the final upshot of all revelation. The last voice that speaks from Scripture has for its special message "God is Love." The last voice that sounds from the completed history of the world will have the same message, and the ultimate word of all revelation, the end of the whole of the majestic unfolding of God's purposes will be the proclamation to the four corners of the universe, as from the trump of the Archangel, of the name of God as Love. The northern and the southern pole of the great sphere are one and the same, a straight axle through the very heart of it, from which the bounding lines swell out to the equator, and towards which they converge again on the opposite side of the world. So mercy is the strong axletree, the northern pole and the southern, on which the whole world of the Divine perfections revolves and moves. The first and last, the Alpha and Omega of God, beginning and crowning and summing up all His being and His work, is His mercy, His lovingkindness.

But next to mercy comes faithfulness. "Thy faithfulness reacheth unto the clouds." God's faithfulness is in its narrowest sense His adherence to His promises. It implies, in that sense, a verbal revelation, and definite words from Him pledging Him to a certain line of action. "He hath said, and shall He not do it." "He will not alter the thing that is gone out of His lips." It is only a God who has actually spoken to men who can be a "faithful God." He will not palter with a double sense, keeping His word of promise to the ear, and breaking it to the hope.

But not only His articulate promises, but also His own past actions, bind Him. He is always true to these; and not only continues to do as He has done, but discharges every obligation which His past imposes on Him. The ostrich was said to leave its eggs to be hatched in the sand. Men bring men into positions of dependence, and then lightly shake responsibility from careless shoulders. But God accepts the cares laid upon Him by His own acts, and discharges them to the last jot. He is a "faithful Creator." Creation brings obligations with it; obligations on the creature; obligations on the Creator. If God makes a being, God is bound to take care of the being that He has made. If He makes a being in a given fashion, He is bound to provide for the necessities that He has created. According to the old proverb, if He makes mouths it is His business to feed them. And He recognizes the obligation. His past binds Him to certain conduct in His future. We can lay hold on the former manifestation, and we can plead it with Him. "Thou hast been, and Therefore Thou must be." "Thou hast taught me to trust in Thee; vindicate and warrant my trust by thy unchangeableness." So His word, His acts, and His own nature, bind God to bless and help. His faithfulness is the expression of His unchangeableness. "Because He could swear by no greater, He swore by Himself."

Take then these two thoughts of God's lovingkindness and of God's faithfulness and weave them together, and see what a strong cord they are to which a man may cling, and in all his weakness be sure that it will never give nor break. Mercy might be transient, and arbitrary, but when you braid in "faithfulness" along with it, it becomes fixed as the pillars of Heaven, and immutable as the throne of God. Only when we are sure of God's faithfulness can we lift up thankful voices to Him, "because His mercy endureth forever." A despotic monarch may be all full of tenderness at this moment, and all full of wrath and sternness the next. He may have a whim of favor today, and a whim of severity tomorrow, and no man can say, "What doest thou?" But God is not a despot. He has, so to speak, "decreed a constitution." He has limited Himself. He has marked out His path across the great, wide region of possibilities of the Divine action; He has buoyed out His channel on that ocean, and declared to us His purposes. So we can reckon on God, as astronomers can foretell the motions of the stars. We can plead His faithfulness along with His love, and feel that the one makes sure that the other shall be from everlasting to everlasting.

The next beam of the Divine brightness is righteousness. "Thy righteousness is like the great mountains." Righteousness is not to be taken here in its narrow sense of stern retribution which gives to the evildoer the punishment that he deserves. There is no thought here, whatever there may be in other places in Scripture, of any opposition between mercy and righteousness, but the notion of righteousness here is a broader and greater one. It is just this, to put it into other words, that God has a law for His being to which He conforms; and that whatsoever things are fair, and lovely, and good, and pure down here, those things are fair, and lovely, and good, and pure up there; that He is the archetype of all excellence, the ideal of all moral completeness: that we can know enough of Him to be sure of this, that what we call right He loves, and what we call right He practices.

Brethren, unless we have that for the very foundation of our thoughts of God, we have no foundation to rest on. Unless we feel and know that "the Judge of all the earth doeth right, and is right, and law and righteousness have their home and seat in His bosom, and are the expression of His inmost being, then I know not where our confidence can be built. Unless 'Thy righteousness, like the great mountains,' surrounds and guards the low plain of our lives, they will lie open to all foes."

Next, we pass from the Divine character to the Divine acts. Mercy, faithfulness, and righteousness all converge and flow into the great river of the Divine "Judgments."

By judgments are not meant merely the acts of God's punitive righteousness, the retributions that destroy evildoers, but all God's decisions and acts in regard to man. Or, to put it into other and briefer words, God's judgments are the whole of the "ways," the methods of the Divine government. So Paul, alluding to this very passage when he says "How unsearchable are Thy judgments," adds, as a parallel clause meaning the same thing, "and Thy ways past finding out." That includes all which men call, in a narrower sense, judgments, but it includes, too, all acts of kindness and loving gifts. God's judgments are the expressions of His thoughts, and these thoughts are thoughts of good and not of evil.

But notice, in the next place, the boundlessness of all these characteristics of the Divine nature.

"Thy mercy is in the heavens," towering up above the stars, and dwelling there, like some Divine ether filling all space. The heavens are the home of light, the source of every blessing, arching over every head, rimming every horizon, holding all the stars, opening into abysses as we gaze, with us by night and by day, undimmed by the mist and smoke of earth, unchanged by the lapse of centuries; ever seen, never reached, bending over us always, always far above us. So the mercy of God towers above us, and stoops down towards us, rims us all about and arches over us all, sheds down its dewy benedictions by night and by day; is filled with a million stars and light-points of beauty and of splendor; is near us ever to bless and succor, and help, and holds us all in its blue round.

"Thy faithfulness reacheth to the clouds." Strange that God's fixed faithfulness should be compared to the very emblems of mutation. The clouds are unstable, they whirl and melt and change. Strange to think of the unalterable faithfulness as reaching to them! May it not be that the very mutability of the mutable may be the means of manifesting the unalterable sameness of God's faithful purpose, of His unchangeable love, and of His ever consistent dealings? May not the apparent incongruity be a part of the felicity of the bold words? Is it not true that earthly things, as they change their forms and melt away, leaving no track behind, phantomlike as they are, do still obey the behests of that Divine faithfulness, and gather and dissolve and break in the brief showers of blessing, or short, sharp crashes of storm at the bidding of that steadfast purpose which works out one unalterable design by a thousand instruments, and changeth all things, being in itself unchanged? The thing that is eternal, even the faithfulness of God, dwells amid, and shows itself through, the things that are temporal, the flying clouds of change.

Again, "Thy righteousness is like the great mountains." Like these, its roots are fast and stable; like these, it stands firm forever; like these, its summits touch the fleeting clouds of human circumstance; like these, it is a shelter and a refuge, inaccessible in its steepest peaks, but affording many a cleft in its rocks, where a man may hide and be safe. But, unlike these, it knew no beginning, and shall know no end. Emblems of permanence as they are, though Olivet looks down on Jerusalem as it did when Melchizedek was its king, and Tabor and Hermon stand as they did before human lips had named them, they are wearing away by winter storms and summer heats. But, as Isaiah has taught us, when the earth is old, God's might and mercy are young; for "the mountains shall depart and the hills be removed, but My kindness shall not depart from thee." "The earth shall wax old like a garment, but My righteousness shall not be abolished." It is more stable than the mountains, and firmer than the firmest things upon earth.

Then, with wonderful poetical beauty and vividness of contrast, there follows upon the emblem of the great mountains of God's righteousness the emblem of the "mighty deep" of His judgments. Here towers Vesuvius; there at its feet lie the waters of the bay. So the Righteousness springs up like some great cliff, rising sheer from the water's edge, while its feet are laved by the sea of the Divine judgments, unfathomable and shoreless. The mountains and the sea are the two grandest things in nature, and in their combination sublime; the one the home of calm and silence, the other in perpetual motion. But the mountain's roots are deeper than the depths of the sea, and though the judgments are a mighty deep, the righteousness is deeper, and is the bed of the ocean.

The metaphor, of course, implies obscurity, but what sort of obscurity? The obscurity of the sea. And what sort of obscurity is that? Not that which comes from mud, or anything added, but that which comes from depth. As far as a man can see down into its blue-green depths they are clear and translucent; but where the light fails and the eye fails, there comes what we call obscurity. The sea is clear, but our sight is limited.

And so there is no arbitrary obscurity in God's dealings, and we know as much about them as it is possible for us to know; but we cannot see to the bottom. A man on the cliff can look much deeper into the ocean than a man on the level beach. The further you climb, the further you will see down into the "sea of glass mingled with fire" that lies placid before God's throne. Let us remember that it is a hazardous thing to judge a picture before it is finished, a building before the scaffolding is pulled down, and it is a hazardous thing for us to say about any deed or any revealed truth that it is inconsistent with the Divine character. Wait a bit; wait a bit! "Thy judgments are a great deep." The deep will be drained off one day, and you will see the bottom of it. Judge nothing before the time.

But as an aid to patience and faith hearken how the Psalmist finishes up his contemplations: "O Lord! Thou preservest man and beast." Very well then, all this mercy, faithfulness, righteousness, judgment, high as the heavens, deep as the ocean, firm as the hills, it is all working for this—to keep the millions of living creatures round about us, and ourselves, in life and well-being. The mountain is high; the deep is profound. Between the mountain and the sea there is a strip of level land. God's righteousness towers above us; God's judgments go down beneath us; we can scarcely measure adequately the one or the other. But upon the level where we live there are the green fields, where the cattle browse, and the birds sing, and men live, and till, and reap, and are fed. That is to say, we have all enough in the plain, patent facts of creation and preservation of man and animal life in this world to make us quite sure of what is the principle that prevails up to the very top of the inaccessible mountains, and down to the very bottom of the unfathomable deep. What we know of Him, in the blessings of His love and providence, ought to interpret for us all that is perplexing. What we understand is good and loving. Let us be sure that what we do not yet understand is good and loving too. The web is of one texture throughout. The least educated ear can catch the music of the simpler melodies which run through the Great Composer's work. We shall one day be able to appreciate the yet fuller music of the more recondite parts, which to us seem only jangling and chaos at present. It is not His melody but our ears that are at fault. But we may well accept the obscurity of the mighty deep of God's judgment, when we can see plainly that, after all, the earth is full of His mercy, and that the eyes of all things wait on God, and He giveth them their meat in due season.

II. So much, then, for the great picture here of these boundless characteristics of the Divine nature. Now let us look for a moment at the picture of man sheltering beneath God's wings.

"How excellent is Thy lovingkindness, O God! Therefore the children of men put their trust under the shadow of Thy wings." God's lovingkindness, or mercy, as I explained the word might be rendered, is *precious,* for that is the true meaning of the word translated "excellent." We are rich when we have that for ours; we are poor without it. Our true wealth is to possess God's love, and to know in thought and realize in feeling and reciprocate in affection His grace and goodness, the beauty and perfectness of His wondrous character. That man is wealthy who has God on his side; that man is a pauper who has not God for his.

"How precious is Thy lovingkindness, *therefore* the children of men put their trust." There is only one thing that will ever win a man's heart to love God, and that is that God should love him first, and let him see it. "We love Him because He first loved us," is the New Testament teaching. Is it not all adumbrated and foretold in these words: "How precious is Thy lovingkindness, O God! Therefore the children of men put their trust"?

We may be driven to worship after a sort by power; we may be smitten into some cold admiration, into some kind of reluctant subjection and trembling reverence, by the manifestation of Divine perfections. But there is one thing that wins a man's heart, and that is the sight of God's heart; and it is only when we know how precious His lovingkindness is that we shall be drawn towards Him.

And then this last verse tells us how we can make God our own: "They put their trust under the shadow of Thy wings." The word here rendered, and accurately rendered, "put their trust," has a very beautiful literal meaning. It means to flee for refuge, as the man-slayer might flee into the strong city, for as Lot did out of Sodom to the little city on the hill, or as David did into the cave from his enemies. So, with such haste, with such intensity, staying for nothing, and with the effort of your whole will and nature, flee to God. That is trust. Go to Him for refuge from all evil, from all harm, from your own souls, from all sin, from hell, and death, and the devil.

Put your trust under "the shadow of his wing." That is a beautiful image, drawn, probably, from the grand words of Deuteronomy, where God is likened to the "eagle stirring up her nest, fluttering over her young," with tenderness in her fierce eye, and protecting strength in the sweep of her mighty pinion. So God spreads the covert of his wing, strong and tender, beneath which we may all gather ourselves and nestle.

And how can we do that? By the simple process of fleeing unto Him, as made known to us in Christ our Savior; to hide ourselves there. For let us not forget how even the tenderness of this metaphor was increased by its shape on the tender lips of the Lord: "How often would I have gathered thy children together, as a hen gathereth her chickens under her wings." The Old Testament took the emblem of the eagle, sovereign, and strong, and fierce; the New Testament took the emblem of the domestic fowl, peaceable, and gentle, and affectionate. Let us flee to that Christ, by humble faith, with the plea on our lips—

> Cover my defenseless head
> With the shadow of Thy wing;

and then all the Godhead in its mercy, its faithfulness, its righteousness, and its judgments will be on our side; and we shall know how precious is the lovingkindness of the Lord, and find in Him the home and hiding-place of our hearts forever.

43

What Men Find
beneath the Wings of God

*They shall be abundantly satisfied with the fatness of
Thy house, and Thou shalt make them drink of the
river of Thy pleasures.*
*For with Thee is the fountain of life; in Thy light
shall we see light—Psalm 36:8, 9.*

In the preceding verses we saw a wonderful picture of the boundless perfections of God; His lovingkindness, faithfulness, righteousness, and of His two-fold act, the depths of His judgments and
the plainness of His merciful preservation of man and beast. In
these verses we have an equally wonderful picture of the blessedness
of the godly, the elements of which consists in four things: satisfaction, represented under the emblem of a feast; joy, represented
under the imagery of full draughts from a flowing river of delight;
life, pouring from God as a fountain; light, streaming from Him as
source.

And this picture is connected with the previous one by a very
simple link. Who are they who "shall be abundantly satisfied?"
The men "who put their trust beneath the shadow of Thy wings."
That is to say, the simple exercise of confidence in God is the channel through which all the fullness of Divinity passes into, and fills
our emptiness.

Observe, too, that the whole of the blessings here promised
are to be regarded as present and not future. "They shall be abundantly satisfied" would be far more truly rendered in consonance
with the Hebrew: "They *are* satisfied"; and so also we should read
"Thou *dost* make them drink of the river of Thy pleasures; in Thy

light *do* we see light." The Psalmist is not speaking of any future blessedness, to be realized in some far-off, indefinite day to come, but of what is possible even in this cloudy and sorrowful life. My text was true on the hills of Palestine, on the day when it was spoken; it may be true amongst the alleys of Manchester today. My purpose this morning is simply to deal with the four elements in which this blessedness consists—satisfaction, joy, life, light.

I. Satisfaction; "They shall be abundantly satisfied with the fatness of Thy house." Now, I suppose, there is a double metaphor in that. There is an allusion, no doubt, to the festal meal of priests and worshipers in the temple, on occasion of the peace-offering. And there is also the simpler metaphor of God as the host at His table, at which we are guests. "Thy house" may either be, in the narrower sense, the temple; and then all life is represented as being a glad sacrificial meal in His presence, of which "the meek shall eat and be satisfied." Or Thy "house" may be taken in a more general sense; and then all life is represented as the gathering of children round the abundant board which their Father's providence spreads for them, and as glad feasting in the mansions of the Father's house.

In either case the plain teaching of the text is, that by the might of a calm trust in God the whole mass of a man's desires are filled and satisfied. What do we want to satisfy us? It is something almost awful to think of the multiplicity, and the variety, and the imperativeness of the raging desires which every human soul carries about within it. The heart is like a nest of callow fledglings, every one of them a great, wide open, gaping beak, that ever needs to have food put into it. Heart, mind, will, appetites, tastes, inclinations, weaknesses, bodily wants—the whole crowd of these are crying for their meat. The Book of Proverbs says there are three things that are never satisfied: the grave, the earth that is not filled with water, and the fire that never says "It is enough." And we may add a fourth, the human heart, insatiable as the grave; thirsty as the sands, on which you may pour Niagara, and it will drink it all up and be ready for more; fierce as the fire that licks up everything within reach and still hungers.

So, though we be poor and weak creatures, we want much to make us restful. We want no less than that every appetite, desire, need, inclination shall be filled to the full; that all shall be filled to the full at once, and that by one thing; that all shall be filled to the full at once, by one thing that shall last forever. Or else we shall be like men whose store of provision gives out before they are halfway across the desert. And we need that all our desires shall be filled at once by one thing that is so much bigger than ourselves that we shall grow up towards it, and towards it, and towards it, and yet never be able to exhaust or surpass it.

Where are you going to get that? There is only one answer, dear brethren, to the question, and that is—God, and God alone is the food of the heart; God, and God alone, will satisfy your need. Let us bring the full Christian truth to bear upon the illustration of these words. Who was it that said, "I am the Bread of Life. He that cometh unto Me shall never hunger?" Christ will feed my mind with truth if I will accept His revelation of Himself, of God, and of all things. Christ will feed my heart with love if I will open my heart for the entrance of His love. Christ will feed my will with blessed commands if I will submit myself to His sweet and gentle, and yet imperative, authority. Christ will satisfy all my longings and desires with His own great fullness. Other food palls upon man's appetite, and we wish for change; and physiologists tell us that a less wholesome and nutritious diet, if varied, is better for a man's health than a more nutritious one if uniform and monotonous. But in Christ there are all constituents that are needed for the building up of the human spirit. And so we never weary of Him if we only know His sweetness. After a world of hungry men have fed upon Him, He remains inexhaustible as at the beginning; like the bread in His own miracles, of which the pieces that were broken, and ready to be given to the eaters were more than the original stock, as it appeared when the meal began. Or like the fabled feast in the Norse Walhalla, to which the gods sit down today, and tomorrow it is all there on the board, as abundant and full as ever. So if we have Christ to live upon, we shall know no hunger; and "in the days of famine we shall be satisfied."

Oh! Brethren, do you know what it is ever to feel that your hungry heart is at rest? Did you ever know what it is to say, "It is enough"? Have you anything that satisfies your appetite and makes you blessed? Surely men's eager haste to get more of the world's dainties shows that there is no satisfaction at its table. Why will you spend "your money for that which is not bread, and your labor for that which satisfies not," as Indians in famine eat clay which fills their stomachs, but neither stays their hunger, nor ministers strength? Eat and your soul shall live.

II. Now, turn to the next of the elements of blessedness here, joy. "Thou makest them drink of the river of Thy pleasures."

There may be a possible reference here, couched in the word "pleasures," to the Garden of Eden, with the river that watered it parting into four heads; for "Eden" is the singular of the word which is here translated "pleasures," or "delight." If we take that reference, which is very questionable, there would be suggested the thought that amidst all the pain and weariness of this desert life of ours, though the gates of Paradise are shut against us, they who dwell beneath the shadow of the Divine wing really have a paradise blooming around them; and have flowing ever by their side, with tinkling music the paradisaical river of delights, in which they may bathe and swim, and of which they may drink. Certainly the joys of communion with God surpass any which unfallen Eden could have boasted.

But, at all events, the plain teaching of the text is that the simple act of trusting beneath the shadow of God's wings brings to us an ever fresh and flowing river of gladness, of which we may drink. The whole conception of religion in the Bible is gladsome. There is no puritanical gloom about it. True, a Christian man has sources of sadness which other men have not. There is the consciousness of his own sin, and the contest that he has daily to wage; and all things take a soberer coloring to the eye that has been accustomed to look, however dimly, upon God. Many of the sources of earthly felicity are dammed up and shut off from us if we are living beneath the shadow of God's wings. Life will seem to be sterner, and graver, and sadder than the lives "that ring with idiot laughter solely," and have no music because they have no melancholy in them. That cannot be helped. But what does it matter though two or three surface streams, which are little better than drains for sewage, be stopped up, if the pure river of the water of life is turned into you hearts? Surely it will be a gain if the sadness, which has joy for its very foundation, is yours, instead of the laughter which is only a mocking mask for a death's head, and of which it is true that even "in laughter the heart is sorrowful, and the end of that mirth is heaviness." Better to be "sorrowful, yet always rejoicing," than to be glad on the surface, with a perpetual sorrow and unrest gnawing at the root of your life.

And if it be true that the whole Biblical conception of religion is of a glad thing, my brother, it is your duty, if you are a Christian man, to be glad, whatever temptations there may be in your way to be sorrowful. It is a hard lesson, and one which is not always insisted upon. We hear a great deal about other Christian duties. We do not hear so much as we ought about the Christian duty of gladness. It takes a very robust faith to say, "Though the fig-tree shall not blossom, neither shall fruit be in the vine, yet I will rejoice in the Lord, I will joy in the God of my salvation." But unless we can say it we have an attainment of Christian life yet unreached, to which we have to aspire.

But be that as it may, my point is simply this—that all real and profound possession of and communion with God in Christ will make us glad; glad with a gladness altogether unlike that of the world round about us; far deeper, far quieter, far nobler, the sister and the ally of all great things, of all pure life, of all generous and lofty thought.

And where is it all to be found? Only in fellowship with Him. "The river of thy pleasures" may mean something yet more solemn and wonderful than pleasures of which He is the Author. It may mean pleasures *which He shares,* the very delights of the Divine nature itself. The more we come into fellowship with Him, the more shall we share in the very joy of God Himself. And what is His joy? He delights in mercy; He delights in self-communication; He is the blessed, the happy God because He is the giving God. "He delights in His love. He rejoices over" His penitent child "with singing."

In that blessedness we may share; or if that be too high and mystical a thought, may we not remember Who it was that said: "These things speak I unto you, that My joy may remain in you"; and Who it is that will one day say to the faithful servant: "Enter thou into the joy of thy Lord"? Christ makes us drink of the river of His pleasures. The Shepherd and the sheep drink from the same stream, and the gladness which filled the heart of the Man of Sorrows, and lay deeper than all His sorrows, He imparts to all them that put their trust in Him.

So, dear brethren, what a blessing it is for us to have, as we may have, a source of joy, frozen by no winter, dried up by no summer, muddied and corrupted by no iridescent scum of putrefaction which ever mantles over the stagnant ponds of earthly joys! Like some citadel that has an unfailing well in its courtyard, we may have a fountain of gladness within ourselves which nothing that touches the outside can cut off. We have but to lap a hasty mouthful of earthly joys as we run, but we cannot drink too full draughts of this pure river of water which makes glad the city of God.

III. We have the third element of the blessedness of the godly represented under the metaphor of life, pouring from the fountain, which is God. "With Thee is the fountain of life." The words are true in regard of the lowest meaning of "life"—physical existence—and they give a wonderful idea of the connection between God and all living creatures. The fountain rises, the spray on the summit catches the sunlight for a moment, and then falls into the basin, jet after jet springing up into the light, and in its turn recoiling into the darkness. The water in the fountain, the water in the spray, the water in the basin, are all one. Wherever there is life there is God. The creature is bound to the Creator by a mystic bond and tie of kinship, by the fact of life. The mystery of life knits all living things with God. It is a spark, wherever it burns, from the central flame. It is a drop, wherever it is found, from the great fountain. It is in man a breath of God's nostrils. It is not a gift given by a Creator who dwells apart, having made living things, as a watchmaker might a watch, and then "seeing them go." But there is a deep mystic union between the God who has life in Himself and all the living creatures who draw their life from Him, which we cannot express better than by that image of our text, "With Thee is the fountain of life."

But my text speaks about a blessing belonging to the men who put their trust under the shadow of God's wing, and therefore it does not refer merely to physical existence, but to something higher than that, namely, to that life of the spirit in communion with God, which is the true and the proper sense of "life"; the one, namely, in which the word is almost always used in the Bible.

There is such a thing as death in life; living men may be "dead in trespasses and sins," "dead in pleasure," dead in selfishness. The awful vision of Coleridge in the "Ancient Mariner," of dead men standing up and pulling at the ropes, is only a picture of the realities of life; where, as on some Witches' Sabbath, corpses move about and take part in the activities of this dead world. There are people full of energy in regard of worldly things, who yet are all dead to that higher region, the realities of which they have never seen, the actions of which they have never done, the emotions of which they have never felt. Am I speaking to such living corpses now? There are some of them here alive to the world, alive to animalism, alive to lust, alive to passion, alive to earth, alive perhaps to thought, alive to duty, alive to conduct of a high and noble kind, but yet dead to God, and, therefore, dead to the highest and noblest of all realities. Answer for yourselves the question—do you belong to this class?

There is life for you in Jesus Christ, who "*is* the Life." Like the great aqueducts that stretch from the hills across the Roman Campagna, His Incarnation brings the waters of the fountain from the mountains of God into the lower levels of our nature, and the fetid alleys of our sins. The cool, sparkling treasure is carried near to every lip. If we drink, we live. If we will not, we die in our sins, and are dead while we live. Stop the fountain, and what becomes of the stream? It fades there between its banks, and is no more. You cannot live the life of the animal except that life were joined to Him. If it could be broken away from God it would disappear as the clouds melt in the sky, and there would be nobody, and you would be nowhere. You cannot break yourself away from God *physically* so completely as to annihilate yourself. You can do so *spiritually,* and some of you do it, and the consequence is that you are dead, *dead*, DEAD! You can be made alive from the dead, if you will lay hold on Jesus Christ, and get His life-giving spirit into your hearts.

IV. Light. "In Thy light shall we see light."

God is "the Father of lights." The sun and all the stars are only lights kindled by Him. It is the very crown of revelation that God is light, and in Him is no darkness at all. Light seems to the unscientific eye, which knows nothing about undulations of a luminiferous ether, to be the least material of material things. All joyous things come with it. It brings warmth and fruit, fullness and life. Purity, and gladness, and knowledge have been symbolized by it in all tongues. The Scripture uses light, and the sun, which is its source, as an emblem for God in His holiness, and blessedness, and omniscience. This great word here seems to point chiefly to light as knowledge.

This saying is true, as the former clause was, in relation to all the light which men have. The inspiration of the Almighty giveth him understanding. The faculty by which men know, and all the exercise of that faculty, is His gift. It is in the measure in which God's light comes to the eye that the eye beholds. "Light" may mean not only the faculty, but the medium of vision. It is in the measure in which God's light comes, and because His light comes, that all light of reason in human nature sees the truth which is its light. God is the author of all true thoughts in all mankind. The spirit of man is a candle kindled by the Lord.

But as I said about life, so I say about light. The material or intellectual aspects of the word are not the main ones here. The reference is to the spiritual gift which belongs to the men "who put their trust beneath the shadow of Thy wings." In communion with Him Who is the Light as well as the Life of men, we see a whole universe of glories, realities, and brightnesses. Where other eyes see only darkness, we behold "the King in His beauty, and the land that is very far off." Where other men see only cloudland and mists, our vision will pierce into the unseen, and there behold "the things which are," the only real things, of which all that the eye of sense sees are only the fleeting shadows, seen as in a dream, while these are the true, and the sight of them is sight indeed. They who see by the light of God, and see light therein, have a vision which is more than imagination, more than opinion, more than belief. It is certitude. Communication with God does not bring with it superior intellectual perspicuity, but it does bring a perception and experience of spiritual realities and relations, which, in respect of clearness and certainty, may be called sight. Many of us walk in darkness, who, if we were but in communion with God, would see the lone hill-side blazing with chariots and horses of fire. Many of us grope in perplexity, who, if we were but hiding under the shadow of God's wings, would see the truth and walk at liberty in the light, which is knowledge and purity and joy.

In communication with God, we see light upon all the paths of duty. It is wonderful how, when a man lives near God, he gets to know what he ought to do. That great Light, which is Christ, is like the star that hung over the Magi, blazing in the heavens, and yet stooping to the lowly task of guiding three wayfaring men along a muddy road upon earth. So the highest Light of God comes down to be a Lantern for our paths and a Light for our feet.

And in the same communion with God, we get light in all seasons of darkness and of sorrow. "To the upright there ariseth light in the darkness"; and the darkest hours of earthly fortune will be like a Greenland summer night, when the sun scarcely dips below the horizon, and even when it is absent, all the heaven is aglow with a calm twilight.

All these great blessings belong today to those who take refuge under the shadow of His wings. But blessed as the present experience is, we have to look for the perfecting of it when we pass from the forecourt to the inner sanctuary, and in that higher house sit with Christ at His table and feast at the marriage supper of the Lamb. Here we drink from the river, but there we shall be carried up to the source. The life of God in the soul is here often feeble in its flow, a fountain sealed and all but shut up in our hearts, but then it will pour through all our being, a fountain springing up into everlasting life. The darkness is scattered even here by the beams of the true light, but here we are only in the morning twilight, and many clouds still fill the sky, and many a deep gorge lies in sunless shadow, but there the light shall be a broad universal blaze, and there shall be nothing hid from the heat thereof.

Now, dear brethren, the sum of the whole matter is, that all this four-fold blessing of satisfaction, joy, life, light, is given to you, if you will take Christ. He will feed you with the bread of God; He will give you His own joy to drink; He will be in you the life of your lives, and "the master-light of all your seeing." And if you will not have Him, you will starve, and your lips will be cracked with thirst; and you will live a life which is death, and you will sink at last into outer darkness.

Is that the fate which you are going to choose? Choose Christ, and He will give you satisfaction, and joy, and life, and light.

44

The Love That
Calls Us Sons

*Behold what manner of love the Father hath be-
stowed upon us, that we should be called the sons of
God*—1 John 3:1.

One or two points of an expository character will serve to introduce what else I have to say on these words.

The text is, I suppose, generally understood as if it pointed to the
fact that we are called the sons of God, as the great exemplification
of the wonderfulness of His love. That is a perfectly possible view
of the connection and meaning of the text. But if we are to translate
with perfect accuracy we must render, not "that we should be
called," but *in order that we should be called the Sons of God."*
The meaning then is that the love bestowed is the means by which
the design that we should be called His sons is accomplished. What
John calls us to contemplate with wonder and gratitude is not only
the fact of this marvelous love, but also the glorious end to which
it has been given to us and works. There seems no reason for slur-
ring over this meaning in favor of the more vague "that" of our version. God gives His great and wonderful love in Jesus Christ, and
all the gifts and powers which live in Him like fragrance in the
rose. All this lavish bestowal of love, unspeakable as it is, may be regarded as having one great end, which God deems worthy of even
such expenditure, namely, that men should become, in the deepest
sense, His children. It is not so much to the contemplation of our
blessedness in being sons, as to the devout gaze on the love which,
by its wonderful process, has made it possible for us to be sons, that
we are summoned here.

Again, you will find a remarkable addition to our text in the Revised Version, namely, "and such we are." Now these words come with a very great weight of manuscript authority, and of internal evidence. They are parenthetical, a kind of rapid "aside" of the writer's, expressing his joyful confidence that he and his brethren are sons of God, not only in name, but in reality. They are the voice of personal assurance, the voice of the spirit "by which we cry Abba, Father," breaking in for a moment on the flow of the sentence, like an irrepressible glad answer to the Father's call. With these explanations let us look at the words.

I. The love that is given.

We are called upon to come with our little vessels to measure the contents of the great ocean, to plumb with our short lines the infinite abyss, and not only to estimate the quantity but the quality of that love, which, in both respects, surpasses all our means of comparison and conception.

Properly speaking, we can do neither the one nor the other, for we have no line long enough to sound its depths, and no experience which will give us a standard with which to compare its quality. But all that we can do, John would have us do, that is, look and ever look at the working of that love till we form some not wholly inadequate idea of it.

We can no more "behold what manner of love the Father has bestowed on us" than we can look with the undimmed eyes right into the middle of the sun. But we can in some measure imagine the tremendous and beneficent forces that ride forth horsed on his beams to distances which the imagination faints in trying to grasp, and reach their journey's end unwearied and ready for their tasks as when it began. Here are we, ninety odd millions of miles from the center of the system, yet warmed by its heat, lighted by its beams, and touched for good by its power in a thousand ways. All that has been going on for no one knows how many eons. How mighty the Power which produces these effects! In like manner, who can gaze into the fiery depths of that infinite Godhead, into the ardors of that immeasurable, incomparable, inconceivable love? But we can look at and measure its activities. We can see what it does, and so can, in some degree, understand it, and feel that after all we have a measure for the Immeasurable, a comparison for the Incomparable, and can *thus* "behold what manner of love the Father hath bestowed on us."

So we have to turn to the work of Christ, and especially to His death, if we would estimate the love of God. According to John's constant teaching, that is the great proof that God loves us. The most wonderful revelation to every heart of man, of the depths of that Divine heart, lies in the gift of Jesus Christ. The Apostle bids me "behold what manner of love." I turn to the Cross, and I see there a love which shrinks from no sacrifice, but gives "Him up to death for us all." I turn to the Cross, and I see there a love which is evoked by no lovableness on my part, but comes from the depth of His own Infinite Being, Who loves because He must, and Who must because He is God. I turn to the Cross, and I see there manifested a love which sighs for recognition, which desires nothing of me but the repayment of my poor affection, and longs to see its own likeness in me. And I see there a love that will not be put away by sinfulness, and shortcomings, and evil, but pours its treasures on the unworthy, like sunshine on a dunghill. So, streaming through the darkness of eclipse, and speaking to me even in the awful silence in which the Son of Man died there for sin, I "behold," and I hear, the "manner of love that the Father hath bestowed upon us," stronger than death and sin, armed with all power, gentler than the fall of the dew, boundless and endless, in its measure measureless in its quality transcendent—the love of God to me in Jesus Christ my Savior.

In like manner we have to think, if we would estimate the "manner of this love," that through and in the great sacrifice of Jesus Christ there comes to us the gift of a Divine life like His own. Perhaps it may be too great a refinement of interpretation; but it certainly does seem to me that that expression "to bestow His love upon" us, is not altogether the same as "to love us," but that there is a greater depth in it. There may be some idea of that love itself being as it were infused into us, and not merely of its consequences or tokens being given to us; as Paul speaks of "the love of God shed abroad in our hearts" by the spirit which is given to us. At all events this communication of Divine life, which is at bottom Divine love—for God's life is God's love—is His great gift to men.

Be that as it may, these two are the great tokens, consequences and measures of God's love to us—the gift of Christ, and that which is the sequel and outcome thereof, the gift of the Spirit which is breathed into Christian spirits. These two gifts, which are one gift, embrace all that the world needs. Christ for us and Christ in us must both be taken into account if you would estimate the manner of the love that God has bestowed upon us.

We may gain another measure of the greatness of this love if we put an emphasis—which I dare say the writer did not intend—on one word of this text, and think of the love given to "*us*," such creatures as we are. Out of the depths we cry to Him. Not only by the voice of our supplications, but even when we raise no call of entreaty, our misery pleads with His merciful heart, and from the heights there comes upon our wretchedness and sin the rush of this great love, like a cataract, which sweeps away all our sins, and floods us with its own blessedness and joy. The more we know ourselves, the more wonderingly and thankfully shall we bow down our hearts before Him as we measure His mercy by our unworthiness.

From all His works the same summons echoes. They all call us to see mirrored in them His loving care. But the Cross of Christ and the gift of a Divine Spirit cry aloud to every ear in tones of more beseeching entreaty and of more imperative command to "behold what manner of love the Father hath bestowed upon us."

II. Look next at the sonship which is the purpose of His given Love. It has often been noticed that the Apostle John uses for that expression "the Sons of God," another word from that which his brother Paul uses. John's phrase would perhaps be a little more accurately translated "Children of God," while Paul, on the other hand, very seldom says "children," but almost always says "sons." Of course the children are sons and the sons are children, but still, the slight distinction of phrase is characteristic of the men, and of the different points of view from which they speak about the same thing. John's word lays stress on the children's kindred nature with their father and on their immature condition.

But without dwelling on that, let us consider this great gift and dignity of being children of God, which is the object that God has in view in all the lavish bestowment of His goodness upon us.

That end is not reached by God's making us men. Over and above that He has to send this great gift of His love, in order that the men whom He has made may become His sons. If you take the context here you will see very clearly that the writer draws a broad distinction between "the Sons of God" and "the world" of men who do not comprehend them, and so far from being themselves sons, do not even know God's sons when they see them. And there is a deeper and solemner word still in the context. John thinks that men (within the range of light and revelation, at all events) are divided into two families—"the children of God and the children of the devil." There *are* two families amongst men.

Thank God! The prodigal son, in his rags amongst the swine, and lying by the swine-troughs in his filth and his husks, and his fever, *is* a son. No doubt about that! He has these three elements and marks of sonship that no man ever gets rid of: he is of a Divine origin, he has a Divine likeness in that he has got mind, and will, spirit, and he is the object of a Divine love.

The doctrine of the New Testament about the Fatherhood of God and the sonship of man does not in the slightest degree interfere with these three great truths, that all men, though the features of the common humanity may be almost battered out of recognition in them, are all children of God because He made them; that they are children of God because still there lives in them something of the likeness of the creative Father; and, blessed be His name! that they are all children of God because He loves, and provides, and cares for everyone of them.

All that is blessedly and eternally true; but it is also true that there is a higher relation than that to which the name "children of God" is more accurately given, and to which in the New Testament that name is confined. If you ask what that relation is, let me quote to you three passages in this Epistle, which will answer the question. "Whoever believeth that Jesus is the Christ is born of God," that is the first; "Everyone that doeth righteousness is born of God," that is the second; "Everyone that loveth is born of God," that is the third. Or, to put them all into one expression which holds them all, in the great words of his prologue in the first chapter of John's Gospel you find this: "To as many as received Him to them gave He power to become the sons of God." Believing in Christ with loving trust produces, and doing righteousness and loving the brethren, as the result of that belief prove the fact of sonship in its highest and its truest sense.

What is implied in that great word by which the Almighty gives us a name and a place as of sons and daughters? Clearly, first, a communicated life, therefore, second, a kindred nature which shall be "pure as He is pure," and, third, growth to full maturity.

This sonship, which is no mere empty name, is the aim and purpose of God's dealings, of all the revelation of His love, and most especially of the great gift of His love in Christ. Has that purpose been accomplished in you? Have you ever looked at that great gift of love that God has given you on purpose to make you His child? If you have, has it made you one? Are you trusting to Jesus Christ, Whom God has sent forth that we might receive the standing of sons in Him? Are you a child of God because a brother of that Savior? Have you received the gift of a Divine life through Him? My friend! Remember the grim alternative. A child of God or a child of the devil! Bitter words, narrow words, uncharitable words—as people call them! And I believe, and therefore, I am bound to say it, *true* words, which it concerns *you* to lay to heart.

III. Now, still further, let me ask you to look at the glad recognition of this sonship by the child's heart.

I have already referred to the clause added in the Revised Version, "and such we are." As I said, it is a kind of "aside," in which John adds the Amen for himself and for his poor brothers and sisters, toiling and moiling obscure among the crowds of Ephesus, to the great truth. He asserts his and their glad consciousness of the reality of the fact of their sonship, which they know to be no empty title. He asserts, too, the present possession of that sonship, realizing it as a fact, amid all the commonplace vulgarities and carping cares and petty aims of life's little day. "Such we are" is the "Here am I, Father," of the child answering the Father's call, "My Son."

He turns doctrine into experience. He is not content with merely having the thought in his creed, but his heart clasps it, and his whole nature responds to the great truth. I ask you, do you do that? Do not be content with hearing the truth, or even with assenting to it, and believing it in your understandings. The truth is nothing to you, unless you have made it your very own by faith. Do not be satisfied with the orthodox confession. Unless it has touched your heart and made your whole soul thrill with thankful gladness and quiet triumph, it is nothing to you. The mere belief of thirty-nine or thirty-nine thousand Articles is nothing; but when a man has a true heart-faith in Him, Whom all articles are meant to make us know and love, then dogma becomes life, and the doctrine feeds the soul. Does it do so with you, my brother? Can *you* say, "And such we are?"

Take another lesson. The Apostle was not afraid to say "I know that I am a child of God." There are many very good people, whose tremulous, timorous lips have never ventured to say "I know." They will say, "Well, I hope" or sometimes, as if that was not uncertain enough, they will put in an adverb or two, and say "I humbly hope that I am." It is a far robuster kind of Christianity, a far truer one, aye, and a humbler one, too, that throws all considerations of my own character and merits, and all the rest of that rubbish, clean behind me, and when God says, "My son!" says "My Father"; and when God calls us His children, leaps up and gladly answers, "And we are!" Do not be afraid of being too confident, if your confidence is built on God, and not on yourselves; but be afraid of being too diffident, and be afraid of having a great deal of self-righteousness masquerading under the guise of such a profound consciousness of your own unworthiness that you dare not call yourself a child of God. It is not a question of worthiness or unworthiness. It is a question in the first place, and mainly, of the truth of Christ's promise and the sufficiency of Christ's Cross; and in a very subordinate degree of anything belonging to you.

IV. We have here, finally, the loving and devout gaze upon this wonderful love. "Behold," at the beginning of my text is not the mere exclamation which you often find both in the Old and in the New Testaments, which is simply intended to emphasize the importance of what follows, but it is a distinct command to do the thing, to look, and ever to look, and to look again, and live in the habitual and devout contemplation of that infinite and wondrous love of God.

I have but two remarks to make about that, and the one is this, that such a habit of devout and thankful meditation upon the love of God, as manifested in the sacrifice of Jesus Christ, and the consequent gift of the Divine Spirit, joined with the humble, thankful conviction that I am a child of God thereby, lies at the foundation of all vigorous and happy Christian life. How can a thing which you do not touch with yours hands and see with your eyes produce any effect upon you, unless you think about it? How can a religion which can only influence through thought and emotion do anything in you, or for you, unless you occupy your thoughts and your feelings with it? It is sheer nonsense to suppose it possible. Things which do not appeal to sense are real to us, and indeed we may say, *are* at all for us, only as we think about them. If you had a dear friend in Australia, and never thought about him, he would even cease to be dear, and it would be all one to you as if he were dead. If he were really dear to you, you *would* think about him. We may say, (though of course, there are other ways of looking at the matter), that in a very intelligible sense, the degree in which we think about Christ, and in Him behold the love of God, is a fairly accurate measure of our Christianity.

Now will you apply that sharp test to yesterday, and the day before, and the day before that, and decide how much of your life was pagan, and how much of it was Christian? You will never make anything of your professed Christianity, you will never get a drop of happiness or any kind of good out of it; it will neither be a strength, nor a joy, nor a defense to you unless you make it your habitual occupation to "behold the manner of love"; and look, and look, and look, until it warms and fills your heart.

The second remark is that we cannot keep that great sight before the eye of our minds without effort. You will have very resolutely to look away from something else, if, amid all the dazzling gauds of earth you are to see the far-off luster of that heavenly love. Just as timorous people in a thunder-storm will light a candle that they may not see the lightning, so many Christians have their hearts filled with the twinkling light of some miserable tapers of earthly care and pursuits, which, though they be dim and smoky, are bright enough to make it hard to see the silent depths of Heaven, though it blaze with myriad stars. If you hold a sixpence close enough up to the pupil of your eye, it will keep you from seeing the sun. And if you hold the world close to mind and heart, as many of you do, you will only see, round the rim of it, the least tiny ring of the overlapping love of God. What the world lets you see you will see, and the world will take care that it will let you see very little—not enough to do you any good, not enough to deliver you from its chains. Wrench yourselves away, my brethren, from the absorbing contemplation of Birmingham jewelry and paste, and look at the true riches. If you have ever had some glimpses of that wondrous love, and have ever been drawn by it to cry, Abba, Father, do not let the trifles which belong not to your true inheritance fill your thoughts, but renew the vision, and by determined turning away of your eyes from beholding vanity, look off from the things that are seen, that you may gaze upon the things that are not seen, and chiefest among them, upon the love of God in Christ Jesus our Lord.

If you have never looked on that love, I beseech you now to turn aside and see this great sight. Do not let that brightness but unnoticed while your eyes are fixed on the ground, like the gaze of men absorbed in gold digging, while a glorious sunshine is flushing the Eastern sky. Look to the unspeakable, incomparable, immeasurable love of God, in giving up His Son to death for us all. Look and be saved. Look and live. "Behold what manner of love the Father hath bestowed on you," and beholding, you will become the sons and daughters of the Lord God Almighty.

45

The Unrevealed Future of the Sons of God

Beloved, now are we the sons of God, and it doth not yet appear what we shall be; but we know that, when He shall appear, we shall be like Him; for we shall see Him as He is—1 John 3:2.

I have hesitated, as you may well believe, whether I should take these words for a text. They seem so far to surpass anything that can be said concerning them, and they cover such immense fields of dim thought that one may well be afraid lest one should spoil them by even attempting to dilate on them. And yet they are so closely connected with the words of the previous verse, which formed the subject of my last sermon, that I felt as if my work were only half done unless I followed that sermon with this.

The present is the prophet of the future, says my text: "Now we are the sons of God, *and*" (not "but") "it doth not yet appear what we shall be." Some men say: "Ah! *Now are* we, but we shall be—nothing!" John does not think so. John thinks that if a man is a son of God he will always be so. There are three things in this verse now, if we are God's children, our sonship makes us quite sure of the future; how our sonship leaves us largely in ignorance of the future, but how our sonship: flings one bright, all-penetrating beams of light on the only important thing about the future, the clear vision of and the perfect likeness to Him Who is our life. "Now are we the sons of God," therefore we shall be. We are the sons; we do not know what we shall be. We are the sons, and therefore, though there be a great circumference of blank ignorance as to our future, yet, blessed be His name! There is a great light burning in the middle of it. "We know that when He shall appear we shall be like Him, for we shall see Him as He is."

I. The fact of sonship makes us quite sure of the future.

I am not concerned to appraise the relative value of the various arguments and proofs, or, it may be, presumptions, which may recommend the doctrine of a future life to men, but it seems to me that the strongest reasons for believing in another world are these two: first, that Jesus Christ was raised from the dead and has gone up there; and, second, that a man here can pray, and trust, and love God, and feel that he is His child. As was noticed in the preceding sermon, the word rendered "sons" might more accurately be translated "children." If so, we may fairly say, "We are the *children* of God now—and if we are children now, we shall be grown up some time." Childhood leads to maturity. The infant becomes a man.

That is to say, he that here, in an infantile way, is stammering with his poor, unskilled lips the name "Abba! Father!" will one day come to speak it fully. He that dimly trusts, he that partially loves, he that can lift up his heart in some more or less unworthy prayer and aspiration after God, in all these emotions and exercises, has the great proof in himself that such emotions, such relationship, can never be put to an end. The roots have gone down through the temporal, and have laid hold of the Eternal. Anything seems to me to be more credible than that a man who can look up and say, "My Father" shall be crushed by what befalls the mere outside of him; anything seems to me to be more believable than to suppose that the nature which is capable of these elevating emotions and aspirations of confidence and hope, which can know God and yearn after Him, and can love Him, is to be wiped out like a gnat by the finger of Death. The material has nothing to do with these feelings, and if I know myself, in however feeble and imperfect a degree, to be the son of God, I carry in the conviction the very pledge and seal of eternal life. That is a thought "whose very sweetness yieldeth proof that it was born for immortality." "We are the sons of God," therefore we shall always be so, in all worlds, and whatsoever may become of this poor wrappage in which the soul is shrouded.

We may notice, also, that not only the fact of our sonship avails to assure us of immortal life, but that also the very form which our religious experience takes points in the same direction.

As I said, infancy is the prophecy of maturity. "The child is father of the man"; the bud foretells the flower. In the same way, the very imperfections of the Christian life, as it is seen here, argue the existence of another state, where all that is here in the germ shall be fully matured, and all that is here incomplete shall attain the perfection which alone will correspond to the power that works in us. Think of the ordinary Christian character. The beginning is there, and evidently no more than the beginning. As one looks at the crudity, the inconsistencies, the failings, the feebleness of the Christian life of others, or of oneself, and then thinks that such a poor, imperfect exhibition is all that so Divine a principle has been able to achieve in this world, one feels that there must be a region and a time where we shall be all which the transforming power of God's spirit can make us. The very inconsistencies of Christians are as strong reasons for believing in the perfect life of heaven as their purities and virtues are. We have a right to say Mighty principles are at work upon Christian souls—the power of the Cross, the power of love issuing in obedience, the power of an indwelling Spirit; and is this all that these great forces are going to effect on human character? Surely a seed so precious and Divine is somewhere, and at some time, to bring forth something better than these few poor, half-developed flowers, something with more lustrous petals and richer fragrance. The plant is clearly an exotic; does not its obviously struggling growth here tell of warmer suns and richer soil, where it will be at home?

There is a great deal in every man, and most of all in Christian men and women, which does not fit this present. All other creatures correspond in their capacities to the place where they are set down; and the world in which the plant or the animal lives, the world of their surroundings, stimulates to activity all their powers. But that is not so with a man. "Foxes have holes, birds of the air have nests." They fit exactly, and correspond to their "environment." But a man! There is an enormous amount of waste faculty about him if he is only to live in this world. There are large capacities in every nature, and most of all in a Christian nature, which are like the packages that emigrants take with them, marked "Not wanted on the voyage." These go down into the hold, and they are only of use after landing in the new world. If I am a son of God I have much in me that is "not wanted on the voyage," and the more I grow into His likeness, the more I am thrown out of harmony with the things round about me, in proportion as I am brought into harmony with the things beyond.

That consciousness of belonging to another order of things, because I am God's child, will make me sure that when I have done with earth, the tie that binds me to my Father will not be broken, but that I shall go home, where I shall be fully and forever all that I so imperfectly began to be here, where all gaps in my character shall be filled up, and the half-completed circle of my heavenly perfectness shall grow like the crescent moon, into full-orbed beauty. "Neither life, nor death, nor things present, nor things to come, nor height, nor depth, nor any other creature" shall be able to break that tie, and banish the child from the conscious grasp of a Father's hand. Dear brother and sister, can you say, "Now am I a child of God!" Then you may patiently and peacefully front that dim future.

II. Now I come to the second point, namely, that we remain ignorant of much in that future.

That happy assurance of the love of God resting upon me, and making me His child through Jesus Christ, does not dissipate all the darkness which lies on that beyond. "We are the sons of God, *and,*" just because we are, "it does not yet appear what we shall be." Or, as the words are rendered in the Revised Version, "it is not yet made manifest what we shall be."

The meaning of that expression, "It doth not yet appear," or, "It is not made manifest," may be put into very plain words. John would simply say to us, "There has never been set forth before men's eyes in this earthly life of ours an example, or an instance, of what the sons of God are to be in another state of being." And so, because men have never had the instance before them, they do not know much about that state.

In some sense there has been a manifestation through the life of Jesus Christ. Christ has died; Christ is risen again. Christ has gone about amongst men upon earth after resurrection. Christ has been raised to the right hand of God, and sits there in the glory of the Father. So far it has been manifested what we shall be. But the risen Christ is not the glorified Christ, and although He has set forth before man's senses irrefragably the fact of another life, and to some extent given glimpses and gleams of knowledge with regard to certain portions of it, I suppose that the "glorious body" of Jesus Christ was not assumed by Him till the cloud "received Him out of their sight," nor, indeed, could it be assumed, while He moved among the material realities of this world, and did eat and drink before them. So that, while we thankfully recognize that Christ's Resurrection and Ascension have "brought life and immortality to light," we must remember that it is the fact, and not the manner of the fact, which they make plain; and that, even after His example, it has not been manifested what is the body of glory which He now wears, and therefore it has not yet been manifested what we shall be when we are fashioned after its likeness.

There has been no manifestation, then, to sense, or to human experience, of that future, and, therefore, there is next to no knowledge about it. You can only know facts when the facts are communicated. You may speculate, and argue, and guess as much as you like, but that does not thin the darkness one bit. The unborn child has no more faculty or opportunity for knowing what the life upon earth is like than man here, in the world, has for knowing that life beyond. The chrysalis' dreams about what it would be when it was a butterfly would be as reliable as a man's imagination of what a future life will be.

So let us feel two things: Let us be thankful that we do not know, for the ignorance is the sign of the greatness; and then, let us be sure that just the very mixture of knowledge and ignorance which we have about another world is precisely the food which is most fitted to nourish imagination and hope. If we had more knowledge, supposing it could be given, of the conditions of that future life, it would lose some of its power to attract. Ignorance does not always prevent the occupation of the mind with a subject. Blank ignorance does, but ignorance, shot with knowledge like a tissue which, when you hold it one way seems all black, and when you tilt it another, seems golden, stimulates desire, hope, and imagination. So let us thankfully acquiesce in the limited knowledge.

Fools can ask questions which wise men cannot answer and will not ask. There are questions which, sometimes, when we are thinking about our own future, and sometimes when we see dear ones go away into the mist, become to us almost torture. It is easy to put them; it is not so easy to say: "Thank God, we cannot answer them yet!" If we could it would only be because the experience of earth was adequate to measure the experience of Heaven; and that would be to bring the future down to the low levels of this present. Let us be thankful then that so long as we can only speak in language derived from the experiences of earth, we have yet to learn the vocabulary of Heaven. Let us be thankful that our best help to know what we shall be is to reverse much of what we are, and that the loftiest and most positive declarations concerning the future lie in negatives like these: "I saw no temple therein." "There shall be no night there." "There shall be no curse there." "There shall be no more sighing nor weeping, for the former things are passed away."

The white mountains keep their secret well; not until we have passed through the black rocks that make the throat of the pass on the summit, shall we see the broad and shining plains beyond the hills. Let us be thankful for, and own the attractions of, the knowledge that is wrapped in ignorance, and thankfully say, "Now are we the sons of God, and it doth not appear what we shall be."

III. Now I must be very brief with the last thought that is here, and I am the less unwilling to be so because we cannot travel one inch beyond the revelations of the Book in reference to the matter. The thought is this, that our sonship flings one all-penetrating beam of light on that future, in the knowledge of our perfect vision and perfect likeness. "We know that when He shall be manifested, we shall be like Him, for we shall see Him as He is."

"When He shall be manifested"—to what period does that refer? It seems most natural to take the manifestation here as being the same as that spoken of only a verse or two before. "And now, little children, abide in Him, that when He shall *be manifested*, we may have confidence, and not be ashamed before Him at His coming (2:28). That "coming," then, is the "manifestation" of Christ; and it is at the period of His coming in His glory that His servants "shall be like Him, and see Him as He is." Clearly then it is Christ whom we shall see and become like, and not the Father invisible.

To behold Christ will be the condition and the means of growing like Him. That way of transformation by beholding, or of assimilation by the power of loving contemplation, is the blessed way of ennobling character, which even here, and in human relationships, has often made it easy to put off old vices and to clothe the soul with unwonted grace. Men have learned to love and gaze upon some fair character, till some image of its beauty has passed into their ruder natures. To love such and to look on them has been an education. The same process is exemplified in more sacred regions, when men here learn to love and look upon Christ by faith, and so become like Him, as the sun stamps a tiny copy of its blazing sphere on the eye that looks at it. But all these are but poor far-off hints and low preludes of the energy with which that blessed vision of the glorified Christ shall work on the happy hearts that behold Him, and of the completeness of the likeness to Him which will be printed in light upon their faces.

It matters not, though it doth not yet appear what we shall be, if to all the questionings of our own hearts we have this for our all-sufficient answer, "we shall be like Him." As good old Richard Baxter has it:

> My knowledge of that life is small,
>   The eye of faith is dim;
> But, 'tis enough that Christ knows all,
>   And I shall be like Him!

"It is enough for the servant that he be as his Lord."

There is no need to go into the dark and difficult questions about the manner of that vision. He Himself prayed, in that great intercessory prayer, "Father, I will that these Whom Thou hast given Me be with Me where I am, that they may behold My glory." That vision of the glorified manhood of Jesus Christ—certain, direct, clear, and worthy, whether it come through sense or through thought, to be called vision is all the sight of God that men in Heaven ever will have. And through the millenniums of a growing glory, Christ as He is will be the manifested Deity. Likeness will clear sight, and clearer sight will increase likeness. So in blessed interchange these two will be cause and effect, and secure the endless progress of the redeemed spirit towards the vision of Christ which never can behold all His Infinite Fullness, and the likeness to Christ which never can reproduce all his Infinite Beauty.

As a bit of glass when the light strikes it flashes into sunny glory, or as every poor little muddy pool on the pavement, when the sunbeams fall upon it, has the sun mirrored even in its shallow mud, so into your poor heart and mine the vision of Christ's glory will come, molding and transforming us to its own beauty. With unveiled face reflecting as a mirror does, the glory of the Lord, we "shall be changed into the same image." "We shall be like Him, for we shall see Him as He is."

Dear brethren! All begins with this: love Christ and trust Him, and you are a child of God. "And if children, then heirs, heirs of God, and joint heirs with Christ."

46

The Lost Sheep and the Seeking Shepherd

If a man hath a hundred sheep, and one of them be gone astray, doth he not leave the ninety-and-nine, and goeth into the mountains, and seeketh that which is gone astray?—Matthew 18:12

We find this simple parable, or germ of a parable, in a somewhat more expanded form, as the first of the incomparable three in the fifteenth chapter of Luke's Gospel. Perhaps our Lord repeated the parable more than once. It is an unveiling of His deepest heart, and therein a revelation of the very heart of God. It touches the deepest things in His relation to men, and sets forth thoughts of Him, such as man never dared to dream. It does all this by the homeliest image and by an appeal to the simplest instincts. The most prosaic shepherd looks for lost sheep, and everybody has peculiar joy over lost things found. They may not be nearly so valuable as things that were not lost. The unstrayed may be many, and the strayed be but one. Still there is a keener joy in the recovery of the one than in the unbroken possession of the ninety-nine. That feeling in a man may be only selfishness, but homely as it is—when the loser is God, and the lost are men, it becomes the means of uttering and illustrating that truth concerning God which no religion but the Cross has ever been bold enough to proclaim, that He cares most for the wanderers, and rejoices over the return of the one that went astray more than over the ninety-nine who never wandered.

There are some significant differences between this edition of the Parable and the form which it assumes in the Gospel according to Luke. There it is spoken in vindication of Christ's consorting with publicans and sinners; here it is spoken in order to point the lesson of not despising the least and most insignificant of the sons of men. There the seeking Shepherd is obviously Christ; here the seeking Shepherd is rather the Divine Father; as appears by the words of the next verse: "For it is not the will of your Father which is in Heaven, that one of these little ones should perish." There the sheep is lost; here the sheep goes astray. There the shepherd seeks till he finds; here the shepherd, perhaps, fails to find; for our Lord says; *"If so be that he finds it."*

But I am not about to venture on all the thoughts which this parable suggests, nor even to deal with the main lesson which it teaches. I wish merely to look at the two figures—the wanderer and the seeker.

I. First, then, let us look at that figure of the one wanderer.

Of course I need scarcely remind you that in the immediate application of the parable in Luke's Gospel, the ninety-nine were the respectable people who thought the publicans and harlots altogether too dirty to touch, and regarded it as very doubtful conduct on the part of this young Rabbi from Nazareth to be mixed up with people whom nobody with a proper regard for whited sepulchers would have anything to do with. To them He answers, in effect, I am a shepherd. That is my vindication. Of course a shepherd goes after and cares for the lost sheep. He does not ask about its worth, or anything else. He simply follows the lost because it is lost. It may be a poor little creature after all, but it is lost, and that is enough. And so He vindicates Himself to the ninety-nine: "You do not need Me, you are found. I take you on your own estimation of yourselves, and tell you that My mission is to the wanderers."

I do not suppose, however, that any of us have need to be reminded that upon a closer and deeper examination of the facts of the case, every hoof of the ninety-nine belonged to a stray sheep too; and that *all* men are wanderers in the wider application of the parable. Remembering then this universal application, I would point out two or three things about the condition of these strayed sheep, which include the whole race. The ninety-nine may shadow for us a number of beings in unfallen worlds immensely greater than even the multitudes of wandering souls that have lived here through weary ages of sin and tears, but that does not concern us now.

The first thought I gather from the parable is that all men are Christ's sheep. That sounds a strange thing to say. What? All these men and women who having run away from Him are plunged in sin, like sheep mired in a black bog, the scoundrels and the profligates, the scum and the outcasts of great cities like this; people with narrow foreheads, and blighted, blasted lives, the despair of our modern civilization, are they all His? And those great, wide-lying heathen lands where men know nothing of His name and of His love, are they all His too? Let Him answer, "Other sheep I have"—though they look like goats today—"which are not of this fold, them also must I bring, and they shall hear My voice." All men are Christ's, because He has been the Agent of Divine creation, and the grand words of the Hundredth Psalm are true about Him. "It is He that hath made us, and we are His. We are His people and the sheep of His pasture." They are His, because His sacrifice has bought them for His. Erring, straying, lost, they still belong to the Shepherd.

Notice next, the picture of the sheep as wandering. The word is, literally, "which *goeth* astray," not "which is gone astray." It pictures the process of wandering, not the result as accomplished. We see the sheep, poor, silly creature, not going anywhere in particular, only there is a sweet tuft of grass here, and it crops that; and here is a bit of ground where there is soft walking, and it goes there; and so, step by step, not meaning anything, not knowing where it is going, or that it *is* going anywhere; it goes, and goes, and goes, and at last it finds out that it is away from its beat on the hillside—for sheep keep to one bit of hillside generally, as any shepherd will tell you—and then it begins to bleat, and most helpless of creatures, fluttering and excited, rushes about amongst the thorns and brambles, or gets mired in some quag or other, and it will never find its way back of itself until somebody comes for it.

"So," says Christ to us, "there are a great many of you that do not mean to go wrong; you are not going anywhere in particular; you do not start on your course with any intentions either way, of doing either right or wrong, of keeping near God, or going away from Him, but you simply go where the grass is sweetest, or the walking easiest; and look at the end of it; where you have got to." You have got away from Him.

Now, if you take that series of parables in Luke 15. and read the stories there, you will see three different sides given of the process by which a man's heart strays away from God. There is the sheep that wanders. That is partly conscious, and voluntary, but in a large measure, simply yielding to inclination and temptation. Then there is the coin that trundles away under some piece of furniture, and is lost—that is a picture of the manner in which a man, without volition, almost mechanically sometimes, slides into sins and disappears as it were, and gets covered over with the dust of evil. And then there is the worst of all, the lad that had full knowledge of what he was doing. "I am going into a far off country; I cannot stand this any longer—all restraint and no liberty, and no power of doing what I like with my own; and always obliged to obey and be dependent on my father for my pocket money! Give me what belongs to me, for good and all, and let me go!" That is the picture of the worst kind of wandering, when a man knows what he is about, and looks at the merciful restraint of the law of God, and says: "No! I had rather be far away; and my own master, and not always be 'cribbed, cabined and confined' with these limitations."

The straying of the half-conscious sheep may seem more innocent, but it carries the poor thing away from the shepherd as completely as if it had been wholly intelligent and voluntary. Let us learn the lesson. In a world like this, if a man does not know very clearly where he is going, he is sure to go wrong. If you do not exercise a distinct determination to do God's will and to follow in His footsteps Who has set us an example; and if your main purpose is to get succulent grass to eat and soft places to walk in, you are certain before long to wander tragically from all that is right and noble and pure. It is no excuse for you to say, "I never meant it; I did not intend any harm; I only followed my own inclinations." "More mischief is wrought"—to the man himself, as well as to other people —"from want of thought than is wrought by" an evil will. And the sheep has strayed as effectually, though, when it set out on its journey, it never thought of straying. Young men and women beginning life remember and take this lesson.

But then there is another thing that I must touch for a moment. In the Revised Version you will find a very tiny alteration in the words of my text, which, yet, makes a large difference in the sense. The last clause of our text, as it stands in our Bible, is, "and seeketh that which is *gone* astray"; the Revised Version, more correctly, reads: "and seeketh that which *is going* astray."

Now, look at the difference in these two renderings. In the former, the process is represented as finished, in the correct rendering it is represented as going on. And that is what I would press on you, the awful, solemn, necessarily progressive character of our wanderings from God. A man never gets to the end of the distance that separates between him and the Father if his face is turned away from God. Every moment the separation is increasing. Two lines start from each other at the acutest angle and diverge further apart from each other the further they are produced, until at last the one may be up by the side of God's throne, and the other down in the deepest depths of hell. So accordingly my text carries with solemn pathos, in a syllable, the tremendous lesson: "The sheep is not gone, *going* astray." Ah! There are some of my hearers who are daily and hourly increasing the distance between themselves and their merciful Father.

Now the last thing here in this picture is the contrast between the description given of the wandering sheep in our text, and that in St. Luke. Here it is represented as wandering; there it is represented as lost. That is very beautiful and has a meaning often not noticed by hasty readers. Who is it that has lost it? We talk about the lost soul and the lost man, as if it were the man that had lost *himself*, and that is true, and a dreadful truth it is! But that is not the truth that is taught in this parable, and meant by us to be gathered from it. Who is it that has lost it? He to Whom it belonged.

That is to say, wherever a heart gets ensnared and entangled with the love of the treasures and pleasures of this life, and so departs in allegiance and confidence and friendship from the living God, there God the Father regards Himself as the poorer by the loss of one of His children, by the loss of one of His sheep. He does not care to possess you by the hold of mere creation and supremacy and rule. He wants you to love Him, and then He thinks He has you. And if you do not love Him, He thinks He has lost you. There is something in the Divine heart that goes out after His lost property. We touch here upon deep things that we cannot speak about intelligibly, only remember this, that what looks like self-regard in man is the purest love in God; and that there is nothing in the whole revelation which Christianity makes of the character of God more wonderful than this, that He judges that He has lost His child when His child has forgotten to love Him.

II. So much, then, for one of the great pictures in this text. I can spare but a sentence or two for the other—the picture of the Seeker. I said that in the one form of the parable it was more distinctly the Father, and in the other more distinctly the Son, who is represented as seeking the sheep. But these two do still coincide in substance, inasmuch as God's chief way of seeking us poor wandering sheep is through the work of His dear Son Jesus, and the coming of Christ is the Father's searching for His sheep in the "cloudy and dark day."

In these words of my text God leaves the ninety-nine and goes into the mountains where the wanderer is, and seeks him. And thus, couched in veiled form, is the great mystery of the Divine love, the Incarnation and Sacrifice of Jesus Christ our Lord. Here is the answer by anticipation to the sarcasm that is often leveled at evangelical Christianity: "You must think a good deal of human nature, and must have a very arrogant notion of the inhabitants of this little speck that floats in the great sea of the heavens, if you suppose that with all these millions of orbs, the Divine nature came down upon this little tiny molehill, and took your nature and died."

Yes! says Christ, not because man was so great, not because man was so valuable in comparison with the rest of creation—he was but one amongst ninety-nine unfallen and unsinful—but because he was so wretched, because he was so small, because he had gone so far away from God; *therefore,* the seeking love came after him, and would draw him to itself. That, I think, is answer enough.

And then, there is the difference between these two versions of the Parable in respect to their representation of the end of the seeking. The one says "seeks until He finds." Oh! The patient, incredible inexhaustibleness of the Divine love. God's long-suffering, if I may take such a metaphor, like a sleuth-hound will follow the object of its search through all its windings and doublings, until it comes up to it. So that great seeking Shepherd follows us through all the devious courses of our wayward wandering footsteps doubling back upon themselves, until He finds us. Though the sheep may increase its distance, the Shepherd follows. The further away we get the more tender His appeal; the more we stop our ears the louder the voice with which He calls. You cannot wear out Jesus Christ, you cannot exhaust the resources of His bounteousness, of His tenderness. However we may have been going wrong, however far we may have been wandering, however vehemently we may be increasing at every moment our distance from Him, He is coming after us, serene, loving, long-suffering, and will not be put away.

Dear friends! Would you only believe that a loving, living Person is really seeking you, seeking you by my poor words now, seeking you by many a providence, seeking you by His Gospel, by His Spirit, and will never be satisfied till He has found you in your finding Him and turning your soul to Him!

But, I beseech you, do not forget the solemn lesson drawn from the other form of the parable which is given in my text: *if so be that He find it*. There is a possibility of failure! What an awful power you have of burying yourself in the sepulcher as it were, of your own self-will, and hiding yourself in the darkness of your own belief! You can frustrate the seeking love of God. Some of you have done so—some of you have done so all your lives! Some of you, perhaps, at this moment are trying to do it, and consciously endeavoring to steel your hearts against some softening that may have been creeping over them while I have been speaking. Are you yielding to His seeking love, or wandering further and further from Him? He has come to find you. Let Him not seek in vain, but let the Good Shepherd draw you to Himself, when, lifted on the Cross, He giveth His life for the sheep. He will restore your soul and carry you back on His strong shoulder or in His bosom near His loving heart to the green pastures and the safe fold. There will be joy in His heart, more than over those who have never wandered; and there will be joy in the heart of the returning wanderer, such as they who had not strayed and learned the misery could never know, for, as the profound Jewish saying has it, "In the place where the penitents stand, the perfectly righteous cannot stand."

47

The Twofold Aspect of the Divine Working

The way of the Lord is strength to the upright; but destruction shall be to the workers of iniquity—Proverbs 10:29.

You observe that the words "shall be," in the last clause, are a supplement. They are quite unnecessary, and in fact they rather hinder the sense. They destroy the completeness of the antithesis between the two halves of the verse. If you leave them out, and suppose that the "way of the Lord" is what is spoken of in both clauses, you get a far deeper and fuller meaning. "The way of the Lord is strength to the upright; but destruction to the workers of iniquity." It is the same way which is strength to one man and ruin to another, and the moral nature of the man determines which it shall be to him. That is a penetrating word, which goes deep down. The unknown thinkers, to whose keen insight into the facts of human life we are indebted for this book of Proverbs, had pondered for many an hour over the perplexed and complicated fates of men, and they crystallized their reflections at last in this thought. They have in it struck upon a principle which explains a great many things, and teaches us a great many solemn lessons. Let us try to get a hold of what is meant, and then to look at some applications and illustrations of the principle.

I. First, then, let me just try to put clearly the meaning and bearing of these words. "The way of the Lord" means, sometimes in the Old Testament and sometimes in the New, religion, considered as the way in which God desires a man to walk. So we read in the New Testament of "the way" as the designation of the profession and practice of Christianity; and "the way of the Lord" is often used in the Psalms for the path which He traces for man by His sovereign will.

But that, of course, is not the meaning here. Here it means, not the road in which God prescribes that we should walk, but that road in which He Himself walks; or, in other words, the sum of the Divine action, the solemn footsteps of God through Creation, Providence, and History. His goings forth are from everlasting. His way is in the sea. His way is in the sanctuary. Modern language has a whole set of phrases which mean the same thing as the Jew meant by "the way of the Lord," only that God is left out. They talk about the "current of events," "the general tendency of things," "the laws of human affairs," and so on. I, for my part, prefer the old-fashioned "Hebraism." To many modern thinkers the whole drift and tendency of human affairs affords no sign of a person directing these. They hear the clashing and grinding of opposing forces, the thunder as of falling avalanches, and the moaning as of a homeless wind, but they hear the sound of no footfalls echoing down the ages. This ancient teacher had keener ears. Well for us if we share his faith, and see in all the else distracting mysteries of life and history, "the way of the Lord!"

But not only does the expression point to the operation of a personal Divine Will in human affairs, but it conceives of that operation as one, a uniform and consistent whole. However complicated, and sometimes apparently contradictory, the individual events were, there was a unity in them, and they all converged on one result. The writer does not speak of "ways," but of "the way," as a grand unity. It is all one continuous, connected, consistent mode of operation from beginning to end.

The author of this proverb believed something more about the way of the Lord. He believed that although it is higher than our way, still, a man can know something about it; and that whatever may be enigmatical, and sometimes almost heart-breaking, in it, one thing is sure—that, as we have been taught of late years in another dialect, it "makes for righteousness." Clouds and darkness are round about Him, but the Old Testament writers never falter in the conviction, which was the soul of all their heroism and the life blood of their religion, that in the hearts of the clouds and darkness, "justice and judgment are the foundations of His throne." The way of the Lord, says this old thinker, *is* hard to understand, very complicated, full of all manner of perplexities and difficulties, and yet on the whole the clear drift and tendency of the whole thing is discernible, and it is this: it is all on the side of good. Everything that is good, and everything that does good, is an ally of God's, and may be sure of the Divine favor and of the Divine blessing resting upon it.

And just because that is so clear, the other side is as true; the same way, the same set of facts, the same continuous stream of tendency, which is all with and for every form of good, is all against every form of evil. Or, as one of the Psalmists puts the same idea, "The eyes of the Lord are upon the righteous, and His ears are open unto their cry. The face of the Lord is against them that do evil." The same eye that beams in lambent love on "the righteous" burns terribly to the evil doer. "The face of the Lord" means the side of the Divine nature which is turned to us, and is manifested by His self-revealing activity, so that the expression comes near in meaning to "the way of the Lord," and the thought in both cases is the same, that by the eternal law of His Being, God's actions must all be for the good and against the evil.

They do not change, but a man's character determines which aspect of them he sees and has to experience. God's way has a bright side and a dark. You may take which you like. You can lay hold of the thing by which ever handle you choose. On the one side it is convex, on the other concave. You can approach it from either side, as you please. "The way of the Lord" must touch *your* "way." You cannot alter that necessity. Your path must either run parallel in the same direction with His, and then all His power will be an impulse to bear you onward; or it must run in the opposite direction, and then all His power will be for your ruin, and the collision with it will crush you as a ship is crushed like an eggshell, when it strikes an iceberg. You *can* choose which of these shall befall you.

And there is a still more striking beauty about the saying, if we give the full literal meaning to the word "strength." It is used by our translators, I suppose, in a somewhat archaic and peculiar signification, namely, that of a stronghold. At all events the Hebrew means a fortress, a place where men may live safe and secure; and if we take that meaning, the passage gains greatly in force and beauty. This "way of the Lord" is like a castle for the shelter of the shelterless good man, and behind those strong bulwarks he dwells impregnable and safe. Just as a fortress is a security to the garrison, and a frowning menace to the besiegers or enemies, so the "name of the Lord is a strong tower," and the "way of the Lord" is a fortress. If you choose to take shelter within it, its massive walls are your security and your joy. If you do not, they frown down grimly upon you, a menace and a terror. How differently, eight hundred years ago, Normans and Saxons looked at the square towers that were built all over England to bridle the inhabitants! To the one they were the sign of the security of their dominion; to the other they were the sign of their slavery and submission. Torture and prison houses they might become; frowning portents they necessarily were. "The way of the Lord" is a castle fortress to the man that does good, and to the man that does evil it is a threatening prison, which may become a hell of torture. It is "ruin to the workers of iniquity." I pray you, settle for yourself which of these it is to be to you.

II. And now let me say a word or two by way of application, or illustration, of these principles that are here.

First, let me remind you how the order of the universe is such that righteousness is life and sin is death. This universe and the fortress of men are complicated and strange. It is hard to trace any laws, except purely physical ones, at work. Still, on the whole, things do work so that goodness is blessedness, and badness is ruin. That is, of course, not always true in regard of outward things, but even about them it is more often and obviously true than we sometimes recognize. Hence all nations have their proverbs, embodying the generalized experience of centuries, and asserting that, on the whole, "honesty is the best policy," and that it is always a blunder to do wrong. What modern phraseology calls "laws of nature," the Bible calls "the way of the Lord"; and the manner in which these help a man who conforms to them, and hurt or kill him if he does not, is an illustration on a lower level of the principle of our text. This tremendous congeries of powers in the midst of which we live does not care whether we go with it or against it, only if we do the one we shall prosper, and if we do the other we shall very likely be made an end of. Try to stop a train, and it will run over you and murder you; get into it, and it will carry you smoothly along. Our lives are surrounded with powers, which will carry our messages and be our slaves if we know how to command nature by obeying it, or will impassively strike us dead if we do not.

Again, in our physical life, as a rule, virtue makes strength, sin brings punishment. "Riotous living" makes diseased bodies. Sins in the flesh are avenged in the flesh, and there is no need for a miracle to bring it about that he who sows to the flesh shall "of the flesh reap corruption." God entrusts the punishment of the breach of the laws of temperance and morality in the body to the "natural" operation of such breach. The inevitable connection between sins against the body and disease in the body, is an instance of the way of the Lord—the same set of principles and facts—being strength to one man and destruction to another. Hundreds of young men in Manchester—some of whom are listening to me now, no doubt— are killing themselves, or at least are ruining their health, by flying in the face of the plain laws of purity and self-control. They think that they must "have their fling," and "obey their instincts," and so on. Well, if they must, then another "must" will insist upon coming into play—and they must reap as they have sown, and drink as they have brewed, and the grim saying of this book about profligate young men will be fulfilled in many of them. "His bones are full of the iniquity of his youth, which shall lie down with him in the grave." Be not deceived, God is not mocked, and His way avenges bodily transgressions by bodily sufferings.

And then, in higher regions, on the whole, goodness makes blessedness, and evil brings ruin. All the powers of God's universe, and all the tenderness of God's heart are on the side of the man that does right. The stars in their courses fight against the man that fights against Him; and, on the other hand, in yielding thyself to the will of God and following the dictates of His commandments, "Thou shalt make a league with the beasts of the field, and the stones of the field shall be at peace with thee." All things serve the soul that serves God, and all war against him who wars against his Maker. The way of the Lord cannot but further and help all who love and serve Him. For them all things must work together for good. By the very laws of God's own being, which necessarily shape all His actions, the whole "stream of tendency without us makes for righteousness." In the one course of life we go with the stream of Divine activity which pours from the throne of God. In the other we are like men trying to row a boat *up* Niagara. All the rush of the mighty torrent will batter us back. Our work will be doomed to destruction, and ourselves to shame. Forever and ever to be good is to be well. An eternal truth lies in the facts that the same word "good" means pleasant and right, and that sin and sorrow are both called "evil." All sin is self-inflicted sorrow, and every "rogue is a round-about fool." So ask yourselves the question: "Is my life in harmony with, or opposed to, these Omnipotent laws which rule the whole field of life?"

Still further, this same fact of the two-fold aspect and operation of the one way of the Lord will be made yet more evident in the future. It becomes us to speak very reverently and reticently about the matter, but I can conceive it possible that the one manifestation of God in a future life may be in substance the same, and yet that it may produce opposite effects upon oppositely disposed souls. According to the old mystical illustration, the same heat that melts wax hardens clay, and the same apocalypse of the Divine nature in another world may to one man be life and joy, and to another man may be terror and despair. I do not dwell upon that; it is far too awful a thing for us to speak about to one another, but it is worth your taking to heart when you are indulging in easy anticipations that of course God is merciful and will bless and save everybody after he dies. Perhaps—I do not go any further than a perhaps—perhaps God cannot, and perhaps if a man has got himself into such a condition as it is possible for a man to get into, perhaps, like light upon a diseased eye, the purest beam may be the most exquisite pain, and the natural instinct may be to "call upon the rocks and the hills to fall upon them" and cover them up in a more genial darkness from that Face, to see which should be life and blessedness.

People speak of the future rewards and punishments as if they were given and inflicted by simple and Divine volition, and did not stand in any necessary connection with holiness on the other hand or with sin on the other. I do not deny that some portion of both bliss and sorrow may be of such a character. But there is a very important and wide region in which our actions here must automatically bring consequences hereafter of joy or sorrow, without any special retributive action of God's.

We have only to keep in view one or two things about the future which we know to be true, and we shall see this. Suppose a man with his memory of all his past life perfect, and his conscience stimulated to greater sensitiveness and clearer judgment, and all opportunities ended of gratifying tastes and appetites, whose food is in this world, while yet the soul has become dependent on them for ease and comfort. What more is needed to make a hell? And the supposition is but the statement of a fact. We seem to forget much; but when the waters are drained off all the lost things will be found at the bottom. Conscience will get dulled and sophisticated here. But the icy cold of death will wake it up, and the new position will give new insight into the true character of our actions. You see how often a man at the end of life has his eyes cleared to see his faults. But how much more will that be the case hereafter! When the rush of passion is past, and you are far enough from your life to view it as a whole, holding it at arm's length, you will see better what it looks like. There is nothing improbable in supposing that inclinations and tastes which have been nourished for a life time may survive the possibility of indulging them in another life, as they often do in this; and what can be worse than such a thirst for one drop of water, which never can be tasted more? These things are certain, and no more is needed to make sin produce, by necessary consequence, misery and ruin; while similarly, goodness brings joy, peace, and blessing.

But again, the self-revelation of God has this same double aspect.

"The way of the Lord" may mean His process by which He reveals His character. Every truth concerning Him may be either a joy or a terror to men. All His "attributes" are built into "a strong tower, into which the righteous runneth, and is safe," or else they are built into a prison and torture-house. So the thought of God may either be a happy and strengthening one, or an unwelcome one. "I remembered God, and was troubled," says one Psalmist. What an awful confession—that the thought of God disturbed him! The thought of God to some of us is a very unwelcome one, as unwelcome as the thought of a detective to a company of thieves. Is not that dreadful? Music is a torture to some ears; and there are people who have so alienated their hearts and wills from God that the Name which should be "their dearest faith" is not only their "ghastliest doubt," but their greatest pain. O, brethren! The thought of God and all that wonderful complex of mighty attributes and beauties which make His Name should be our delight, the key to all treasures, the end of all sorrows, our light in darkness, our life in death, our all in all. It is either that to us, or it is something that we would fain forget. Which is it to you?

Especially the Gospel has this double aspect. Our text speaks of the distinction between the righteous and the evil doers; but how to pass from the one class to the other, it does not tell us. The Gospel is the answer to that question. It tells us that though we are all "workers of iniquity," and must, therefore, if such a text as this were the last word to be spoken on the matter, share in the ruin which smites the opponent of the Divine will, we may pass from that class; and by simple faith in Him who died on the Cross for all workers of iniquity, may become of those righteous on whose side God works in all His way, who have all His attributes drawn up like an embattled army in their defense, and have His mighty name for their refuge.

As the very crown of the ways of God, the work of Christ and the record of it in the Gospel have most eminently this double aspect. God meant nothing but the salvation of the whole world when He sent us this Gospel. His "way" therein was pure, unmingled, universal love. We can make that great message untroubled blessing by simply accepting it. Nothing more is needed but to take God at His word, and to close with His sincere and earnest invitation. Then Christ's work becomes the fortress in which we are guarded from sin and guilt, from the arrows of conscience, and the fiery darts of temptation. But if not accepted, then it is not passive, it is not nothing. If rejected, it does more harm to a man than anything else can, just because, if accepted, it would have done him more good. The brighter the light, the darker the shadow.

The pillar which symbolized the presence of God sent down influences on either side; to the trembling crowd of the Israelites on the one hand, to the pursuing ranks of the Egyptians on the other; and though the pillar was one, opposite effects streamed from it, and it was "a cloud and darkness to them, but it gave light by night to these." Everything depends on which side of the pillar you choose to see. The ark of God, which brought dismay and death among false gods and their worshipers, brought blessing into the humble house of Obed Edom, the man of Gath, with whom it rested for three months before it was set in its place in the city of David. That which is meant to be the savor of life unto life must either be that or the savor of death unto death.

Jesus Christ is *something* to each of us. For you who have heard His name ever since you were children, your relation to Him settles your condition and your prospects, and molds your character. Either He is for you the tried Corner-stone, the sure Foundation, on which whosoever builds will not be confounded, or He is the stone of stumbling, against which whosoever stumbles will be broken, and which will crush to powder whomsoever it falls upon. "This Child is set for the rise" or for the fall of all who hear His name. He leaves no man at the level which He found him, but either lifts him up nearer to God, and purity and joy, or sinks him into an ever-descending pit of darkening separation from all these. Which is He to you? Something He must be—your strength or your ruin. If you commit your souls to Him in humble faith, He will be your Peace, your Life, your Heaven. If you turn from His offered grace, He will be your Pain, your Death, your Torture. "What maketh Heaven, that maketh hell." Which do you choose Him to be?

48

The Unwearied God and Wearied Men

The everlasting God, the Lord, the Creator of the ends of the earth; fainteth not neither is weary. . . . He giveth power to the faint. . . . Even the youths shall faint and be weary. . . . but they that wait upon the Lord shall renew their strength; they shall mount up with wings as eagles; they shall run, and not be weary; and they shall walk, and not faint—Isaiah 40:28–31.

This magnificent chapter is the prelude or overture to the grand music of the second part of the prophecies of Isaiah. Whatever differences of opinion there may be as to the date or the authorship of that half of the book, there can be no question that it forms a connected whole, and that it is spoken as if from the midst, and for the encouragement of the exiles in Babylon. Its first words are its keynote: "Comfort ye, comfort ye My people." That purpose is kept steadily in view throughout; and in this introductory chapter the prophet points as the only foundation of hope and consolation for Babylonian exiles, or for modern Englishmen, to that grand vision of the enthroned God "sitting on the circle of the earth, before Whom the inhabitants thereof are as grasshoppers.†

For nations and for individuals, in view of political disasters or of private sorrows, the only holdfast to which cheerful hope may cling is the old conviction, "The Lord God Omnipotent reigneth."

The final verses of this introductory chapter are remarkable for the frequent occurrence of "fainteth" and "is weary." They come in every sentence, and if we note their use we shall get the

---

† They build too low, who build beneath the sky.

essence of the hope and consolation which the prophet was anointed to pour into the wounds of his own people, and of every heavy-laden soul since then. Notice how, first, the prophet points to the unwearied God; and then his eyes drop from Heaven to the clouded, saddened earth, where there are the faint and the weak, and the strong becoming faint, and the youths fading and becoming weak with age. Then he binds together these two opposites—the unwearied God and the fainting man—in the grand thought that He is the Giving God, who bestows all His power on the weary. And see how, finally, he rises to the blessed conception of the wearied man becoming like the Unwearied God. "*They* shall run, and not be weary; they shall walk, and not faint."

So the recurrence of these two significant words shapes the flow of the prophet's thoughts. And my object now is simply to follow his meditations, and to gather for ourselves their abundant lessons of hope and encouragement.

I. We have, first, his appeal to the familiar thought of an unchangeable God, as the antidote to all despondency, and the foundation of all hope. "Hast thou not known; hast thou not heard that the everlasting God, the Lord, the Creator of the ends of the earth, fainteth not, neither is weary?"

To whom is he speaking? The words of the previous verse tell us, in which he addresses himself to Jacob, or Israel, who is represented as complaining: "My way is hid from the Lord." That is to say, he speaks to the believing, but despondent part of the exiles in Babylon; and to them He comes with this vehement question in our text, which implies that they were in danger, in their despondency, of practically forgetting the great thought. There is wonder in the question, there is a tinge of rebuke in it, and there is distinctly implied this: that whensoever there steals over our spirits despondency or perplexity about our own individual history, or about the peace and the fortunes of the Church or the world, the one sovereign antidote against gloom and low spirits, and the one secret of unbroken cheer and confidence, is to lift our eyes to the unwearied God. The prophet takes his stand upon the most elementary truths of Revelation. His appeal to His people is: What do you call God? You call Him the Lord, do you not? What do you mean by calling

Him that? Do you ever ask yourselves that question? You mean this if you mean anything: "He fainteth not, neither is wearied."

And that is a philological truth, and theological truth, and a truth all round. "Jehovah" is interpreted from the lips of God Himself: "I am that I am." That is the expression of what metaphysicians call absolute, underived, eternal Being, shaped and determined by none else, flowing from none else; eternal, lifted up above the fashions of time. Of Him men cannot say "He was," or "He will be," but only "He is"; by Himself, of Himself, forever changed.

The life of men and of creatures is like a river, with its source and its course and its end. The life of God is like the ocean, with joyous movement of tides and currents of life and energy and purpose, but ever the same, and ever returning upon Itself. "The Everlasting God" is "the Lord." Jehovah, the Unchanged, Unchangeable, Inexhaustible Being, spends, and is unspent; gives, and is none the poorer; works, and is never wearied; lives, and with no tendency to death in His life; flames with no tendency to extinction in the blaze. The bush burned and was not consumed: "He fainteth not, neither is weary."

And let me say, before I go further, here is a lesson for us to learn, of meditative reflection upon the veriest commonplaces of our religion. There is a tendency among us all to forget the indubitable, and to let our religious thought be occupied with the disputable and secondary parts of revelation, rather than with the plain deep verities which form its heart and center. The commonplaces of religion are the most important. Everybody needs air, light, bread and water. Dainties are for the few, but the table which our "religion" sometimes spreads for us is like that at a rich man's feast—plenty of rare dishes but never a bit of bread; plenty of wine and wineglasses, but not a tumbler-full of spring water to be had. There are parts of our faith that are of less importance. The most valuable parts are the well-worn truths, the familiar commonplaces that every little child knows.

Meditate, then, upon the things most surely believed, and ever meditate until the dry stick of the commonplace truth puts forth buds and blossoms like Aaron's rod. Every pebble that you kick with your foot, if thought about and treasured, contains the secret of the universe. The commonplaces of our faith are the food upon which our faith will most richly feed.

And so here, dear brethren, in the old, old truth, that we all take for granted, as being so true that we do not need to think about it, lies the source of all consolation, and hope for men, for churches, for the world. We all have times, depending on mood or circumstances, when things seem black and we are weary. This great truth will shine into our gloom, like a star into a dungeon. Are our hearts to tremble for God's truth today? Are we to share in the pessimist views of some faint-hearted and little-faith Christians? Surely as long as we can remember the name of the Lord, and His unwearied arm, we have nothing to do with fear or sadness for ourselves or for His Church, or for His world.

II. But we turn next to notice the unwearied God giving strength to wearied man.

The eye that looked hopefully and buoyantly up to Heaven, falls to earth and is shaded and sad as it sees the contrast between the serene and immortal strength above, and the burdened fainting souls here. "Even the youths shall faint and be weary, and the young man shall utterly fall." Earth knows no independent strength. All earthly power is limited in range and duration, and, by the very law of its being, is steadily tending to weakness.

But though that has a sad side, it has also a grand and blessed one. Man's needs are the open mouth—if I may so say—into which God puts His gifts. The more sad and pathetic the condition of feeble humanity by contrast with the strength, the immortal strength of God, the more wondrous that grace and power of His which are not contented with hanging there in the heavens above us, but bend right down to bless us, and to turn us into their own likeness. The low earth stretches, gray and sorrowful, flat and dreary, beneath the blue arched heaven, but the heaven stoops to encompass—ay! to touch it. "He giveth power to the faint, and to them that have no might He increaseth strength."

All creatural life digs its own grave. The youths shall faint with the weakness of physical decay, the weakness of burdened hearts, the weakness of consciously distracted natures, the weakness of agonizing conscience. They shall be weary with the weariness of dreary monotony, of uncongenial tasks, of long-continued toil, of hope deferred, of disappointed wishes, of bitter disenchantments, of learning the lesson that all is vanity—the weariness that creeps over us all as life goes on. All these are the occasions for the inward strength of God to manifest itself even in us; according to the great word that He spoke once and means ever: "My grace is sufficient for thee, and My strength is made perfect in weakness."

Notice the words preceding my text, "Lift up your eyes on high, and behold Who hath created these things, that bringeth out their host by number. He calleth then all by name by the greatness of His might; for that He is strong in power, not one faileth." There in those heavens, that unwearied strength brings forth their embattled hosts like a ranked army; and every one of the mighty orbs answers to the call of the Commander, like a legion to the muster-roll.

In the simple astronomy of those early times, there was no failure nor decay, nor change in the calm heavens. The planets, year by year, returned punctually to their places; and, unhasting and unresting, rolled upon their way. Weakness and weariness had no place there, and the power by which "the most ancient heavens" were upheld and maintained was God's unwearied might.

And then Israel, with singular self-tormenting ingenuity, having obeyed the prophet's injunction to "lift up the eyes on high" and look at the ordained order and undecaying bright strength there, finds in it all the exacerbation of the bitterness of his own lot. He complains that his path is hid, his course on earth seems so sad, and cloudy, and weary, as compared with the paths of those great stars that move without friction, effort, confusion, dust, or noise, while all these things—friction, effort, confusion, dust, noise—beset our little carts as we tug them along the dreary road of life.

But, says Isaiah, His power does not show itself so nobly up there as it does down here. It is not so much to keep the strong in their strength as to give strength to the weak. It is much to "preserve the stars from wrong," it is more to restore and to bring power to feeble men. It is much to uphold all those that are falling so that they may not fall; but it is more to raise up all those that have fallen and are bowed down. So, brethren, what God does with poor, weak men like us, when He lifts up our weakness and replenishes our weariness; pouring oil and wine into our wounds and a cordial into our lips, and sending us, with the joy of pardon, upon our road again—that is a greater thing than when He rolls Neptune in its mighty orbit round the central sun, or upholds with unwearied arms, from cycle to cycle, the circle of the heavens with all its stars. To give "power to the faint" is His divinest work.

Isaiah did not know—or, if he did, he knew it very dimly—what every Christian child knows: that the highest revelation of the power of Him that "fainteth not, neither is weary," is found in Him Who "being weary with His journey, sat thus on the well," and being worn out with the long work and excitement of a hard day slept the sleep of the laboring man, on the wooden pillow of the little boat amid the whistle of the tempest and the dash of the waves.

And Isaiah did not know—or if he did, he knew it very dimly and as from afar—that the highest fulfillment of his own word: "He giveth power to the faint, and to them that have no might He increaseth strength"—would be found when a gentle voice from amidst the woes of humanity said: "Come unto Me! All ye that labor and are heavy laden, and I will give you rest. Take My yoke upon you; and ye shall find rest unto your souls."

III. And so the last thing in these words is: the wearied man lifted to the level of the unwearied God, and to His likeness—"They that wait upon the Lord shall *renew their strength.*" That phrase means, of course, the continuous bestowment in unintermitting sequence of fresh gifts of power, as each former gift becomes exhausted, and more is required. Instant by instant, with unbroken flow, as golden shafts of light travel from the central sun, and each beam is linked with the source from which it comes by a line that stretches through millions and millions of miles, so God's gift of strength pours into us as we need. Grace abhors a vacuum, as nature does; and just as the endless procession of the waves rises on the beach, or as the restless network of the moonlight irradiation of the billows stretches all across the darkness of the sea, so that unbroken continuity of strength after strength gives grace for grace according to our need, and as each former supply is expended and used up, God pours Himself into our hearts anew.

That continuous communication leads to the perpetual youth of the Christian soul. For the words of the text, "They shall mount up with wings as eagles," might, perhaps more accurately be rendered, "They shall put forth their pinions as eagles"—the allusion being to the popular belief that in extreme old age the eagle molted, and renewed its feathers—that popular belief, which is referred to in Psalm 103 (which is itself later in date than this chapter). "Who satisfieth thy mouth with good things, so that thy youth is renewed like the eagle's."

According to the law of physical life, decaying strength and advancing years tame and sober and disenchant, and often make weary, because we become familiar with all things and the edge is taken off everything. Though these tell upon us whether we are Christians or not, and in some important respects tell upon us all alike, yet, if we are "waiting upon God," keeping our hearts near Him, living on His love, trying to realize His inward presence and His outstretched hand, then we shall have such a continuous communication of His grace, strength, and beauty, as that we shall grow younger as we grow older, and, as the good old Scotch psalm has it—

> In old age, when others fade,
> They fruit still forth shall bring.

"The oldest angels are the youngest," said Swedenborg. They that wait upon the Lord have drunk of the fountain of perpetual youth, for the buoyancy and the inextinguishable hope which are the richest possessions of youth may abide with them whose hopes are set on things beyond the sky.

And then, still further, my text goes on to portray the blessed consequences of this continuous communication of Divine strength in these words: "They shall run and not be weary." That is to say: this strength of God's poured into our hearts, if we wait upon Him, shall fit us for the moments of special hard effort, for the crises which require more than an ordinary amount of energy to be put forth. It will fit us too for the long, dreary hours which require nothing but keeping doggedly at monotonous duties, "They shall walk and not faint." It is a great deal easier to be up to the occasion in some shining moment of a man's life, when he knows that a supreme crisis has come, than it is to keep that high tone when plodding over all the dreary plateaus of uneventful, monotonous travel and dull duties. It is easier to run fast for five minutes than to grind along the dusty road for a day.

Many a vessel has stood the tempest and then has gone down in the harbor, because its timbers have been gnawed by dry rot. And many a man can do what is wanted in the trying moments, and yet make shipwreck of his faith in uneventful times—

> Like ships that have gone down at sea
> When heaven was all tranquillity.

Soldiers who could stand firm and strike with all their might in the hour of battle will fall asleep or have their courage ooze out at their fingers' ends when they have to keep solitary watch at their posts through a long winter's night. We have all a few moments in life of hard, glorious running, but we have days and years of walking, the uneventful discharge of small duties. We need strength for both; but, paradoxical as it my sound, we need it most for the multitude of smaller duties. We know where to get it. Let us keep close to "Christ, the Power of God," and open our hearts to the entering in of His unwearied strength. "Then shall the lame man leap as a hart," and we shall "run with patience the race that is set before us," if we look to Jesus, and follow in His steps.

49

Christ's Present Love and Its Great Act

Unto Him that loved us, and washed us from our sins in His own blood—Revelation 1:5.

There are two alterations made upon these words in the Revised Version which present the true reading of the original. They are very slight in themselves, but they make a considerable difference in the meaning. In the first clause we ought to read not "Unto Him that loved," but "Unto Him that loveth." The alteration in the Greek is about equivalent in magnitude to the alteration in English,—a "th" instead of a "d,"—but the deepening of the sense is wonderful. We are pointed not to a past love, however precious that may be, but to the ever present love, timeless and changeless, with which Jesus Christ holds the whole world in His grasp.

In the second clause the omission of one letter in the original turns "washed" into "loosed." Though that change does not materially affect the meaning, it substitutes another metaphor. Both are directly Apocalyptic. We read a great deal in this Book of Revelation of men washing their robes and making them white in the blood of the Lamb, and equivalent expressions. But we also read about men being redeemed and loosed from sin by the blood of the Lamb. The one expression regards sin as a stain from which we have to be cleansed; the other as a bondage or chain, from which we have to be set free. In the present case, the authority of manuscripts is in favor of "loosed," and the context, perhaps, slightly favors it also, as the contrast between emancipated slaves and "kings and priests," who are spoken of in the next clause, heightens the conception of the love which, not content with setting us free, goes on to place on our heads the miter of the priest and the diadem of the king.

Taking, then, the clauses thus read and rendered, and remembering that they form the first words of a doxology which bursts irrepressibly from the lips of the seer as he contemplates what he and his brethren owe to Jesus Christ, we have brought before us the ever-present, timeless love of Jesus, the great act which is the outcome and proof of His love, and the praise which it should call out.

I. First, then, consider the ever-present, timeless love of Jesus Christ.

John is writing these words of our text nearly half a century after Jesus Christ was buried. He is speaking to Asiatic Christians, Greeks and foreigners, most of whom had not been born when Jesus Christ died, none of whom had probably ever seen Him in this world. To these people he proclaims, not a past love, not a Christ that loved these Asiatic Greeks at the moment when John was writing, a Christ that loves us nineteenth century Englishmen at the moment when we read.

Another thing must be remembered. He who thus speaks is "the disciple whom Jesus loved." Is it not beautiful that he thus takes all his brethren up to the same level as himself, and delights to sink all that was special and personal in that which was common to all? He unites himself with his brethren, in that significant "us," which in effect says to the seven churches of Asia, "I stood no nearer the Master than you do. I had nothing which you may not possess if you will."

Of course all this is unintelligible, and has really no meaning at all unless we believe Christ to be Divine. Did he who wrote these words, "unto Him that *loveth* us," think of his Master as dead and in His grave half-a-century ago? Did he think of Him even as a man who lived still, no doubt in the spirit-world, and perhaps might be or perhaps might not be cognizant of what passed on earth? Could he have thought of Him as only human, and attributed to Him an actual love to men whom He had never seen in His earthly life? What exaggerated unreality it would be to look back over the centuries to the purest and noblest souls who gave themselves for their fellows, and to say that they, dead and gone, had any knowledge of or any love for men who had not been born till long after they had died! Why, the benevolence with which the warmest lover of his kind looks on the multitudes in far-off lands who are his own contemporaries, is much too tepid a sentiment to be called love, or to evoke answering thanks. Still less warm and substantial must he the ghost of the same feeling which such a man cherishes for coming generations. But if he is dead and gone, who would think of believing that his heart still throbbed with love for men on earth? The heart that can hold all the units of all successive generations, and so love each that each may claim a share in the grandest issues of its love, must be a Divine heart, for only there is there room for the millions to stand, all distinguishable and all enriched and blessed by that love. Is there anything but unmeaning exaggeration in this word of my text, anything that will do for a poor heart struggling with its own evil, and with the world's miseries and deviltries, to rest upon, unless we believe that Christ is Divine, and loves us with an everlasting love, because He is God manifest in the flesh?

That Divine nature of the Lord Jesus Christ is woven through the whole of the Book of Revelation, like a golden thread, and manifestly is needed to explain the fact of this solemn ascription of praise to Him, as well as to warrant the application of each clause of it to His work. For John to lift up his voice in this grand Doxology to Jesus Christ was blasphemy, if it was not adoration of Him as Divine. He may have been right or wrong in his belief, but surely the man who sang such a hymn to his Master believed Him to be the Incarnate Word, God manifest in the flesh. If we share that faith, we can believe in Christ's present love to us all. It is no misty sentiment or rhetorical exaggeration to believe that every man, woman, and child that is or shall be on the earth till the end of time has a distinct place in His heart, and is an object of His knowledge and of His love.

This one word, then, is the revelation to us of Christ's love, as unaffected by time. Our thoughts are carried by it up into the region where dwells the Divine nature, above the various phases of the fleeting moments which we call past, present, and future. These are but the lower layer of clouds which drive before the wind, and melt from shape to shape. He dwells above in the naked, changeless blue.

As of all His nature, so, blessed be His name, of His love; we can be sure that time cannot bound it. We say not, "It was," or "It will be," but "It is." Our text proclaims the changeless, timeless, majestic present of that love which burns, and is not consumed, but glows with as warm a flame for the latest generations as for those men who stood within the reach of its rays while He was on earth. "I am the first and the last," says Christ, and His love partakes of that eternity. It is like a golden fringe which keeps the web of creation from raveling out. Before the earliest of creatures was this love. After the latest it shall be. It circles them all around, and locks them all in its enclosure. It is the love of a Divine heart, for it is the same yesterday, and today, and forever. It is the love of a human heart, for that heart could shed its blood, to loose us from our sins. Shall we not take this love for ours? The foundation of all our hopes and all our joys, and all our strength in our work should be this firm conviction, that we are wrapped about by, and evermore in, an endless ocean of the present Divine love of the present loving Christ.

Then, further, that love is not disturbed or absorbed by multitudes. He loveth *us*, says John to these Asiatic Christians; and he speaks to all ages and people. The units of each generation and of every land have a right to feel themselves included in that word, and every human being is entitled to turn the "us" into "me." For no crowds block the access to His heart, nor empty the cup of His love before it reaches the thirsty lips on the farthest outskirts of the multitude. When He was here on earth, the multitude thronged Him and pressed Him, but the wasted forefinger of one poor timid woman could reach the garment's hem for all the crowd. He recognized the difference between the touch that had sickness and supplication in it and the jostlings of the mob, and His healing power passed at once to her who needed and asked it, though so many were surging round Him. So He still knows and answers the silent prayer of the loving and the needy heart. Howsoever tremulous and palsied the finger; howsoever imperfect and ignorant the faith, His love delights to answer and to over answer it, as He did with that woman, who not only got the healing which she craved, but bore away besides the consciousness of His love and the cleansing of her sins. He does with all the multitude who hang on Him as he did when he fed the thousands. He ranks them all on the grass, and in order ministers to each his portion in due season. We do not jostle each other. There is room in that heart of Christ for us all.

> The glorious sky, embracing all,
>> Is like its Maker's love;
> Wherewith encircled, great and small
>> In peace and order move.

Every star has its separate place in the great round, "and He calleth them all by name," and holds them in His mind. So we, and all our brethren, have each our own orbit and our station in the Heaven of Christ's heart, and it embraces, distinguishes, and sustains us all, "Unto Him that loveth *us.*"

Another thought may be suggested, too, of how this present timeless love of Christ is unexhausted by exercise, pouring itself ever out, and ever full notwithstanding. They tell us that the sun is fed by impact of fuel from without, and that the day will come when its furnace-flames shall be quenched into gray ashes. But this love is fed by no contributions from without, and will outlast the burnt-out sun and gladden the ages of ages forever. All generations, all thirty lips and ravenous desires, may slake their thirst and satisfy themselves at that great fountain, and it shall not sink one inch in its marble basin. Christ's love, after all creatures have received from it, is as full as at the beginning; and unto us upon whom the ends of the earth are come, this precious and all-sufficing love pours as full a tide as when first it blessed that little handful that gathered round about Him on earth. Other rivers run shallow as they broaden, but this "river of God" is as deep when it spreads over the world as if it were poured through the narrows of one heart.

Again, it is a love unchilled by the sovereignty and glory of His exaltation. There is a wonderful difference between the Christ of the Gospels and the Christ of the Revelation. People have exaggerated the difference into contradiction, and then, running to the other extreme others have been tempted to deny that there was any. But one thing is not different. The Nature behind the circumstances is the same. The Christ of the Gospels is the Christ in His lowliness, bearing the weight of man's sins; the Christ of the Apocalypse is the Christ in His loftiness, ruling over the world and time. But it is the same Christ. The one is surrounded by weakness and the other is girded with strength, but it is the same Christ. The one is treading the weary road of earth, the other is sitting at the right hand of God the Father Almighty; but it is the same Christ. The one is the "Man of sorrows and acquainted with grief," the other is the Man glorified and a Companion of Divinity; but it is the same Christ. The hand that holds the seven stars is as loving as the hand that was laid in blessing upon little children. The face that is as the sun shining in its strength beams with as much love as when it drew publicans and harlots to His feet. The breast that is girt with the golden girdle is the same breast upon which John leaned his happy head. The Christ is the same, and the love is unaltered. From the midst of the glory and the sevenfold brilliancy of the light which is inaccessible, the same tender heart bends down over us that bent down over all the weary and the distressed when He Himself was weary; and we can lift up our eyes above stars, and systems, and material splendors, right up to the central point of the universe, where the throned Christ is, and see "Him that loveth us"—even *us!*

II. Notice, secondly the great act in time which is the outcome and proof of this endless love.

"He loosed us from our sins by His own blood." The metaphor is that of bondage. "He that committeth sin is the slave of sin." Every wrong thing that we do tends to become our master and our tyrant. We are held and bound in the chains of our sins. The awful influence of habit, the dreadful effect of a corrupted conscience, the power of regretful memories, the pollution arising from the very knowledge of what is wrong—these are some of the strands out of which the ropes that bind us are twisted. We know how tight they grip. I am speaking now, no doubt, to people who are as completely manacled and bound by evils of some sort— evils of flesh, of sense, of lust, of intemperance, of pride, and avarice, and worldliness, of vanity, and frivolity, and selfishness—as completely manacled as if there were iron gyves upon their wrists, and fetters upon their ankles.

You remember the old story of the prisoner in his tower, delivered by his friend, who sent a beetle to crawl up the wall, fastening a silken thread to it, which had a thread a little heavier attached to the end of that, and so on, and so on, each thickening in diameter until the got to a cable. That is how the devil has got hold of a great many of us. He weaves round us silken threads to begin with, slight, as if we could break them with a touch of our fingers, and they draw after them, as certainly as destiny, "at each remove a" thickening "chain," until, at last, we are tied and bound, and our captor laughs at our mad plunges for freedom, which are as vain as a wild bull's in the hunter's net. Some of you have made an attempt at shaking off sin—how have you got on with it? As a man would do who with a file made out of an old soft knife tried to work through his fetters. He might make a little impression on the surface, but he would mostly scratch his own skin, and wear his own fingers, and to very little purpose.

But the chains can be got off. Christ looses them by "His blood." Like corrosive acid, that blood, falling upon the fetters, dissolves them, and the prisoner goes free, emancipated by the Son. That death has power to deliver us from the guilt and penalty of sin. The Bible does not give us the whole theory of an atonement, but the fact is plainly proclaimed that Christ died for us, and that the bitter consequences of sin in their most intense bitterness, even that separation from God which is the true death, were borne by Him for our sakes, on our account, and in our stead. By the shedding of His blood is remission of our sins. His blood looses the fetters of our sins, inasmuch as His death, touching our hearts, and also bringing to us new powers through His Spirit, which is shed forth in consequence of His finished work, frees us from the power of sin, and brings into operation new powers and motives which deliver us from our ancient slavery. The chains which bound us shrivel and melt as the ropes that bound the Hebrew youths in the fire, before the warmth of His manifested love and the glow of His Spirit's power.

I beseech each heart that listens to me now to yield to the redeeming power of the blood which cleanses from all sin. You cannot deliver yourselves from the slavery of sin, but Jesus Christ, by His own blood, has delivered the whole world, and you amongst the rest. He did it because he loves us, and He has done it once and for all.

The one act in time, which is the proof and outcome of His love, is this deliverance from sin by His blood. What a pathos that thought gives to His death! It was the willing token of His love. He gave Himself up to the cross of shame because He held us in His heart. There was no reason for His death, but only that "He loveth us." And with what a solemn power that thought invests His death! Even His love could not reach its end by any other means—not by mere good will, nor by any small sacrifice. Nothing short of the bitter Cross could accomplish His heart's desire for men. There was a needs be for His death, but the necessity was, if we may so say, of His own making. He must die, for He loved the world so much that He must accept the mission of the Father, who so loved it that He sent the Son to die. His love in His death embraced us each, as it does today. Each man of all the race may be quite sure that he had a place in that Divine-human love of Christ's as He hung upon the Cross. I may take it all to myself, as the whole rainbow is mirrored on each eye that looks.

We have no proof of Christ's love to us, and no reason for loving Him, except His death for our sins. But if we believe, as John believed, that He tasted death for every man, and that by that death every poor, sin-mastered soul that trusts in Him may shake off the demon that sits upon his shoulders and be free from the guilt, the punishment, and the tyranny of sin, then we need not despair, however obstinate may be the conflict, but go into it with good heart, happy in the love and confident in the power of the Eternal Lover and Purifier of our souls, whose blood looses us from our sins, whose grace makes us kings and priests to God.

III. One final word as to the praise which should be our answer to this great love.

Irrepressible gratitude bursts into a doxology from John's lips, even here at the beginning of the book, as the seer thinks of the love of Christ, and all through the Apocalypse we hear the shout of praise from earth or Heaven. The book which closes the New Testament "shuts up all with a sevenfold chorus of hallelujahs and harping symphonies," as Milton says, in his stately diction, and may well represent for us in that perpetual cloud of incense rising up fragrant to the throne of God and of the Lamb, the unceasing love and thanksgiving which should be man's answer to Christ's love and sacrifice.

Our praise of Christ is but the expression of our recognition of Him for what He is, and our delight in and love towards Him. Such love, which is but our love speaking, is all which He asks. Love can only be paid by love. Any other recompense offered to it is coinage of another currency, that is not current in its kingdom. The only recompense that satisfies love is its own image reflected in another heart. That is what Jesus Christ wants of you. He does not want your admiration, your outward reverence, your lip homage, your grudging obedience. His heart hungers for more and other gifts from you. He wants your love, and is unsatisfied without it. He desired it so much that he was willing to die to procure it, as if a mother might think "My children have been cold to me while I lived; perhaps, if I were to give my life to help them, their hearts might melt." All the awful expenditure of love stronger than death is meant to draw forth our love. He comes to each of us, and pleads with us for our hearts, wooing us to love Him by showing us all which He has done for us, and all which He will do. Surely the Cross borne for us should move us. Surely the throne prepared for us should touch us into gratitude.

That Lord Who died and lives dwells now in the Heavens, the center of a mighty chorus and tempest of praise which surges round His throne, loud as the voice of many waters, and sweet as harpers harping on their harps. The main question for us is, Does He hear our voice in it? Are our lips shut? Are our hearts cold? Do we meet His fire of love with icy indifference? Do we repay His sacrifice with unmoved self-regard, and meet His pleading with closed ears? "Do ye thus requite the Lord, O foolish people and unwise?"

Take this question home to your heart, How much owest thou unto thy Lord? He has loved thee, has given Himself for thee, and His sacrifice will unlock the fetters and set thee free. Will you be silent in the presence of such transcendent mercy? Shall we not rather, moved by His dying love, and joyful in the possession of deliverance through His Cross, lift up our voices and hearts in a perpetual song of praise, to which our lives of glad obedience shall be as perfect music accompanying noble words, "Unto Him that loveth us, and looseth us from our sins by His own blood"?

50

The Cross, the Glory of Christ and God

Therefore, when He was gone out, Jesus said, Now is the Son of Man glorified, and God is glorified in Him. If God be glorified in Him, God shall also glorify Him in Himself, and shall straightway glorify Him —John 13:31, 32.

There is something very weird and awful in the brief note of time with which the Evangelist sends Judas on his dark errand. "He . . . went immediately out, and it was night." Into the darkness that dark soul went. That hour was "the power of darkness," the very keystone of the black arch of man's sin, and some shadow of it fell upon the soul of Christ Himself.

In immediate connection with the departure of the traitor comes this singular burst of triumph in our text. The Evangelist emphasizes the connection by that: "*Therefore,* when he was gone out, Jesus said." There is a wonderful touch of truth and naturalness in that connection. The traitor was gone. His presence had been a restraint; and now that that "spot in their feast of charity" had disappeared, the Master felt at ease; and like some stream, out of the bed of which a black rock has been taken, His words flow more freely. How intensely real and human the narrative becomes when we see that Christ, too, felt the oppression of an uncongenial presence, and was relieved and glad at its removal! The departure of the traitor evoked these words of triumph in another way, too. At his going away, we may say, the match was lit that was to be applied to the train. He had gone out on his dark errand, and that brought the Cross within measurable distance of our Lord. Out of a new sense of its nearness He speaks here. So the note of time not only explains

471

to us why our Lord spoke, but puts us on the right track for understanding His words, and makes any other interpretation of them than one impossible. What Judas went to do was the beginning of Christ's glorifying. We have here, then, a triple glorification—the Son of Man glorified in His Cross; God glorified in the Son of Man; and the Son of Man glorified in God. Let us look at these three things for a few moments now.

I. First, we have here the Son of Man glorified in His Cross.

The words are a paradox. Strange, that at such a moment, when there rose up before Christ all the vision of the shame and the suffering, the pain and the death, and the mysterious sense of abandonment, which was worse than them all, He should seem to stretch out His hands to bring the Cross nearer to Himself, and that His soul should fill with triumph!

There is a double aspect under which our Lord regarded His sufferings. On the one hand we mark in Him an unmistakable shrinking from the Cross, the innocent shrinking of His manhood expressed in such words as "I have a baptism to be baptized with, and how am I straitened till it be accomplished"; and in such incidents as the agony in Gethsemane. And yet, side by side with that, not overcome by it, but not overcoming it, there is the opposite feeling, the reaching out almost with eagerness to bring the Cross nearer to Himself. These two lie close by each other in His heart. Like the pellucid waters of the Rhine and the turbid stream of the Moselle, that flow side by side over a long space, neither of them blending discernibly with the other, so the shrinking and the desire were contemporaneous in Christ's mind. Here we have the triumphant anticipation rising to the surface, and conquering for a time the shrinking.

Why did Christ think of His Cross as a glorifying? The New Testament generally represents it as the very lowest point of His degradation; John's Gospel always represents it as the very highest point of His glory. And the two things are both true; just as the zenith of our sky is the nadir of the sky for those on the other side of the world. The same fact which in one aspect sounds the very lowest depth of Christ's humiliation, in another aspect is the very highest culminating point of His glory.

How did the Cross glorify Christ? In two ways. It was the revelation of His heart; it was the throne of His sovereign power.

It was the revelation of His heart. All His life long He had been trying to tell the world how much He loved it. His love had been, as it were, filtered by drops through His words, through His deeds, through His whole demeanor and bearing; but in His death it comes in a flood, and pours itself upon the world. All His life long He had been revealing His heart, through the narrow rifts of His deeds, like some slender lancet windows; but in His death all the barriers are thrown down, and the brightness blazes out upon men. All through His life He had been trying to communicate His love to the world, and the fragrance came from the box of ointment exceeding precious, but when the box was broken the house was filled with the odor.

For Him to be known was to be glorified. So pure and perfect was He that revelation of His character and glorification of Himself were one and the same thing. Because His Cross reveals to the world for all time, and for eternity, too, a love which shrinks from no sacrifice, a love which is capable of the most entire abandonment, a love which is diffused over the whole surface of humanity and through all the ages, a love which comes laden with the richest and the highest gifts, even the turning of selfish and sinful hearts into its own pure and perfect likeness, therefore does He say, in contemplation of that Cross which was to reveal Him for what He was to the world, and to bring His love to every one of us, "Now is the Son of Man glorified."

We can fancy a mother, for instance, in the anticipation of shame, and ignominy, and suffering, and sorrow, and death which she encounters for the sake of some prodigal child, forgetting all the ignominy, and the shame, and the suffering, and the sorrow, and the death, because all these are absorbed in the one thought: "If I bear them, my poor, wandering, rebellious child will know at last how much I loved him." So Christ yearns to impart the knowledge of Himself to us, because by that knowledge we may be won to His love and service; and hence when He looks forward to the agony, and contumely, and sorrow of the close, every other thought is swallowed up in this one: "They shall be the means by which the

whole world will find out how deep My heart of love to it was."
Therefore does He triumph and say, "Now is the Son of Man glorified."

Still further, He regards His Cross as the means of His glorifying, because it is His throne of saving power. The paradoxical words of our text rest upon His profound conviction that in His death He was about to put forth a mightier and Diviner power than ever he had manifested in His life. They are the same in effect and in tone as the great words: "I, if I be lifted up, will draw all men unto Me." Now I want you to ask yourselves one question: In what sense is Christ's Cross Christ's glorifying, unless His Cross bears an altogether different relation to His life from what the death of a great teacher or benefactor ordinarily bears to His? It is impossible that Christ could have spoken such words as these of my text if He had simply thought of His death as a Plato or a John Howard might have thought of his, as being the close of his activity for the welfare of his fellows. Unless Christ's death has in it some substantive value, unless it is something more than the mere termination of His work for the world, I see not how the words before us can be interpreted. If His death is His glorifying, it must be because in that death something is done which was not completed by the life, however fair; by the words, however wise and tender; by the works of power, however restorative and healing. Here is something more than these present. What more? This more, that His Cross is the propitiation for the sins of the whole world. He is glorified therein, not as a Socrates might be glorified by his calm and noble death; not because nothing in His life became Him better than the leaving of it; not because the page that tells the story of His passion is turned to by us as the tenderest and most sacred in the world's records; but because in that death He wrestled with and overcame our foes, and because, like the Jewish hero of old, dying, He pulled down the house which our tyrants had built, and overwhelmed them in its ruins. "Now is the Son of Man glorified."

And so, brethren, there blend, in that last act of our Lord's—for His death was His act—in strange fashion, the two contradictory ideas of glory and shame; like some sky, all full of dark thunderclouds, and yet between them the brightest blue and the blazing sunshine. In the Cross Death crowns Him the Prince of Life, and His Cross is His throne. All His life long He was the Light of the World, but the very noontide hour of His glory was that hour when the shadow of eclipse lay over all the land, and He hung on the Cross dying in the dark. At His eventide "it was light." "He endured the Cross, despising the shame"; and lo! The shame flashed up into the very brightness of glory, and the ignominy and the suffering became the jewels of His crown. "Now is the Son of Man glorified."

II. Now let us turn for a moment to the second of the three-fold glorifications that are set forth here: God glorified in the Son of Man.

The mystery deepens as we advance. That God shall be glorified in a man is not strange, but that He shall be so glorified in the eminent and especial fashion in which it is spoken of here, is strange; and stranger still when we think that the act in which He was glorified was the death of an innocent Man. If God, in any special and eminent manner, is glorified in the Cross of Jesus Christ, that implies, as it seems to me, two things at all events—many more which I have not time to touch upon, but two things very plainly. One is that God was in Christ, in some singular and eminent manner. If all His life was a continual manifestation of the Divine character, if Christ's words were the Divine wisdom, if Christ's compassion was the Divine pity, if Christ's lowliness was the Divine gentleness, if His whole human life and nature were the brightest and clearest manifestation to the world of what God is, we can understand that the Cross was the highest point of the revelation of the Divine nature to the world, and so was the glorifying of God in Him. But if we take any lower view of the relation between God and Christ, I know not how we can acquit these words of our Master of the charge of being a world too wide for the facts of the case.

The words involve, as it seems to me, not only that idea of a close, unique union and indwelling of God in Christ, but they involve also this other: that these sufferings bore no relation to the deserts of the person who endured them. If Christ, with His pure and perfect character—the innocency and nobleness of which all that read the Gospels admit—if Christ suffered so; if the highest virtue that was ever seen in this world brought no better wages than shame and spitting and the Cross; if Christ's life and Christ's death are simply a typical example of the world's treatment of its greatest benefactors; then, if they have any bearing at all on the character of God, they cast a shadow rather than a light upon the Divine government, and become not the least formidable of the difficulties and knots that will have to be untied hereafter before it shall be clear that God did everything well. But if we can say, "He hath borne our griefs and carried our sorrows"; if we can say "God was in Christ reconciling the world to Himself"; if we can say that His death was the death of Him Whom God had appointed to live and die for us, and to bear our sins in His own body on the tree, then, though deep mysteries come with the thought, still we can see that, in a very unique manner, God is glorified and exalted in His death.

For, if the dying Christ be the Son of God dying for us, then the Cross glorifies God, because it teaches us that the glory of the Divine character is the Divine love. Of wisdom, or of power, or of any of the more "majestic" attributes of the Divine nature, that weak Man, hanging dying on the Cross, was a strange embodiment; but if the very heart of the Divine brightness be the pure white fire of love; if there be nothing Diviner in God than His giving of Himself to His creatures; if the highest glory of the Divine nature be to pity and to bestow, then the Cross upon which Christ died towers above all other revelations as the most awful, the most sacred, the most tender, the most complete, the most heart-touching, the most soul-subduing manifestation of the Divine nature; and stars and worlds, and angels and mighty creatures, and things in the heights and things in the depths, to each of which have been entrusted some broken syllables of the Divine character to make known to the world, dwindle and fade before the brightness, the lambent, gentle brightness that beams out from the Cross of Christ which proclaims—God is love, is pity, is pardon.

And is it not so—is it not so? Is not the thought that has flowed from Christ's Cross through Christendom about what our Father in Heaven is, the highest and the most blessed that the world has ever had? Has it not scattered doubts that lay like mountains of ice upon man's heart? Has it not swept the heavens clear of clouds that wrapped it in darkness? Has it not delivered men from the dreams of gods angry, god capricious, gods vengeful, gods indifferent, gods simply mighty, and vast and awful, and unspeakable? Has it not taught us that love is God, and God is love; and so brought to the whole world the true Gospel, the Gospel of the grace of God? In that Cross the Father is glorified.

III. Now, lastly, we have here the Son of Man glorified in the Father.

The mysteries and the paradoxes seem to deepen as we advance. "If God be glorified in Him, God shall also glorify Him in Himself, and shall straightway glorify Him." Do these words sound to you as if they expressed no more than the confidence of a good man, who, when he was dying, believed that he would be accepted of a loving Father, and would be at rest from his sufferings? To me they seem to say infinitely more than that. "He shall also glorify Him in Himself." Mark that—"in Himself." That is the obvious antithesis to what has been spoken about in the previous clause, a glorifying which consisted in a manifestation to the external universe, whereas this is a glorifying within the depths of the Divine nature. And the best commentary upon it is our Lord's own words: "Father! Glorify Thou Me with the glory which I had with Thee before the world was." We get a glimpse, as it were, into the very center of the brightness of God; and there, walking in that beneficent furnace, we see "One like unto the Son of Man." Christ anticipates that, in some profound and unspeakable sense, He shall, as it were, be caught up into Divinity, and shall dwell, as indeed He did dwell from the beginning, "in the bosom of the Father." "He shall glorify Him in Himself."

But then mark, still further, that this reception into the bosom of the Father is given to the Son of Man. That is to say, the Man Christ Jesus, the Son of Mary, the Brother of us all, "bone of our bone and flesh of our flesh," the very Person that walked upon earth and dwelt amongst us—He is taken up into the heart of God, and in His manhood enters into that same glory, which, from the beginning, the Eternal Word had with God.

And still further, not only have we here set forth, in most wondrous language, the reception and incorporation, if we may use such words, into the very center of Divinity, as granted to the Son of Man, but we have that glorifying set forth as commencing immediately upon the completion of God's glorifying by Christ upon the Cross. "He shall straightway glorify Him." At the instant, then, that He said, "It is finished," and all that the Cross could do to glorify God was done, at that instant there began, with not a pin point of interval between them, God's glorifying of the Son in Himself. It began in that Paradise into which we know that upon that day He entered. It was manifested to the world when He raised Him from the dead and gave Him glory. It reached a still higher point when they brought Him near unto the Ancient of Days, and ascending up on high, a dominion and throne and a glory were given to Him which last now, while the Son of Man sits in the Heaven on the Throne of His glory, wielding the attributes of Divinity, and administering the laws of the universe and the mysteries of providence. It shall rise to its highest manifestation before an assembled world, when He shall come in His glory, and before Him shall be gathered all nations.

This, then, was the vision that lay before the Christ in that upper room, the vision of Himself glorified in His extreme shame because His Cross manifested His love and His saving power; of God glorified in Him above all other of His acts of manifestation when He died on the Cross, and revealed the very heart of God; and of Himself glorified in the Father when, exalted high above all creatures, He sitteth upon the Father's throne and rules the Father's realm.

And yet from that high, and, to us, inaccessible and all but inconceivable summit of His elevation, He looks down ready to bless each poor creature here, toiling and moiling amidst sufferings, and meannesses, and commonplaces, and monotony, if we will only put our trust in Him, and love Him, and see the brightness of the Father's face in Him. He cares for us all; and if we will but take Him as our Savior, His all-prevalent prayer, presented within the veil for us, will certainly be fulfilled at last: "Father, I will that they also whom Thou hast given Me may be with Me where I am, that they may behold My glory."

51

The Greatest in the Kingdom, and Their Reward

He that receiveth a prophet in the name of a prophet shall receive a prophet's reward, and he that receiveth a righteous man in the name of a righteous man shall receive a righteous man's reward. And whosoever shall give to drink unto one of these little ones, a cup of cold water only, in the name of a disciple, verily I say unto you he shall in no wise lose his reward—Matthew 10:41, 42.

There is nothing in these words to show whether they refer to the present or to the future. We shall probably not go wrong if we regard them as having reference to both. For all godliness has "promise of the life that now is, as well as of that which is to come," and *"in* keeping God's commandments," as well as *for* keeping them, "there is great reward," a reward realized in the present, even although death holds the keys of the treasure house in which the richest rewards are stored. No act of holy obedience here is left without foretastes of joy, which, though they be but "brooks by the way," contain the same water of life which hereafter swells to an ocean.

Some people tell us that it is defective morality in Christianity to bribe men to be good by promising them Heaven, and that he who is actuated by such a motive is selfish. Now that fantastic and over-strained objection may be very simply answered by two considerations; self-regard is not selfishness, and Christianity does not propose the future reward as the motive for goodness. The motive for goodness is love to Jesus Christ; and if ever there was a man who did acts of Christian goodness only for the sake of what he would get by them, the acts were not Christian goodness, because the motive was wrong. But it is a piece of fastidiousness to forbid us to reinforce the great Christian motive, which is love to Jesus Christ, by the thought of the recompense of reward. It is a stimulus and an encouragement, not the motive for goodness. This text shows us that it is a subordinate motive, for it says that the reception of a prophet, or of a righteous man, or of "one of these little ones," which is rewardable, is the reception "in the name of" a prophet, a disciple, and so on, or, in other words, recognizing the prophet, or the righteous man, or the disciple for what he is, and because he is that, and not because of the reward, receiving him with sympathy and solace and help.

So, with that explanation, let us look for a moment or two at these very remarkable words of our text.

I. The first thing which I wish to observe in them is the three classes of character which are dealt with—"prophet," "righteous man," "these little ones."

Now the question that I would suggest is this: Is there any meaning in the order in which these are arranged? If so, what is it? Do we begin at the bottom, or at the top? Have we to do with an ascending or with a descending scale? Is the prophet thought to be greater than the righteous man, or less? Is the righteous man thought to be higher than the little one, or to be lower? The question is an important one, and worth considering.

Now, at first sight, it certainly does look as if we had here to do with a descending scale, as if we began at the top and went downwards. A prophet, a man honored with a distinct commission from God to declare His will, is, in certain very obvious respects, loftier than a man who is not so honored, however pure and righteous he may be. The dim and venerable figures, for instance, of Isaiah and Jeremiah, tower high above all their contemporaries; and the godly men who hung upon their lips, like Baruch on Jeremiah's, and others, felt themselves to be, and were, inferior to them. And, in like manner, the little child who believes in Christ may seem to be insignificant in comparison with the prophet with his God-touched lips, or the righteous man of the old dispensation with his austere purity; as a humble violet may seem by the side of a rose with its heart of fire, or a white lily regal and tall. But one remembers that Jesus Christ Himself declared that "the least of the little ones" was greater than the greatest who had gone before; and it is not at all likely that He who has just been saying that whosoever received His followers received Himself, should classify these followers beneath the righteous men of old. The Christian type of character is distinctly higher than the Old Testament type; and the humblest believer is blessed above prophets and righteous men because his eyes behold and his heart welcomes the Christ.

Therefore I am inclined to believe that we have here an ascending series—that we begin at the bottom and not at the top; that the prophet is less than the righteous man, and the righteous man less than the little one who believes in Christ. For, suppose there were a prophet who was not righteous, and a righteous man who was not a prophet. Suppose the separation between the two characters were complete, which of them is the greater? Balaam was a prophet; Balaam was not a righteous man; Balaam was immeasurably inferior to the righteous whose lives he did not emulate, though he could not but envy their deaths. In like manner the humblest believer in Jesus Christ has something that a prophet, if he be not a disciple, does not possess; and that which he has, and the prophet has not, is higher than the endowment that is peculiar to the prophet alone.

May we say the same thing about the difference between the righteous man and the disciple? Can there be a righteous man that is not a disciple? Can there be a disciple that is not a righteous man? Can the separation between these two classes be perfect and complete? No! In the profoundest sense, certainly not. But then at the time when Christ spoke there were some men standing round Him, who, "as touching the righteousness which is of the law," were "blameless." And there are many men today, with much that is noble and admirable in their characters, who stand apart from the faith that is in Jesus Christ; and if the separation be so complete as that, then it is to be emphatically and decisively pronounced that if we have regard to all that a man ought to be; and if we estimate men in the measure in which they approximate to that ideal in their lives and conduct, "the Christian is the highest style of man." The disciple is above the righteous men adorned with many graces of character, who, if they be not Christians, have a worm at the root of all their goodness because it lacks the supreme refinement and consecration of faith; and above the fiery-tongued prophet, if he be not a disciple.

Now, brethren, this thought is full of very important practical inferences. Faith is better than genius. Faith is better than brilliant gifts. Faith is better than large requirements. The poet's imagination, the philosopher's calm reasoning, the orator's tongue of fire, even the inspiration of men that may have their lips touched to proclaim God to their brethren, are all less than the bond of living trust that knits a soul to Jesus Christ, and makes it thereby partaker of that indwelling Savior.

And, in like manner, if there be men, as there are, and no doubt some of them in this congregation, adorned with virtues and graces of character, but who have not rested their souls on Jesus Christ, then high above these, too, stands the lowliest person who has set his faith and love on that Savior. Neither intellectual endowments nor moral character is the highest, but faith in Jesus Christ. A man may be endowed with all brilliancy of intellect and fair with many beauties of character, and he may be lost; and on the other hand simple faith, rudimentary and germlike as it often is, carries in itself the prophecy of all goodness, and knits a man to the source of all blessedness. "Whether there be tongues, they shall cease; whether there be knowledge, it shall vanish away. Now abideth these three, faith hope, charity." "Rejoice not that the spirits are subject unto you, but rather rejoice because your names are written in Heaven."

Ah! Brethren, if we believed in Christ's classification of men, and in the order of importance and dignity in which He arranges them, it would make a wonderful practical difference to the lives, to the desires, and to the efforts of a great many of us. Some of you students before me this morning, young men and young women that are working at college or your classes, if you believed that it were better to trust in Jesus Christ than to be wise, and gave one-tenth, ay! one-hundredth part of the attention and the effort to secure the one which you do to secure the other, you would be different people. "Not many wise men after the flesh," but humble trusters in Jesus Christ, are the victors in the world. Believe you that, and order your lives accordingly.

Oh! What a reversal of this world's estimates is coming one day, when the names that stand high in the roll of fame shall pale, like photographs that have been shut up in a portfolio, and when you take them out have faded off the paper. "The world knows nothing of its greatest men," but there is a time coming when the spurious mushroom aristocracy that the world has worshiped, will be forgotten; like the nobility of some conquered land, who are brushed aside and relegated to private life by the new nobility of the conquerors, and when the true nobles, God's greatest, the righteous, who are righteous because they have trusted in Christ, shall shine forth like the sun "in the Kingdom of My Father."

Here is the climax: gifts and endowments at the bottom, character and morality in the middle, and at the top faith in Jesus Christ.

II. Now notice briefly in the second place the variety of the reward according to the character.

The prophet has his, the righteous man has his, the little one has his. That is to say, each level of spiritual or moral stature receives its own prize. There is no difficulty in seeing that this is so in regard to the rewards of this life. Every faithful message delivered by a prophet increases that prophet's own blessedness, and has joys in the receiving of it from God, in the speaking of it to men, in the marking of its effects as it spreads through the world, which belong to him alone. In all these, and in many other ways, the "prophet" has rewards that no stranger can intermeddle with. All courses of obedient conduct have their own appropriate consequences and satisfaction. Every character is adapted to receive, and does receive, in the measure of its goodness, certain blessings and joys, here and now. "Surely the righteous shall be recompensed in the earth."

And the same principle, of course, applies if we think of the reward as altogether future. It must be remembered, however, that Christianity does not teach, as I believe, that if there be a prophet or a righteous man who is not a disciple, that prophet or righteous man will get rewards in the future life. It must be remembered, too, that every disciple is righteous in the measure of his faith. Discipleship being presupposed, then the disciple-prophet will have one reward, and the disciple-righteous man shall have another; and where all three characteristics coincide, there shall be a triple crown of glory upon his head.

That is all plain and obvious enough if only we get rid of the prejudice that the rewards of a future life are merely bestowed upon men by God's arbitrary good pleasure. What is the reward of Heaven? "Eternal life," people say. Yes! "Blessedness." Yes! But where does the life come from, and where does the blessedness come from? They are both derived, they come from God in Christ; and in the deepest sense, and in the only true sense, God is Heaven, and God is the reward of Heaven. "I am thy shield," so long as dangers need to be guarded against, and then, thereafter, "I am thine exceeding great Reward." It is the possession of God that makes all the Heaven of Heaven, the immortal life which His children receive, and the blessedness with which they are enraptured. We are heirs of immortality, we are heirs of life, we are heirs of blessedness, because, and in the measure in which, we become heirs of God.

And if that be so, then there is no difficulty in seeing that in Heaven, as on earth, men will get just as much of God as they can hold; and that in Heaven as on earth, capacity for receiving God is determined by character. The gift is one, the reward is one, and yet the reward is infinitely various. It is the same light which glows in all the stars, but "star differeth from star in glory." It is the same wine, the new wine of the Kingdom, that is poured into all the vessels, but the vessels are of diverse magnitudes, though each be full to the brim.

And so in those two sister parables of our Master's, which are so remarkably discriminated and so remarkably alike, we have both these aspects of the Heavenly reward set forth—both that which declares its identity in all cases, and the other which declares its variety according to the recipient's character. All the servants receive the same welcome, the same prize, the same entrance into the same joy; although one of them had ten talents, and another five, and another two. But the servants who were each sent out to trade with one poor pound in their hands, and by their varying diligence reaped varying profits, were rewarded according to the returns that they had brought; and one received ten, and the other five, and the other two cities, over which to have authority and rule. So the reward is one, and yet infinitely diverse. It is not the same thing whether a man or a woman, being a Christian, is an earnest, and devoted, and growing Christian here on earth, or a selfish, and an idle, and a stagnant one. It is not the same thing whether you content yourselves with simply laying hold on Christ, and keeping a tremulous and feeble hold of Him for the rest of your lives, or whether you grow in the grace and knowledge of our Lord and Savior. There is such a fate as being saved, yet so as by fire, and going into the brightness with the smell of the fire on your garments. There is such a fate as having just, as it were, squeezed into Heaven, and got there by the skin of your teeth. And there is such a thing as having an abundant entrance ministered, when its portals are thrown wide open. Some imperfect Christians die with but little capacity for possessing God, and therefore their Heaven will not be as bright, nor studded with as majestic constellations, as that of others. The starry vault that bends above us so far away, is the same in the number of its stars when gazed on by the savage with his unaided eye, and by the astronomer with the strongest telescope; and the Infinite God, who arches above us, but comes near to us, discloses galaxies of beauty and oceans of abysmal light in Himself according to the strength and clearness of the eye that looks upon Him. So, brethren, remember the one glory has infinite degrees; and faith, and conduct, and character here determine the capacity for God which we shall have when we go to receive our reward.

III. The last point that is here is the substantial identity of the reward to all that stand on the same level, however different may be the form of their lives.

"He that receiveth a prophet in the name of a prophet shall receive a prophet's reward." And so in the case of the others. The active prophet, righteous man, or disciple, and the passive recognizer of each in that character, who receives each as a prophet, or righteous man, or disciple, stand practically and substantially on the same level, though the one of them may have his lips glowing with the Divine inspiration and the other may never have opened his mouth for God.

That is beautiful and deep. The power of sympathizing with any character is the partial possession of that character for ourselves. A man who is capable of having his soul bowed by the stormy thunder of Beethoven, or lifted to Heaven by the ethereal melody of Mendelssohn, is a musician, though he never composed a bar. The man who recognizes and feels the grandeur of the organ music of "Paradise Lost" has some fiber of a poet in him, though he be but "a mute, inglorious Milton."

All sympathy and recognition of character involves some likeness to that character. The poor woman who brought the sticks and prepared food for the prophet entered into the prophet's mission and shared in the prophet's work and reward, though his task was to beard Ahab, and hers was only to bake his bread. The old knight that clapped Luther on the back when he went into the Diet of Worms, and said to him: "Well done, little monk!" shared in Luther's victory and in Luther's crown. He that helps a prophet because he is a prophet, has got the making of a prophet in himself.

As all work done from the same motive is the same in God's eyes, whatever be the outward shape of it, so the work that involves the same type of spiritual character will involve the same reward. You find the Egyptian medal on the breasts of the soldiers that kept the base of communication as well as on the breasts of the men that stormed the works at Tel-el-Kebir. It was a law in Israel, and it is a law in Heaven: "As his part is that goeth down into the battle, so shall his part be that tarrieth by the stuff, they shall part alike."

"I am going down into the pit, you hold the ropes," said Carey, the pioneer missionary. They that hold the ropes, and the daring miner that swings away down in the blackness, are one in the work, may be one in the motive, and, if they are, shall be one in the reward. So, brethren, though no coal of fire may be laid upon your lips, if you sympathize with the workers that are trying to serve God, and do what you can to help them, and identify yourself with them, and so hold the ropes, my text will be true about you. "He that receiveth a prophet in the name of a prophet shall receive a prophet's reward." They who by reason of circumstances, by deficiency of power, or by the weight of other tasks and duties, can only give silent sympathy, and prayer, and help, are one with the men whom they help.

Dear brethren! Remember that this awful, mystical life of ours is full everywhere of consequences that cannot be escaped. What we sow we reap, and we grind it, and we bake it, and we live upon it. We have to drink as we have brewed; we have to lie on the beds that we have made. "Be not deceived: God is not mocked." The doctrine of reward has two sides to it. "Nothing human ever dies." All our deeds drag after them inevitable consequences; but if you will put your trust in Jesus Christ He will not deal with you according to your sins, nor reward you according to your iniquities; and the darkest features of the recompense of your evil will all be taken away by the forgiveness which we have in His blood. If you will trust yourselves to Him you will have that eternal life, which is not wages, but a gift; which is not reward, but a free bestowment of God's love. And then, built upon that foundation on which alone men can build their hopes, their thoughts, their characters, their lives, however feeble may be our efforts, however narrow may be our sphere, though we be neither prophets nor sons of prophets, and though our righteousness may be all stained and imperfect, yet, to our own amazement and to God's glory, we shall find when the fire is kindled which reveals and tests our works, that, by the might of humble faith in Christ, we have built upon that foundation, gold and silver and precious stones; and shall receive the reward given to every man whose work abides that trial by fire.

52

One Saying with Two Meanings

Then said Jesus unto them, Yet a little while am I with you, and then I go unto Him that sent Me. Ye shall seek Me, and shall not find Me, and where I am thither ye cannot come—John 7:33, 34.

Little children, yet a little while I am with you. Ye shall seek Me; and as I said unto the Jews, whither I go ye cannot come, so now I say to you—John 13:33.

No greater contrast can be conceived than that between these two groups to whom such singularly similar words were addressed. The one consists of the officers, tools of the Pharisees and of the priests, who had been sent to seize Christ, and would fain have carried our their masters' commission, but were restrained by a strange awe, inexplicable even to themselves. The other consists of the little company of His faithful, though slow, scholars, who made a great many mistakes, and sometimes all but tired out even His patience, and yet were forgiven much because they loved much. Hatred animated one group, loving sorrow the other.

Christ speaks to them both in nearly the same words, but with what a different tone, meaning, and application! To the officers the saying is an exhibition of His triumphant confidence that their malice is impotent and their arms paralyzed; that when He wills He will *go*, not be dragged by them or any man, but go to a safe asylum, where foes can neither find nor follow. The officers do not understand what He means. They think that, bad Jew as they have always believed Him to be, He may very possibly consummate His apostasy by going over to the Gentiles altogether; but, at any rate, they feel that He is to escape their hands.

The disciples understand little more as to whither He goes, as they themselves confess a moment after; but they gather from His words His loving pity, and though the upper side of the saying seems to be menacing and full of separation, there is an under side that suggests the possibility of a reunion for them.

The words are nearly the same in both cases, but they are not absolutely identical. There are significant omissions and additions in the second form of them. "Little children," the tenderest of all the names that ever came from Christ's lips to His disciples, and never was heard on His lips except on this one occasion, for parting words ought to be very loving words. "A little time I am with you," but He does not say, "And then I go to Him that sent me." "Ye shall seek Me," but He does not say "And shall not find Me." "As I said unto the Jews, whither I go ye cannot come, so now say I to you." That little word "now" makes the announcement a truth for the present only. His disciples shall not seek Him in vain, but when they seek they shall find. And though for a moment they be parted from Him, it is with the prospect and the confidence of reunion. Let us, then, look at the two main thoughts here. First, the two "seekings," the seeking which is vain, and the seeking which is never vain; and the two "cannots," the inability of His enemies forevermore to come where He is, and the inability of His friends, for a little season, to come where He is.

I. The two seekings. As I have observed, there is a very significant omission in one of the forms of the words. The enemies are told they will never find Him, but no such dark words are spoken to the friends. So, then, hostile seeking of the Christ is in vain, and loving seeking of Him by His friends, though they understand Him but very poorly, and therefore seek Him that they may know Him better, is always answered and over-answered.

Let me deal just for a moment or two with each of these. In their simplest use the words of my first text merely mean this: "You cannot touch Me, I am passing into a safe asylum where your hands can never reach Me."

We may generalize that for a moment, though it does not lie directly in my path, and preach the old blessed truth that no man with hostile intent seeking for Christ in His person, in His Gospel, or in

His followers and friends, can ever find Him. All the antagonism that has stormed against Him and His cause and words, and His followers and lovers, has been impotent and vain. The pursuers are like dogs chasing a bird, sniffing along the ground after their prey, which all the while sits out of their reach on a bough, and carols to the sky. As in the days of His flesh, His foes could not touch His person till He chose, and vainly sought Him when it pleased Him to hide from them, so ever since, in regard of His cause, and in regard of all hearts that love Him, no weapon that is formed against them shall prosper. They shall be wrapped, when need be, in a cloud of protecting darkness, and stand safe within its shelter. Take good cheer all you that are trying to do anything, however little, however secular it may appear to be, for the good and well-being of your fellows! All such service is a prolongation of Christ's work, and an effluence from His, if there be any good in it at all; and it is immortal and safe, as is His. "Ye shall seek Me and shall not find Me."

But then, besides that, there is another thought. It is not merely hostile seeking of Him that is hopeless and vain. When the dark days come over Israel, under the growing pressure of the Roman yoke, and amidst the agonies of that last siege, and the unutterable sufferings which all but annihilated the nation, do you not think that there were many of these people who said to themselves: "Ah! If we had only that Jesus of Nazareth back with us for a day or two; if we had only listened to Him!" Do you not think that before Israel dissolved in blood there were many of those who had stood hostile or alienated, who desired to see "one of the days of the Son of Man," and did not see it? They sought Him, not in anger any more; they sought Him, not in penitence, or else they would have found Him; but they sought Him simply in distress, and wishing that they could have back again what they had cared so little for when they had it.

And are there no people listening to me now to whom these words apply—

> He that will not, when he may,
> When he will it shall be—Nay!

Although it is (blessed be His name) always true that a seeking heart finds Him, and whensoever there is the faintest trace of penitent desire to get hold of Christ's hand we do get the hand, it is also true that things neglected once cannot be brought back; that the sowing time allowed to pass can never return; and that they who have turned, as some of you have turned, dear friends, all your lives, a deaf ear to the Christ that asks you to love Him and trust Him, may one day wish that it had been otherwise, and go to look for Him and not find Him.

There is another kind of seeking that is vain, an intellectual seeking without the preparation of the heart. There are no doubt some people here today that would say, "We have been seeking the truth about religion all our lives, and we have not got to it yet." Well, I do not want to judge either your motives or your methods, but I know this, that there is many a man who goes on the quest for religious certainty, and looks *at,* if not *for* Jesus Christ, and is not really capable of discerning Him when he sees Him, because his eye is not single, or because his heart is full of worldliness or indifference; or because he begins with a foregone conclusion, and looks for facts to that; or because he will not lay down and put away evil things that rise up between him and his Master.

My brother! If you go to look for Jesus Christ with a heart full of the world, if you go to look for Him, while you wish to hold on by all the habitudes and earthlinesses of your past, you will never find Him. The sensualist seeks for Him, the covetous man seeks for Him, the passionate, ill-tempered man seeks for Him; the woman plunged in frivolities, or steeped to the eyebrows in domestic cares—these may in some feeble fashion go to look for Him and they do not find Him, because they have sought for Him with hearts overcharged with other things and filled with the affairs of this life, its trifles and its sins.

I turn for a moment to the seeking that is not vain. "Ye shall seek Me," is not on Christ's lips to any heart that loves Him, however imperfectly, a sentence of separation or an appointment of a sorrowful lot, but it is a blessed law, the law of the Christian life.

That life is all one great seeking after Christ. Love seeks the absent when removed from our sight. If we care anything about Him at all, our hearts will turn to Him as naturally as, when the winter begins to pinch, the migrating birds seek the sunny South, impelled by an instinct that they do not themselves understand.

The same law which sends loving thoughts out across the globe to seek for husband, child, or friend when absent, sets the really Christian heart seeking for the Christ, whom, having not seen, it loves, as surely as the ivy tendril feels out for a support. As surely as the roots of a mountain-ash growing on the top of a boulder feel down the side of the rock till they reach the soil; as sure as the stork follows the warmth to the sunny Mediterranean, so surely, if your heart loves Christ, will the very heart and motive of your action be the search for Him.

And if you do *not* seek Him, brother, as surely as He is parted from our sense you will lose Him, and He will be parted from you wholly, for there is no way by which a person who is not before our eyes may be kept near us except only by diligent effort on our part to keep thought and love and will all in contact with Him; thought meditating, love going out towards Him, will submitting. Unless there be this effort you will lose your Master as surely as a little child in a crowd will lose his nurse and his guide, if his hand slips from out the protecting hand. The dark shadow of the earth on which you stand will slowly steal over His silvery brightness, as when the moon is eclipsed, and you will not know how you have lost Him, but only be sadly aware that your Heaven is darkened. "Ye shall seek Me," is the condition of all happy communion between Christ and us.

And that seeking effort, dear brother, in the three-fold form in which I have spoken of it, to keep Him in our thoughts, in our love, and over our will, is neither a seeking which starts from a sense that we do not possess Him, nor one which ends in disappointment. But we seek for Him because we already have Him in a measure, and we seek Him that we may possess Him more abundantly, and anything is possible rather than that such a search shall be vain. Men may go to created wells, and find no water, and return ashamed, and with their vessels empty, but every one who seeks for that Fountain of salvation shall draw from it with joy. It is as impossible that a heart which wants Jesus Christ shall not have Him, as it is that lungs dilated shall not fill with air, or as it is that an empty vessel put out in a rainfall shall not be replenished. He does not hide Himself, but He desires to be found. May I say that as a mother will sometimes pretend to her child to hide, that the child's delight may be the greater in searching and in finding, so Christ has gone away from our sight in order, for one reason, that He may stimulate our desires to feel after Him! If we seek Him hid in God we shall find Him for the joy of our hearts.

A great thinker once said that he would rather have the search after truth than the possession of truth. It was a rash word, but it pointed to the fact that there is a search which is only one shade less blessed than the possession. And if that be so in regard to any pure and high truth, it is still more so about Christ Himself. To seek for Him is joy; to find Him is joy. What can be a happier life than the life of constant pursuit after an infinitely precious object, which is ever being sought and ever being found; sought with a profound consciousness of its preciousness, found with a widening appreciation and capacity for its enjoyment? "Ye shall seek Me" is a word not of evil but of good cheer; for buried in the depth of the commandment to search is the promise that we shall find.

II. Secondly, let us look for a moment at these two "cannots." "Whither I go, ye cannot come," says He to the enemies, with no limitation, with no condition. The "cannot" is absolute and permanent, so long as they retain their enmity. To His friends, on the other hand, He says, "So *now* I say to you," the law for today, the law for this side the flood, but not the law for the beyond, as He explains more fully in the subsequent words: "Thou canst not follow Me now, but thou shalt follow Me afterwards."

So, then, Christ is *somewhere*. When He passed from life it was not into a state only, but into a place; and He took with Him a material body, howsoever changed. He is somewhere, and there friend and enemy alike cannot enter, so long as they are compassed with "the earthly house of this tabernacle." But the incapacity is deeper than that. No sinful man can pass thither. Where has He gone? The preceding words give us the answer. "God shall glorify Him in Himself." The prospect of that assumption into the inmost glory of the Divine nature directly led our Lord to think of the change it would bring about in the relation of His humble friends to Him. While for Himself He triumphs in the prospect, He cannot but turn a thought to their lonesomeness, and hence come the words of our text. He has passed into the bosom and blaze of Divinity. Can I walk there, can I pass into that tremendous fiery furnace? "Who shall dwell with the everlasting burnings?" "Ye cannot follow Me now." No man can go thither except Christ goes thither.

There are deep mysteries lying in that word of our Lord's—"I go to prepare a place for you." We know not what manner of activity on His part that definitely means. It seems as if somehow or other the presence in Heaven of our Brother in His glorified humanity was necessary in order that the golden pavement should be trodden by our feet, and that our poor, feeble manhood should live and not be shriveled up in the blaze of that central brightness.

We know not how He prepares the place, but Heaven, whatever it be, is no place for a man unless the Man, Christ Jesus, be there. He is the revealer of God, not only for earth, but for Heaven; not only for time, but for eternity. "No man cometh unto the Father but by Me," is true everywhere and always, here as there. So I suppose that, but for His presence, Heaven itself would be dark, and its King invisible, and if a man could enter there he would either be blasted with unbearable flashes of brightness or grope at its noon-day as the blind, because his eye is not adapted to such beams. Be that as it may, "the Forerunner is for us entered." He has gone before, because He knows the great City, "His own calm home, His habitation from eternity." He has gone before to make ready a lodging for us, in whose land He has dwelt so long, and He will meet us, who would else be bewildered like some dweller in a desert if brought to the capital, when we reach the gates, and guide our unaccustomed steps to the mansion prepared for us.

But the power to enter there, even when He is there, depends on our union with Christ by faith. When we are joined to Him, the absolute "cannot," based upon flesh, and still more upon sin, which is a radical and permanent impossibility, is changed into a relative and temporary incapacity. If we have faith in Christ, and are thereby drawing a kindred life from Him, our nature will be in the process of being changed into that which is capable of bearing the brilliance of the felicities of Heaven. But just as these friends of Christ, though they loved Him very truly, and understood Him a little, were a long way from being ready to follow Him, and needed the schooling of the Cross, and Olivet, and Pentecost, as well as the discipline of life and toil, before they were fully ripe for the harvest, so we, for the most part, have to pass through analogous training before we are prepared for the place which Christ has prepared for us. Certainly, so soon as a heart has trusted Christ, it is capable of entering where He is, and the real reason why the disciples could not come where He went was that they did not yet clearly know Him as the Divine Sacrifice for theirs and the world's sins, and, however much they believed in Him as Messiah, had not yet, nor could have, the knowledge on which they could found their trust in Him as their Savior.

But, while that is true, it is also true that each advance in the grace and knowledge of our Lord and Savior will bring with it capacity to advance further into the heart of the far-off land, and to see more of the King in His beauty. So, as long as His friends were wrapped in such dark clouds of misconception and error, as long as their Christian characters were so imperfect and incomplete as they were at the time of my text being spoken, they could not go thither and follow Him. But it was a diminishing impossibility, and day by day they approximated more and more to His likeness, because they understood Him more, and trusted Him more, and loved Him more, and grew towards Him, and, therefore, day by day became more and more able to enter into that Kingdom.

Are you growing in power so to do? Is the only thing which unfits you for Heaven the fact that you have a mortal body? In other respects are you fit to go into that Heaven, and walk in its brightness and not be consumed? The answer to the question is found in another one—Are you joined to Jesus Christ by simple faith? The incapacity is absolute and eternal if the enmity is eternal.

State and place are determined yonder by character, and character is determined by faith. Take a bottle of some solution in which heterogeneous matters have all been melted up together, and let it stand on a shelf and gradually settle down, and its contents will settle in regular layers, the heaviest at the bottom and the lightest at the top, and stratify themselves according to gravity. And that is how the other world is arranged—stratified. When all the confusions of this present are at an end, and all the moisture is driven off, men and women will be left in layers, like drawing to like. As Peter said about Judas with equal wisdom and reticence, "he went to his own place." That is where we shall all go, to the place we are fit for.

God does not slam the door of Heaven in anybody's face; it stands wide open. But there is a mystic barrier, unseen, but most real, more repellent than cherub and flaming sword, which makes it impossible for any foot to cross that threshold except the foot of the man whose heart and nature have been made Christ-like, and fitted for Heaven by simple faith in Him.

Love Him and trust Him, and then your life on earth will be a blessed seeking and a blessed finding of Him whom to seek is joyous effort, whom to find is an Elysium of rest. You will walk here not parted from Him, but with your thoughts and your love, which are your truest self, going up where He is, until you drop "the muddy vesture of decay" which unfits you while you wear it for the presence-chamber of the King, and so you will enter in and be forever with the Lord.